CONTOURS OF THE MIDDLE AGES

CONTOURS OF THE MIDDLE AGES

by

LÉOPOLD GENICOT

Translated from the French

by

LAURENCE AND RONA WOOD

LONDON

ROUTLEDGE & KEGAN PAUL

Translated from the French
LES LIGNES DE FAÎTE DU MOYEN ÂGE
© *Casterman 1961*

First published in Great Britain 1967
by Routledge & Kegan Paul Ltd
Broadway House, 68–74 Carter Lane
London, E.C.4

Printed in Great Britain by
Cox & Wyman Ltd
London, Fakenham and Reading

English translation
© *Routledge & Kegan Paul Ltd 1967*

SBN 7100 6015 7

CONTENTS

ILLUSTRATIONS

MAPS

PREFACE

Every historian is familiar with the painful labour of deducing general principles from the facts he has taken so much pleasure in unearthing. A feeling made up partly of the thrill of discovery, partly of a conviction of rightness, gives place to the torment of composition, the difficulty of shaping recalcitrant material into a neat, carefully argued exposition. He feels he is losing contact with reality, his choice of facts seems arbitrary, his conclusions artificial. In place of a single line he is impelled to write ten, or twenty, in order to bring out shades of meaning, to make reservations, or convey exact degrees of probability. The more ambitious his theme, the more anxious his task.

It is nonetheless essential to make these general interpretations of history and, in presenting them to a wide public, it may be necessary to reduce the history of centuries to a few hundred pages. History is not the privilege of the few: when the labour of scholars brings truth to light it is their duty to make it known to all, and truth is not betrayed if essentials are emphasized at the expense of detail. This basic trend is what I have tried to establish for the history of the Middle Ages.

My work fell into two stages. First I examined the different aspects of medieval life, political, economic, social, religious and artistic, which gave me a collection of 'curves', ranging from demography to canonical studies. The next stage was to superimpose the 'curves' in order to see how far they were in harmony, and the concordance between them was so exact that I was able to deduce a single 'curve', which constitutes the substance of this book.

I need scarcely point out that this task, whose final product is all that the reader sees, was very long, and required the help of many books and many learned friends. In the twelfth century one of the teachers of the Chartres school is reported by John of Salisbury as saying: 'We are like dwarfs sitting on the shoulders of giants. We see farther than the ancients, not because our eyes are sharper, or because we ourselves are taller, but because they have raised us up above their own gigantic height.' The idea has some truth in it still, but one must add that the researcher today, in an age of specialization, owes a debt not only to his forerunners but also to great numbers of fellow-workers.

Other consequences flow from the nature and objects to the work. It would be falsified by gving too much importance fo dates: in history, as in economic development, modifications of the current are gradual, often spread over a long period of time. The great movements I have attempted to trace developed slowly and exact dates have been put in only as markers to sharpen my exposition. I should like to emphasize that this is not a general history of the Middle Ages; it is a history of medieval civilization. Then again, the book only deals with the Middle Ages. It is true that the age between the founding of Constantinople and the Renaissance did not include only what was medieval: after 1300 there was much that was created in a modern spirit, and there were many who drew attention to values and aspects of reality which had been previously neglected, insisting on freedom for the individual, or affirming the goodness and beauty of Nature, not as reflections of the Godhead, but as important in their own right. But to treat at length of this new spirit would be outside the scope of this book. It deals not with the fall of Rome or the birth of the modern age, but with the origin, development and decay of the Middle Ages, presented as a general outline and illustrated with examples drawn from different domains. Among the mass of available material the book picks out the positive elements, which spelled progress for mankind, and takes little note of certain retrograde aspects, which would have distracted the reader's attention from the main theme.

The reader is given a frame-work which he can fill with more detail, should he so wish, and to help him in his studies I have made the bibliographical notes more generous than is usual in a work of this scope. The general bibliography was designed for readers with a knowledge of French and includes the most reliable books in that language; English translations have been given where they exist.

Admiration for the Middle Ages has not made me, nor should it make anyone, despise other periods of history or desire a return to the past. Every period has its good points; each one, our own included, can be great only if it works out its own solutions to contemporary problems, and does not attempt to apply those evolved in previous centuries.

I am delighted that there is now an English translation of my book. To me, England means the precincts of Canterbury, Ely or Wells, and the cathedrals which dominate them, the flower-bordered quadrangles on the banks of the Cam, Rochester's keep and Kenilworths' great gate-house, the villages of Kent and Wiltshire with their lanes meandering through grass and flowers, houses weathered by time, and the blessed peace of their churchyards; it means the Lindisfarne Gospels, Durham's massive columns, the vaulted roofs of King's College Chapel and Lincoln chapter-house; all these, and many more, have given me hours of pleasure and inspiration.

English readers will see that I have devoted considerable attention to their country and its saints, scholars and craftsmen. I think that the book has already played a small part in making medieval England and its important contribution to Western civilization better known on the Continent. I hope that now it will help the English public to know and appreciate the Europe of the past.

I trust it may be a bridge of understanding between us; it has proved so in the case of Germany, and Poland, rising above long-standing enmities and modern ideologies. I myself consider the true value of any human achievement depends on how far it succeeds in persuading mankind to unite and co-operate.

Louvain, 22 June 1967

INTRODUCTION

The term 'Middle Ages' dates from the Renaissance. Humanists were the first to use it, and it appears occasionally during the latter half of the fifteenth century and more frequently during the sixteenth. In the seventeenth century, when historians took it over, it became the accepted term.[1]

The expression itself indicates a certain attitude of mind; it conveys the disdain felt by religious reformers, scholars and artists for those centuries lying between classical Greece and Rome and their Renaissance.[2] Reformers only saw in them a long period during which the virtues of primitive Christianity were systematically undermined, and evangelical ideals gradually stifled. Scholars and artists called these ages 'dark', or, as in Italy, 'Gothic', and found them dull and unproductive, or even barbarous and decadent.

The work of Herder in Germany, Burke in England and de Maistre in France brought about a change: philosophers, aesthetes, writers, historians, all 'discovered' the Middle Ages. In Romantic circles the resultant enthusiasm was feverish and short-lived, but enduring interest was aroused among scholars, and many special studies were undertaken. Light was gradually thrown on this period and it began to take its rightful place in the evolution of history.

This place is in the forefront. Nowadays no one treats the Middle Ages as uniformly Dark, or even as just a period of transition. On the contrary, there is a growing consensus of opinion that they should be regarded as the 'First Ages', and given credit for laying the foundations of Christian civilization in the West – a civilization which, with the classical culture it inherited, still provides whatever is most permanent in the present-day world.

If one accepts this as the chief contribution of the Middle Ages, the medievalist's principal task is then to discover how this civilization was built up, what was particularly characteristic of it at its best, when and why it lost its impetus and withered away. The purpose of this book is to answer these questions.

We must therefore begin with the great migrations during the last part of the fourth century and the beginning of the fifth. There has

1

been, and still is, much discussion amongst historians as to when the Middle Ages, as such, begin. Should one date them from the Roman crisis, in the middle of the third century, which sounded the knell of classical civilization and caused the schism between East and West, or from the foundation of Constantinople in 330, which set the seal on the division of the Roman Empire? Early historians favoured one or other of these dates, and some English, French and Roumanian scholars still do, though they are influenced by different considerations.[3] Or does our period date rather from the time when the Roman Empire was invaded on a large scale by barbarians who were untouched by Roman culture, and determined to destroy it in order to build a new world? The Romantics thought so.[4] Or even from the fall of the Empire in the West? Many text-books take this view. From the arrival of the Muslims in the Mediterranean? That was Pirenne's thesis.[5] Most of these theories are arguable; there is a good deal of truth in all of them, as we shall see when we examine them more closely. But as far as we can tell, the event of cardinal importance was the crossing of the Rhine and the Danube by the Germanic peoples. Medieval civilization sprang from the meeting and interaction of Rome, the barbarians and the Church. So the Middle Ages must begin at the moment when these three forces first came into close contact, that is, during the great waves of invasion.

The terminal date has given rise to less controversy. Such great changes took place between 1450 and 1550 that scholars are in little doubt. It is undeniably at that time that a new world, which had been gradually emerging since the thirteenth century, and even earlier in some spheres and in some religious or intellectual centres,[6] took definite shape.[7] It was the result of a series of contemporaneous, interrelated events in many sectors – in the Church, among intellectuals, in economics and politics.

The Reformation aimed to put an end to long-standing abuses, but, not content with disciplinary action, it moved into the field of dogma. Its heterodox doctrines shattered the religious unity of the West, and paved the way to civil war, if one can use the term at this date. Although it does not appear to have especially favoured the rise of capitalism,[8] whatever may have been said on the subject, it certainly strengthened the trend towards individualism by its teaching on the individual examination of conscience.

In the economic world there was a widening of horizons and a change in organization. The great discoveries, due as much to the enterprise and competitiveness of the Mediterranean and Atlantic peoples as to the advance of the Turks,[9] opened up the West, and thus the future, for a world which till then had been looking towards the East, the South, and the past. Towns like London, Antwerp, Amsterdam and Hamburg now outstripped Venice, Genoa, Pisa, Marseilles and Barcelona in importance, and in general the North of Europe became predominant at the expense of the South. The great discoveries did even more than political changes to encourage the rise of capitalism. States were claiming wider powers and spending lavishly, and were therefore driven to borrow on a large scale; men of wealth and enterprise, with money to lend, seized the chance of enrichment. The discoveries gave scope to even more remunerative investments; trade with the new territories, which meant bartering cheap goods for rare and valuable raw materials, was highly profitable. Men of the sixteenth century found wide opportunities to *'proufiter et trafiquer'*, they had few scruples and aimed to exploit them for private gain; in this they were assisted by the techniques improved or perfected by the great Italian merchants, beginning in the thirteenth century, and by the rise in prices brought about by the increased supply of gold and silver. At the same time they were discarding the old Christian ideas of the guilds on the 'just price', the common good, and other moral or social restraints.

Humanists even shook off the yoke of scholarship; they maintained that the springs of culture and religion which they sought to tap lay beyond it. Even men who, like Erasmus, remained profoundly Catholic, and *a fortiori* others like Valla, paved the way in philosophy to individualism, critical rationalism and even materialistic naturalism.[10]

In politics despotism was the order of the day, based in theory on Roman concepts.

The civilization that this book sets out to study came to an end, therefore, about the year 1500. The medieval ideal of Christian obedience was routed on all sides by the modern ideal of liberty. The community spirit, the transcending of geographical boundaries, which were so characteristic of the Middle Ages at their height, were destroyed by the forces now unleashed both in individuals and in states. Separatism was triumphant.

Western civilization subsisted, but was based now either on the more or less conscious effort of some individuals who could still be called medieval, or on a new element, more limited and fragile than the old unity in one faith – the veneration of the same classical past. The close-knit bonds of Europe, and the decisive influence of the Church both came to an end with the end of the Middle Ages.

The geographical limits of our study enclose all those countries – and they are numerous and far-flung – which have made a contribution to the Christian civilization of the West. Britain, Belgium, Western Germany, Northern Italy, Catalonia, Northern and Southern France, for example, are of special interest because there the raw materials of this civilization, though distinctive and individual, were yet worked and woven into the same pattern.

Given these limits of space and time, we find that the period falls logically into certain divisions.

The first leads up to the middle of the ninth century. The period opened in confusion, a time of violent clashes, but gradually order was imposed and the pattern of future developments can be discerned. New organizations were set up, basic necessities for civilized life were saved from the shipwreck of Rome, the Church extended its hold over individuals and society, and breathed its spirit into them. Soon, within this framework, with these basic materials and in this spirit, the Carolingian dynasty sketched a first rough draft of a civilization. It was premature, but not sterile; later it was to bear fruit.

But this was only to be when order had been largely reimposed on further chaos, and the Church, which for a time had declined into worldliness and sloth, had revived and renewed its inspiration. New cultural elements were eventually acquired and a vigorous population increase was to affect all Europe. Then our civilization took shape, in time to flower vividly in the France of Saint Louis. About a hundred years of stability followed, beginning about 1125 or 1150ᶜ and constituting one of the great periods in history.

Mankind never remains long on such peaks. The magic equilibrium is disturbed. Soon the Church was in retreat before an advancing secularization; slowly it had to loose its hold on its political power, on science and art. The spirit of nationalism sprang up everywhere, in the spheres of politics, economics, even religion, scholarship and art. The disintegration of the Middle Ages inexorably followed. Their fate was sealed by the Reformation, the Renaissance, the rise of capitalism and despotism.

But the Middle Ages did not wholly die. They have left within and around us a heritage whose value and importance we can recognize today.

PART ONE

DAWN

'Between a world that is dying and a world emerging into life there is always an area of chaos. It is both a tomb and a cradle. In its death throes, the dying world tries to crush the new world which is struggling into life, blind as a kitten and still without a name. In that chaos every kind of disaster looms: economic crises, social revolutions, wars. Empires rise and fall, whole countries are swallowed up, new nations, new forces appear; there is general instability, intellectual doubt and physical destruction. The flame of civilization flickers, and there is a return to barbarism.' Gustave de Reynold's words can be applied, point by point, to the history of the West from the fifth or perhaps even the third, to the eighth century.[1]

This period was dark and gloomy from many points of view. It endured invasions, not perhaps as brutal as they have been described, but nevertheless with their share of massacres, looting and disorder. It saw endless struggles for power between tribal rulers, and subsequently between Clovis's descendants, who used any means at hand to rid themselves of their rivals. Government withered away at the centre; officials were left free to extort money, and landowners to increase their holdings, at the expense of the peasants. Trade dwindled, regional specialization almost completely disappeared; most production was of a low standard and for a local market; the only important merchants were now foreigners from the East, mostly Jews or Syrians. The arts suffered a decline – stonemasonry perhaps less than some have supposed, but monumental sculpture certainly; there were no ventures into high relief, no representation of the human body or natural forms. Sculpture became two-dimensional, formal and purely decorative, with motifs drawn from plant and animal life. In literature the classical wells of inspiration dried up, and even in official documents Latin was no longer correctly written. The standard of morality was also low; it followed the example of the court; debauchery led to the degeneration and early eclipse of the Merovingian dynasty. The chronicler known as the Pseudo-Fredegarius described it in a disenchanted phrase: 'The world is growing old.'

But rays of light, gathering strength, pierced through the gloom. As the Mediterranean world disintegrated, new entities took shape; the emerging West broke away from Byzantium and from Africa;

Central and Southern Gaul, the British Isles and the German Rhine-land, which were to cradle the new civilization, became increasingly important. Here and there, against all odds, men had continued to cultivate the classical love of learning and the arts, and these seeds were destined eventually to flower in a new environment. Missionaries of burning faith shouldered again the task of conversion, turning their steps towards the barbarians, whether pagan or Arian, and won them for the Church. Its influence began to permeate society and individuals, in different ways, by accident rather than design. Such was the dearth of able men to fill posts of authority in the secular world that bishops inevitably were drawn into politics, and monks into scholarship and cultivation of the arts. The Church was equipping itself for its mission of civilizing the West. After three hundred years all these efforts were rewarded: in the Carolingian period the Middle Ages appear on the horizon.

The four chapters of Part One are devoted to an analysis of this achievement in construction. They will only touch in passing on what one might call the negative aspect of the period. Their object is not to describe the fall of the classical civilization of the Roman Empire, but to follow the rise of a young culture in a new Europe.

Chapter 1

THE SETTING: FROM THE ANCIENT WORLD
TO WESTERN EUROPE

Its geographical location set medieval civilization apart. Its fabric was based on that of the classical world; Christianity, already ancient, inspired its thought; its setting was new.

Classical civilization had been Mediterranean in origin. It had been the common property of all the countries on the shores of 'Mare nostrum', linked together in the Empire of Rome. It had been their own, because only they had played a part in its formation and evolution; countries inland had received it but had neither influenced nor enriched it.

Medieval civilization, however, belonged to Western Europe. Only a fraction of the Roman Empire was concerned in it. It was nourished by England, Belgium, the Rhineland, Burgundy, Normandy and the Île de France, more than by Catalonia, Aquitaine, Provence and Italy.

So a double revolution took place in that time of transition between the Empire and the Middle Ages, from the third to the seventh century. On the one hand, Western Europe became detached from Eastern Europe and Africa, and on the other its boundaries spread and its natural centre moved northwards.[1]

In this chapter we shall study these two parallel movements. First, we shall recall in passing the close-knit unity of the Graeco-Roman world at its apogee; then we shall analyse in some detail the different events which drove a wedge between the West, East and South of the ancient world, and the results which followed. We shall sum up the relative situation of the central and southern parts of the Western world at the beginning of the Middle Ages, and set out the factors which contributed to the new and soon predominant importance of the North.

In the first century of our era all the inhabitants of the Mediterranean

9

coast shared the same civilization. They maintained close contact with each other, thanks to the sea. They exchanged their agricultural and industrial products, their artistic and literary ideas, even their religions and philosophies. Southern Europe, Asia Minor and North Africa formed one cultural entity. It would be outside the province of this book to argue this point fully. In any case one has ample proof in the 'Piazza delle corporazioni' at Ostia, with its mosaics advertising shipping companies which undertook transport to all parts of the civilized world.

But a break-up of East and West was conceivable at any time because the dominance of Byzantium set the fulcrum too far to the East. It became inevitable after the great crisis in the middle of the third century. The Germanic invasions in the fifth century finally triggered it off, and Justinian's efforts to reverse the movement at the beginning of the sixth century were fruitless.

A hundred years later another fissure opened in the Mediterranean world. The Arabs, in the name of Muhammad, threw themselves upon the Infidel, and captured Spain, North Africa and Syria from Christendom.

The Empire's unity was not destroyed by a single, brutal blow; it was the victim of five hundred years of change. Now to study these changes, stage by stage.

Rome, by its conquests, had no sooner consolidated the unity of the ancient world than a new danger had arisen. The influence of the Eastern Mediterranean had begun to constitute a growing menace; it increasingly dominated the Empire. In religion for example it engendered Mithraism, and, more important, Christianity; the first bishops and martyrs in Gaul came from Smyrna and Pergamus.[2] It was the East too which furnished the majority of the Empire's officials and governors[3] – another sign of a dangerous imbalance.

This inequality was made more pronounced by the great crisis in the third century.[4] A violent upheaval, lasting thirty years, from about 235 to 268, shook the Roman world to its foundations. Its several armies, now rivals, each demanded the purple for their leader. So frequent were these pronunciamentos that anarchy reigned. Within the Empire armed bands spread terror, and the Barbarians without were encouraged by this situation of weakness and disunity. They made repeated inroads at different points into Imperial territory; one thrust carried the Franks as far as Spain, the Alamans appeared in Auvergne, in Italy, and in the Rhaetian Alps, the Goths almost occupied the Balkans, and the Persians conquered Armenia, Cilicia and Syria. At the same time economic life was brought to a standstill by repeated drastic devaluations which conveniently wiped out budgetary deficits; in two decades prices increased tenfold. Worse

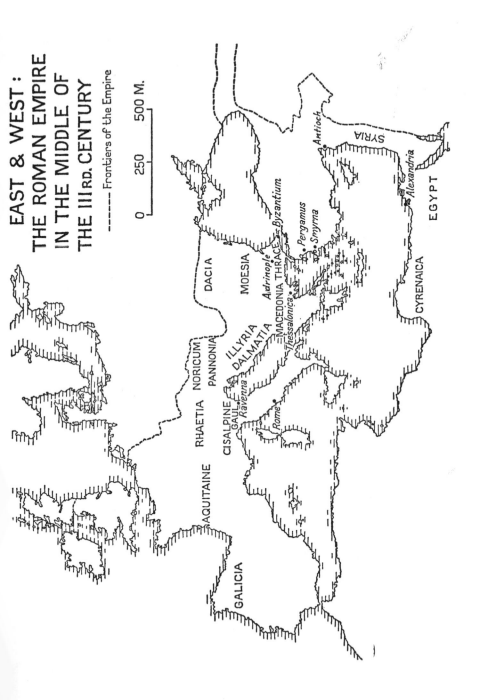

EAST & WEST:
THE ROMAN EMPIRE
IN THE MIDDLE OF
THE IIIrd. CENTURY

------- Frontiers of the Empire

0   250   500 M.

GALICIA

AQUITAINE

RHAETIA NORICUM
PANNONIA

DACIA

CISALPINE
GAUL
Ravenna

ILLYRIA
DALMATIA

MOESIA

Rome

MACEDONIA THRACE
Adrinople
Thessalonica

Byzantium
Pergamus
Smyrna

CYRENAICA

SYRIA

Antioch

Alexandria

EGYPT

was to come: an epidemic of plague, which lasted for many years. The Empire seemed about to collapse under its cruel burdens, and in fact only survived thanks to the arrival on the scene of talented military leaders from Illyria. It had suffered many changes, and Byzantine influence was more than ever predominant.[5]

The Western Empire had been particularly hard hit: its economy had received a mortal blow, its towns had been ravaged, its artistic inspiration was exhausted. Industry, which had flourished in Italy, Gaul and Spain in the first century, and even in Britain in the second, declined rapidly at the end of the third.[6] Soon only low-quality goods for a local market were produced, in all but a few areas. Trade inevitably slackened. Agriculture alone remained relatively prosperous, but specialization was abandoned, and with it contact with a wider community; the great estates, which swallowed up most of the small and medium-sized holdings, became self-sufficient. The towns were affected by these economic changes, by the barbarian raids, and by the crushing taxes levied on their richer inhabitants – perhaps even by peasant hostility and a certain primeval mistrust of urban life. They had not been remarkable for their size, and now they lost a considerable proportion of their population and business. Within the protecting walls that they built for themselves they vegetated.[7]

Under these conditions cultural life came to a standstill. This was the intensification of a process which had been going on since the second century. Pagan literature could boast of only one or two writers of moderate talent. Christianity had seemed to tap a richer vein, but it was soon exhausted. In art technical skills were lost irretrievably. In the West the general picture presaged the predominantly rural life of the early Middle Ages.

But in the Eastern Mediterranean things were different. Town life was busy and cultivated: the tone was set by cities like Byzantium, which was destined to play a great future role, Thessalonica, which was to prosper for centuries, Antioch and Alexandria.[8] These were cosmopolitan centres, throbbing with trade and industry, especially the production of luxury goods; in their schools there was no lack of philosophical speculation and religious argument; their wealth was poured into new art forms redolent of Asia. The life of the ancient world was centred round the shores of the Bosphorus and the coasts of Asia Minor and Egypt. It was not surprising that Constantine moved his capital there in 330.

Undoubtedly the most serious consequence of the crisis in the middle of the third century was the creation of a marked contrast between East and West. At the heart of the Empire there was now not merely inequality but rivalry. This fact did not escape those wielding power. They tightened the central government's hold and strengthened bureaucracy; but at the same time they abandoned a unified civil and military command: from 286 there were two *Augusti*. The establishment of the Diarchy was significant: it was an admission that relations between the two halves of the Roman world had become strained and that a breach might be expected.

It took place in fact at the time of the 'great invasions', as they are called, although more accurately one would term them 'great migrations'. They form the first phase of an outstanding phenomenon which was destined to recur throughout the early Middle Ages and disrupt the West. Two magnetic forces originally caused the migrations: Germanic tribes in their misty northern marshes were attracted by the fertility, sunshine and ease of the South, and the nomads of the desert lands of Central Asia were drawn to the alluvial plains on their borders.[9] The arrival of the Huns brought things to a head. About 355, after a repulse in China they reached the banks of the Volga and, still surging westwards, defeated the tribes settled along the Danube and the Rhine and pushed them towards the Imperial frontiers. Inadequate garrisons were powerless against such hordes at bay.

In the East the Visigoths defeated Valens at Adrianople in 378 and set out on the wanderings which were to take them from Moesia to Illyria, Dalmatia, Italy and finally Aquitania and Spain, where they settled between 418 and 475. One tribe of Ostrogoths made a sally into Italy in 405, but was wiped out; another followed in 488, led by Theodoric. In 406 the Alans and the Sueves harried the Roman defences, sacked Gaul and spread into the Iberian peninsula; the vanguard reached Africa in 428, the rearguard were finally halted by the Visigoths in Galicia. The Franks, Alamans and Burgundians penetrated southwards along the valleys of the Scheldt and Moselle, into Alsace and the Palatinate, and through Burgundy as far as Provence. Finally, farther west, the Saxons swooped on both shores of the North Sea and the English Channel; together with Angles, Jutes, and possibly some Frisians, Franks and Chauci, they established three bridgeheads in England, and made their way farther inland during the second half of the fifth century. There they remained for two generations, and then moved forward again, pushing the Britons as far as Cornwall and Wales, and gaining control of most of England.[10]

Obviously only certain provinces were thrown into the melting-pot. By means of diplomacy more than force of arms the *Basileus* had managed to deflect those barbarians who had crossed the lower Danube towards Italy, Gaul and Spain. The East remained intact, while the West was profoundly changed. Naturally the links – political, cultural and even material – between the two zones were broken. Political unity disappeared, in fact, if not in theory. Theoretically there was still one Empire and, after the deposition of Romulus Augustulus in 476, only one Emperor. But in practice he only controlled the East. The barbarian chiefs who had shared the West between them sometimes described themselves as his representatives. For several generations longer they struck coins in his name and they paraded their imperial titles of consul or patrician. None of this would imply recognition of more than an honorific title to pre-eminence.[11]

The administrative structure changed also. In Byzantium little was altered before Heraclius (610–41): the organization remained comprehensive, logical and coherent. However, in the kingdoms of the Visigoths and Anglo-Saxons, for example, there was an incoherent jumble of Roman and Germanic elements which resulted in a rudimentary and inefficient organization.[12]

The levels of culture, as we have already seen, began to diverge still further. Pirenne has an apt phrase: 'The West went out of cultivation.'[13] Whether intentionally or not, the invaders hastened the collapse of civilization; its decline can be measured in the West by the dwindling number of scholars with any knowledge of the Greek language and literature.[14] Byzantium on the other hand increasingly turned its back on its Latin traditions, cultivated Hellenism and laid itself open to Asiatic influences. Byzantine art, whose masterpiece was Santa Sophia at Constantinople (532–7), betrays its twofold origin: in its technical skill, its richness and colour it is Asiatic; in its preoccupation with line and its simplicity of form it is Greek.[15]

In the long run the barbarian invasions were to separate the two parts of ancient '*Romania*' from each other. As the Germanic tribes invaded the Empire, Slavs occupied their former territories. After 650, groups of them, either of their own accord or at Heraclius's invitation, crossed the Danube themselves and settled in what is now Yugoslavia, forming a wedge between West and East.[16]

The religious bond remained, but it was fragile and easily broken. The break was final in some of the countries situated at a great distance from the imperial capital and only partially Romanized: in Syria and Egypt, for example, the Monophysite heresy, which had been condemned in 448 and 451, was encouraged by a certain latent separatism, and developed into what was almost a state church; it paved the way for the Muslim domination in the seventh century.[17] In other cases there was only intermittent contact; many diverse events gave rise to frequent disputes between Byzantium and Rome after Constantine's death and presaged the schism of the Greek provinces at the eastern limits of the Empire.

This was not to come about until 1054, under the leadership of

Michael Cerularius, but its causes dated from the fourth and fifth centuries. One source of trouble was intervention by the *Basileus* in the Church's affairs, even in questions of dogma;[18] he was tempted to interfere because there was no clear demarcation between the civil and religious spheres of influence; he was also concerned to maintain religious unity, which would ensure peace; and he was recognized as having a certain sacred quality as emperor. The ambitions of the patriarch of Constantinople also led to serious difficulties; as Bishop of the New Rome he stood first in the Eastern hierarchy and was often inclined to dispute the supremacy of Peter's successors.[19] Friction over secondary matters such as ethnic rivalry, differences in language, theological formulae, ritual and disciplinary rules, became increasingly bitter.[20]

Thus, at the very beginning of the Middle Ages, in which religious unity was to play such a major part, papal authority was overthrown in one area of the East and was proving extremely weak in the remainder.[21] The division of the Roman Empire was complete.

Justinian's reign, ironically, provided proof of this. His repeated efforts to turn the tide which was bearing Byzantium nearer to Asia, and to strengthen its links with Rome and the West were to end only in failure.[22] The 'Emperor who never sleeps' had been given joint power in 518 by his uncle, whom he succeeded in 527. He cherished one ambition: to continue and complete the work of the Caesars, re-establish '*Romania*' as a territorial and cultural entity, and give it a Christian crown. In other words, he proposed to restore political unity in the Mediterranean world by reconquering the West; to do the same for religious unity by reconciling the Patriarchate with the Papacy, and by bringing Egypt and Syria back to the true faith. He even hoped to make Latin the first language in Constantinople, and thus restore linguistic and cultural unity, trusting it would lead to a classical renaissance.

He failed to accomplish this ambitious programme; his successes were only minor ones. He did not succeed in conquering Gaul or most of Spain. He did not destroy heresy in the East, and his frequent interference in doctrinal disputes only increased the Western Church's mistrust. He was not able to dislodge the Greek language from its strong position east of Illyria; and except in Sicily he could not impose an art style which was Byzantine and strongly influenced by Syria, Armenia and Persia, or a literary style which had nothing Roman about it. Any progress he made was short-lived. Africa, Italy and the coasts of Spain, which he conquered after 533, were destined in little more than a hundred years to fall into the hands of the Arabs, Lombards and Visigoths. The link with Rome, which he had re-established after 519, was to be broken again in 640, and after 681 no Western bishops participated in any council held in Constantinople. In the eastern Mediterranean Latin, and with it Roman traditions, was completely forgotten.

Should the blame be laid solely on a lack of persistence, or a scarcity of men, money and time? On the contrary. If Justinian's achievement seems slight and ephemeral the fundamental reason is that to Western eyes Byzantium, with its Greek officials, its merchants from Asia Minor, its German, Slav or Persian soldiers, was utterly foreign. His religious policy failed because Byzantium was riddled with Monophysitism, and the Emperor's intervention led only to sterile disputes over dogma. A common culture made no headway against the Roman and barbarian heritage on the one side and the Greek and Asiatic on the other. The incompatibility of the two ways of life is the significant factor, and the fundamental cause of Justinian's failure.

It was to have serious consequences. An enemy was to arise which would rob both East and West of much territory and incorporate it in an Arab Muslim empire, creating a further split in the Mediterranean world.

The attack was brutally sudden.[23] Between leaving his birthplace for Medina in 622 and his death in 632, Muhammad had managed to unite the Arabs under him, as much by his military and diplomatic successes as by his religious preaching. He turned their natural ardour to good use in spreading abroad his doctrine. He persuaded them to direct their superabundant aggression against the infidel by convincing them that as God is One so must the faithful be, and by forbidding internecine strife. Heavenly rewards were also promised to all who died for the faith. Consequently, under his successors, the Arabs launched a furious attack on the world as they knew it. In ten years they had conquered Syria and Persia, Egypt and Cyrenaica; then they captured Armenia, defeated the Berbers, and reached the frontiers of Europe. One frontier was crossed: in 711 in a single battle they gained control of Visigothic Spain. Fortunately for medieval Europe Constantinople succeeded in holding out against them between 711 and 718, and at the other end of the continent Duke Eudes of Aquitaine in 720 and 721, and Charles Martel in 732 and 737, inflicted decisive defeats on them. They did not manage to penetrate farther, but they remained masters of the Mediterranean coasts, and eventually captured the major islands – Crete in 825, Sicily after 827 and Malta in 870.

The expansion of Islam and especially the conquest of 'Mare nostrum' by the Saracens had serious consequences. One well-known theory holds that they opened a new era in history by overthrowing the ordered classical world.[24] They had in effect closed the main, if not the only highway, between East and West and forced the latter to be self-supporting. About 700 an Arab wrote: 'The Christians cannot sail so much as a plank on the sea now.' For centuries to come life was to be uncertain and hazardous along the shores of Italy, Provence and Catalonia, and as a result the cultural and political supremacy that the southern regions had enjoyed was destined to move northwards. So, it is claimed, the result of Arab victories was to destroy the two chief characteristics of the ancient world – the unity of Imperial Rome and the dominance of the Mediterranean – and bring to birth the Middle Ages.

This is an attractive theory, but it claims too much, and few scholars now favour it.[25] The arguments on which it was based, especially the economic ones, are now seen to be less solid than they appeared thirty years ago. We were told that many Syrian and Jewish wholesale merchants traded in Oriental spices and wines, Egyptian papyrus and African oil, with Frankish Gaul, with Italy under Theodoric and Visigothic Spain; ports and inland towns hummed with activity, and the money in use was a close copy of Byzantine coinage. But in the Carolingian period there were no foreign merchants, no exotic imports, nor were there any busy commercial centres or gold coinage on the Imperial model; the coins were silver *denarii* worth one-thirtieth of the gold. Is not this marked change a proof that before the advent of Muhammad the Mediterranean peoples had remained in close contact, but that after the Arab advance they had become isolated and cut off? Indeed not! First of all, economic prosperity under the Merovingians has been exaggerated. It is difficult to believe, for example, that spices, wines or papyrus were in great demand or that Marseilles, with its eight or nine thousand inhabitants inside a perimeter one and a half miles long, could be called a *large* port, through which poured merchandise destined for Gaul and even Britain. Then too, a more plausible explanation has been passed over: the scarcity of precious metals, which is so evident in a museum like the Metropolitan in New York when one compares Byzantine goldsmiths' work with jewels from the barbarian kingdoms. The dwindling barbarian trade with the East can be explained by the scarcity of exchangeable commodities on their side, since they hardly produced any silver or gold and found it more and more difficult to pay for their imports. The change from the *solidus* to the *denarius* was probably to cover up the scarcity of precious metal, and to link the value of the currency to the price of the metal, a price which increased as the quantity decreased. We must not forget either that, as we shall point out at the end of this chapter, contact between the eastern and western parts of '*Romania*' was not severed in 750 or 800.[26]

The true, or at least the more important consequences of Arab expansion were felt elsewhere. It did for a time hamper relations between the West and Byzantium. It brought humiliating dismemberment to the latter, which was already suffering from the reaction of the barbarians to Justinian's rule, and the attacks of the Slavs. Only Greece, Macedonia, Thrace, Asia Minor and remnants of Italy were left to her. She had been a universal empire, but now she was the kingdom of the Straits. So much had been achieved by the Arab advance. But more important was the loss to Christianity of Syria, with its memories of Romanos the Melodist, the Egypt of Origen and Clement, Augustine's Africa, Prudentius's Spain. Of course, in some of these countries religious disputes had already given rise to separatist ideas; in others Romanization had been less effective than elsewhere and they had been more affected by the Germanic invasions;[27] but it was Muhammad's sword which had cut through remaining links or wiped out earlier influences. Its effect was so drastic that we now find it difficult to imagine that Algeria and Tunisia were once part of the Latin world, and the forum at Djemila, the theatre at Timgad and the capitol at Sbeitla take us by surprise. The most significant result of the Saracen invasions was undoubtedly the establishment of the rule, religion and culture of Islam in more than half the lands washed by the Mediterranean sea.

Byzantium, Western Europe, Islam were three different worlds; the first in a state of metamorphosis, the second emergent, the third strange and foreign. No one could doubt that the close-knit classical world was dead.

The widening of frontiers in the West and the change in its centre of gravity, like the process of separation, did not happen overnight. They too were the fruits of a long period of change, in which the important events for the North were the Germanic invasions, and for the South Justinian's activities and the Islamic expansion. We must now sum up the position of Belgic Gaul, the Rhineland and England on the one hand, and Italy, Provence, Aquitaine and Spain on the other, in the disintegrating ancient world, and then look at events again, but from a different point of view.

From the second century before our era Rome had established a foothold in the Mediterranean countries near the Latium coast, where the soil and natural resources promised well, and which were easy to reach by water. Groups of colonists had been sent out, and from centres like Cremona and Placentia, Narbonne and Arles, Tarragona and Cordova, Roman culture had spread and taken root. Already under the first Caesars some of the best schools were as far distant as Marseilles and Autun, and some of the best Latin was being written by Seneca and Lucan, born far from Rome. In the fourth century

Spain had produced Orosius and Prudentius, while the 'universities' of Bordeaux, Toulouse and Narbonne were more highly thought of than their Italian counterparts. These examples, and many others, which the religious, social and economic history of the region can provide, demonstrate clearly both the level of culture achieved in the South by about 400, and the lead it held over the rest of Western Europe.

Then came the barbarian invasions. The heritage left by Rome in the North was largely destroyed, and so the contrast presented by North and South was accentuated. There was however at the same time a certain access of youthful energy and a foreshadowing of the time when, under the Carolingians, the North would recapture the lead.

But to begin with the North fell back still farther. From 250 onwards the Germanic tribes had sporadically attacked and ravaged

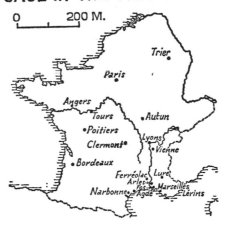

NORTH & SOUTH: GAUL IN THE Vᴛʜ. CENTURY

it, and, beginning in 406, they had begun to settle in close-knit communities. Eventually they totalled 15 to 25 per cent of the population of Northern France and Wallonia, and more than 50 per cent in Alsace, the Rhine Basin, Flanders and Central and Eastern Britain. In the South however, except for certain areas like the Toulouse region, they were swallowed up by the original inhabitants. In addition, those who settled along the Mediterranean shores, the Goths, were less primitive. At home in the Lower Danube–Black Sea area their contact with the Roman Empire had left its mark on them; and so the Visigoths, and possibly the Burgundians, were more easily assimilated than the Angles, Saxons, Franks or Alamans. During the fifth century these discrepancies in the type and number of the invaders widened still further the gap between Southern Gaul and the regions north of the Loire and the Alps.

Intellectually they were poles apart. Scholarship still flourished in Italy, at Milan, Ravenna, Rome and other centres. Spain was to be the home of Isidore of Seville. Literary life went on, though with some setbacks, in Aquitaine and Provence, producing Sidonius

Apollinaris (431–89), educated in Lyons and Arles, typical of the over-sophistication of the late Empire, Avitus (†513), bishop of Vienne, 'the most outstanding of the Christian poets between the sixth century and the eighth', and the historian Gennadius, who was a priest at Marseilles (†494). The North could show nothing like this; Trier, the only intellectual centre to achieve a certain measure of fame in the fourth century, was engulfed in the invasions, and Salvian, who came either from there or from Cologne, wrote his *De Gubernatione Dei* in the South between 439 and 451.[28]

The religious climate offered equally striking contrasts. In Britain Christianity was still struggling to overcome strong opposition at the beginning of the fifth century, when further pagan reinforcements arrived in the shape of the Anglo-Saxons. In Belgium, and even more in the Rhineland, the first missionaries had made some headway, but it was jeopardized by the advance of the Franks and the Alamans. The Christian communities were probably dispersed; they certainly were not revived there.[29] But in the South, particularly in Southern Gaul, Catholicism was clearly a living force. There were regular councils, at Narbonne and Angers in 453, Arles in 455, Lyons in 460, Tours in 461, and so on. Monasteries were founded – at Lérins in 410, Marseilles in 418, then at Ferréolac, Sainte Marie de Lure, in the Isère valley and in the Lyons district. Before long Caesarius of Arles promulgated the first Western rule of monastic life. There was lively theological debate on the doctrine of grace: Hilary of Arles (†449), Vincent of Lérins (†450) and above all Faustus of Riez (†late fifth century) attacked Augustinian teaching more or less openly, whilst Claudianus Mamertus at Vienne (†474), Julianus Pomerius at Arles and Prosper of Aquitaine put up a brilliant and vigorous defence. It must be pointed out that some of these writers were foreigners: Faustus was born in Britain and Julian in Mauretania. Their presence is indicative of the fame then enjoyed by the southern Church as a whole, and by the Lérins monastery and the see of Arles in particular.

A similar but less striking contrast is discernible in economic affairs. From about 250 onwards barbarian raids brought ruin to most of the flourishing industries of Belgium and the Rhineland, and about 400 to their smaller-scale counterparts in Britain. When raids were followed by wholesale colonization during the fifth century, trade between these three areas came to a standstill. Commercial intercourse across the North Sea was broken off for a time, and the principal ports serving it on the continent, Boulogne and Vechten, disappeared. In central and southern Gaul trade was less affected: it only slackened later, and more slowly, so that its harbours, Marseilles, Agde, Fos, Bordeaux, and the towns they served – Arles, Narbonne, Clermont, Poitiers – still attracted eastern traders.

20

The heart of the West, pulsating in its literature, scholarship, religion, industry and commerce, was by 500 more firmly fixed than ever in a Mediterranean setting.

But the sixth century saw the tide turn. The North began to show signs of discipline and energy, a legacy, though slow to take effect, of the great invasions. As we have already seen, the invasions had left behind the Angles, Saxons, Franks and Alamans, as either the majority or a very substantial minority of the population in the former provinces of Britain, Belgic Gaul and both Upper and Lower Germany. The Lombards had arrived later, but were now settled in most of Venetia, Transpadane and Cispadane Gaul, Etruria and Umbria. This transfusion of new blood had brought fresh vigour to all these areas.[30] At first it was simply wasted in internal struggles for power; but from about 550 in some places, 600 to 650 in others, it began to be used for constructive purposes. Calm and order were largely restored and men began to fashion a new civilization. They took what was to hand, and they added the contribution brought mostly by missionaries and monks from the South and Ireland. In every field advances were made which were to find their culmination in the flowering of the ninth century. Northern Gaul's part in this process is so significant that it merits closer study.[31]

The victories of Clovis were the starting-point. In the course of the invasions Gaul had been dismembered by Visigoths, Burgundians, Gallo-Romans, Bretons, Saxons, Alamans and Franks. It had lost its identity, and seemed destined to disappear completely, when Clovis appeared on the scene. He was remarkable, not for his brains but for his exceptional vitality. In victory after victory he pieced Gaul together, and when death carried him off his sons completed his work. In a few decades these men from the North had remade Gaul; and the effects of this were to be of vast importance.

The South may well have held some attraction for Clovis, but however that may be it was Paris that the Merovingian chose for his capital; his successors clung to the Île de France region, and from then onwards the political centre of the whole of Gaul, including rebellious Aquitaine, was firmly fixed north of the Loire.[32] The history of the councils of the Church is impressive on this point. Not one was held north of the Loire in the fifth century, but in the sixth the picture changes; the most important councils of the period met in Orleans in 511, 533, 538, 541 and 549, then in Paris in 552, 573, 577 and 614, in Clichy in 626 or 627, and so on. They were becoming 'national' councils, which brought together bishops from all over Gaul; in Orleans in 541, for example, the bishops of Bordeaux, Eauze, Toulon, Narbonne, Dax, Limoges, Vaison, Apte, Javols, Uzés, Poitiers and Cieutat rubbed shoulders with their colleagues from Northern Gaul, whilst the latter only rarely appeared at councils in the South after 517. By then only provincial councils were held there.

This astonishing change of fortune was the beginning of a transformation of the North. It did not become a brilliant cultural centre overnight; but, leaning gratefully on the South, it took its first steps away from barbarism.[33]

The Church grew, favoured by kings out of political interest as well as for reasons of conscience, and by high officials and great landowners; there were missionaries from Aquitaine and Ireland, and probably more local proselytizers than some historians allow. New sees were created at Arras, Tournai, Laon, Thérouanne, possibly also at Soissons and St. Quentin. Parishes were marked out, and chapels built in towns and on country estates. Many monasteries were founded, especially from the fifth century onward; by then there were several in each of the dioceses of Bayeux, Rouen, Beauvais, Langres, Trier, for example. In the seventh century the arrival of Columbanus and his Scots followers led to the foundation of Luxeuil, nursery of so many bishops, abbots and missionaries, Fontaine, Jouarre, Rebais, Laon, St. Dié, Moyenmoutier, Remiremont, Nivelles, Fosses and many others.

The spread of Christianity was accompanied by a revival of intellectual life. Monks began to take up the pen in northern abbeys and cloisters; what they wrote was of a low standard, as it was in the South, but it was a beginning. Here, as elsewhere, the vast majority of early works were lives of saints; the first was a life of Saint Genevieve, written in Paris about 530, by a monk or clerk who came from the Meaux district; in the same century it was followed by a life of Remigius of Rheims, and in the seventh century by lives of Lubin of Chartres, the Irish saint Fursy, Arnould of Metz, Wandrille, who gave his name to the village originally called Fontenelle, in Normandy, Eligius of Noyon and Géry of Cambrai. A few chronicles were written; one part of the chronicle of the Pseudo-Fredegarius, which is a continuation of the *Historia Francorum* by that famous native of Auvergne, Gregory of Tours, has been attributed, very improbably, to an Austrasian writer; but the *Liber historiae Francorum*, almost our only source book for the years 657 to 757, is undoubtedly the work of a St. Denis monk who was himself a native of the region.

The other arts also made progress. Kings, bishops and abbots commissioned many buildings in the North. It is impossible to know whether they were better or worse than those in the South: all one can say from the meagre information available is that, although there may not have been much skill shown in the construction of a building, it was decorated with some care; Aquitaine marbles were used, and panels of the local limestone, carved *in situ* into interwoven patterns and geometric designs; after the middle of the eighth century this was the only form of ornamentation.[34]

Economic life revived too. In the seventh century the volume of trade, especially in woollen cloth and possibly metals, increased. Contact was re-established with England, when Quentovic replaced Roman Boulogne, and it seems likely that at the St. Denis fair, which was instituted in the reign of Dagobert, the 'Saxons' seen there were Anglo-Saxons.[35] The port of Duurstede replaced Vechten and from it Frisians sailed up the Rhine, and northwards as far as Scandinavia. Inland along the waterways of the Meuse, Scheldt and Seine local coinage was minted everywhere, and taxes and tolls brought in a rich harvest. One could already foresee economic conditions in the eighth and ninth centuries, when the trade of the lands north of the Seine, or the Loire, was to outstrip that of the rest of the country.

The great invasions were not the sole reason for the changed status of North and South. They had thrust the area between the Loire and the Rhine unexpectedly into the foreground; but in the same period Italy, Spain and Aquitaine were affected by equally serious events.

Until 525 or 530 Italy had suffered little, and had even enjoyed a renaissance under Theodoric.[36] When he died it was Italy's turn to become medieval. Justinian embarked on a campaign of reconquest. The Ostrogoths resisted desperately, struggling for twenty years, until their leaders were wiped out. With them the peninsula lost her ablest protectors. From then on she was a tempting prey, and almost immediately she was attacked by a '*gens germana ferocior*', a particularly brutal Germanic tribe, the Lombards. War, invasion, chaos: the brilliance of Theodoric's reign was followed by an alarmingly rapid collapse of cultural standards.[37]

Fifty years later the Arabs attacked in the south-west. They conquered most of Spain, a country where the arts were in a flourishing state.[38] They did not destroy its civilization: in comparison with Cordova Aix in the Carolingian period was but a straggling village;[39] but they imposed a foreign civilization on a society which was Roman and Christian.[40] Beyond the Pyrenees they brought ruin to towns and industries. Isidore of Seville, Ildefonsus of Toledo, the Spanish writers of the seventh century left no heirs, and no more marble was exported from Aquitaine.

But we should be rash to conclude from all this that Byzantium no longer influenced the West, or that Southern Europe was henceforward to be ineffectual.

During the very early Middle Ages the West had drawn away from Byzantium; it had become more and more different from it and shown progressively less interest in it; gradually mention of Byzantium was even left out of its universal histories.[41] But that is not to say that they were in any respect cut off from one another. In the economic sphere, for example, Henri Pirenne based his theories on proved phenomena, though he may have exaggerated or misinterpreted them. Intellectual rapport is proved by the fact that Boethius, that 'last of the Romans',[42] published his monographs in Constantinople between 522 and 526. There was no aesthetic gulf; although clearly the basic essentials of the future Romanesque style were to be found in Italy and Gaul from the fourth and fifth centuries onwards, we cannot deny that the buildings and even more the mosaics, silks, jewels, ivories and miniatures of Byzantium and Asia continued for a long time to have an influence on the arts of the West.[43] In religious matters interaction became less common, but it by no means ceased. The Papacy was continually interfering in matters concerning the Patriarch of Constantinople; between 640 and 741 about a dozen churchmen from the East sat on the throne of Saint Peter. Saint Theodore of Canterbury, who was born in Tarsus and educated in Athens, left one of the thriving Greek monasteries in Rome in 668 to become head of the Church in England. From about 500 the *Kyrie* and the *Gloria* began to be used in the Latin form of the Mass; Byzantine festivals in honour of the Crucifixion and the Blessed Virgin were adopted by the Western Church; pilgrimages to holy places became popular. Other significant examples could be added to this list.

All through the Middle Ages this was to continue. Carolingian merchants bought more Eastern spices and silks than their Merovingian predecessors.[44] Tenth-century illuminators and Ottonian metalworkers were imbued with Byzantine hieraticism. After the year 1000 those who devoted their lives to pious works followed the customs of the Eastern Church.[45] And so on, until the fifteenth century. Only when the Levant had fallen into Turkish hands did the West turn away, and this act marked the opening of a new period of history.

Within the West itself the South was not destined to stagnate, though during the Carolingian period it was the North which took the lead. Southern cities had their own contribution to make to medieval civilization. From the eleventh century they contributed more than the North, in part because they had preserved more of their classical heritage; it was reborn, for example, in the Romanesque art of Provence and Burgundy, which drew its inspiration from the Roman cities of Arles and Autun, and in the legal researches inspired in Bologna by the recovery of the *Digest*. They were in direct contact with the Arab world and through it with the Orient and Asia; from

24

these sources new knowledge was available to them which they diffused through the rest of Europe. Art forms like lyric poetry reflected the warmth of the climate and the exuberance of the people and complemented the outpourings of the rough uncivilized North. Between the fifth and the eighth centuries there was a widening of Western frontiers, but no wholesale movement of civilization towards the North.

This two-fold movement, growing and developing for four hundred years, created the setting of medieval civilization. The detail was not filled in till the time of Charlemagne, but by the middle of the eighth century the main trends can be discerned.

Chapter 2

RAW MATERIALS: GERMANY AND ROME

The essential raw materials of the new civilization were being gathered together within this setting. There was little that was original about them. During the very early Middle Ages the West did not venture in any new directions, but was content to preserve and mould together elements bequeathed by the past or received from abroad.

Although drawn from widely separated sources and different historical periods these legacies and loans blended harmoniously enough. Prehistory, the era of Constantine, Persia, Asia Minor, Syria, Egypt, Africa, Gaul and Ireland are all represented. But this enumeration might mislead, for it was the Germanic peoples and Latin and Christian antiquity which made by far the greatest contribution to medieval civilization. The contributions of other peoples and periods were much less important. In the pages which follow we shall discuss this, analysing the political, social and economic structure of the West for the period from 450 to about 750, and its artistic, literary and scientific heritage.

Recognition of the legacy of Rome prompts a question: who saved it from the shipwreck to hand it on to succeeding generations? The second part of the chapter will answer this, by listing the chief cultural centres of the West from the period of the great invasions to the Carolingians, and briefly assessing their influence.

Merovingian Gaul, Anglo-Saxon England, Visigoth Spain or Lombard Italy had all borrowed the essential features of their systems of government from Germany. Tacitus's account makes it clear that they were significantly different from Roman imperial institutions, which were too complex to survive the invasions. The new conquerors did not abandon their political system; they did not manage to preserve the Roman administrative network; but they took over one institution of practical use, the office of Count, though they failed to perpetuate more complicated ones like the land-tax. The West was therefore on a highly precarious admini-

26

strative basis after 406 and was to remain so for eight hundred years.[1]

Everything turned upon the conception of kingship,[2] which itself had been transformed by the experience of the migrations and subsequently by contact with Rome. The king's powers had originally been small, but the need for a strong central authority to lead in the search for new lands and overcome resistance, the increase of wealth and prestige that victories brought to such a leader, and the inherited example of Roman absolutism, all led to their being enlarged. However, they remained vested in the king's person.

The idea of the king as the personification of the State had disappeared. Abstract notions made no appeal to the Germanic mind; it was concerned with people and the material world; from it stemmed the medieval passion for relics and pilgrimages, an expression of a desire for tangible contact with holiness. The concept of one person expressing the collective will, existing on a different plane from other people but taking a human form, meant nothing to them. They could only recognize flesh-and-blood kings. Scholars looked back to the Roman Empire and tried to represent the monarchy as a type of Roman magistrature, and Christian theologians argued that it was a divine delegacy. They were trying to separate the office from the person who occupied it, but they were only partly successful. The *Mirror of Princes* was to be a much more common form throughout the Middle Ages than the *Ars Politica*. Until the twelfth century the sovereign exacted obedience because he belonged to a family regarded by pagans as god-like and by Christians as divinely appointed and endowed with charismatic powers; but also because his subjects had chosen him, he was their rallying point, the one to whom homage was due.

Such 'personalization', as German historians call it, brought dangers in its train. The king came to be identified with his kingdom, and his birthright, revenues and power with its size, its wealth and its resources. It was one of the root causes of the financial difficulties which dogged so many of the rulers of this period. Some felt justified in sharing out between them the domain inherited from a dead father, with bitter enmity as a frequent result. Worst of all, the well-being of the kingdom was at the mercy of one man; if he was brave, rich and clever, everyone prospered; if cowardly, poor and unlucky, there was no peace, security or justice for anyone.

The role assigned to the great nobles of the State was another legacy to these Western European monarchies from their own barbarian past, and it was a common source of embarrassment to their rulers. The origins of the nobility are disputed: they may be traced to the *'nobiles'* and *'principes'* mentioned by Tacitus, to Imperial senators, or the loyal henchmen of Merovingian kings.[3] In any case the concept was Germanic. The nobles shared some of the king's authority; they had elected him from amongst his royal brothers,[4] and he took counsel with them on all matters of importance. They were independent within their own estates; no official had the right of entry.[5] The necessity of limiting their freedom and integrating their territory with the rest of the kingdom became the monarchy's thorniest problem. It was to be most difficult to solve in Germany, though her kings tried one method after another: feudal subordination, by making them vassals; setting up prince-bishops as a counter-weight to their power; playing them off against the common people. Even so they had to admit defeat.[6] How in fact could they hope to restrain such independent factions with the organization available to them? There were no longer any specialized services, no bodies of trained administrators; the old hierarchy of State officials had gone, and central control had become weak; civil and military powers were no longer separated. The main administrative work was now carried out by a few officials, whose duties were ill-defined, and a handful of amanuenses, whose faulty education is evident in the documents they have left. Regional government was in the hands of one man, the count; he took charge of what today would be a province or a shire, in all kinds of capacities, maintaining law and order, raising taxes, and, in time of war, leading his own army of freemen.[7]

And so we see the factors which for so long bred disorder in a half-barbarian society: at the top an autocrat on a seesaw, with insubordinate nobles, and a government so rudimentary that it could not calculate probable revenues or budget for expenditure. In the semi-autonomous provinces a few officers of the State had a monopoly of all essential functions, but lacked the power to compel the obedience of the rich.

Social life in the early medieval period owed more to its barbarian than to its Roman past. As its political structure shows it was aristocratic and to a large extent individualistic. In order to form a satisfactory picture of it we must study these two aspects, and a third which is derived from the part played by the family.

Scholars studying the peoples who inhabited the territories beyond the Rhine before the fourth century have reached two main conclusions. The theory formulated by historians of the Romantic period, that Germanic societies were based on equality and communal ownership, was only an *a priori* one; their society did not consist of freemen only. It was dominated by an aristocracy of birth, wealth or political power.[8] It remained so after the invasions. In the West up till 1100 the prime mover was the nobility, with the monarchy, whose prerogatives it shared, and the Church, which it largely furnished with bishops and abbots. It was the nobles who founded monasteries; gold- and silversmiths' work adorned their weapons; bards composed epics for them. Social life revolved around them.

In the second place, society was rooted in the individual and his personal ties. As we have seen, the monarchy was much less an institution than the particular man who embodied it. Laws were not based on territorial divisions; people were subject to the customs of the tribe they belonged to, not the area they occupied, but there were survivals of what Tacitus called the 'comitatus'.[9] As he described it, barbarian chiefs surrounded themselves with 'boon companions' who lived at their expense and under their protection, and fought for them in return, a practice which was continued and extended in the Merovingian era. It was advantageous to the ruler in binding his nobles more closely to him, and to the ambitious who found opportunities of advancement at the court; the weaker profited by becoming the vassals of the stronger. Agreements to support each other, probably sworn on oath, became customary, and paved the way to feudalism and a world founded on loyalty and trust.

Ties of kinship were even stronger: according to Tacitus again, the patriarchal family or 'Sippe' was the assize court of Germanic society, 'where custom was more efficacious than law elsewhere'.[10] Although the family was a very large unit, like marriage it was indissoluble; its strength lay in this, and in the solidarity of its members. They had equal rights in the family estate, which was administered by the head of the family on their behalf. They had a legal right and a moral obligation to avenge a wrong inflicted on any of their number, just as they were held collectively responsible for any individual member's crime.

The medieval family structure was looser and its sphere of action more limited. It came to consist of fewer members, so that finally it comprised only father, mother and their dependent offspring, eating at the same table; this is reflected in the splitting-up of estates. The family system gave way to single-family homes. In time the right of married couples to dispose of their landed property appeared; and the law frowned on private vengeance.

Even so, until the eleventh and twelfth centuries deeds of alienation of land carried the express consent of near relations, and right up to the French Revolution they had the right to buy back property sold or mortgaged to outsiders. Throughout the feudal period too, anyone in difficulty would still turn to his blood-brothers, and vendettas continued to rage.[11] Family feeling obviously remained strong, and still provided a unifying motive. It is not too far-fetched to see in it the seed, or the seedbed, of that urge to band together which is so characteristically medieval.

Roman influences, then, hardly counted in the social system of the time and the same may be said of Christianity. In the Carolingian period the Church took it over, reformed it in some aspects, strengthened it and set it on spiritual foundations;[12] it may be said to have renewed but not created it. It remained a Germanic institution.

The economic structure of the early Middle Ages was dominated by agriculture in the form of great estates, and it is difficult to decide on its origins. In Germany, certainly, the manpower engaged in commerce and industry was inconsiderable, and although most holdings were small, large domains did exist. In the Roman Empire after the third century there had been an increasing tendency to amalgamate estates. In any case it is difficult to generalize. In all probability barbarian influences predominated in the North, while in the South the characteristic Roman villas with their twin functions steadily increased in numbers.

As Pirenne maintained, and as the post-Clovis history of Gaul shows, trade did not disappear from the Merovingian West, but it dwindled noticeably.[13] Contractual agreements became so rare that the law of obligation almost disappears from the legal sources.[14] The one occupation of any importance was agriculture, so that the Latin verb *laborare*, to work, became in French *labourer*, to plough. The soil was the basis of the economy.

Most of the land was in the hands of a few men. The tendency towards large-scale landholding had slackened during the invasions, especially in areas where barbarians had settled in great numbers, but it soon revived. During the period of Rome's decline a peasant would part with his land to a rich neighbour for various reasons: as a result of threats or chicanery, in return for protection or a precarious life interest in a larger holding, or because he could not pay the heavy taxes. The sixth- or seventh-century peasant did the same, for the same reasons: the knavery and violence of contemporary nobles, denounced by the Council of Mâcon, lack of security, the offer of a larger piece of land or a concession to clear waste, the burden of taxes and services. Soon many small farms were swallowed up by larger, and often huge, estates.

On the largest estates there would be a score or so of '*villae*', on the smaller only one. The way in which they were organized varied: it depended on their size and situation, and on the period in question.[15] Sometimes the land was directly cultivated by the lord and his servants, and sometimes it was leased to others; most commonly it was a combination of the two – demesne land on the one hand and tenant exploitation on the other. In what was to become Germany ten per cent of the land was in direct exploitation, and in France twenty-five to seventy-five per cent. It was worked by the lord's serfs, who were tied to the land, and by peasants who owed labour-service to their master. His estate would be essentially a large farm, with the usual buildings, gardens, ploughland, grazing and woods, but it also included several craftsmen – shoemakers, smiths and so on – as well as a mill and a bakery, often a brewery and a wine press, which, at least from the ninth century, everyone on the estate was compelled to use, and of course to pay for. Land was leased usually in the form of a *mansus*, that is to say a house with its garth, fields, sometimes land for grazing, and certain rights in the lord's forest; in size it could vary between 7 and 75 acres.[16] In theory, though often not in practice, each *mansus* would be occupied by one family; in Italy usually for a short term, north of the Alps for life or in perpetuity. In return an annual rent was payable in money and in kind, as well as three days' work a week on the lord's land.

Unlike his equivalent today the great landowner did not limit himself to collecting his dues. Because of his privileged position and the weak and bankrupt state of the central authority, he very quickly acquired, in full or in part, the rights of jurisdiction exercised elsewhere by the king and his officers. His wide authority enabled him to hold courts for the people living on his estate. They were his men, and he was already their lord.[17] During the Merovingian period the traditions of the late Empire were perpetuated; at the same time the broad lines of a West European economy were laid down, to remain practically unchanged through the early Middle Ages until the tenth century.

Germanic influence on the development of the arts was very slight. Their primitive village life in houses of untrimmed timber, plastered with clay, was not conducive to the cultivation of architecture, sculpture or painting. Their only artistic influence was on metalwork and eventually, through it, on manuscript illumination.

Their goldsmiths' work enjoyed an unprecedented vogue; witness the number of necklaces, bracelets, rings, earrings, brooches, buckles or sword-hilts found in burials of the period, and the rarer crowns, vases and chalices that formed part of the treasure of kings and cathedrals. The style of decoration changed.[18] Craftsmen adopted and developed the features of some Celtic, Gallo-Roman and Romano-British works of art, such as the buckles from Anthée-lez-Dinant or the Mildenhall Treasure dishes;[19] there the artist had been concerned with purely decorative use of interwoven lines and curves, and some stylized objects, rather than representing man and the natural world.[20] Cloisonné enamelling, a technique that had probably been introduced to the West by Egyptians in the Coptic period, but only rarely used, now became popular; instead of hollowing the surface to be decorated it was divided into compartments by thin metal walls, into which enamel was poured or uncut stones inserted. Motifs drawn from the animal kingdom were borrowed from the Scythians and Sarmatians,[21] neighbours of the Germanic hordes before the invasions; and it was they who inspired the practice of decorating objects with jewels or glass, and the lavish use of colour.

This strangely beautiful and compelling style of decoration influenced illuminators. When sculpture revived it too felt the impact. But the Germanic contribution to the future of Western art was confined to this geometrical, abstract style or to a few themes that artists would come across in treasuries and libraries. The Roman heritage was of far greater importance.

This heritage was in fact Roman, rather than Byzantine. Undoubtedly during the early part of the Middle Ages Western Europe adopted certain architectural ideas from Byzantium, Asia Minor or Syria: harmonizing the interior and the exterior of buildings, dividing the height of the aisles to provide a gallery, or adding extensions to an apse. But the latest research seems to show that the future Romanesque arch, and the other basic elements of that style of architecture, were already known of before the great invasions. Whether they had been invented on the spot or imported from the Levant at the beginning of our period is a question beyond the scope of this book.[22] For us the point of interest is that there was little fundamental difference between Merovingian basilicas and baptisteries, and buildings erected when Constantine was emperor; both followed a centralized layout – usually oblong, sometimes cruciform, with nave and apse, and both made use of mosaics or other superimposed ornament as decoration.

The same was true of sculpture. Classical traditions, which were growing weak by the third century, became less and less operative in the fifth and sixth, but they did not disappear altogether. Triumphal arches and sarcophagi survived to serve as models. A few artists continued to work in the classical styles in Southern Gaul, and in Italy, and influenced England[23] in the early part of our period: they carved in relief and tried to reproduce the human form, instead of merely incising or engraving stone in geometric, curving patterns, or twisted designs of plants. They were not very skilled, but that was unimportant compared with the fact that they were upholding the ideal of art as both monumental and man-centred. Without the combination of faultless works of art bequeathed by the Romans and clumsily executed barbarian copies of them, how could the great Romanesque school of sculpture ever have emerged?

Medieval literature owed equally little to the Germanic peoples. There was a tradition of epic poetry relating the exploits of early heroes. This survived the migrations and the conversion to Christianity, even the Church's disapproval of them as pagan works. At the end of the seventh century or the beginning of the eighth the famous epic poem of *Beowulf*, on the deeds, death and burial of a king of Gothland, in South Sweden, was written down by Anglo-Saxons. About a hundred years later Charlemagne ordered an anthology to be made of the '*barbara et antiquissima carmina quibus veterum regum actus et bella canebantur*', which has unfortunately disappeared. Even about 900 Bishop Radbod of Utrecht railed against the '*monstruosa fabula*' which were the form of entertainment at banquets.[24] Given this, it is difficult to believe with Bédier[25] that the *chanson de geste* owed nothing to the Germanic tribes. But that was all they contributed: apart from it, all the mental and literary equipment of the early Middle Ages was derived from classical antiquity, or, to be more precise, from Rome and Christianity.

In Western Europe at this time nothing was known of Hellenism except through the writings of Romans, Christians and a few Eastern authors, in particular those who arrived in Italy and Spain as a result of Justinian's reconquest. In philosophy Plato's *Timaeus* and Aristotle's *Logic* were both known, and something of Neo-Platonism was seen through the eyes of pagan writers in Latin as well as the Fathers of the Church.[26] Science had not appealed to the Roman mind, but the facts that the elder Pliny had collected and tabulated in his *Natural History* were available, with some notions of mathematics and astronomy, invaluable in drawing up the liturgical calendar. In literature Hellenism counted for even less, which is not surprising when one remembers that its decline in Western Europe dates from the late Empire, and that Christian scholars were particularly hostile to Greek literature.

Rome was the presiding genius of education in Europe.[27] Latin texts existed in wide variety. Research into the sources of early medieval writers, as well as the catalogues of the oldest monastic libraries, or the reconstructions of Carolingian *scriptoria*[28] give a good idea of their scope. Arator, an Italian poet of the mid-sixth century, imitated Virgil, Ovid and Horace. Isidore of Seville, who came fifty years later, and will be mentioned again, in drawing up his *Etymologies*, used Pliny the Elder, Sallust and Suetonius, Virgil and Ovid again, Lucan and Juvenal, Columella and others. In the abbey at Rebais, founded forty miles to the east of Paris by Irish monks, copies were still being made of Virgil, Cicero, Horace, Terence, Donatus and Priscian. In the great monasteries of the early Middle Ages, Bobbio in Northern Italy, St. Gallen in Switzerland, Fleury-sur-Loire, Corbie-lez-Amiens, or Lorsch on the Rhine, manuscripts of all the classical writers were carefully preserved; this was especially true of Virgil, because of the beauty of his style and the nobility of

33

his sentiments, and because many saw in him a prophet of Christianity.

The West also inherited a Roman syllabus of studies, laid down by Martianus Capella about 420:[29] the *trivium*, the formal disciplines of grammar, rhetoric and dialectic, or logic, and the *quadrivium*, the natural sciences, arithmetic, geometry, astronomy and music. A few years later it was adopted by Saint Augustine, but he gave it a new *raison d'être*: it was to assist in the understanding and exposition of Holy Scripture. From then on the *septem artes liberales* had a definite objective and a firm place in the cultural framework of the Middle Ages; in the thirteenth-century universities they were still the core of Arts Faculty teaching. But until then they were usually regarded only as the pillars supporting the architrave of philosophy, so far as it was seen as a separate discipline, and the pediment of theology.

Finally Western Europe inherited from the classical Roman period a preference for certain literary forms, particularly history, as a tool of moral education rather than a scientific study; and from the period of decadence a lack of taste which appears, especially in the early Middle Ages, in works both affected in style and meretricious in content.

The early Christian period is fairly well represented in the '*armaria*' of the barbarian kingdoms and the Carolingian era:[30] the Fathers of the Church, poets sacred and profane, spiritual writers and historians. There were the Greek fathers, like Clement and Origen, leading lights of the Alexandrian school of theology, John Chrysostom's Homilies, Eusebius of Caesarea's history of the Church, all translated into Latin.[31] Above all there were the important writers of the West, such as Tertullian, the vehement apologist from Africa, Prudentius, the Spanish poet, whose *Psychomachia* inspired medieval artists as much as writers, Ambrose of Milan, famous for his hymns, Jerome, a Roman by adoption, admired as an exegete and biographer; there was Sulpicius Severus, from Gaul, who continued the work of Eusebius of Caesarea, and Orosius, another Spaniard, whose universal history, *Adversus paganos*, was to be widely read and discussed for ten centuries. Finally, and supremely, came Augustine, who was to influence the Middle Ages so widely and so deeply, in the general direction and the basic principles of their theology, in their essential political ideas, which were more or less correctly interpreted from the *City of God*, and, in a wider way, in their conception of the outward and visible world as a reflection of the invisible, that 'exemplarism' which is woven into the history of the next thousand years.[32]

And so we may say that the Germanic peoples gave the new world the main elements of its political and social, though perhaps not its economic, structure. Since they were its masters that is almost self-evident. But the Romans had contributed all that was important in its cultural life. Herein lies a problem. Classical civilization might well have disappeared in the invasions and the anarchy which followed them. How did it manage to survive?

The credit for its survival belonged chiefly to the Church. In a very short time it became practically the only patron of literature and the arts. Kings and nobles might commission metalworkers and architects, they might even occasionally manifest an interest in a writer's work; as a general principle they favoured the spread of culture as a stabilizing influence, but their role was a somewhat passive one, encouraging rather than initiating or guiding.

Theodoric was the exception.[33] An intelligent, ambitious Ostrogoth prince, he had spent ten years in his youth at the Imperial court of Constantinople, where he had come to know and value classical civilization. When he became ruler of the Ostrogoths, and, about 490, master of Italy, he planned a classical renaissance there. He established Roman institutions and Roman law in his kingdom. He supported scholars, poets and orators. He even tried to recreate the atmosphere of town life by encouraging games in the arena. Thanks to him classical antiquity flowered again for a time on the banks of the Tiber, the Montone and the Po, or rather, since Theodoric's inspiration was Byzantine, Rome, Ravenna and Pavia took on an eastern brilliance. Ostrogothic Italy, like a gleam of light in the troubled, barbarian darkness of the West, was the chief refuge of Roman and Christian culture in the late fifth and early sixth centuries, a stable kingdom 'where writers are read and held in esteem'.

There were many schools for the education of the governing class, where literature was studied; contemporary writers, all things considered, were not without merit; one thinks of Ennodius, bishop of Pavia, and especially of the celebrated Boethius.[34] Anicius Manilius Severinus Boethius was born about 480 of a distinguished family whose members had for several generations played an important part in government; his only ambition was to serve his fellow citizens, which he did as a high official. He was a consul when still in his thirties and was noted for the probity and devotion with which he carried out the duties of all the high offices to which Theodoric had promoted him; in 523 he was arrested on a trumped-up charge of treason and beheaded in 524. He was even more outstanding, perhaps, as a man of learning; in his own phrase, he aimed to 'enrich the city's life with the arts and wisdom of Greece', in other words to put Goths and Romans who understood only Latin in contact with Aristotle and Plato. He even dreamed of reconciling the two and 'showing that it

35

is untrue that they disagree on all points; on the contrary they have the same view of many of the great philosophical problems'. He attacked this great enterprise with enthusiasm. He wrote first some short treatises on the *quadrivium*, which he considered indispensable if one was to understand philosophy. Then he turned his attention to Aristotle; he translated and explained part of his *Logic*, including the *Categories*, and the *Isagoge*, Porphyry's commentary on them. But little interest was aroused by his efforts in this direction and he did not continue them. Theology drew him, and he attempted to resolve the difficulties inherent in the doctrine of the Trinity by the light of reason – philosophy again. Finally in prison he wrote his *De consolatione philosophiae*; four hundred manuscripts of this, his most famous work, are extant and it will continue to be published.[35] In it he remained a philosopher, calling on Wisdom to sustain him in his trials; in his pagan cast of mind he remains the last true representative of classical culture. Yet in Boethius the emphasis was on all that turns the soul towards God, a creative Providence, in fact a Christian God, and in his concern that intellect should serve faith and in his cult of the syllogism Theodoric's minister was already a man of the medieval type. He was to have a considerable influence on such men[36] – to introduce them to arithmetic, geometry and music; to convince them in the field of theology that dogma must be based on reason; and to teach them the practice of logical argument; finally, with the rediscovery of several of his treatises in the tenth century, philosophical speculation had enough food for thought to last until the twelfth century.[37]

Ostrogoth Italy produced no artists of the stature of Boethius, but at least an artistic tradition was maintained, itself an achievement at this period. In Rome, Ravenna and Pavia palaces, basilicas, baptisteries and great mausolea were constructed, basically in the style of the Constantine era, with some eastern influence. They were still decorated with mosaics and frescoes. Sculpture included equestrian statues; relief carving and the realistic portrayal of human forms were still in vogue.

The fundamentally secular culture that the great king promoted hardly outlived him. With his death Italy was fated to enter upon a calamitous period of her history. The relentless struggles between the Goths under Totila and Justinian's Byzantine troops were followed by the Lombardic invasions.[38] Civilization suffered a bitter blow and would hardly have survived but for the protection of the Church. When peace returned a few grammarians and rhetoricians and some jurists were to be found in the scholastic centres in Northern Italy, especially at the court of Pavia, but they were men of limited vision and no great influence.[39] From about 550 the responsibility for safeguarding the classical tradition in art and literature fell largely to the clergy; fortunately they showed more enthusiasm for the task than they had done in earlier centuries.

The firmly established Church of this period did in fact regard Graeco-Roman culture with more favour than the early Church had done. It had adopted classical techniques and even classical themes in art with very little reluctance, but from the beginning it had despised and mistrusted pagan literature.[40] Saint Paul had condemned as useless and dangerous 'the wisdom sought after by the Greeks', and early generations of Christians had followed his ruling. Eventually, however, a few leaders of thought had reacted against it and taken a more liberal attitude. Poets like Saint Ambrose and Prudentius had read and imitated Virgil and Horace. Exegetes and theologians had immersed themselves in secular learning. As early as the end of the second century Clement of Alexandria had boldly suggested enlisting Greek philosophy in the service of the faith, because 'it prepares man's mind for God's word, encourages understanding, sharpens intelligence and awakens the spirit'. Two hundred years later Augustine had included the liberal arts in his educational programme. It came to be thought that classical learning could assist in the understanding of Scripture and in the formulation of theological doctrines. Just at the time when the secular world abandoned literary studies monastic doors opened to them and formally welcomed them.

From the earliest Middle Ages intellectual activity had been carried on in the abbeys of Western Europe. Their founders had ordained meditation on the Bible and recommended the transcription of manuscripts.[41] In the early sixth century Saint Benedict reaffirmed this, laying down that his followers were to occupy themselves chiefly with the divine office and '*lectio divina*'. But how could they devote themselves to 'reading on the things belonging to God' without some background of culture and some authoritative guidance? The Rule mentioned writings, especially those of the 'holy Catholic fathers', which were to be available to the members of the community,[42] like the Testaments and accepted commentaries on them, but not, apparently, classical works.[43]

It was left to one of Benedict's contemporaries, Cassiodorus, and to Theodore of Tarsus and Hadrian, who established the Anglo-Saxon branch of Christianity a hundred years later, to include the classics in the monastic syllabus of studies. About 540 Cassiodorus founded what he called a '*schola christiana*' at Vivarium, on his estate in Calabria, where the Holy Scriptures and secular literature were studied. He does not seem, however, to have enjoyed the success some have claimed.[44] A hundred years later Theodore and Hadrian

D

made a place in the programme of studies of their schools for pagan writings, and thus laid the foundation stone.[45] Henceforward the abbeys of the British Isles fostered classical culture, and continental houses soon followed their example.

But we must have no illusions as to the state of mind of priests and monks of the period. In the eyes of many the study of pagan writers was merely a necessary evil; they would not have wasted any time on them if they had possessed Christian epitomes, anthologies of all the ideas useful in exegesis and theology to be found in classical authors. The result was a demand for encyclopedic works which was to continue for centuries. All the clergy would have agreed that the classics were not an end in themselves and were only justified in so far as they helped to pave the way to spiritual wisdom. 'Scholarship directed only towards erudition is but idle curiosity and alienates the soul from God. The spirit's true aim must be the knowledge and the love of God.' In these words Augustine was also expressing the attitude of churchmen in general, of Cassiodorus in Italy and Alcuin in England.[46] One seems to hear an echo in Alcuin's own letter to the Irish: 'Children should be taught grammar and other branches of philosophy, so that by degrees of wisdom they may rise to the perfection enshrined in the Gospels.'[47]

From then on classical studies were bound up with the Church and with its prosperity. They made little progress in places like Italy and Southern Gaul, where Catholicism had long ago taken root and was now somewhat dormant, but they flourished in countries which had just seen the defeat of Arianism or paganism, such as Spain and the British Isles.

Even after the destruction caused by the Gothic wars, and the brutality of the Lombard invasion, Italy in the sixth and the seventh centuries was still a centre from which civilization radiated. It had lost most of its energy and creative force, but something remained. The focal point of Byzantine Italy was Ravenna, where Justinian completed S. Vitale and S. Apollinare about 550, and with them rounded off a group of buildings which were to influence the architecture of the Palatine Chapel in Aix, and perhaps the early Kentish churches.[48] The only Merovingian poet, Fortunatus, who wrote the *Vexilla Regis* some time between 520 and 600, was educated in Ravenna.[49] Lombardy could boast one or two cultivated clerics in Como and Milan, and at Pavia kings were happy to surround themselves with lively-minded courtiers; Charlemagne's councillor, Paul the Deacon, was one of them, and Peter of Pisa may have been another. In spite of the damage inflicted on her by Justinian's generals, papal Rome was one of Europe's important artistic and intellectual centres. Christian and pagan manuscripts transcribed there were in use in Gaul, Spain and England. England imported Roman monumental sculpture, painting and illumination. Benedict Biscop, who founded the Northumbrian abbeys at Jarrow and Wearmouth, went to Rome five times and brought back all kinds of books, '*innumerabilis librorum omnis generis copia*', religious paintings showing Christ, the Virgin Mary and the Apostles, and illustrating Gospel stories, as well as beautiful materials, and even artists to decorate his monasteries.[50] The ruling Popes and Roman priests were not the absolute Boeotians that some have claimed. It is true that Gregory the Great, who ascended the throne of Saint Peter in 590, had harsh words for those who cultivated literature for its own sake. He recognized however the uses of profane learning when it 'was a help in the ascent to the glories of Holy Writ', and when it acted as the handmaiden of the approved sacred studies. He himself took pains to compose religious texts which raised the prestige of the Eternal City in the eyes of the Christian world and continued to be the chosen reading matter of the Middle Ages. His successors, or their Curia, showed some ability in composing graceful Latin epitaphs. Even some relics of Hellenism survived in the region south of Rome. And so even in her state of weakness Italy was preparing the way directly and indirectly for Charlemagne's Renaissance, with Britain as intermediary.

Gaul was less prominent at the time, particularly in literature and science. Even before 475[51] its schools had disappeared and the private tutors who replaced them could do little to delay the drift to decadence, which, after three generations, was very marked. In the second half of the sixth century the country of Sidonius Apollinaris and Avitus of Vienne, of Vincent of Lérins and Prosper of Aquitaine could boast of no more poets or theologians, only chroniclers and hagiographers of doubtful merit. The best of them, Gregory of Tours, was only familiar with Virgil among the ancients, and could make no high claims for his own literary style; he himself described his Latin as 'rustic', and he was not over-modest; his works are full of inaccuracies, and are no more than a list of events, with little attempt at synthesis. Even so he was head and shoulders above his successors. The barbarity of thought and expression in Merovingian documents is well matched by the chaotic hand in which they are written. In Gaul contact with classical antiquity lapsed and little remained as intellectual pabulum for the Carolingian Renaissance but monastic copies of a few manuscripts – Jerome, Augustine, Virgil and possibly Horace.[52]

Until recently it was maintained that the arts were equally impoverished,[53] but recent research has brought about a new assessment.[54] Illuminated manuscripts were few, but the frescoes of the period must have been of high standard, to judge by their Carolingian descendants,[55] and the technique of stained glass was very advanced; it was not to be improved on until the twelfth century, and Gallic windows were the envy of England at the time.[56] In general sculpture was not common and was often little more than engraving; there was nevertheless some work on ivories, on sarcophagi and on capitals, from which true relief and representation of the human figure were not altogether absent.[57] Stonemasons constructed churches of quite considerable dimensions, built strong walls in both large and small bond, threw vaults across small buildings and were the first to put bells into a lantern tower or porch. In the seventh century Gallic artisans were so highly thought of that, after recruiting his sculptors in Italy, Benedict Biscop went northwards, probably to Provence, to engage his stonemasons, and it is thought that the early churches of Northumbria bear their mark.[58] Monuments of the Gallo-Roman period were kept in repair, and were later to serve as models; in all this Gaul can be said to have been important in handing on to the Middle Ages classical ideas and techniques in painting and architecture, even in sculpture.

As we have seen, culture did not disappear in Italy, or even in Gaul, but it lacked drive. In seventh-century Spain, on the other hand, it leapt forward.[59]

The Iberian peninsula became one of the chief intellectual and artistic centres in the West, by virtue of a series of fortunate circumstances. The Roman occupation had left its mark. The Visigothic invaders who settled there in the fifth and early sixth centuries had been relatively civilized; for example in 475 their rulers had promulgated the first barbarian 'law', the *Codex Euricianus*, and in 506 the *Breviarium Alaricianum*, which remained the chief source of Roman law north of the Alps throughout the early medieval period. Spain's geographical position had made possible easy contact by sea with Italy, Africa, Egypt, Syria and Byzantium, and many foreigners had settled there, like Donatus, who arrived with his monks and his library in 571, driven from his African monastery by the Berbers. The last of these happy accidents was Justinian's partial reconquest, since artists and men of letters followed on the heels of the Emperor's troops.

Such favourable conditions were not exploited, because of a long period of political and religious strife. But by the end of the sixth century the Visigoth state was at last stable; it had ceded Aquitaine to Clovis and the Franks, but south of the Pyrenees it threw the Byzantine forces back to the sea and overcame the Sueves; it was sole ruler of the peninsula, and with the absence of any threat to its security its warlike instincts slackened. Simultaneously its leaders, who up till then had been fiercely Arian, like their people, were converted to Catholicism; this assisted the assimilation of Goths and Hispano-Romans, and gave greater freedom to the clergy, who were thus able to engage in cultural activities.

One man, Isidore of Seville, epitomizes the Spanish Church's intellectual achievement at this period.[60] Born about 560, he became archbishop of Seville about 600; Braulio and Tajo were to hold the see of Saragossa, and Julian, Ildefonsus and Eugenius that of Toledo. He set up a college for his clergy, and, clearly at his instigation, a national Council decided in 633 that the example should be followed in every diocese. He created or at least improved a library which was as rich in sacred and profane, ancient and modern works as those of Saragossa and Toledo. He presided over the most famous of the Toledo councils: they continued until 701, and produced a sound system of dogma which may not have been altogether original, but, for its period, was remarkable.[61] In addition to writings on morals such as his *De viris illustribus*, later continued by Ildefonsus, and on science, history, scripture and theology, he composed the famous *Etymologiae*. In them he included all that he had learnt, directly or indirectly, about classical science, and they were to constitute the sum of scientific knowledge for the whole of the early Middle Ages; Isidore's encyclopedia was not only the most exhaustive, it was the most read.

The practice of the arts was no less distinguished than that of literature:[62] the Isidorian era, which was the heir to Roman traditions, but at the same time receptive to Byzantine styles and techniques, saw the rise of a remarkable group of buildings north of the Tagus. They were notable for their ground-plan, which was a combination of the basilica and the Greek cross, and for their roofs – barrel vaulting, groined arches and domes. Remarkable also were their carved capitals and friezes, with their mixture of key patterns, rosettes, vine-leaves, wild animals and birds, and sometimes, as in San Pedro de la Nave, human figures.

Just when its future seemed particularly bright, Spain fell unexpectedly victim to the Arab advance. Peace had made men soft, and they were unable to withstand Tarik's forces; a single battle at Xeres in 711 settled the issue. The mainstream of culture changed course,[63] but all was not lost for Christianity. Asturia remained independent, and Charlemagne soon freed Catalonia; together they were destined to be the cradle of Romanesque art. There Beatus wrote his commentary on the Apocalypse, with its illuminations which were to have such an influence on sculpture; there also architects constructed churches with barrel vaulting resting on supporting arches, using decorative tricks like blind arcades; in all this they were pioneers of the first art style of Western Europe. Moorish government in Spain was not intolerant and Christian society could still produce such men as Theodulf and Agobard, the Carolingian Empire's best poet and its only jurist. Last but not least, Spanish manuscripts had already crossed the mountains, and the key works of the seventh century, especially those of Isidore of Seville, were soon known beyond the Pyrenees, even in England.[64] It fell to England to rekindle the flame which was soon glowing everywhere in Western Europe.

At this point there is a temptation to use the expression 'English miracle' to describe the apparently sudden development of art and scholarship in early eighth-century Britain. Such a description would however be false, in view of the fact that the descendants of the barbarous Anglo-Saxons, especially the nobles, had enjoyed and cultivated an indigenous literature of epic and lyric poetry,[65] and that contact with Roman missionaries and Irish monks had been highly fruitful. The influence of these 'Scots' on England, and, through her, on Western Europe is undeniable, but it was probably less important than many earlier historians have claimed.[66] Inspired by Bretons and Gauls, probably since the fifth century, certainly the sixth, they had devoted themselves to Biblical studies with the convert's enthusiasm, and their monasteries had become centres of religious education; historical sources make this quite clear. Documents prove that they had a good knowledge of Latin, since they read the scriptures and the authoritative commentaries by the early Fathers. There is nothing however which proves that they had read or discussed secular and pagan writers, nor introduced them to the Anglo-Saxons and Gauls who went to Hibernia '*legendarum gratia scripturarum*', nor yet taught them in their numerous abbeys scattered throughout Britain and the continent: Lindisfarne, Malmesbury, Luxeuil, Bobbio, Lorsch, St. Gallen, Würzburg. . . . It is therefore unlikely that in the transmission of classical culture they did in fact play the part which some writers still claim for them. But at least they must be credited with having stimulated a taste for learning and with having encouraged more liberal studies in all their institutions, particularly those on English soil.

In South-Eastern England the Roman missionaries under Augustine had brought with them Bible manuscripts, patristic writings and liturgical treatises, and at Canterbury they had set up a seminary for the clergy. Their work, like that of the Irish missionaries, helped to pave the way for Saint Theodore and his companions.

The flowering of culture in Britain dates in fact from the time of Theodore, who became archbishop of Canterbury in 668. Political struggles were becoming less bitter at the time when he travelled from Rome to the shores of Kent; the sixteen or seventeen Anglo-Saxon kingdoms had managed to establish a rudimentary balance of power.

Religious quarrels too were being settled; paganism had almost disappeared and the Council of Whitby, five years earlier, had put an end to the acrimonious and wasteful disputes between the 'Romans', followers of Saint Augustine of Canterbury and Saint Paulinus of York on the one hand, and the Celtic clergy of the North on the other. In spite of his age – he was sixty-seven when he arrived – Theodore was full of energy, and he seized every advantage that the situation offered. He laid down the organization of the English Church under a single primate, filled the empty bishoprics and set up six new dioceses. He called together councils, which drew up canons for the conduct of the clergy and relations between the secular and regular branches. This product of Athenian education, who had made a reputation for himself in Rome as a scholar, encouraged the spread of learning. Hadrian, a monk whose origins and education were in Africa and Byzantine Italy, and Benedict Biscop, an Anglo-Saxon who had spent some time in Gaul and Italy, were his lieutenants in this movement; adopted and transformed by Boniface, Alcuin and their fellows, it was to emerge finally as a great cultural renaissance under Charlemagne.

Nestling near cathedrals and in the shadow of English cloisters, schools were set up, equipped with splendid libraries; there illustrious men taught and wrote.[67] In the beginning the school of Canterbury, with Hadrian as its head for forty years, enjoyed the highest reputation; then Monkwearmouth and Jarrow, in Northumbria, set up in 674 and 681 respectively by Benedict Biscop; somewhat later the school of York, in its turn the most brilliant. In their tireless search for breadth and accuracy of knowledge they laid their hands on all the available manuscripts, whether in Italy, Gaul, Spain or Ireland; from 733 they could claim to possess all the works of important medieval writers, like Boethius, Arator, Cassiodorus and Gregory the Great, Gennadius and Fortunatus, Isidore of Seville, Eugenius and Julian of Toledo, and, more important, most of the classical writers then known.[68] As a result the standard of the teachers was high: they wrote impeccable Latin, and were renowned for the breadth of their knowledge and their love of scholarship. In theory, like their precursors and their continental contemporaries, they made secular learning the handmaiden of religious studies, but in practice they were often carried away by the spirit of research and made the means an end in itself.

The greatest of them was the Venerable Bede.[69] Probably born about 675 in Jarrow, he entered the local abbey and there produced his many and varied works: they included scientific treatises, dealing especially with chronology, Biblical commentaries which put him on a par with the early Fathers, and the *Historia ecclesiastica gentis*

Anglorum, the first historical work of the Middle Ages, amazing in its grasp and intelligence.[70] As late as the thirteenth century his writings wielded great influence,[71] but as a teacher he made an even greater mark; among his pupils was Egbert, the most outstanding personality of the York school, and himself the master of Alcuin, who was to be the pillar of the Carolingian Renaissance.

It was not only classical literature that the 'Romans' transplanted into England; they brought works of art too, paintings and books, whose influence can be traced in the miniatures of the period.[72] The early eighth-century Lindisfarne Gospels, for example, show a combination of the barbarian style of abstract ornamentation with a representational tradition. The *Codex Amiatinus*, written in Jarrow at the same period, is illustrated almost solely with figures. At the same time Italian sculptors and stonemasons from Gaul were teaching their art to local builders. The churches of Kent and Northumbria probably did not influence Carolingian buildings – rather the other way about.[73] But undoubtedly Anglo-Saxon illuminated manuscripts and carvings helped in the ninth century to restore the humanistic ideals enshrined in classical art.

These then were the elements of the Western European civilization to come. They were not new, and they were not sufficient in themselves. In the very early Middle Ages men were so preoccupied with disasters, and so fascinated by Rome that they concentrated on a kind of salvage operation. In this spirit they copied pagan writings, wrote manuals of spelling, grammar or chronology, compiled encyclopedias and chronicles, and aimed at imitating classical architecture, sculpture and painting. They did not, however, take over the classical heritage *en bloc*, and it was not their sole inspiration. Their music, for example, was derived more from Jewish sources.[74] They rejected classical philosophy as such, and refused to accept it as a way of life.

Even these borrowed elements were transformed and added to. They may have been classical in origin, but the Christian, and some-what uncomprehending, viewpoint from which they were interpreted modified their spirit and its implications. Two elements stand out: the new theology, which took the place of pagan philosophy; and the Gregorian chant, which gave a new character to the Divine office.

The Church was by now a dominant influence in Western Europe and a significant factor in ensuring that the nascent civilization would not be a mere copy of its classical precursor.

Chapter 3

SPIRIT: THE CHURCH AND WESTERN EUROPE

The Germanic invasions brought Christians face to face with a difficult problem. Since the end of the fourth century under Theodosius, even since Constantine, their church had been closely linked with the Empire, and Christianity had become the state religion. When Rome and the Empire began visibly to weaken under the barbarian threat, Christians were brought up against a dilemma: should they remain a national church and refuse to collaborate with the invaders, or should they abandon their classical past and go over to them?

It was left to a few to make the decision for the rest. Thoughtful men like Saint Augustine in the *City of God* and Salvian in his *De Gubernatione Dei* surveyed the situation with the calm eyes of faith: the world was only too familiar with such events, and Christians should not be perturbed or disconcerted but should learn from them.[1] Men of action followed the example of Saint Germanus of Auxerre and carried out their daily tasks without worrying about what the future held in store.[2] Their co-religionists followed their lead; some of them, as patriotic Romans, defended and mourned the Empire in its last days, but, believing as they did in the Father's good providence, the Son's intercession and the grace of the Holy Ghost, they were able to face the new circumstances of the West with resignation rather than regret.[3]

In three centuries much was accomplished by bishops, priests and monks. Individual souls were won over and converted from Arianism and paganism, and even the most rustic peasant was claimed for the Church; after conversion came the less spectacular but more difficult task of 'Christianization'. Churchmen began to intervene more often in public affairs; they had inherited the organizing ability of Rome, and were able to give valuable assistance to barbarian kingdoms at grips with problems of government; in a decadent society they alone were equipped for the task of education and the practice of scholarship, literature and the arts. In all this they were laying the foundations of that unity of spirit which was to be the keynote of the Middle Ages.

In the beginning by no means all of Western Europe was Catholic. During the fourth century the Church had won over the marches of the old Roman world, installed bishops at Tongeren and York and set up strong Christian communities on the banks of the Rhine. But it had not converted all the peoples within the Empire's boundaries: like the civil administration it was based on the towns, and in some country areas its influence was not felt. There were villagers still to be reached, and, after 406, Arians – Goths, Vandals, Burgundians, Sueves, and pagans – Franks and Anglo-Saxons; sizeable numbers still to be converted and then Christianized.

Fortunately circumstances were favourable. In Southern Gaul and Spain some of the barbarian rulers, especially among the Visigoths, did indeed subject the Church to an under-cover persecution, chiefly because they were worried by the number of its adherents. Farther north, the Catholic population was not so dense and many pagan rulers – the Frankish Clovis, Ethelbert of Kent and Edwin of Northumbria – made the missionaries welcome, gave them moral and financial support and helped to make possible mass conversions, which were speedy, but not always long-lived. There was rarely any violent resistance, and consequently few martyrs; on the contrary, sympathy was widespread.

The work of the missionaries was co-operative, though not on any systematic basis; popes did not impose precise plans but they co-ordinated activity to a limited extent. There were vast numbers of missionaries; recruits came from all sides to swell the multitude. They came from longstanding Catholic areas in the West like Italy and Aquitaine: Saint Augustine of Canterbury and Saint Paulinus of York were both Romans, Saint Amand who proselytized the Scheldt valley was born south of the Loire.[4] They came, too, from countries only recently converted – compact groups of rough, noisy Irishmen were scattered over England and the Continent; they were imbued with Celtic dynamism, a determination to follow the example of the first apostles, and a burning zeal for asceticism which could only be satisfied by a period of exile amongst peoples ignorant of the faith.[5] In the mission field the lives of Remigius of Rheims, Leander of Seville, Wilfrid of York and Lambert of Maastricht were by no means unique.[6] There was the same enthusiasm in the Byzantine empire; Martin, who converted the Sueves and founded the monastery at Braga in Portugal, came from Pannonia. Wherever a missionary was in a dangerous situation or unable to complete his task, a replacement would be at hand immediately to take over; if the Church was forced to retreat at any point she would push forward a salient not far away.

The missionaries were relatively well-trained. Most of them were monks or had spent several years in an abbey. Monasticism, which had been brought to Western Europe in the fourth century, had quickly spread in three waves during the following two hundred years.[7] The first wave originated in central and southern Gaul, at Lérins (410) and Auxerre (some time before 418).[8] Saint Patrick, who studied in both places, introduced monasticism into Ireland, where it immediately took hold;[9] from there it spread to Iona (563), and to England, through Saint Aidan, who had been a monk at Iona and founded Lindisfarne Abbey (635); another impetus brought it back to Europe with Saint Columbanus, who founded Luxeuil in the Vosges and Bobbio in Italy. He was the first and greatest of the Scots who undertook the conversion of the Franks, Alamans, Thuringians and Bavarians from 590 onwards.[10] The second main wave was Spanish in origin, and remained so. Very early in the Middle Ages the

MONASTICISM IN EUROPE AT THE BEGINNING OF THE MIDDLE AGES

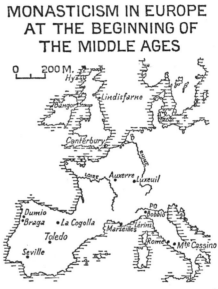

monastic way of life took root there – at Dumio, Braga, Toledo, La Cogolla and Seville; much the same rule was followed until after the year 1000.[11] The third, and the most important, wave started with Saint Benedict (†547) and his monasteries at Subiaco and Monte Cassino. Whatever view one takes of his rule,[12] he was the patriarch of West European monasticism, and many of his spiritual sons settled in southern England. At a later stage, with their better-organized community life, they gradually supplanted other orders, in particular the Irish ones;[13] and between 400 and 600 their monastic houses multiplied. In no sense did they specialize in training missionaries, but they did provide a higher level of education than secular clergy usually enjoyed; they gave them a grounding in the Scriptures; and they encouraged those evangelistic virtues of non-attachment, charity, poverty, humility, steadfastness and faith which were to bear fruit in the work amongst the Arian and pagan inhabitants of the old Empire.

In the dawn of the Middle Ages Arianism revived. It had been crushed in the Roman world after the condemnations at Nicaea in 325 and Constantinople in 381, but the Visigoths had taken it up and had become very zealous.[14] During the wanderings which led them from Moesia in the Balkan peninsula to Dacia, Italy, Aquitaine and Spain, they introduced it to the peoples with whom they came in contact – the Ostrogoths, Vandals, Burgundians and Sueves. About A.D. 500 it figured as the national religion of the Germanic peoples as opposed to the Catholicism of the Latins.[15]

This was, however, only a short-lived revival. Arianism was not strong enough to defend itself against orthodoxy, still less to engage in opposition to it. By regarding the Word as a created being it had deprived itself of what Christians found a great source of strength: the certainty that God had come down to live among men, and had proved His infinite love by redeeming them with His blood. In addition it lacked unity; it might claim to be Catholic, but since it was subservient to local rulers (it is possible that its liturgy was in the vernacular) each people had its own church. Latter-day Romans regarded it as an inferior religion, fit for rough, uneducated barbarians; a few subscribed to it for reasons of self-interest, but in general it and its illiterate clergy were looked upon with contempt. Its chance of gaining adherents was therefore slight, indeed it was certain to lose them in the process of integration, as the invading peoples tended to discard whatever differentiated them from the indigenous population.

In such conditions Arianism survived thanks only to royal support, and if that was withdrawn its days were numbered. This happened in 516 to the Burgundians, in 563 to the Sueves, and in 587 to the Visigoths. Avitus of Vienne and his fellow bishops, Martin of Braga and Leander of Seville, converted their rulers, Sigismund, Theodomir and Recared, to Catholicism. The conversion of the Lombards, who had replaced the Ostrogoths, decimated by Justinian, was begun about 600 by Gregory the Great and Queen Theodelinda, but for various reasons was not completed till 671. The date marked the definitive end of Arianism.

Since the heresy was spread by the Visigoths it made little headway among barbarian peoples farther north, outside their sphere of influence. The Bavarians, Thuringians, Alamans and Franks remained pagan. It was soon clear that the Franks would outstrip the others, and missionaries turned their attention first to them.

They were not long in achieving a striking success in the conversion of Clovis.[16] Since 482, when he came to power, his attitude to the priests, their flock, and all that they stood for, had been benevolent. His wife Chlotilde and Remigius, the bishop of Rheims, had been very persuasive, and he had almost taken the final step of becoming a Catholic; but he hesitated. His companions-in-arms were still loyal to their gods, and he might lose their confidence if he changed his religion. He might also lay himself open to an attack from the Arian princes of the Burgundians and Visigoths on his southern borders, just when the Alamans were threatening him from the east. His first move was therefore to persuade the Burgundians to remain neutral while he defeated the Alamans. He was then ready to make the decision. His long record of successes meant that he was no longer anxious about alienating his warriors. His only remaining enemies were the Visigoths, and by becoming a Catholic he could win over the orthodox population persecuted by their Arian leaders. So, with nothing to lose and much to gain, he asked to be baptized, and this one event secured the future for Catholicism.

It was some time, however, before all the Franks were converted. Catholicism made slow progress in the country around the Meuse and the Scheldt. Saint Remigius had established bishoprics at Arras and Tournai, but fifty years later they were amalgamated with Cambrai and Noyon because the faithful were so few in number.[17] Seventh-century tombs in cemeteries of Lorraine show none of the characteristic Christian emblems.[18] It was not until after 625 that the first monasteries were founded in what is now Belgium. It took over two hundred years of effort on the part of native Christians, such as Géry, Omer, Lambert and Hubert, Amand and his fellow Aquitainians, and Irish missionaries, to stamp out paganism among the Franks; they accomplished it by about 725.

Meanwhile, the victorious battles of Clovis and his descendants had influenced Alemania, Bavaria and Thuringia in favour of Christianity.[19] But in these regions, especially in Thuringia which had never been part of the Roman Empire and had not experienced Christianity in that period, there was more opposition to be faced than in southern Gaul. Officials, Frankish missionaries and Irish monks such as Gallus, Eustasius of Luxeuil, and Kilian, were only partly successful. The work was taken up again in the Carolingian period.

The conversion of the Franks facilitated missionary work among the Anglo-Saxons, the last remaining barbarian group within the limits of the Roman Empire. Bede himself says that the king of Kent welcomed Augustine of Canterbury and his companions, partly because his wife, a Frankish princess, had already told him about Christianity: '*nam et antea fama ad eum Christianae religionis pervenerat, utpote qui et uxorem habebat Christianam de gente*

Francorum regia.'[20] Augustine was destined to be the first primate of Britain.

The Britons of Wales and Cornwall had not attempted to convert the Angles and Saxons. They nursed too much resentment at having been driven from their richest lands. They had not communicated the faith which they had received from Rome in the fourth century. After 597 Italians, and then Irishmen, came to fill the gap.

The story goes that it was a chance conversation in Rome between 574 and 578 that drew Gregory the Great's attention to England. He decided to go himself and win it for Christ. At the time he was dissuaded; fifteen years of absorbing work followed, and in the end his election to the Papacy meant that he could hardly leave Italy. He did not, however, abandon his plan, but entrusted it to a man in whom he had complete confidence, Augustine, the prior of Saint Andrew's on the Coelian.[21]

THE CONVERSION OF ENGLAND

Lindisfarne
Jarrow
NORTHUMBRIA
Bangor
Whitby
York
MERCIA
LINDSEY
MIDDLE-ANGLIA
Dunwich
EAST-ANGLIA
WALES
ESSEX
Dorchester
London
Malmesbury
WESSEX
Rochester
Canterbury
KENT
CORNWALL

Augustine arrived in Kent, the most populous and well-cultivated part of the island, and firmly planted Christianity there, instituting the primate's see at Canterbury and the first suffragan see at Rochester. He also went to Essex, which at the time was a dependency of Kent, and set up a see at London. About twenty years later another Italian, Paulinus, who had arrived in 601 with a second group of Benedictine monks, baptized Edwin, king of Northumbria, who had married the king of Kent's daughter; Paulinus founded what was to be the archbishopric of York and spread the gospel throughout Lindsey. At the same time Augustine's successor at Canterbury sent Felix of Burgundy to Dunwich to convert East Anglia, while Brixinus, who came from somewhere on the continent, was based on Dorchester and was proselytizing Wessex with the approval of the Pope. Within a period of fifty years emissaries from Rome had made contact with most of Anglo-Saxon England.

50

Their conversions were not always blessed with permanence. In 616 there was a return to paganism in Essex. Paulinus's work in the north did not outlive Edwin, who was killed in 632 in a battle against Cadwallon, king of Gwynedd. The task of reconversion in these areas was undertaken by Irish missionaries. Oswald of Northumbria, who defeated Cadwallon in 633, summoned monks whom he had known in his youth from Iona. In 634 one of them, Aidan, settled with a few companions on Lindisfarne. In less than twenty years they had brought Northumbria, Lindsey and Essex back to the faith, and had won over Mercia and Middle Anglia. By about 660 the whole of England had been converted – in the north by the Scots, in the south by the 'Romans'.

The result, for several years, was discord. The Celtic Church had developed in a kind of vacuum, and its customs were different from Roman ones, in particular its method of calculating the date of Easter. Adherence to these customs led to quarrels between the Celts and the heirs of Augustine of Canterbury. But in 664 the Synod of Whitby decided the matter: Wilfrid, who was to occupy the see of York in the following year, upheld the Roman rule and it prevailed. Unity was thus established. The way was open for Theodore of Tarsus to come and lay down the framework of a thriving Anglo-Saxon Christianity;[22] in the eighth century that church was to send Willibrord, Boniface and their followers to convert Frisia and Germany.

Bringing the Gospel to pagan peoples, and baptizing them, was only an introduction. The real task was to truly 'Christianize' them, in other words, to change their way of life radically. The essence of Christianity did not lie merely in repeating set forms of words, in ritual observances or even intellectual acceptance of dogma; it implied a deep-rooted attitude of mind. The true Christian not only publicly declared his belief in Christ's teaching, he behaved like Christ, or at least, since the old Adam never quite dies, he sincerely and assiduously tried to follow Christ's example.

To purge old poisons, eradicate pagan traditions, and replace them by a Christian way of looking at life was not something which could be done in a matter of days or even years. Some of the Frankish or Saxon audience in a sixth- or seventh-century crowd who listened to the strange missionary preaching a new religion may have grasped its significance at once; in that word so dear to the medieval mind their 'conversio' may have meant a revolution in their lives. But what of the rest? Gregory of Tours records that 'in those times there was more lamentation than in the time of Diocletian's persecution'. Even the greatest of missionaries could only sow the seed. It had to be left to the patient care of others to see that it was not trodden underfoot, but was allowed to germinate, take root and multiply.

Such basic husbandry was especially called for in pagan Europe, where the seed often fell on soil which had not been properly prepared. Conversions were often too hastily made, frequently for material motives; nobles might be improving their political prospects, or trying to keep up with the Romans culturally by adopting their religion, peasants might be afraid of angering a newly-converted lord. The missionaries themselves may have soft-pedalled the catechism and played down the differences between idolatry and Catholicism. They purveyed the essentials of doctrine, but they were not concerned to make their source-book, the Bible,[23] available to the common people in the vernacular – nor the liturgy which was, so to speak, a dramatized version of the doctrine.[24] They built churches on the ruins of pagan temples, dedicated holy springs to the saints, transformed ancient rites into Christian feasts, and in this way they may have encouraged the survival of pagan practices and attitudes of mind.[25] The somewhat tarnished Christianity of the early Middle Ages, its dogma reduced to a few set forms, its morality inspired by fear rather than love, its undue emphasis on the miraculous – relics used as lucky charms, blessings as magic incantations – is not solely accounted for by a superstitious population. People may have been swayed by emotion and overwhelmed by a feeling of helplessness in the face of nature, but some blame must be laid at the door of the priests who followed the first missionaries; possibly they were too anxious to ensure that the transition from paganism to Christianity should be painless.

The problem of rooting out under-cover paganism, and gradually giving the new converts a fuller understanding of their religion was to be met by setting up monasteries and grouping the faithful laity into parishes. In the monasteries men could see the example of a fully Christian life; with their better education, and better material and moral conditions, the monks could follow the gospel teaching in their lives more easily than the secular clergy. Parish organization would ensure spiritual guidance for the mass of the population; parish priests would consolidate and gradually improve on the results already achieved by missionaries; they would be always on the spot to set right doctrinal mistakes or moral lapses. And so, from the fifth to the eighth centuries abbeys and churches sprang up all over Western Europe.

There was nothing very systematic about their creation; churches, in particular, were founded for a host of different reasons. Sometimes the initiative came from the bishop, or from missionaries, sometimes from groups of peasants who managed to raise the necessary money to build and endow a church; but more often the prime mover was a noble who felt that his estate was not complete without it. Often there was considerable delay before a resident priest was appointed and the collection of parish dues authorized. Parishes varied in importance and in the size of their population according to their geographical location. In the south their number increased rapidly, but they remained few in the north until the eighth and ninth centuries.[26]

Once the framework was laid down the work of 'Christianization' could begin in earnest. It was a somewhat thankless task and proceeded only slowly; those who undertook it often lacked the necessary qualities. Monks tended to lead too comfortable a life, and did not always set a good example. Parish priests were usually appointed, in fact if not in theory, by secular nobles descended from the founder of the local church, and the only training they received was on the spot, from their predecessor; they were often ill-informed, apathetic and lax in their morals, especially where they were recruited from rough, uncivilized peoples like the Franks. In such conditions the true spirit of Christianity was slow to have an effect on individuals. The result was the striking contrast one notices in Western Europe in the early medieval period, and indeed later, between superstition and faith, cruelty and charity, pride and humility, lechery and chastity, greed and generosity. Respect for the Church did not protect it from outrage, and churches were sacked on the one hand and impressively endowed on the other. Such antitheses strike and even shock modern observers all the more because of the prevailing 'clericalism' or 'confessionalism' of medieval society.

At an early stage, the Church had gone beyond the limits of the religious sphere, and had intervened in social, political and cultural matters.[27]

Good works came first. The poor were assisted, the aged cared for, the sick nursed, serfs were freed, and prisoners of war, slaves and common law criminals were ransomed. In all this it was fulfilling its vocation to show that God is love and can only be reached through love. The State, of course, was indifferent to the lot of ordinary people; the Church was alone in showing compassion for the poor.

Its interference in political affairs was the result of a combination of ideas and events. The Church's duty was felt to be not to dominate the State but to guide it.[28] Christ had, after all, broken with pagan tradition in pronouncing that temporal authority was supreme in temporal matters. In 494, through the mouth of Pope Gelasius, the Church had reiterated that the civil power was divinely appointed and had complete freedom of movement within its own sphere; but, as Saint Augustine added, its chief task was to ensure the salvation of its subjects. As God's representative on earth the Church felt a responsibility to see that the temporal power fulfilled its mission, so it kept a watchful eye on the administration of justice and on taxation, with the tacit or express approval of the local ruler. In Spain under the Visigoths criticisms were made of royal decisions, and Church councils took it upon themselves to legislate.[29]

The force of circumstance was operating in that direction. As the only organized force and the sole European repository of Roman traditions in administration and culture, the Church was almost forced to fill the gaps in a barbarian society; and its moral authority and wealth were rapidly growing. State officials were often allowed too much freedom by the civil power and tended to abuse it;[30] Church dignitaries were best qualified to prevent or minimize the effect of their arbitrary actions. On certain occasions and for certain missions kings needed men of some education – only priests could fill the bill.

They had, to all intents and purposes, a cultural monopoly. Until the urban renaissance, centres of civilization were to be found only in religious and monastic communities; they constituted the towns of what was essentially a rural society. They provided practically the only academic education.

The classical tradition was the hallmark of their education, as we have already seen.[31] Teachers in the schools followed Roman programmes of studies and writers were too inclined to imitate classical authors. But the Church was beginning to influence education and literature, and the perspective was changing. The aim of the liberal arts was no longer to produce a whole man, but to be the handmaidens of exegesis and theology. The essential spirit of most writings was modified radically: their authors based their philosophy and scale of values on the Gospel rather than on paganism or the natural law.

The Church left its mark on the arts too. To take only one example, mosaic style changed subtly on coming into contact with Christianity: the realism which had been a legacy from the classical past gave way to something more grandiose which could express the Christian ideal better.[32]

The Church, then, was active in every sphere. Its influence was not decisive everywhere, but its presence was felt. The first stage had been reached, and further advances would follow.

Such an expansion of activity into the different realms of public life, and among Arians and pagans, somewhat endangered the Church's unity – both doctrinal and disciplinary – but the perils were surmounted without too much difficulty.

In Western Europe the faith was never seriously threatened. Catholicism's rivals were far from being mature philosophies or organized religions. The Germanic tribes' Arianism was only a survival and their ignorant priesthood could make no headway against cultured Romans. It is true that paganism could and did, as we have seen, mark Christian attitudes of mind,[33] but it was too crude to be able to distort articles of faith. Europeans of the West were less subtle and more disciplined than those farther east, and in the long run, not much attracted by heresies. They were bored by the cerebral controversies about the nature of Christ which Byzantium found so absorbing; in the eighth century the adoptianists under Felix of Urgel made little stir.[34] They did discuss one practical question, which was how the concepts of grace and freedom, God's power and man's free will, could be reconciled. In the early fifth century the Celt, Pelagius, came to grief on this point, and overstressed the importance of free will.[35] In the Carolingian period Gottschalk, a Saxon, took up the opposite stand, and came down on the side of unqualified predestination.[36] However, both their doctrines were condemned with some dispatch. This problem, which might be termed 'the problem of the West' did not lead to a doctrinal schism until the end of the Middle Ages, with the coming of Luther and Calvin.

On questions of discipline, however, unity was sometimes difficult to achieve. In several particulars Ireland followed its own practices; it based them on Saint John's authority rather than on that of Peter's successors, and refused to change them for Roman customs.[37] Spain declared that the Pope had 'a tender care for all churches', but it was proud of its theologians, and claimed the right to examine papal decisions in councils convoked by the king.[38] After its reconquest by Byzantium, Italy fell a prey to Near Eastern disputes on dogma, and in the middle of the sixth century a revival of Origenism led to a schism of the bishops of Milan and, in particular, Aquileia.[39] Lastly, in Gaul the king was responsible for choosing bishops, or at least for confirming the appointee of clergy and people; he also convoked or authorized councils and in general exerted an influence which dangerously rivalled that of the Holy See.[40] Although some historians have exaggerated the possibility that Western Christendom might have split into a number of different state churches, that danger did exist.

It was averted by one of the greatest popes in history. Towards the end of the sixth century Gregory I gave real personality to the Papacy.[41] His *Liber regulae pastoralis*, with its portrait of an ideal pastor, his *Moralia* or Commentaries on Job, his *Dialogi* – stories of miracles performed by holy men of the recent past – his *Antiphonale*, which was the origin of Gregorian chant, and his other writings, all had a wide circulation and reflected considerable prestige on the author and his office.[42] In Italy his efforts paved the way for the end of the Aquileian schism, and in spite of Byzantium he opened negotiations with the Lombards which were to lead to their conversion. His letters to Spanish and Gallic bishops demonstrate conclusively the supreme authority he enjoyed, by nature of his office. His initiative in undertaking the conversion of the Anglo-Saxons was to bear fruit – the creation of two churches, the English and the German, closely dependent on the Papacy. It was also a determining factor in the Irish adoption of Roman usages in 704,[43] a hundred years after his death, which marked the end of effective opposition to the Holy See.

The Church conferred more than a religion as it spread throughout Western Europe; through the mere fact that it remained one and indivisible it unified Europe. Its doctrines might be only superficially understood, but they implied a single vision of the world, rising above individuals and their personal ideas. It rose above divisions into races and kingdoms and even the potentially dangerous hostility between Barbarians and Romans: 'there are no more Scythians, Aquitainians, Lombards or Alamans . . . for Christ shed his blood so that those who were far off should be brought near, to make an end of separation'.[44] It rose above differences in culture; unlike Islam and other faiths outside the Roman tradition, Christianity, which was born within the empire and became its state church, could provide the link between the classical and the new world. One faith, interpreted by one spiritual leader: the corner-stone of the Middle Ages was in place.

Chapter 4

FIRST LIGHT: THE CAROLINGIANS

In 639 the death of Dagobert I led to a critical situation in the chief barbarian kingdoms. Frankish Gaul was breaking up into separate, weaker states. Aquitaine followed an independent line, while Austrasia's attitude to Neustria and Burgundy was hostile. In all their dominions the last, debauched Merovingians could no longer impose their authority. Clovis's achievement was in jeopardy.

In this crisis a new, masterful dynasty emerged. Its early leaders were mayors of the palace, Austrasian nobles; they succeeded in restoring unity and order. After the victory at Tertry in 687 Neustria and Burgundy submitted to Austrasia, and the new rulers took control.[1] A few decades passed, and then the *de facto* government became *de jure:* Pepin the Short, who was descended from four generations of this rich, intelligent, energetic clan, was acclaimed king by the nobles in 751.

In its hundred years the dynasty he founded was destined to bring to completion changes which had been brewing in Western Europe from the fifth to the seventh centuries. It was to define political structures, encourage literature and the arts, and support the establishment of Christianity. It was to strive to impose peace and unity in its dominions, and so make possible the first flowering of medieval civilization.

Such a vast programme was too extensive for one man, however brilliant, and it was in fact the achievement of a whole royal house. It takes its name justifiably from Charlemagne; but Pepin the Short laid excellent foundations, and Charlemagne's work was carried on, though in a less spectacular fashion, by Louis the Pious and Charles the Bald. It would be false and unjust to forget them and attribute the 'renaissance' to Charlemagne alone.

Since 250 the western and eastern ends of Europe had been drawing apart. After 500 the West's centre of gravity had moved northwards.

Around the year 800 Carolingian victories, which turned a kingdom into an empire, sharply emphasized these two tendencies.

Politically and strategically it was essential for Pepin and Charlemagne to embark on empire-building in the Merovingian style. To the north and east Merovingian forces had pushed beyond Gaul's natural frontiers;[2] the result was that 'greater Francia' included several trouble spots. The Frisians, Saxons, Alamans and Bavarians had often been defeated but they had never been tamed. They had to be subjugated at all costs, to make certain of peace in the region. In the process, Carolingian forces were to reach the valley of the Elbe before establishing a frontier. In the south, Eudes of Aquitaine and Charles Martel had halted the Arab advance, but with such dangerous neighbours, a mountain frontier was desirable. In the south-east the Lombards were exerting pressure on the Papacy; if it should become their vassal they would reap the advantage of the prestige it had enjoyed since Gregory I, and would take first rank among the barbarians.

Religious considerations were no less important. It was impossible for Pepin the Short not to answer the Holy See's agonized appeal, since the Church had crowned him and thereby, in effect, supported him in his struggle against Merovingian 'legitimists'. Charlemagne styled himself 'King and priest, Christendom's leader and guide', so that he could hardly tolerate the existence of paganism between the Rhine and the Elbe, or Moorish domination of the faithful in Spain.

So, one campaign followed another – closely in the first Carolingian's reign, without respite at all under the second. Victories came thick and fast. Frisia capitulated, and so, finally, did the rebellious Saxons. Bohemia entered the Frankish sphere of influence. Bavaria, which had been to all intents and purposes an independent duchy, was absorbed, and its dependent Carinthia with it. Carniola and Istria were annexed. The Lombard kingdom was dismembered, and that part of it which became the Papal state was allowed little freedom of action. The Arabs abandoned Septimania, and even yielded one of the bridgeheads beyond the Pyrenees, which later provided a starting-point for the *Reconquista*. Forces penetrated even into unconquerable Brittany. In 814 Francia *'longe lateque dilatata,'* to quote Jonas of Orleans,[3] stretched from the English Channel and the river Vilaine to Trieste and Brindisi, and from the Elbe to Barcelona.

All Western Europe was included in it. It embraced the Saxony of Widukind and Roswitha, Saint Gall's Alemania, Notger and Renier de Huy's Lotharingia. All the great centres of medieval civilization lay within those frontiers: Flanders with its free cities and its cloth trade, the Abbaye aux Hommes in Normandy, the Champagne fairs, the Île de France with its soaring Gothic and proud scholarship, Chartres and Beauce, Burgundy's Cluny and Cîteaux, Aquitaine and the early troubadours, the 'first Romanesque art' of Catalonia and Lombardy, and Romagna with the jurists of Ravenna and Bologna. Even England maintained close relations with the Carolingians; Canterbury sent them Boniface, and York Alcuin; Carolingian art arrived in return.[4]

It was men from the north, once again, who succeeded in linking so many disparate kingdoms in one culture and one political grouping. The Merovingians' birthplace had been Tournai. The Carolingians, as descendants of Arnulf of Metz and Pepin of Landen were men of Lorraine, and the Meuse valley in particular. Their estates were there, their deer forests, and the monasteries they founded.[5] It was natural that they should establish their capital in this part of the country that they knew and loved. In fact, after the conquest of Frisia and Saxony, Aix was at the heart of the kingdom, and no longer on the frontier.

This was the culmination of a shift that had started in the time of Clovis; the political centre of Western Europe moved a few degrees farther north, and cultural centres sprang up in its wake. It was at St.-Wandrille, St.-Denis, Laon, Corbie, St.-Bertin, St.-Riquier, Rheims, Metz, Utrecht, Aix, Cologne, Fulda, Lorsch, Corvey, Reichenau and St.-Gallen, with Tours, Ferrières, Orleans, Fleury-sur-Loire, Lyons and Aniane that the famous schools and chief 'scriptoria' of the period were to be found.

Their political achievement was destined to be short-lived, for the empire soon broke up. But attitudes of mind persisted, just as they did among the Arabs after the break-up of the Arab empire. Western European nations had been refined and moulded by the same powerful influences – kings, missionaries and monks – so that they had fundamental characteristics in common. Until the early Renaissance the lead was to come from the country between the Loire and the Rhine.

Frankish expansion had other results too. It made Charlemagne ruler of vast territories, master of the historic capital of the Caesars, protector of the Papacy, defender of the Catholic church, and in all this the equal of the 'Basileus', with a better claim than his to be the heir of the fourth-century emperors. It led inevitably to his assumption of the purple. In some ways Western Europeans could regard the coronations of 751 and 800 as consecrating a *fait accompli*.[6]

Charlemagne's coronation was, however, also a gesture of independence *vis-à-vis* Byzantium.[7] It destroyed the illusion of universal power enjoyed by Constantine's successors, an illusion which had been fostered from the time of the Germanic invasions. It dashed any hope of restoring the Roman Empire by grouping all the peoples west of the Rhine and the Danube under one leader. Henceforth, the only conceivable empire was a Christian one, with little in common with its predecessor.[8] The 'Basileis' were no fools, and they protested against Carolingian 'usurpation'; but they were powerless to act, and after a few years they had to grant recognition. The removal of the imperial capital from Tiber's banks to the shores of the Bosphorus had set off a reaction that was by now almost complete: West and East were only united by a weak religious link, one which had already given way several times and which was soon to suffer a definitive break.

Within these new frontiers of medieval Europe the Carolingian dynasty became patrons of literature and the arts. Their aim was first of all to ensure the education of the priesthood, and then the creation of a lay *élite* from which the governing class would spring; admiration for Rome, and the desire to establish a similarly national culture was another incentive. They therefore sought out and drew in any and every element which might have something to contribute. Their tastes were catholic, and included Latin literary masterpieces, Greek philosophical treatises, Christian sermons, early medieval anthologies and miscellanies, canonical books and Germanic epic poems. Their net was cast wide – as far as England, Spain and even Ireland.

England proved a particularly rich source,[9] willing to share with Francia treasures collected there from the time of Theodore of Canterbury and Benedict Biscop. Continental students had free access to its schools and libraries: a Frisian, Ludger, for example, is known to have begun his studies at Utrecht but finished them at York, and brought a number of books back home with him. Even more important was the fact that, throughout the eighth century all the most intelligent and learned Englishmen were sent across the Channel. Among the serried ranks of these scholarly missionaries and teachers, with manuscripts as their luggage, Saint Boniface and Alcuin were the most impressive. Boniface was one of the greatest and most compelling of medieval missionaries, a sensitive spirit, quickly swinging from burning zeal to deep discouragement, but always moved to charity and pity.[10] Before leaving England he had been a teacher and grammarian, and had composed poetry, and throughout his apostolic work he remained a humanist. He was convinced of the value of profane studies as part of spiritual education, and he communicated his enthusiasm for them to people like young Nithard, Charlemagne's grandson, and Sturm of Bavaria, who later founded the great German cultural centre, the abbey of Fulda. In all his travels he urged Christians, especially priests, not to neglect the liberal arts. '*Ut liberalium litterarum scientiam et divini intellectus*

flagrantem spiritualiter ignem non extinguas,' he wrote.[11] Two generations later, Alcuin followed in his footsteps.

Alcuin himself has often been called 'Charlemagne's Minister of
Education'; he was not a great writer or full of originality, but he had
qualities of mind which were more important at the time: he was the
intellectual heir of Bede, and an outstanding teacher – and as Gaul
prepared for its renaissance its need was for teachers.[12] He used
different means to make his pedagogy memorable and effective; he
wrote many clear, simple manuals in a readable dialogue form, and
made use of the 'disputation' method between teacher and students;
and he set up libraries. The best proof of his gift for teaching, and the
depth of his influence on his pupils, lies in their own merits and in the
affection he aroused in them.

The Carolingians looked beyond the treasures heaped on them by
Boniface, Alcuin and numerous other Anglo-Saxons; external
politics drew them towards Italy, which still retained some of its
antique aura. They brought manuscripts[13] back with them, mostly
from Rome, and after 774, teachers and writers like Peter of Pisa,
Paulinus of Aquileia and Paul the Deacon arrived from Lombardy.
Political events – the Moorish invasion – decided the Visigoths to
leave Isidore of Seville's province. They were hospitably received by
the Carolingians, who favoured the most cultivated of them, Theodulf, with a place of honour at court. Another invasion threat, this
time from the Vikings, led Irish monks, followers of Saint Columbanus, to abandon Holy Island. They also were welcomed, their
advice and help were sought, and some of them were given charge of
the palace school. The intellectual heritage from barbarian Europe
was concentrated there, and more besides – for Rome and Constantinople provided Greek manuscripts and Hellenic and Byzantine
translators.[14]

Carolingian Gaul also acted as a magnet to works of art. Many
different styles and influences converged there – from Anglo-Saxon
and Italian miniatures to Oriental silks and jewels. In architecture,
construction and decoration used in classical and Christian Rome,
Byzantine Ravenna, and even the Visigoths' Terrassa left their mark,
though they did not change the fundamentals of traditional style.[15]
The Merovingians had shown considerable skill in architecture, and
had decorated their monumental buildings with frescoes, so that
their descendants were not forced to borrow from neighbouring
peoples, as they were in the realms of literature. It was Eudes of
Metz, a Frankish contemporary of intellectuals like the Englishman
Alcuin, the Lombard Paul the Deacon and the Spaniard Theodulf,
who was the architect of the Palatine Chapel at Aix.

Both mayors of the palace and Carolingian kings left no stone unturned in their efforts to spread Catholicism among the pagans, and the Gospel spirit in the life of the community; they were inspired in this by religious enthusiasm, but also by self-interest. They clearly realized the political significance of religion. The transition from independence to membership of the *Regnum Francorum* was obviously made easier if the peoples concerned were also converted to Catholicism. Within the empire Christianity could act as a unifying force, one which was badly needed to bind together so many different peoples scattered over a vast, inadequately administered area. But Charlemagne and Louis the Pious were not solely swayed by political considerations, however powerful they might be; they were moved as much by true missionary zeal.

The result was that evangelizing priests were always supported, and were often actually dispatched on their missions by Pepin the Short or one of his successors. In the territories directly under their control they put the missionaries under the local lord's protection. In neighbouring countries they fought to gain a foothold for them. In Saxony Charlemagne himself directed operations; he decided the objectives, shared out the tasks, and at one stage threatened death to any of the vanquished who refused baptism, in spite of Alcuin's remonstrance that 'one can persuade men to believe but one cannot force them'. Such unflagging support from the secular arm enabled Anglo-Saxon monks and their European brothers to win over Germany and Frisia, which in turn served as a forward base for new advances.

The names Germany and Frisia conjure up pictures of Boniface, a coward made bold by faith, and Willibrord, a brave, fearless man. They were rightly revered as the Apostles of these regions. On the other hand, it is in no way denigratory of their outstanding qualities if one calls to mind the other brave men who participated in their work at every stage.[16] Hesse, Thuringia and Bavaria had been introduced to Christianity before Boniface arrived.[17] As early as the eighth century priests had been recruited and bishops consecrated from among the local flock, but paganism was still endemic, and it began to have an adverse effect on Christian dogma and practice. From 722 to 753 Rome entrusted Boniface with the task of reconversion; he was to expurgate doubtful doctrines and idol-worship and set up churches and monasteries; he had also to reform clerical life and complete the organization of the church hierarchy. In all his work he was supported by Charles Martel and Pepin the Short and assisted by other Englishmen. When he died a martyr's death in 753 his dream of a Christian Germany had become a reality. But across the lower Rhine Willibrord was less fortunate. The first Anglo-Saxon missionaries, Wilfrid of York and Wigbert, had not been able to make much headway there, and the local people fought against Christianity as they did against foreign domination. When Willibrord died in 739 he had only just embarked on the conversion of Frisia.[18] The northern part of the region held out until after 770, when it succumbed to another Englishman, Willehad, who was assisted by two local men, Alberic and Ludger.[19]

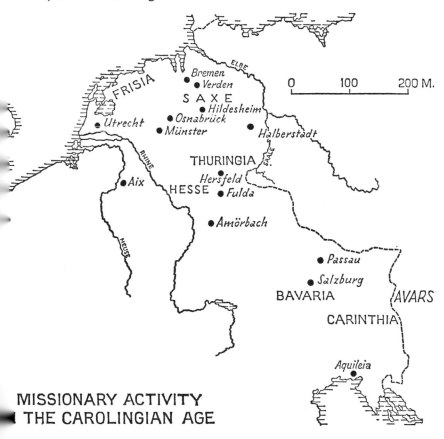

MISSIONARY ACTIVITY
THE CAROLINGIAN AGE

Success had only just crowned these efforts in the Frankish marches and border regions when missionaries were called to a new field. The Utrecht diocese had already been made famous by Willibrord and could boast of Fulda and Hersfeld, abbeys which Boniface and his followers had founded, as well as the older foundation at Amörbach in Bavaria; in 777 Charlemagne called upon it to join in the evangelization of Saxony.[20] In 787 he appointed Willehad and Patto of Amörbach as its first bishops; they were to hold the new sees of

Bremen and Verden.[21] A few years later he summoned Ludger and Wiho from Frisia, and made them bishops of Münster and Osnabrück. About 820 Louis the Pious set up the dioceses of Halberstadt and Hildesheim, and so completed the task which his father had embarked on with perhaps excessive enthusiasm. Farther south, Salzburg Christians led by Pepin the Short's appointee, the Irishman Virgilius, had made considerable headway in Slovene Carinthia by the middle of the eighth century. In 796 Alcuin encouraged his pupil Arno to extend his efforts there; with the help of Passau and Aquileia, the Gospel was brought to the Avars and their Slav dependencies. With them, the entire Empire finally became Christian.

Christianity thus reached ever further into pagan areas, and in regions where it was already well-established religious fervour increased. 'Christianization' and evangelization advanced hand in hand. The secular clergy had much to do with it. Their numbers had increased – especially in the north where many new parishes were created in the eighth and ninth centuries. Their quality also improved; higher dignitaries of Church and State began to show concern about their level of education, tried to keep up their enthusiasm and watched over their behaviour; both civil and ecclesiastical decrees insisted on certain minimum standards of theological knowledge, and on the duty of the priest to be at his flock's disposition at all times; they laid much stress on the value of good preaching and wise example.[22]

Christian precepts did not only apply in private life; their effect began to be felt in public life, particularly in the political sphere. The Church began to play its distinctive part in the drafting of laws and the administration of the kingdom.[23] Important ecclesiastical figures were at the court, close to the king; they mixed with the secular nobility in the courts of law; in council they discussed temporal matters such as coinage, weights and measures;[24] as bishops in their bishopric, or 'missi' on tours of inspection, they were in charge of the civil administrators. But Christianity's most significant influence was on the king, and on his conception of his divine mission.[25]

Both Holy Scripture and Saint Augustine led the Carolingian King in his meditations to the same conclusion: he was the Lord's anointed, it was his duty to lead his subjects to the Promised Land or build the 'City of God' with them, a city where God's word would be law. In the final analysis, he saw himself faced with the task of ordering all things in God's name, in other words, of making God's peace and His justice prevail; he had to encourage all his subjects to lead a Christian life, or even force them into the right path by royal decree.

It is not surprising, then, that he did not confine himself to the things of this world. Given the trust which the Almighty had reposed in him to guide and save his people, how could he dissociate himself from such religious matters as clerical morals, for example, or even disputes about doctrine? Lapsed priests or heresiarchs might lead the faithful astray. It might be argued that such matters came within the jurisdiction of the Church hierarchy, and he should do no more than ratify its decisions. However, the Old Testament did not recognize such a distinction between the spiritual and temporal powers, and neither did that second David, Charlemagne. He did not admit formally that he regarded himself as emperor-pope, but his actions suggested it. He did not systematically try to make the civil power supreme over the religious, simply because he did not make any distinction between the two. The idea of himself as the sole embodiment of civil authority, with the Pope and bishops sole representatives of religious authority, would have been quite alien to his way of thinking. He himself took sides in disputes over dogma, and he accepted the fact that priests should exert influence over his own actions, even in the sphere of politics. Far from trying to make one aspect subordinate to the other, he regarded them as one.[26]

This attitude is understandable but it was none the less fraught with danger, as subsequent history was to demonstrate. Charlemagne's ideas when he was '*Rex Francorum et Langobardorum atque patricius Romanorum*' were still the same when he became '*magnus et pacificus imperator*', and they were handed on to his imperial successors. A new conception of the 'Imperium', characteristic of medieval Western Europe, began to take shape. The Emperor was the divinely-appointed leader of a new chosen race; the coronation rite invested him with the duty of guiding Christianity and protecting it from its enemies within and without. His power over lesser kings was based on this right but also limited by it: he could order them to obey in the interests of Christianity and in its defence. But the Pope, too, received his universal power from the Almighty; which of the two men was pre-eminent? The question was not put explicitly in 800, but it inevitably would be; when the spiritual and temporal power were not in agreement, the necessity for unity would bring it to the fore. This was the origin of the conflicts known as the Investiture and '*Dominium Mundi*' controversies.

The increasingly common practice of appointing important churchmen to secular office was also to prove prejudicial. It inevitably led the civil authority to claim the privilege of selecting bishops, and it was normally the safe, clever candidate who was chosen, rather than the man who was noted for piety and zeal. Even the best of them was unable to devote himself wholly to his pastoral duties, and some were inclined to neglect them completely. It was to be one of the factors leading to the decadence of the Church in the tenth and eleventh centuries.

But we must not be unjust to the Carolingians, or forget the circumstances of the time. The unfortunate results of their policies were largely due to a dwindling of the spirit that inspired them. In any case, they were not striking out on a new line; with the Old Testament as their guide, they were following the one opened up by the early Middle Ages. It also embodied the views of the contemporary church, which was no more anxious than the State to cause a rift between them. Such a policy was essential: the Frankish Church needed the firm hand of the State, and the kingdom needed a supply of wise counsellors furnished by the Church. For a time, results were positive: Christianity became the religion of a unified Western Europe, and linked men together in a close-knit society imbued with its ideals. In many ways – religious, geo-political, cultural – the Carolingians were completing an edifice whose foundations had been laid at the end of the classical period.

They hoped to go even further; so they aimed first at establishing law and order within the kingdom. Their watchword might have been unity with stability. The beginning of the dynasty in 751 saw Western Europe in a state of unresolved ferment. For several centuries there had been no clear lines of development or general tendencies; everything had been in a state of flux and change. The Carolingians grasped the situation, and sought to alter it.

They worked indefatigably to establish a measure of uniformity and centralization. They even laid down the weights and measures to be used throughout their territory. They reformed the monetary system. Their concern was not so much to fix a rate of exchange in keeping with a weak trading position, as to by-pass the gold shortage and link up with the silver monometallism used by the Scandinavians and Arabs. They therefore replaced the old solidus by a silver denarius, and gave it legal currency and a fixed standard of metallic content and weight; it was soon accepted readily throughout the West.[27] They debated as to how the different legal systems operating in different areas might best be unified, and considered making one of them, the Salic law, apply to the whole country.[28] This came to nothing, but they did achieve a certain measure of uniformity in common and criminal law by making changes in the 'Leges', and making more capitularies and *per se scribenda* prescriptions generally applicable to all their subjects, whatever their place of origin. They concentrated, however, on the political and religious spheres.

The Frankish kingdom had evolved empirically, in Germanic

rather than Roman style, and, like other barbarian kingdoms, it was loosely constructed and lacked cohesion. It was based on the rule of one man, supported by a very rudimentary administrative system, and was ill-adapted to weather political storms. Its weaknesses had already been demonstrated; several cracks had appeared and parts of the structure had fallen away. Its original construction had been piecemeal, the result of a series of victorious campaigns. The Carolingians, and Charlemagne in particular, felt impelled to take a number of measures to achieve some solidity and uniformity. Frontiers were therefore guarded by a system of 'marches' whose rulers were granted extensive military powers so that they could take immediate action in any threat of invasion. The duchies of Aquitaine and Bavaria, which had been almost completely autonomous, were named 'kingdoms', like Italy, under princely rulers subservient to Aix; it was a clever move which appeared to satisfy demands for independence, while ensuring centralized control. Throughout the Empire, especially in conquered territories, government officials and Austrasian or Alaman vassals were in positions of power; they were people who had thrown in their lot with the reigning dynasty and accepted its plans for unification.[29] '*Missi dominici*', 'the lord's envoys', were charged with keeping the central government in touch with its regional representatives; they made tours of inspection, as many as four a year, to see that orders were carried out, and to nip in the bud any abuses or tendencies to stray in an independent direction. General assemblies, or '*placita*' were held yearly, and all men of rank, secular or ecclesiastical, attended. Most of the lands belonging to the Church were granted immunity; but the counts' loyalty was often in doubt, and in many places the bishop or abbot acted as the government representative; he was considered to be more reliable, and more likely to make sure that every citizen carried out his military and other duties.[30] Written administrative records – 'those prerequisites of order and stability' – became usual.[31] After 800, the period when the Empire first showed signs of decline, power began to be concentrated in the king's hands. At coronations, the ceremony of the anointing, which had not been a Frankish custom, was introduced; it endowed the king with special religious significance in the eyes of his Christian subjects.[32] The oath of obedience due from all adult males was re-established;[33] and the special relationship between a vassal and his lord became more general.[34] When all men of importance, high officials of church and state and rich landowners, were made 'the king's men', and, as Richer said, brought to '*regis manibus sese militaturum committant fidemque spondeant ac sacramenta firment*',[35] they were bound by the strongest conceivable tie: the '*Treue*', reinforced by a sacred oath. After solemnly swearing allegiance they were likely to hesitate before betraying him. Farther down the scale, if a poor freeman looked to one of these great men as his lord that was an insurance, at second hand, so to speak, that he would not fail to present himself at the '*placitum*' and on the field of battle. If the army were summoned, for example, counts would answer the call not only as the king's subjects but as his vassals, and the freemen would accompany them for the same reasons; the first duty of a '*vassus*' was to support his '*senior*' in war. All means were used, as the preceding enumeration shows, to confer unity and stability on Francia; but it demonstrates too how ineffective these means were to prove. The old ways, the rule-of-thumb methods, continued. The Carolingians did their best with the situation they found, but they had no overall plan.[36] They did not go beyond the Germanic conception of power; for them it was rooted in the king's person, and therefore weak to the extent that he was weak. The rite of consecration, oaths of loyalty and the feudal system strengthened the idea of kingship, but they did not prevent the kingdom from breaking up into ever smaller fragments. Louis the Pious and his advisers were alone in looking ahead and putting the accent on the Empire, that is, the State itself.[37] However, they did not realize their ambition, which was to reorganize the kingdom on that basis; they merely covered up some cracks.

The Carolingians attached as much importance to a lively religious life as they did to political stability. For spiritual, and temporal, reasons they looked for a dedicated and powerful church.[38]

The mid-eighth-century church, however, was in a weak and divided condition. Intellectually and morally the priesthood lacked quality. They were recruited in a haphazard fashion: parish priests were chosen by the local lord of the manor, bishops by the king or the nobles, abbots by the descendants of the abbey's founder; monks tended to be awkward characters put into a monastery out of harm's way. They were only half-educated; some of them did not understand, for example, the baptismal rite. They were half-hearted too; parish priests were only granted a bare living by their lord, and spent too much time bemoaning their lot; aristocratic bishops were politicians rather than pastors, and their lives were rarely edifying, sometimes scandalous. More efficient organization, by better men, could improve the situation or at least lessen its ill-effects. Unfortunately bishops had little authority and their orders were ignored; many of the metropolitan dioceses had disappeared; the Pope was a long way away; abbeys took small notice of their Ordinary, and were not yet grouped under mother-houses.

As soon as Carloman, who was devout and pious, succeeded his father on the throne of Austrasia, he was disturbed at the state of affairs he found.[39] He at once requested Saint Boniface to 'call a synod to correct and improve the situation of the churches and of religion'. The great missionary did so, and in April 742 a '*Synodum germanicum*' was held under his direction; it was soon followed by the council of Les Estinnes, and in Neustria Pepin followed his elder brother's example and called the council of Soissons. The decrees which these assemblies passed were promulgated by the civil power in the form of capitularies, aimed at 'restoring ecclesiastical order'.[40] On a practical level it was decided to 'reform' the regular and secular Frankish clergy;[41] the latter were to have a minimum knowledge of doctrine and to be seemly in their lives, and Saint Benedict's rule was to apply to all monks. Organization had to be tightened up, otherwise even the best arrangements would remain dead-letters; so the hierarchy was to be re-planned and closer contact established at each level. Parish priests were to be answerable to their bishop. He himself would have sole authority in his diocese, would live in its chief town and be responsible to the archbishop. The archbishop would be in charge of his province, and would be the Pope's representative,[42] linking Papacy and people. National or regional synods would maintain contact between the different dignitaries and ensure that they acted together; they would keep a close watch on the religious climate, and settle any problems which might arise. In all, a wise programme of reforms, largely based on Anglo-Saxon and Germanic experience.

Carloman's successors approved and continued it. They saw to it that councils met at more frequent intervals; more precise and detailed capitularies were issued.[43] Priests were continually reminded that it was their duty to be all things to all men and to set a good example; they were exhorted to model themselves on Gregory I's '*Liber regulae pastoralis*'; it was laid down that they should teach their flock, visit the sick, comfort the poor, give shelter to travellers; they were forbidden to have relations with women, frequent taverns or indulge in riotous pleasures. Schools were set up or enlarged to improve their educational standard. Scholars like Alcuin himself compiled collections of homilies to help make preaching more effective. Some chapters followed the model of Bishop Chrodegang's reform at Metz and decided to live as communities vowed to individual poverty. Saint Benedict's rule was adopted on a wider scale. Lastly, episcopal authority began to assert itself;[44] many metropolitan sees were re-established, and the archbishops re-affirmed the Pope's overriding authority. The Papacy and the dynasty were closely linked in ties of mutual gratitude; pontiffs gave assistance to Carolingians to oust the Merovingians, Carolingians delivered pontiffs from the Lombard threat and, in the Patrimony of Saint Peter, provided a territorial

F
69

basis for papal authority. The Church was gradually setting its house in order.

But Pepin the Short and Charlemagne were not satisfied. They went further than Carloman, and strove to make liturgy and canon law uniform throughout the kingdom. They realized the importance of outward signs, particularly when the vast majority of the population was illiterate and bound to rely on symbolic interpretation. They knew that the Church's strength would lie in a high degree of regimentation. So they set to work to clear up the muddle that existed in liturgical practice and canon law.

In the early Middle Ages almost all Western Europe followed either the Gallican or Roman observance. During the Merovingian period the Gallican observance suffered many alterations and corruptions because its use was so widespread and it lacked a centralized control.[45] The Roman, on the other hand, which had developed in Rome and Southern Italy under papal protection, had kept its original purity of form. As papal prestige grew the Roman observance had tended to spread and deform the Gallican. Some of its forms of words and ceremonies reached Gaul after the sixth century. By the end of the seventh century there were copies of the whole of the Gelasian 'sacramentary' in the Paris area. In 754 the Church at Metz accepted it. It seemed that the best way of re-introducing some order into Francia's observance was to insist throughout on the use of Roman ritual, and this is what Pepin and Charlemagne did.[46] '*Ob unanimitatem Apostolicae Sedis et sanctae Dei Ecclesiae pacificam concordiam*', they insisted on the adoption of all the Roman liturgy: '*cantilena*' or Gregorian chant, Gregorian '*sacramentary*', '*ordo*' and '*cursus*'.[47] But it was a liturgy in which Alcuin included borrowings from the Frankish manuals, both Gallican and Gelasian.[48]

Charlemagne applied the same methods to canon law reform. After 744 the council of Les Estinnes had laid down that the '*antiquorum patrum canones*' should be observed. But the problem was where to find these ancient ecclesiastical laws, in which of the compilations in force in the Frankish kingdom. In 774, in order to settle the matter, the king sent for an authentic collection of the old canons from Rome, and he appears to have imposed it on the clergy as a whole. Even so, the '*Collectio Dyonisiana-Hadriana*' did not eliminate another, the '*Hispana*', and subsequent efforts to combine them into a single code were not entirely successful.[49]

Louis the Pious was even more of an enthusiast for order and uniformity than his ancestors – as exemplified in his vision of a single legal system and his stress on the conception of empire; he completed the reform by ordering all religious communities to use the same rule.

Although Chrodegang of Metz's statutes had circulated through the chapter houses, and since 742 monastic houses had had to conform to the Benedictine rule, at the beginning of Louis' reign monks and canons were still lax and haphazard in their observance. He therefore convoked a first assembly at Aix in 816, which produced the 'De institutione canonicorum'.[50] This influential document underlined the essential distinction between the canonical and the monastic state, which hinged on the attitude to private property. It laid down strict standards to be followed by all the communities of canons in the Empire.[51] A year later a second synod met at Aix, this time composed of monks; it was entrusted with the setting-up of what was called the 'ordo regularis' and 'una consuetudo' in monastic houses. The capitulary which contained these decisions is an adaptation of, and commentary on, the Benedictine rule. In itself it was of even greater significance than the 'De institutione' because of the emphasis it put on the importance of the Divine Office; this began to encroach on time formerly devoted to work, even such outstanding missionary work as Anglo-Saxon monks had accomplished, and brought about a change in Benedictine priorities which was to last for centuries.[52] In 818, again at Aix, certain monasteries received the right to elect their superior; but, to preserve the others from possible depredations of wicked abbots, it was decided to divide their possessions into two, one part to be used only to supply the needs of the brethren. Meanwhile Benedict of Aniane, the great inspiration behind all these reforms, 'the second Saint Benedict', set himself to ensure that they were carried out. By dint of unremitting effort he was on the whole reasonably successful.[53]

This incessant activity in the different aspects of religious life had no very immediate or definitive results. Ignorance, indolence and disobedience did not disappear at the first capitulary injunction, nor did traditional liturgies, customary law or the idiosyncrasies of particular chapters and monasteries. We know this to be so because the same ordinances had to be repeated over and over again. The future looked black. Bishops were more than ever immersed in politics.[54] Almost all abbeys were under some secular lord's thumb. Church estates were no better protected against disastrous 'secularization'.[55] Even so, great strides were made, and in three generations, after 820, Frankish priests were ready to play a major part in the 'Carolingian Renaissance'.

The movement of intellectual and artistic revival planned by Charlemagne began to take definite and hopeful shape at just about that time. As yet there was not much to be seen, but it was taking root in the area between the Loire and the Rhine in such a positive fashion that it was able to survive, in some form, that 'lead', or 'iron', century which followed the death of Charlemagne.

The interest shown in cultural matters by the greatest of the Carolingians is well known; it originated principally in his concern for religion. For example, he held the Anglo-Saxon view that an uneducated priesthood was useless. 'It may be better to act rather than to know,' he said, 'but one must know before one acts.'[56] He ordered schools to be set up throughout his kingdom. Their curriculum was tailor-made; would-be priests learnt enough to follow scriptural and liturgical texts and conduct church ceremonies – the elements of music, arithmetic and grammar,[57] which formed only a small part of the seven branches of the '*trivium*' and '*quadrivium*'. But that was only the minimum standard, there was nothing to prevent them widening their horizons. In capitularies the '*studia litterarum et liberalium artium*'[58] were encouraged. Grammar was not as narrow as it might sound: it required study of the written language in recommended texts, and therefore often turned into literary appreciation.

Charlemagne laid less stress on the arts, but he did not ignore them. It was unlikely that he would, for the splendid ceremonies he set such store by would have been out of place in a poor, dilapidated church. On several occasions he urged bishops and '*missi*' to make sure that their churches were well-constructed and maintained, and suitably embellished.[59] In ordering that the Roman rite should replace the Gallican, and in encouraging learning he incidentally provided great scope for illuminators. He insisted that religious houses and chapters should replace their liturgical manuscripts and gather together serious libraries. Some of them managed to buy the essential books abroad, especially in England and Italy, but most had them copied on the spot or in a local scriptorium.[60] So the reform of the liturgy and the intellectual revival gave Frankish illuminators their chance to develop, and provided them with fine contemporary models: Anglo-Saxon codices are usually works of art, because English priests had a passion for beautiful manuscripts,[61] and Italian ones are full of valuable reminders of the classical period.

If the political situation had not been stable these first steps would have led nowhere. But, as we have seen, order prevailed; the king was authoritarian, and his decisions were implemented. New schools were set up, and old ones reorganized, especially within the abbeys, at Tours and in the north at St. Wandrille, St. Riquier, Corbie, Gorze, Fulda, Lorsch, St. Gallen and Reichenau.[62] They were furnished with libraries which were well enough stocked for the masters and their best pupils to find material well outside the elementary curriculum of the '*Admonitio generalis*'; they could dip into dialectic, for example, or astronomy. Foreign teachers stayed at the palace, and wrote text-books; contact with them was very stimulating and beneficial to the better educated clergy.[63] The emperor and his entourage – Theodulf, Angilbert and Hildebald – were responsible for fine buildings at Aix, Germigny-des-Prés, St. Riquier and Cologne.[64] The demand for service books gave rise to a school of illumination at Trier and Aix which, in the Ada Gospel books,[65]

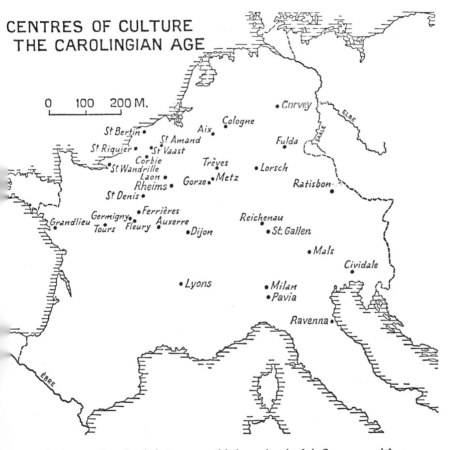

CENTRES OF CULTURE
THE CAROLINGIAN AGE

0   100   200 M.

St Bertin
St Riquier
St Wandrille
St Amand
St Vaast
Corbie
Aix
Cologne
Corvey
Fulda
Lorsch
Tréves
Laon
Rheims
St Denis
Gorze
Metz
Ratisbon
Grandlieu
Germigny
Tours
Fleury
Ferrières
Auxerre
Dijon
Reichenau
St. Gallen
Mals
Cividale
Lyons
Milan
Pavia
Ravenna
ELBE
SAALE
ÈBRE

created a style of miniature combining classical influences with a marked degree of originality. Goldsmiths demonstrated their skill, and all that they had learnt from ancient Rome, and England, in such masterpieces as the Tassilo chalice.[66] To sum up, thanks to the political calm that prevailed, the movement was getting under way.

During Charlemagne's reign, however, it lacked conviction, especially as far as literature was concerned. Apart from Angilbert, who was a skilled administrator but a third-rate thinker and writer, all the scholars were foreigners. The leading figures in theological argument were the Anglo-Saxon Alcuin, Paulinus of Aquileia, who was a Lombard, and Theodulf, a Visigoth.[67] Literary output was small and poor in quality. The only things worth mentioning are Theodulf's poems, especially his lovely Palm Sunday hymn, and the '*Historia Langobardorum*' of Paul the Deacon, who was himself from Lombardy.[68]

Works of architecture were possibly even more rare,[69] but they were successful and promising. The chapel at Aix was a masterpiece of originality, harmony and technical skill; its architecture was full of symbols, and it was destined to play an influential role in architectural history. For more than two centuries its polygonal ground plan, symbolizing the new Jerusalem,[70] was frequently copied in Northern Europe.[71] Its complicated roofing – wagon-vaulting, groin-vaulting and domes – pointed the way to more ambitious vaulted buildings. St. Riquier's abbey church rivalled it in size – it was nearly three hundred feet long – and still more by the originality of its great 'westwork'.[72] This building, with a vaulted ground-floor opening on to the nave, and a first floor containing a galleried chapel (the church proper), with an open lantern tower reaching a height of two hundred feet, was one of the prototypes of what experts call a porch-church. Cologne cathedral was an adaptation, on an equally grand scale, of a ground plan with two apses, one at each end of the structure, which had already been used in the fourth century in St. Maurice at Agaune in the Valais.[73] And so, along the banks of the Rhine and in Picardy, a monumental style was developing, one which was destined to be pre-eminent for many years, especially in Germany, and then to bequeath its best points, its east end structure and its sense of proportion, to the Romanesque style which followed it.

Around 810 to 820 a new generation of men, and the first-fruits of the religious reforms, gave a new impetus to the movement, even in the literary field.

Intellectually the most striking change was the predominance of the Franks in this renaissance. Its artisans were largely drawn from the original kingdom. A few foreigners took part, Italians like Anastasius the Librarian, Irishmen in particular – John the Scot, Sedulius and their compatriots at Laon; but they were in a minority. From the reign of Louis the Pious, Rabanus Maurus, born at Mainz, Walafrid Strabo, a Suabian, and Einhard, whose name shows his Germanic ancestry, replaced men like Alcuin, Theodulf and Paul the Deacon.

The renaissance spread, to include an increasing number of abbeys and chapters in the northern and central Empire. There was renewed activity in monastic schools like Corbie, Fulda, Reichenau and St.

Gallen, which were well known even in Charlemagne's time; and newer or more modest foundations at places such as Lyons, Auxerre and Corvey began to rival them. The scribes attached to monasteries like Fleury-sur-Loire, St. Germain des Prés, St. Denis, St. Bertin and St. Amand worked assiduously and supplied an increasing number of libraries.[74] Literary productions of all types followed close upon each other. Writers and teachers of theology tended to become less narrow in their outlook; Servatus Lupus of Ferrières was by no means the only one to appreciate that study of the liberal arts was more than just an aid to the understanding of the Scriptures, and that 'knowledge is valuable in itself' without reference to problems of exegesis.

Such an environment was likely to encourage talent, whether literary or scientific, and there was no lack of it during most of the ninth century.[75] Paschasius Radbert of Corbie could well be considered the first real theologian of the Middle Ages. In the Eucharist controversy, initiated by the liturgist Amalric, of Trier and Metz, continued by the deacon Florus of Lyons and made famous by another Corbie monk, Ratramnus, who was diametrically opposed to him, Radbert argued forcibly for the doctrine of the real presence; his contribution, the '*Liber de corpore et sanguine Domini*' was impressive in a debate which broke new ground, if not in a very original way.[76] In '*De divisione naturae*' the theology was as interesting as the philosophy; the two were still hardly distinguishable. Its author, John Scotus Erigena, the most intelligent and widely-read scholar of the time, tried to illumine faith with the light of reason; he produced an explanation of the universe by means of neoplatonic concepts which were familiar to him through his knowledge of Greek. Everything about the work – its aim, style and even its ideas – was unfamiliar to the barbarian West, so that he gained no great following as a result of it.[77] Walafrid Strabo, Sedulius Scottus, Gottschalk and Wandalbert of Prüm were equally brilliant in another way; they were all gifted poets in their different styles. Walafrid, the abbot of Reichenau, takes the palm for his freshness, sensibility and delight in nature; his description of the monastery garden in '*Hortulus*' still charms us.[78] The Irish poet's best qualities are his liveliness and musical use of words. Gottschalk is impressive because of his sincerity, and his sense of rhythm, but Wandalbert chose an unfortunate subject; it is difficult to make a 'Lives of the Martyrs' lyrical.[79] There are anonymous works which are as good as these, the '*Ave Maris Stella*', '*Veni Creator*' and the early liturgical sequences. In history Einhard's '*Vita Karoli magni*' is the Carolingian Renaissance's most famous prose work, and its style is fascinating, if not its content;[80] the reverse is true of the '*Vita Ludovici Pii*' by the 'Astronomer' and Agnellus's

Liber pontificalis ecclesiae Ravennatis'.[81] The letters of Servatus Lupus reveal his hellenism and the similarities between his outlook and that of later humanists of the twelfth, or sixteenth, centuries.[82]

It would be possible to cite other names and titles, but one would run the risk of giving the impression that the writers of the period were all very individual; nothing would be further from the truth. Even the writers we have just mentioned did not always use a personal style, and the same is even more true of the rest, who were scholars rather than thinkers, craftsmen rather than artists. Their works, which were almost always in poetry because everything was expressed in metrical form, were usually stilted; they were correctly expressed in elegant versification and varied turns of phrase, but they lacked life. Historical writers usually came to grief in the same way as their predecessors: in Lives of saints commonplaces and verbiage abounded, and there was no grasp of synthesis in the 'Annals' or 'Acts' of bishops and abbots. Treatises on theology, exegesis, asceticism or politics largely consisted of quotation from Biblical or patristic texts, or documents issued by the Councils; the passages themselves did duty as arguments, and reference to 'authoritative works' dispensed with discussion.[83] There was no notable progress here. In the reigns of Louis the Pious and Charles the Bald, writers, again usually Franks, were more numerous, and works of real interest were less rare. But spontaneity and originality were still stifled by imitation and quotation. Even after two or three generations had passed the Renaissance still bore the marks of its early days in school.

Perhaps it did not really matter. Carolingian scholars and writers, especially the best of them, had lost some of their originality by taking such great pains to imitate classical models. But it was not all loss. They had steeped themselves in classical culture and had begun where necessary to adapt it to a Christian setting. They had learnt how to write. They had made medieval Latin the language of the educated West, a language rich enough to satisfy contemporary needs and supple enough to adapt itself to new ones. Untiring copying of manuscripts had saved many of them from oblivion, and in the process scribes had learnt to respect texts, and not to scorn their predecessors' opinions. In so doing they were laying sound foundations, as much so, perhaps, as if they had been producing beautiful poetry or new ideas.

The Carolingian Renaissance might have been less enduring if it had been more glitteringly independent. It might have lacked a firm base, or remained localized and thus disastrously involved in the political and religious disorder of the end of the ninth century. The fact that it managed to survive was probably due to its solidly classical foundations and its limited objectives: it was not too exalted to be out of reach for average, hard-working talents; a few of them, at least, in face of great difficulties, managed to preserve their heritage and bequeath it to those who came after. Sturdy, solid buildings can weather a storm better than slender spires.

The reigns of Charlemagne's son and grandson saw great activity in the arts. Along the Loire valley, farther north too, and in Lombardy architects, painters and sculptors were at work, and were paving the way for the future Romanesque style.

From 815 a considerable increase in the amount of building undertaken meant that the architectural achievements of the previous period were consolidated and perfected. At Rheims in Champagne, Corvey in Westphalia, and Reichenau on Lake Constance great buildings with a sense of space and proportion were constructed. At St. Gallen and elsewhere a proper chancel took shape, in the form of a bay interposed between apse and transept. Piers replaced simple columns, and in St. Philibert at Grandlieu, in 836, they were already cruciform in section, and ready to support a vaulted roof. In St. Philibert's chevet and in the crypt of St. Germain at Auxerre there were three apses joined side by side, a foretaste of the so-called Benedictine ground plan. Enlargement of the same two churches, in 847 and 859 respectively, included ambulatories with chapels opening off them.[84] The culmination of this productive period in Frankish building was the first appearance of early Romanesque art, with its characteristic decoration, consisting of bands and blind arcades, derived from Ravenna.

In the decoration and embellishment of these monuments, and to satisfy the extravagant tastes of the period, other artists were to exercise their considerable talents. Painters, and artists in mosaic and glass vied with each other in decorating church and palace walls, which glowed in a vibrant harmony of gold, blue and Byzantine purple at Aix and Germigny; in St. Germain at Auxerre the tone was more subdued, in the red, ochre, grey and white which were to become the distinguishing mark of 'French' frescoes.[85] Sculptors were engaged in works of art for the nobility, decorating buildings and occasionally sculpting capitals and chevets. They may have found stone a difficult or unattractive medium, for they preferred to work in more malleable or luxurious materials – stucco, terracotta, bronze, gold, silver and ivory; they made statues and figurines, tables and altar fronts, ambo plaques, armour and crowns, chandeliers and crucifixes, chalices and patens, eagle lecterns, bindings, combs and diptychs. Almost all such works of art have disappeared; they were too fragile, too easily stolen or melted down in bad times; those which survive bear witness to the high quality of the rest; several of them are astonishingly finished: notably Cividale del Friuli's stucco statues, the Milan 'pallioto' in chased silver, the Waulsort rock-crystal disc, the Metz carved ivory gospel-book cover. The bronze doors at Aix, and the statuette presumed to be of Charlemagne, foreshadow the great achievements of Rhenish and Mosan metalwork.[86] Illuminators set themselves to produce wonderful books, especially liturgical works, decorating them with ornamental capitals and miniatures, sometimes with 'insular' geometric designs as at St. Vaast, St. Amand or, before 867, at St. Denis, but in other cases using a representational style with a vivid sense of drama. This latter was used at Tours under Count Vivian, at St. Denis towards the end of the century and in the Rheims district. It was there that the real masterpieces were produced such as the Hautvillers gospel-book, the Utrecht psalter, in which colour takes second place to line, Charles the Bald's first Bible, the Loisel gospel-book and the Bible of S. Paolo fuori le Mura.

A wide variety of skills existed; there were artists in mosaic and glass, fresco painters, sculptors in stone and other materials, metal-founders, goldsmiths, engravers, jewellers and illuminators. The sources of inspiration were varied too, but classical influences became more and more marked. Carolingian art was eclectic. The best products of Rome, the Greek kingdoms, Persia, Syria, the nomadic Asian tribes and their descendants, Italy, Byzantium, England, Spain and Gaul itself were all admired and imitated in turn. The result was a serious loss of individuality because the greater the influx of new ideas the more difficult it was to control them and weld them into a new and original style. The gain was in fecundity, which augured well for the future; the supply of themes, forms and techniques available to Romanesque artists was amazingly rich. Without Byzantine influence, for example, the Berzé-la-Ville frescoes would not have been painted; if the barbarian heritage had been rejected ornamental sculpture would have been less lively. The relative lack of individuality in the ninth century, which in any case did not apply in the art of illumination, was the foundation for the originality of the eleventh and twelfth centuries. But the streams of inspiration which watered the Carolingian era did not all flow in the same direction. The one whose source was in classical antiquity broadened and deepened as its course lengthened.[87] Significantly, Man himself came to the forefront. The West had, of course, always been interested in him; from the fifth to the eighth centuries he had been the subject for Frankish painters, and sculptors, and especially for Italian and Anglo-Saxon illuminators. But pure decoration had ousted him from the place of prime importance, and now he began to recapture it. He appeared everywhere – on the cover of Charles the Bald's psalter, in low-reliefs on the portable altar in St. Emmeran at Ratisbon, in the Tyrol in

St. Benedict's chevet at Mals, on St. Remigius's reliquary at Rheims, and even in the stained glass of St. Bénigne at Dijon. Carolingian artists still worked in decorative styles but now they were more concerned to point a moral and tell a story, and in this too they foreshadowed their Romanesque counterparts.

Cantors followed the fashion; some parts of the office were set to music more elaborate than plainsong, and this '*organum*' was the first step on the road to polyphony.[88]

The traditions which formed the artistic springboard were themselves Gallic; by contrast, scholarship and literature which were 'imported articles' tended to be less personal and creative. With the exception of music, all forms of culture suffered from the same lack of originality. In learning and literature the Carolingian period made no vigorous progress, hardly broke any new ground, in fact, because of reluctance to abandon fruitful sources or difficulty in integrating them. Only a rare man like John the Scot could succeed in reconciling philosophy and revelation; and in architecture there was as yet no thought of making techniques subordinate to the production of an over-all effect. A beginning had been made: basic materials had been collected or discovered, especially in architecture; new tools, like medieval Latin, had been forged; but these were signposts for a future age. There was still no fusion, no synthesis.

This point marks the true beginning of medieval civilization; the main features have fallen into place. The setting was right: centred midway between the Loire and the Rhine, accessible to the whole of Christian Europe; Reichenau scribes and St. Gallen goldsmiths belonged to the same family as their brother craftsmen in Auxerre or Oviedo; Carolingian architecture influenced building in the Asturias;[89] soon Grimbald was to bring European literature and scholarship to England and help Alfred the Great to revive learning in his ravaged country, while Oswald was to become archbishop of York after years of preparation at Fleury-sur-Loire.[90] The essential elements were to hand. For centuries to come they were diverse in origin; they were Byzantine, oriental, barbarian, and classical; the last of the list was the most influential and important and destined to remain so throughout the Middle Ages. The climate of opinion on which everything rested was Christian. The term 'Renaissance' is misleading if it is applied to the intellectual and artistic movement of the ninth century: the Carolingian period drew largely on Rome, even more than did its more self-confident descendants, but it was by no means solely concerned with pagan models, or blindly uncritical of them, and it did not accept their ideology. Its foundation stone, and the object of its devotion, was Christianity. Walafrid Strabo may have admired Virgil and Ovid, but his own poetry has a different ring. Like classical writers, illuminators were more concerned with the story they were illustrating than with the picture itself; but their story was the Bible, their characters were Christ or His disciples, the apostles and evangelists, His friends the saints, His successors the popes, and His delegates the kings. Man reappeared in ninth-century art, in the context of religion.[91]

There was to be no unbroken continuity from the Carolingians to Saint Louis. The cultural achievements of Charles Martel's descendants were soon in jeopardy because of the ineffectiveness of their political and religious reforms. Ground was lost to some extent everywhere; but there remained a foothold from which a new step forward could be taken when the way was clear.

PART II

NOON

The death of the last Carolingian king was immediately followed by the destruction, actual or threatened, of all that the dynasty had achieved. The kingdom broke apart in disorder and discord. The increasing secularization of the Church undermined the effects of the religious reforms. In conditions of anarchy and indiscipline civilization was hard put to it to resist a new impulse towards barbarism. About the year 900 Charlemagne's reign looked like a mere interval, and history seemed to be continuing on a course which had only been interrupted two centuries earlier by the mayors of the palace.

Political unity was the first of their achievements to disappear, not surprisingly in view of the difficulties experienced by a single authority in ruling different peoples scattered over a vast territory. We have seen the fundamental weakness in this case: the constitution which the Frankish kingdom inherited from its Germanic founders. Carolingian measures had proved ineffective. Some of them fell flat; the 'missi dominici', for example, enjoyed no real power as soon as the emperor agreed not to dispatch them except with the nobles' consent, and to choose them from among the bishops and counts of the region in question. Such a concession removed their whole raison d'être: people could not inspect themselves objectively, and they were not likely to reprimand their neighbours whose help they might one day need. Other innovations tended to make the situation worse, in particular the extension of vassaldom; it changed officials into vassals, and so accentuated the personal factor which was already the weak point of the central authority. After Charlemagne the country's stability depended more than ever on the king.[1] There would have been no problem if his descendants had been men of his stamp. But his son was nondescript and vague: he was easily swayed, and instead of husbanding his resources he sacrificed his estates in pious donations.[2] Lothar, his eldest grandson, was cleverer and more energetic, but he fell victim to another custom inherited from the barbarian past: his brothers attacked him, demanding a share of his inheritance, and obtained it. In 843 the Empire, which had never really formed a viable state, broke into three. The parts came together again, but only temporarily, between 884 and 888.[3]

This was only a beginning. It was soon followed by the impact of

Norse and Magyar invasions. The last Carolingians had no fleet, no army, no revenue, and therefore no means of stopping them; they were despised and discredited. The nobles came to the fore as leaders of the resistance. This marked a second stage in political disintegration: princes, dukes, marquises, counts and bishops took the place of kings.

They attempted to contest the nobility's traditionally independent attitude, for a time successfully; but sooner or later they had to admit defeat, temporarily at least. The local lords became almost autonomous, and carved up the Empire between them.

The church reforms of Carloman and his successors fared better, on the whole, though they did not survive intact. Chroniclers bemoaned the horrors of invasion and the brutality of the nobles, and at the dawn of the tenth century the second abbot of Cluny also raised his voice: 'The ministers of the Church are glutted with flesh meat,' Saint Odo wrote, 'they are drunk with pride, shrivelled with avarice, weakened by voluptuousness, tormented by wickedness, inflamed by anger, at odds with one another; envy twists them and lechery kills.'[4] Neglect of their duties, together with greed and debauchery, were the bitter but natural fruits of insecurity, and of practices which the Carolingians had introduced or tolerated. Bishops had become important politicians and had often been chosen for their skill and loyalty rather than their piety. It was to be expected that they would develop a taste for the good things of the world, neglect their pastoral duties and despise spiritual riches. Monks were under the jurisdiction of lay lords or their retainers, their estates had been secularized, they had been harried, hunted, often left homeless by Norse or Magyar hordes. It was hardly surprising if they neglected their choirs, libraries and scriptoria.

The decadence of the Church and the political disturbances seriously undermined cultural standards. The Carolingians had tried to diffuse culture through various channels, but the Church had remained the chief, almost the only, '*Kulturträger*', to use the expressive German term. Now it, too, had cast off the burden.

But gradually, in fits and starts, more consistently in some areas than others, peace was restored: the wave of invasions died away, and order reigned once more. In one diocese after another the Church set itself to rights, and began to savour spiritual joys again. There was a rapid rise in population, and an upsurge of energy. In such happier circumstances civilization took root, grafting itself on to the vigorous stock which remained from the Carolingian Renaissance.

For it had not perished completely, in spite of all that had happened. Some scholars had kept faith, and had trained their followers to uphold the ideals of truth and beauty. Most of the monumental architecture had survived. Enough remained for civilization to revive in peaceful Ottonian Germany, protected by the dignity of the Imperial Church.

Progress was swift. The tentative preparatory period was over. Art and scholarship were now full of confidence in themselves and in the power of reason guided by faith, and were ready to attack any problem; inexorable logic carried them upward to realms where difficulty and opposition disappeared.

In the second part of this book, as in the first, we shall deliberately ignore what might be called the 'negative' of history, and we shall examine, step by step, that amazing progression by which the Middle Ages reached their glorious peak in the France of Saint Louis – when, as Joinville says, 'the throne glowed like a resplendent sun'.

Chapter 5

THE POLITICAL CLIMATE: THE STRUGGLE
FOR PEACE

'The complaints of the poor never cease, neither do the treacherous attacks of those who, like dogs, savage Saint Peter's followers. . . . Nearly every day these men fall to massacring each other. They assault each other blindly, like wild animals, because they are drunk or jealous, or even for no reason at all. In one year thirty-five of Saint Peter's innocent serfs were murdered, and far from repenting of their crime, the murderers reaped honour and glory from it.' – 'In the councils when the peace of God was proclaimed, all those present were fired with enthusiasm and, raising their hands to heaven, cried with one voice: peace, peace, peace. . . . But in no time at all, since men are by their nature inclined to follow evil and turn away from God's mercy, they went back on their sworn oath, like dogs returning to their vomit or pigs to their filth. Men of power, prisoners of their own greed, began to plunder even more fiercely than before. The common people followed the example of the great, and gave themselves up to all kinds of debauchery.' – 'The men of substance and rank in this part of the country spend most of their time in fighting and killing; so they pile up huge mounds of earth, dig ditches and erect fences round them; from such strongholds they can the better defend themselves from their enemies, defeat their peers and oppress the weak.'[1] These representative quotations, semi-official accounts, the first written between 1023 and 1025 about the Rhineland, the second between 1044 and 1050 about France, and the last between 1130 and 1140 about Flanders, give a vivid picture of the atmosphere of the time. One must not go too far[2] and imagine Western Europe a continual prey to groups of soldiers or bandits. Between 850 and 1100, public or private wars, pillaging forays and feudal revolts did not affect everybody all the time. But uncertainty, fear and distress were always present. Everyone longed for peace.

There were two main threats to peace: invasions, and civil war due to the weakness of the central government and the ambitions of the nobles and their confederate knights. To ensure peace there had to be an end to attacks from without, and governmental control had to be strengthened within; it was easy enough to formulate the programme but difficult to carry it out. The instigators of trouble were powerful men, and it would need a grand alliance of those on the side of law and order to defeat them or render them harmless. All the assistance, both moral and material that could be mustered from priesthood, kings, feudal lords and cities, would be required.

The Norse and Magyar invasions unleashed chaos. They lasted for a century in Europe, and even longer in England. Though they had some positive results, in general they contributed to disintegration and cultural decadence. From about 834 or 840 waves of Norsemen had set sail for Western Europe;[3] they had been spurred to action by the over-population of their country, had become skilled in navigation and had encountered only slight resistance to their preliminary raids. A Norwegian tidal wave submerged Ireland, and simultaneously a horde of Danes attacked both shores of the North Sea and the Atlantic coasts; they penetrated up river estuaries and many inland areas were threatened. The Magyars, who were Asiatic nomads, a later equivalent of the fourth- and fifth-century Huns, settled in Central Europe about 860. Forty years later they began to make cavalry raids each year on Germany east of the Rhine and northern Italy.[4]

Devastating, murderous attacks continued in Europe for two or three generations, and then they began to slacken. The booty began to grow less: there was not much left when the country had already been pillaged several times. The invaders found increased difficulties and dangers. The Scandinavian and Magyar world began to change, and their victims started to organize defence against them.

Economic and political changes were working against the invaders. Their very success tied them to the land. The Norsemen were not mere pirates; they cleared and ploughed the land. They took stock of the fertile regions they had conquered and set to work to get the best out of them. Soon, their only ambition was to settle down peacefully under their old leaders and in their old way of life in a new country. It was the same with the nomad Magyars; they turned into peasants. At the same time monarchical authority asserted itself and established control over the Nordic countries and over the plains around the Danube and the Theiss. A halt was called to expeditions which had served as a source of supplies to the king's enemies and kept alive the spirit of aggression.[5]

Western Europe, too, was stirring. It had been observed that the invaders were often very inadept at siege warfare. So ancient fortifications were restored, new ones constructed, walled towns sprang up, and castles where the population could take shelter with their treasures, and which could withstand attack. Marches were established against the Magyars – Aquileia, Verona, then in Austria – following the Carolingian formula. Several victories were won in open country, at Louvain in 891, Argenteuil in 898, Chartres in 911, Unstrut in 933 and Augsburg (Lechfeld) in 955.

They were decisive victories. They marked the end of Norse and Magyar invasions in the area which had formed the Carolingian empire.

England was free of Scandinavian attacks from 954, but less than a generation later they were resumed with renewed violence.

Until then the island had suffered more from the Vikings than any other country except Ireland. At one time, after forty years of continuous raids, it was on the point of falling completely into Viking hands. It was only the genius of one of its kings, Alfred of Wessex, which saved it. In 870 he had decided to cut his losses and cede the eastern part of the country to the enemy; they had already settled there and given it the name 'Danelaw'. He had barricaded them out of the rest of the country by building forts along the frontier. His descendants had continued the same policy. They had allied themselves with all the rest of unoccupied England, and together they had formed a force strong enough to check the sallies which were made from the Danelaw. From the defensive they had passed to the offensive, and had succeeded in forcing the Vikings to recognize their sovereignty. From 926 the king could call himself 'rex totius Britanniae'. In the years that followed, the Norsemen in France had tried to recover their independence and continue the advance towards the South and West, but they gave up after a final defeat in 954. By the middle of the ninth century peace reigned again, more completely than before. In the melting-pot of the same tribulations and triumphs the Anglo-Saxon kingdoms, which till then had been jealous rivals, were fused into one, and for the first time since the early Middle Ages one monarch ruled over all the old Heptarchy. But it was to be only a truce. Twenty-five years later the invasions began again. This time they were not raids organized by brigands, with plunder as their chief object; they were wars of conquest, led by the king in person at the head of a full-scale army. England struggled desperately, but in 1017 had to admit defeat and bow to Canute the Great; it was absorbed into the great maritime Nordic empire that he had conquered around the Baltic and North Seas. But his artificial construction did not long survive him. In 1035 England had its own king again; there, as in Europe, the Scandinavian invasions were at an end.

What was even more important was that all invasions now ceased.

The West was not liable to be shattered by barbarian attacks, whether launched from the misty Baltic, the Arabian deserts or the plateaux of Central Asia; civilization could follow its normal course. The period of the 'great migrations', which began towards the end of the fourth century, was now over.

Its last phase had some positive value: Western Europe gained more territory, a protective screen on its eastern frontier, and an access of energy. Once contact had been established the Scandinavian world entered into commercial relations, adopted Christianity, copied Western art forms and forged close links with the rest of Europe. Hungary was converted to Christianity, and became its strong bastion in face of another Asiatic adversary, this time the Turks. Finally, those Vikings who made their home on the shores of the Atlantic brought with them their abounding energy and their genius for organization. A group of them who were defeated at Chartres in 911 had agreed not to carry out any more raids, but to settle peacefully in the Rouen district; and it was their descendants who conquered England in a single battle at Hastings in 1066, and set up an efficient government. They were to do the same later in Southern Italy and the Near East.[6]

The Scandinavian and Magyar raids had further consequences. They disrupted or endangered civilized life in the British islands. In Europe they helped to strengthen the power of the great lords at the expense of that of the king.

The earliest Norwegian and Danish raids struck grievous blows at England and Ireland. In the Island of Saints civilization foundered. In the Heptarchy it lost the lustre it had enjoyed since the 'Anglo-Saxon pre-renaissance' in the eighth century. Forty critical years followed. Then there was a slow recovery under Alfred the Great. He undertook far-reaching measures in political and military matters, and not least in the realm of the spirit. He set up a palace school, brought learned men over from Francia, and himself translated the most notable Christian classics so that his subjects could study them: Gregory I's '*Regula pastoralis*', the '*Adversus paganos*' of Orosius, Bede's '*Historia ecclesiastica gentis Anglorum*', Boethius's '*De consolatione philosophiae*', and extracts from Saint Augustine's writings. His successors continued along the same lines; and the return of peace and a monastic reform hastened the process.[7] The arts revived – architecture and especially illumination.[8] However, the second series of raids turned back the clock. Then the Norman conquest changed the course of English culture, and had an especially damaging effect on its most interesting development, vernacular literature.[9] The conquerors brought with them their French and Latin culture and imposed it. After 1066 England was blessed with long periods of calm. William the Conqueror, Henry I and especially Henry II were anxious to make the court an intellectual and artistic centre:[10] and by the twelfth and thirteenth centuries it had developed its own individual and fruitful version of Western civilization. But it had suffered too profoundly for two centuries to be able to regain its central position.

In the former Frankish empire the effect of the invasions was more marked in the political sphere. They tended to encourage particularism and the break-up of larger units into small. They absorbed the central government's attention so that it could not keep the nobles under surveillance, and encouraged the leaders among them to usurp its already undermined authority. The kings of western Francia – from now on we shall call it France – were usually powerless against the Vikings. In eastern Francia – Germany – the kings submitted to the Magyars during a certain period. The people turned against leaders who could not protect them, and rallied to a few powerful nobles. The Carolingians had entrusted control over vast areas – duchies, marquisates or groups of counties – to members of these families, and they had enjoyed royal authority in their lands.[11] They had organized defence, kept the peace, administered justice, appointed bishops, and sometimes even enforced oaths of loyalty from their subjects.[12] This was the origin of French principalities and German 'national duchies'.[13]

Once the invasions were over the problem of how to curb the power of the leading nobles, one of the chief political dilemmas of the Middle Ages, stood out in sharp relief.

The German rulers settled it in their favour for a century and a half. They increased their own ascendancy and reduced that of the nobles in the lifetime of the Saxon and Salian dynasties. It was inevitable that the great lords should hit back. They did so in 1075, supported by one section of the Church, and they were successful. The new royal house of Hohenstaufen intervened to little purpose in 1150. A hundred years later the struggle ended with the nobles in control of a divided country.

The problem was, as ever, to strengthen royal authority, which was always vulnerable because it was vested in the king's person. The best solution, clearly, was to restore the concept of the State; the idea of power should be separated from the individual men who exercised it; fixed, clear rules should govern its devolution. But this was not possible in 900. Carolingian classical scholars like Servatus Lupus, who admired Cicero, used the term '*respublica*', but the notion behind it was still vague. It only became clear in the course of the juridical renaissance of the eleventh and twelfth centuries, and did not take definite form in Europe till the thirteenth century. German rulers, however, managed to achieve a stable measure of authority by a combination of fortunate circumstances and an intelligent policy.

In their country, as in the rest of Western Europe during the tenth century, theological speculation and historical events together emphasized two ideas which were of positive value: the indivisibility and the specific nature of royal authority. The tradition that a dead king's sons should inherit jointly disappeared. It is not clear why this happened; the practice of anointing the king which had been adopted as a Frankish custom may have had some influence, or the rebuilding of the Empire in 800; men's minds may have harked back to classical traditions, or it may have been a severely practical decision.[14] In any case it ended the troubles that had been caused by each royal demise. At about the same time the Church in council pronounced definitively on the royal charge from God. At Mainz in 888 and Trosly in 909 it reiterated the Paris pronouncement of 829: 'The king's duty is to govern and rule over God's people with equity and justice, and to safeguard peace and concord.'[15] Bishop Gerard of Cambrai's attitude in 1023 shows the deep impression those words had made on the German mind; when his French brothers asked him to promulgate the 'Peace of God' in his diocese he first of all declined to do so because, he said: 'It is the king's responsibility, not the priest's, to suppress disturbances, settle disputes and promote peace.'[16] The king was entrusted by the Almighty with the task of maintaining order and justice. It followed that he was indispensable to the kingdom, and that he had no equal.

German rulers did more than merely make the most of the current of opinion. They used practical means to ensure the achievement of their aim, which was to establish a moral superiority. They were not the first or the only monarchs to designate their successor in their own lifetime, but the practice guaranteed that son followed father and frustrated aristocratic attempts at usurpation: nobles could no longer elect as king either a man of irresolute character who was unlikely to curb their freedom of action, or one who seemed willing to weaken the monarchy by making concessions to them. In the tenth century Otto I shed great glory on his Saxon dynasty, and his successors inherited his dazzling prestige. He penetrated farther than the Carolingian frontier of the Elbe and the Saale, and imposed Germanic influence on the Slav areas of Europe.[17] He crushed the Magyars at Lechfeld, and put an end to their marauding practices. He dominated the three areas of central Francia, which, with the Imperial title, had been Lothar's inheritance; his father had annexed Lotharingia, he himself conquered Italy and subjugated Burgundy.[18] He considered that he had a right to inherit Lothar's crown as well as his lands. It was placed on his head in 962, and henceforward the most important secular title in Christendom was linked with the German monarchy. Finally, in the eleventh century the Salian kings, Conrad II and Henry IV reorganized and developed their domain. Henry was particularly energetic. He made an inventory of his possessions, and improved the system of collection of taxes and tolls. He recovered both lands and rights from the nobles who had claimed or usurped them; he decided to lay hands on the profits which for many years had accrued to them from the administration of criminal justice; he claimed ownership of forest areas where they had planted new villages and monasteries. He brought more land into cultivation, and increased the value of his patrimony; he planned to incorporate in it large areas of the land east of the Saale which he had conquered from the Slavs. He even thought of exploiting the silver mines which had just been discovered at Rammelsberg, to provide bullion for his mint and so produce enough coinage to pay his numerous officials and the soldiers of his powerful private army.

While they were consolidating their power by these means German rulers also made sure of allies in their struggle to dominate the most important nobles and keep the rank and file under control. Otto I and his successors relied largely on the Church's help. They entrusted certain specially selected and loyal bishops with comital powers over extensive territories. They in effect set up ecclesiastical principalities, ruled by faithful vassals, at key points in the kingdom.[19] The Salian kings went further. Conrad II tried, but without much success, to win over the lesser nobility. Henry IV cultivated the growing class of bourgeois town dwellers and the peasants. He realized that the bourgeois needed peace if trade was to prosper, and that the peasants were often the worst sufferers from disturbed conditions. With this in mind he promulgated regional settlements, '*Landfrieden*'. He made bold use of his inferior officials. They were serfs, whose families had held '*ministeria*' for several generations so that socially they were regarded as superior to their fellows, though legally they were still the king's bondmen and had no freedom of action.[20] It was among such men that he would find his councillors, provincial officials, military leaders, and even sometimes bishops. The royal power was at its zenith.

However, the nobles were seething with resentment. Their pride was hurt, and so were their pockets. They demanded the privilege of directing policy, which was their due according to ancient Germanic custom. They complained that the king had given their places on the royal councils to 'men of no standing', 'who have insignificant ancestors, or none at all'.[21] A lord was absolute master in his domain, but the king claimed the right to intervene, if necessary, to keep the peace and administer justice. The great lords had become rich; they had annexed land and cultivated it on a large scale. The king had now recovered what his predecessors had lost, and was claiming sole rights in the forests. Saxony was up in arms. Henry IV was of South German Salian stock, and he did not trust this northern duchy which had nurtured the previous dynasty. He studded it with castles, filled them with southerners, and forced heiresses to marry his officials. In 1073 a rebellion broke out.

It was a failure. The nobles, with their estates, fortified keeps and vassals, were a force to be reckoned with, but they were not yet strong enough. They needed allies. The Gregorian reform movement gave them invaluable support from an unexpected quarter, in the shape of a group of the clergy and the Holy See itself.

The rebellion in fact brought about a breach between Rome, and many German and Italian bishops and clergy, and the king. It was claimed that the Pope was the supreme ruler in Christendom, in everything, even in political matters, and was above all persons, even kings. The emperor, Henry IV, could not afford to accept such a hypothesis. The reform laid down that no lay person could bestow ecclesiastical benefices, and it reminded the holders of such offices that their duties were chiefly, even solely, spiritual. This was to weaken the very cornerstone of the political structure that Otto I and his descendants had built. The king could hardly rely on his bishops unless he had appointed them himself. Could he be sure of full co-operation from them, in any case, if their time was to be given up to their pastoral duties? As a king, Henry IV found it even more difficult to comply with such decisions. He collected together at Worms an assembly of bishops who were ready to disobey the Pope. The latter reacted violently. In a synod in Rome on 14th February, 1076, he pronounced the man 'who was so mad with pride that he had set himself up against the Church' to be unfit to govern, absolved his subjects from their oath of allegiance, and solemnly excommunicated him. The Quarrel of the Investitures had begun.

It was to be a disaster for the German monarchy. Little by little, all that the Saxons and Salians had achieved was whittled away. As early as 1077 the first of the anti-kings supported by the papacy formally repudiated the hereditary principle. Henry was forced to buy his nobles' loyalty with grants from the royal estates. The Church was no longer a trusty ally: many of the higher clergy were ranged behind the Holy See. The harassed king was often away in Italy and the great lords naturally took every advantage of his difficulties and of the disturbed situation to present themselves as protectors of the weak. They greatly extended their authority, persuading the lesser

94

nobles to become their vassals, making the peasantry dependent on them, arrogating regalities to themselves. In less than two generations the cleverest of them, the '*Fürsten*', that is, the princes, or, literally, the 'first', were the real masters of the kingdom.

In 1125 and 1138 the application of the elective rather than the hereditary principle dealt another blow to the monarchy. The kings who were elected were the weakest claimants in the lists, and they could obtain votes only by mortgaging their authority. Each had different theories, methods, personnel, so that there was no continuity of policy or day-to-day administration. They tended not to make a distinction between crown properties and their personal possessions, so that what should have been inherited by later kings was sometimes passed down to their blood relations instead. By 1152 the German monarchy's fate seemed sealed.

But it was not yet to be. The greatest of medieval statesmen, Frederick I, appeared on the scene. There was a general longing for peace after eighty years of strife, the Pope's claims to temporal power were widely disapproved, even by churchmen, and Frederick was a highly intelligent man; it is not surprising that he was able to restore the monarchy to its former position. He used all the means invented by all his predecessors, whether Carolingians, Ottonians or Salians, and even referred back to Roman theories on absolute government; he was very flexible, and varied his tactics according to circumstances. Where he could do so with impunity he used threats, even force, but he would compromise where a head-on clash seemed fruitless. He realized that it was no use, for the moment, conducting an open campaign against the 'princes', so he treated with them. He agreed to recognize their seizures of land, give them a role in the government, discuss policy on equal terms with them, even help them to subjugate their vassals, if they acknowledged him as their sole overlord. He could not as yet crush these great feudal lords, so he brought them into the administration under his leadership as the Carolingians had done. However, he did decide to abolish certain of the duchies, and he revived the policy of '*Landfrieden*' to control the nobles to a certain extent and mollify the common people. He encouraged the growth of towns and the creation of free villages, whose inhabitants were the prototype of what he hoped to achieve eventually throughout the Empire: subjects in the old pattern, whose relationship was with the state in the person of the king, who would receive their orders only from him or his officers. He aimed to make the Church once more the tower of strength it had been under the Ottos, and he therefore took advantage of obscure or vague passages in the Worms concordat to nominate bishops or abbots. Above all, he followed in the Salians' footsteps by recruiting a large body of administrators who formed a reliable army of dedicated public servants; and he systematically and persistently enlarged his landholdings.[22]

But already he began to come up against the stumbling block which was destined to frustrate his efforts, namely the conflict between his two selves, the imperial and the regal.[23] The emperor should be master of all Italy, of Rome as well as Lombardy and the great commercial centres. The king must be master of the German nobles. It was doubtful whether one man could do both. Even Frederick I found it difficult: in dealing with the lords at home he was handicapped by his conflicts with the Po valley towns. His grandson, Frederick II, deliberately chose to concentrate on the Empire and Italy, and he conciliated the North in order to have his hands free for action south of the Alps. When he died, the monarchy had ceased to be a force of any importance, and as a result, Germany lost the chief factor making for unity and stability;[24] this was at a time when the French monarchy was once again full of vigour and vitality.

It had suffered a long eclipse. The nobles had at first had the upper hand, and the king had lost control over the great princes. Subsequently the lesser nobility had defied the princes. By the year 1000 law and order were at such a low ebb that the Church had to intervene and suggest a settlement. As a result the process was reversed. Townspeople, dukes and counts followed suit. From about 1050 or 1100 the monarchs began to recover, and remould and consolidate their authority step by step. They strengthened it, making it domanial, then feudal, then regal. Eventually they enjoyed such power that early in the fourteenth century people could say, 'God's coat of arms is the fleur-de-lis.'[25]

In the tenth century untoward circumstances and outdated ninth-century customs and ideas prevented French kings from effectively holding the great nobles in check. The inroads into their territory had been made earlier and more disastrously, and lasted longer than in the rest of the old Empire. The central government was proportionately weakened and discredited, and centrifugal tendencies took hold. An even worse effect was the reopening of dynastic quarrels in 888, just when similar ones in the East were being settled. The great lords of Western Francia who were alarmed by the Norse threat did not choose to crown the legitimate heir, a child of eight who was later to become Charles the Simple; even though a regency council would have been set up, they voted instead for Eudes, comte de Paris, the Capetians' ancestor;[26] they thought he would be a strong leader. And so, rivalry amongst Carolingians was followed, until 988, by strife between Carolingians and Capetians; it was just as bad for the monarchy's wealth and prestige, and just as good for nobles grasping at land, privilege and independence. The 'vassalization' that Charlemagne and his successors had imposed on their ancestors had been only too effective west of the Rhine.[27] There, dukes and counts had regarded their duties as a fief, and since all fiefs had become hereditary, they automatically handed them down to their descendants. Since the king had not appointed these descendants he could not dismiss them either, and they did not see any advantage in obeying him. And there was no question of playing the bishops off against them. In Germany the Church had followed Carolingian traditions and supported the secular arm, but in ninth-century France it tried to take control over it. So from about 900 or 950, France was at the mercy of its princes. They no doubt recalled that they were the king's representatives in their principalities, but they swore allegiance to him only when they saw fit, and they obeyed the dictates of self-interest rather than his orders.[28]

But before the end of the tenth century they themselves were in dire straits. Their estates broke up into domains which were almost completely independent.[29] They were grouped around fortified castles where the lords defied authority. They dispensed justice in their domain, undertook to protect their villeins and in return established all sorts of rights over them, such as tallage and various obligatory services. The contemporary hero of a *chanson de geste* was not Roland, the Emperor's lieutenant, or William, the great feudal lord who took a faltering monarch's place, but Raoul de Cambrai, the proud, overweening knight.[30]

The division of the country in itself encouraged violent reaction. The nobility's traditions of independence, even their physical make-up and temperament made the use of force attractive to them. As children they were trained in the use of arms so that when they were grown up they could 'shine in the midst of the fray'.[31] They felt innately superior, looked down on people who did not belong to their caste and were indifferent to their lot. The brutality shown by the Norsemen inured them to violence, and they were encouraged in it by their way of life – the idleness and boredom of existence in gloomy castles and the delights of roaming the countryside. In practice their immunity was complete: in the eleventh century there was no court which had jurisdiction over the feudal nobility.[32] Their customary code was exceedingly sensitive about points of honour; vendettas were the normal way for people of a certain rank to obtain reparation, and as they were waged by every member of the injured family against all the guilty ones, they were often disastrous for a whole district. Private wars between neighbours and surprise raids were common currency. Sometimes, like Garin of Lorraine, 'they set out.

The fire raisers and scouts went ahead and the foragers followed to collect up the booty. . . . In one place they would make a clean sweep of everything, in another take the sheep, donkeys and oxen. Smoke rose, fires spread, peasants fled terrified in all directions.'[33] Or, like the six Brabant knights who were later to found Affligem abbey on the site of their exploits, they would lie in ambush 'in a lonely spot near a high road frequented by merchants and many pilgrims' and fall upon travellers and rob them.[34] Even at the beginning of the twelfth century the highest praise that his biographer, Galbert of Bruges, could bestow on Charles the Good, Count of Flanders, one of the principalities with the longest settled history, was that during his reign all his subjects, peasants or townspeople, could go about their business unarmed![35]

There was only one partial curb on such licence, the feudal oath. Carolingian policy had been to widen the scope of the feudal system and speedily establish the hereditary principle in Western Francia, so the nobles who were the heirs of ninth-century lords were brought into the system. Of course the vassal had a leader, his lord, whom he was obliged to assist and never to injure in any way. But at that time there was no formal pyramid with the king at the top, going down by stages through princes, counts, those who owned castles, to plain knights, so that everyone of a certain status had his place in the system and his link with the central government. In some cases the feudal link was firm, in others it either did not exist or had become weak; and as everyone could have several lords, loyalties crossed, were difficult to disentangle and often practically cancelled each other out.[36] Then too, the vassal was not accountable to his lord in all his actions; his complete allegiance to his lord did not prevent his pitting his strength against one of his peers or attacking peasants, merchants or clerks. He had also plenty of arguments or pretexts for going back on his oath.

A reaction was inevitable. As the chief organized force the Church was best situated to take the lead. Selfish as well as disinterested motives combined to make it an opponent of violence and disorder. In its wealth and relative weakness it was an easy prey. Countless ecclesiastical domains had been ravaged by feudal nobles or brutally seized, on feeble pretexts or none at all, or burdened with excessive dues. As early as the beginning of the tenth century it had had to take measures against such inroads and depredations. At the council of Trosly in 909 it had denounced as sacrilege the theft or pillage of ecclesiastical goods, and threatened the guilty with excommunication. Then, as the reform movement took root,[37] it was realized that it was not simply a question of protecting Church property, but that the Church itself had a greater mission: to remind men of their brotherhood in Christ and to try to establish His peace and amity among them.[38]

Henceforward its policy was twofold, one line of action being concerned with the outside world and conducted publicly in a phased campaign, the other concerned with its own soul and difficult to analyse historically. The aim of the first was to extend to merchants, peasants and the poor the permanent protection that clerks and their property already enjoyed, and also to stop all military action during certain days of the week and at certain periods of the liturgical year. With this object the nobles of a diocese, or of several dioceses, were brought together in council, and made to swear solemnly and collectively never to attack non-belligerents, and not to pursue their quarrels between Wednesday evening and Monday morning, during Advent to the Sunday after Epiphany, during Lent until Low Sunday, between the Rogation days and the Octave of Whitsun and on some of the special days dedicated to the Virgin and the saints. This system, which originated at Le Puy in 990 and was known as 'the Peace of God' or 'the Truce of God' spread quickly through France and was finally taken up and promulgated by the Pope himself in 1095. At the same time, the Church continued its secular task of 'Christianizing' society.[39] It strove to teach the faithful a better understanding of the Gospel truths, and a greater respect for them. It reiterated the commandment 'Thou shalt not kill',[40] and taught that, as the famous pronouncement of the council of Narbonne went, 'to kill a Christian is to spill Christ's blood'. But it concentrated on the nobles as the chief engineers of disorder. They were not told to sheath their swords, but to use them 'in the defence of churches, widows, orphans and all God's servants against the enmity of pagans and the fearful terror and alarm of wicked men'.[41] The ideal knight held up as a model was wise and courageous, self-disciplined, loyal to his king as well as his lord, quick to punish injustice and succour the weak; he was a sincere believer, ready to sacrifice his life for his faith. He was a combination of feudal and Christian virtues, a soldier but a man of God, whose weapons had been blessed. At his initiation ceremony the prayers had reminded him of his duties as 'defender of Law and Right'; he must be as pure and single-minded as Saint George or the stone Saint Theodore in the porch at Chartres.

It is difficult to decide just how effective it all was. The Church's powers of coercion were limited; an army would have been more effective to keep the Peace than threats, or even pronouncements of anathema on those who broke it. Sometimes the standard set was too high; when, for example, feudal lords were forbidden to engage in their profitable forays, and were ordered to desist from war, their favourite pastime, for two-thirds of the year. It was an almost impossible task, from the psychological point of view, to effect a quick change of mentality in the ruling class by methods of persuasion or moral pressure, and to try to make silk purses out of sows' ears in a few decades. Complete success was not possible, and it certainly was not achieved, but it was not a complete failure. Excommunication was often a more effective method than we might think; it put the guilty man beyond the pale of Christendom, and of society as a whole, because the two were co-extensive, and its seal of opprobrium meant his inevitable damnation. Even if all the nobles did not become soldier monks like the Templars or Hospitallers, or like Saint Louis, most of them were to some extent, whether fleetingly, superficially or deeply, influenced by ideals of chivalry. This was underlined by the first flush of enthusiasm for the Crusades,[42] and by the fact that the feudal system gradually became less rigid and more human. There were indirect results, too; the Church had launched the movement to restore public order; others followed its example.

Some of those who did so were drawn from the urban middle class. From the end of the tenth century towns began to develop and spread, largely because of a marked rise in population.[43] They were dependent on trade, which itself needed a peaceful environment if it was to flourish. Townspeople, therefore, began to copy the Church's methods; they banded together, swore oaths to keep the peace and help one another, and banished anyone who broke the vow.

Princes took action on a wider scale.[44] They had taken the king's place in their territories, and so theirs was the responsibility for keeping law and order. They also saw an opportunity for strengthening their hold on the lesser nobility in the measures the Church was undertaking; they decided to collaborate. They and the bishops together promulgated 'the Peace of God', and they constituted themselves its guardians. Next they proclaimed their own 'Peace'.[45] They reorganized the administration of justice: they tried to recover their former control, or at least ensure that those responsible were answerable to them.[46] They forbade the building of castles without their consent in case they might be used as redoubts, and they punished disobedience by razing the offending building to the ground. They tried in all sorts of ways to win the nobles to their side; by marriage alliances, conceding fiefs to them, and appointing younger sons to positions in the Church.[47] Eventually, very large stretches of the country were relatively peaceful.

Robert the Pious, son of Hugues, was the only one of the early Capetians to follow the princes in supporting the Church's measures. The others were preoccupied with different aims, of which the chief was to increase their material wealth, and thus strengthen their weakened authority. They still enjoyed a certain prestige conferred by the coronation ritual and the doctrine that it embodied, but it did not grow. The fact that they were very unremarkable monarchs did not matter. The Church insisted more forcibly than ever that they must 'govern the kingdom in its totality', and that they were its law-givers.[48] No feudal lord, however bold and powerful, could forget that holy oil had anointed their foreheads; he would not dare to proclaim himself their equal or raise an impious hand against them: it would be 'vile temerity' to strike them, even for an enemy on the field of battle.[49] The common people began to believe that some diseases could be cured just by touching a king. Kings were the feudal superiors of princes, and through them of most of the nobles, and theoretically they could demand loyalty, military or financial help, and advice. They were fortunate enough to engender heirs who could be trained in their father's lifetime, so that the hereditary system soon became established; they were spared both the bargaining and juggling for power among the magnates, and long periods when priests as guardians exercised control. They still had some trump cards; to play them well they needed one thing – money. They might be born in the purple, consecrated by Holy Mother Church, feudal dignitaries – but as landed proprietors they were on a somewhat small scale, and tended to be looked down on.[50] Their Île de France was well-situated, rich in men and resources, but unfortunately less extensive than some principalities, and partly dominated by rebellious barons. When kings were hardly any richer than many of their vassals they could not expect to carry much weight. It would be very difficult for them to mount expensive expeditions to bring anyone at a distance to heel. The best they could do was to hold on to what they had, and defend themselves when they were made the target of attack. Henry I did so, and in his case it was not easy.[51] But more backing – and in practice that meant a large domain – was necessary before they could make progress.

The credit for realizing this belongs to Henry's son, Philip I. He took every opportunity of enlarging his inheritance: in 1069 he obtained the Gâtinais, Corbie in 1074, in 1077 French Vexin, and in 1100 Bourges and Dun. They did not amount to much, but they counted for something to a modestly endowed king. His successors would now follow the trail he had blazed.

However, it was one thing to gain more territory, but another to exercise effective control over it. The first priority was to curb all the unruly lords and barons of Montlhéry, Courcy and other places; they made the country round the Capetian capital one of the most insecure parts of the kingdom. Louis VI set to work vigorously, indefatigably.[52] Brandishing his sword he led the assaults and dashed first into the breach, followed by crucifix and clergy, and equal numbers of knights and quickly-assembled foot soldiers; and he cleared his land of trouble-makers. When he called a halt after thirty years' struggle he had crushed Thomas de Marle, Hugues du Puiset and other brigands, and confiscated their lands; he had made communications between Orleans, Sens, Melun, Senlis, Mantes and Paris safe. A definite stage had now been reached: the monarchy had an assured base in a loyal Île de France. It had also found faithful allies: in fulfilling, albeit in a limited area, its task of establishing law and order, it had won over all those groups of priests, townspeople, country villeins and serfs who had suffered from misrule. The first objectives had been reached.

In embarking on the second stage, which was to extend its field of action and enlarge its estates outside the Île de France, the monarchy's justification rested on feudal laws. The king had remained the nobles' feudal lord, no matter what happened. This had only been true in theory: in practice, when he wanted to make sure of his vassals' support he had sometimes had to conclude alliances with them.[53] Louis VII, son of Louis VI, now proposed to reorganize feudalism and give it some practical value. In Burgundy, for example, he insisted that all the great lords should hold their rights and their castles in fief from him, and that knights should swear allegiance to the nobles. He tried to close up the holes in the 'feudal pyramid' and make it the workable framework of the kingdom.[54] The king also made use of several possibilities that feudal customs offered: he could assure the succession of any of his vassals who died without heirs, act as guardian while an heir was a minor, marry off heiresses, bring a traitorous vassal to trial before his peers and confiscate his fief, or intervene in a fief if the holder ruled it unjustly.

The last custom was the one which Louis' successor, Philip Augustus, invoked in settling the 'Angevin empire' problem, incidentally increasing his own domain fourfold. William I's conquest of England, the subsequent passage of his throne to Henry II, and the marriage of the latter to Eleanor of Aquitaine had united France's Atlantic seaboard in John Lackland's hands. 1202 was a significant date: in that year John carried off the betrothed of one of his Poitiers vassals, and refused to compensate him. The victim summoned him before a higher feudal court, and when John did not appear his French fiefs were declared forfeit. He rebelled against the sentence, but he was decisively defeated at Bouvines in 1214. He lost Normandy, Anjou, Maine, Poitou and had to renounce his claim over the Auvergne.

By this time the monarchy had become powerful enough to dominate the feudal scene; it had once more become sovereign. The king was now above ordinary feudal relationships. Henceforth he was the liege lord of all his vassals, whether they were linked directly to him, or indirectly through the intermediary of a noble or prince; in other words, he had a prior claim on his vassals' services, and he could overrule all other obligations. Conversely, the king was immune from attack: the feudal processes which permitted the vassal in certain cases to take vengeance on a felon overlord did not apply to him.[55] The monarch once more took control of the administration of justice; Saint Louis allowed appeals on all court decisions to be made to what was later called the 'Parlement'.[56] The maintenance of internal peace and order was a chief preoccupation, and any violation of it was declared to be an offence against the crown, to be tried by the king's judges. The king could issue Ordinances which applied to the whole country.

During this period the opportunity occurred for the monarchy to establish itself in the South, an area hitherto outside its sphere of influence, and very different from the North from the point of view of its people, language, literature, law, customs and even religion. In the second half of the twelfth century it had been infiltrated by a heresy known as Albigensianism or Catharism.[57] Cistercians had urged the Papacy to action, but verbal onslaughts had been ineffective. In 1208 the murder of the Papal legate by one of the Count of Toulouse's men led to a decision to take drastic measures; a crusade was preached against the murderer and the whole sect. Simon de Montfort, one of the lesser Île de France nobles, plunged into a Holy War, continued fighting when higher-ranking crusaders had withdrawn from the field, and ended up as victor of Toulouse, Narbonne, Béziers and Carcassonne. When he died the southerners turned on the French savagely. His son had few good qualities and was soon in such desperate straits that he had first to enlist the king's help and then to cede his rights to him; in fact the king virtually annexed the vast estates belonging to the Counts of Toulouse.[58] In 1271 they were recognized as part of the Capetian patrimony; Champagne was absorbed in 1285, and there only remained four great detached fiefs on the frontiers: Guyenne, Brittany, Flanders and Burgundy.

Conditions were becoming less and less favourable to the nobles. They spent far too much money on luxuries – the Crusades had given them expensive tastes – and on the finer points of armour and fortification. Devaluations of the currency reduced their income from rents and dues, many of which were payable in depreciating deniers. West of the Alps towns were sworn enemies of the nobility, and as trade grew towns became stronger. Kings and the surviving territorial princes henceforth had enough resources and enough liquid assets to pay officials and mercenaries, so that they could do without the nobles' services. Before long a series of great battles – at Courtrai in

1302, Mortgarten in 1315, Crécy in 1346 – inflicted heavy losses on the aristocracy, and proved that pikemen and archers were tactically superior to cavalry. Strength was ebbing out of the feudal system itself; its position was vulnerable and exposed, threatened as it was by the king and the middle classes; in its exhausted state it was becoming an anachronism, politically and militarily.

Clearly much had been achieved – a royal house, wielding power over obedient nobles, in a domain which was to all intents and purposes coterminous with France.

The movement to restore a settled form of government, which had just reached its apogee, had been set in motion by the Church at the very end of the tenth century, taken up by the ruling dynasty, and quickly set France in a dominant position in European civilization. She was much better placed than England, first the victim of the Norse invasions, and after 1066 often ill-governed and torn by rebellions. From 1075 Germany too was split by the Investitute Controversy, and Italy's political lot was linked to Germany's. Spain was in an exposed position on the frontiers of the Christian world, and was absorbed in reconquering her territory from the Moors. In the early stages, in a feudal France, decentralizing forces had produced different regional styles of architecture and sculpture, and the birth of vernacular literature was due to the dominance of feudal lords who knew no Latin. Now, under a strong monarchy, political unity led to a cultural regrouping, and an upsurge of power and prestige gave such an impetus that French art and thought reached and influenced the whole of Christendom.

However, politics were not the sole determining factor. One might ask why Flanders, which enjoyed stable government early in its history, played only a minor role in cultural development in this second part of the Middle Ages. There is a simple explanation for this: there were few religious centres in Flanders, and the advance of civilization was dependent, at this period and until the thirteenth century on the existence of a powerful, dedicated Church.

Chapter 6

THE ECCLESIASTICAL SPHERE: FROM CLUNY TO ROME

The Church's greatest peril sprang from its success. Although in essence a spiritual community it could not cut itself off from secular society: the Church was created for man, and to touch men's hearts it must assume a human form. And so, as its influence spread wider, it strove to fit missionary tactics to local conditions, to establish the organization essential to continuous and coherent action, to build up resources which would enable its ministers to devote themselves wholly to their spiritual task, and to achieve a legal status which would ensure its freedom of action. These aims were never accomplished without trial and error, without toil and strife. At times they were only partially achieved. But where the Church was successful, with its techniques perfected, its constitution established, where its needs were supplied and its existence recognized, its activity supported by civil authority – then a terrible temptation opened before it: that of resting on its laurels and rapidly lapsing into a formal and apathetic routine. The appeal of sloth and ease was often difficult to resist, for the rank and file and even the spiritual leaders were mere men, sensible therefore of the seductions of comfort, wealth and power. Decadence ensued; until some reformer arose to remind the Church that it was 'in the world but not of the world', to lift it out of the rut, and to set it again on the straight and narrow path of its vocation.

At the human level this explains the often disconcerting history of the Christian Church, characterized by a natural alternation of periods of tension and relaxation, of enthusiasm and apathy. It follows a cycle in which reform is born of crises, which are themselves engendered by too great success.

One such cycle is analysed in this chapter. By unremitting labour the Church had at length assured itself an unequalled position in the Frankish Empire. It alone was recognized, indeed helped and

105

protected, by the civil power; it enjoyed great wealth and played a considerable part in temporal matters. Imperceptibly it became the prisoner of its own power, its wealth and its political role. It became the slave of that authority which appeared to serve it so well. It became attached to the worldly success which gave it a vast and comfortable living, and intoxicated with the power that derived from its political and administrative functions. So marked was the consequent laxity of morals, both personal and institutional, that reformers soon rose up to correct it. From the beginning of the tenth century a few chosen spirits were endeavouring to give the Church back its freedom, to instil again the taste for poverty which is the true mark of Christianity and to bring it back to a realization of its mission. In 910 a movement sprang up, increasingly strong and radical, whose repercussions spread far beyond the domain of religion.

For the Church, the end of the ninth century was a period of undoubted crisis: its causes are clear but its intensity and size are difficult to discern. All the documents – canons of the councils, the 'Liber pontificalis', diocesan histories, monastic chronicles, pastoral letters, treatises, pamphlets, and letters of reformers – tally in giving a sad picture of the clergy of the time. There are innumerable reports of worthless popes, of prelates indistinguishable in their behaviour from the nobles (some went so far as to bequeath their sees to their sons), priests as ignorant as they were covetous and immoral, monks who ignored the provisions of their Rule and the duties of their calling, who had personal chattels, and lived in the cloister with wife and children.[1]

The hard times in which they lived account for such laxity. Dynastic quarrels, invasions, private wars, violence and banditry made an environment unfavourable to the exercise of priestly or monastic virtue. Secular society set up force as law, and violent pleasures were its ideal. The clergy were swept from their moorings by this compulsive current and drifted with the stream, the more so because they were the dependents of this world of brigands.

Bishoprics, monasteries and churches were controlled by the king or by a noble, who chose incumbents from among their lieges to advance their own interests. Bishops, abbots and parish priests were the vassals or 'men' of a lord. Bishops, for example, owed fealty and homage to king or prince, were invested by him with their office and insignia, crozier and ring; they were the feudal lords of their own domain, though they ruled theoretically in the king's name; they provided contingents in time of war and attended his court as members of his council or of his judiciary. Thus their duties were the same as those of the secular magnates, and their lives were in no way different. For those who lacked vocation, and they were by no means few, the temptation was irresistible. Indeed, precisely because bishoprics were fiefs, and important fiefs, conferring wide political influence and abundant revenues, they were often given to the most politically useful candidate, to a scion of some great family, in exchange for his influence, or even sold at a high price to totally unscrupulous persons. What was true of the bishops was true at other levels of the hierarchy, of popes and parish priests, and in a different sector, of abbots.[2] The whole Church was tied to secular society and followed in its wake.

It is difficult to decide the extent of this dependence; the question remains open for lack of detailed information.[3] We must not draw too hasty a conclusion from the available documents. Their authors were for the most part ardent reformers whose anxiety to persuade the reader and justify their thesis led them into extravagances and unfounded generalizations.[4] Even the official archives, which as it happens draw a less sombre picture of the Church in the early feudal period, do not reflect the plain, humble reality of everyday life. Invariably history records the scandalous acts of wrongdoers and says little or nothing of the simple and the virtuous: they lived their quiet lives and faded away without leaving any mark in the written records. For a whole generation, for example, an entire monastic community may have observed the rule of the order and the records are silent. But after this long period let but one of its members commit some grave breach and the fact was inevitably recorded in the judicial roll.

In all probability the answer to the riddle of the clerical crisis, from the ninth to the eleventh century, will vary according to time, place and person.

As for the Papacy, the case is simpler and the verdict already given. From 896 to 964 the incumbents were the creatures of the great Roman families, and most of them rank amongst the worst pontiffs the Church has ever had at its head. From 1012 to 1045 they were again the tools of the ruling families of Rome and although their lives were less blatantly immoral in this period they had lost all independence of action.[5]

With the bishops the facts are less clear. There were amongst them pure simoniacs who purchased their office and busied themselves above all with money-making by innumerable methods; there were younger brothers imbued with the feudal spirit and more concerned with political activities than with matters of religion; there were weak characters whose lack of vocation laid them open to every temptation set in their path by the society in which their high office had placed them. But it is highly questionable whether they formed a majority everywhere, and at every time. The German and Lotharingian prelates of the tenth and eleventh centuries in particular do not appear to have been unequal to their task, and many of them indeed were remarkable for their 'signal piety'.[6] Doubtless they were faithful lieutenants of the Emperor, both by their education, trained as they were in the royal chapel, or at least nominated by its officers,[7] and by their vocation, for, like all the clerics of the time, they were convinced that a political unity which ensured peace was the healthiest environment for the growth of Christianity and that the Emperor was the cornerstone of that unity. The punctilious execution of their secular duties however did not interfere with vigilant attention to their spiritual ministry.

Thus at Liège, in a period of less than a hundred years, three great bishops followed one another: Eraclius, Notger and Wazo.[8] The first of these, whom we know to have been a Saxon, founded, or revived, schools which were soon to become celebrated throughout the West. Notger, a Swabian noble, appointed directly from the court circle, was not only the 'founder of the Fatherland' still venerated by the people of Liège, but also a model of priestly virtue. Wazo, born of a humble family of the region, and like the others attached to the Palatine chapel, though only for a short time, showed by his actions that it was possible to serve the Emperor without forgetting God. In 1046, when all the nobles revolted against Henry III, he remained unshakably loyal. 'Let no one doubt,' he said to his friends, 'that I shall continue to serve him with all my mind and all my power, however he shall serve me. If he should put out my right eye I should serve him and honour him with my left.' Yet a few months earlier, pressed by Henry to condemn the Archbishop of Ravenna, he replied firmly: 'We owe obedience to the sovereign pontiff, and to you fealty. We are answerable to you for our secular administration and to him for what touches the Divine office. This is my verdict: if the accused has offended against ecclesiastical discipline he is answerable to the papal envoy; if he has failed in diligence and fidelity in the secular duties you have entrusted to him, then he is in your hands.'[9]

France and Italy had similar prelates in the tenth century, but more of them perhaps in the eleventh and twelfth: Fulbert at Chartres for instance, or, a hundred and fifty years later, Maurice de Sully in Paris.

The Chapters of the collegiate churches too were perhaps less affected. As far as one can judge from the documents they generally appear to have observed the rule imposed by the Council of Aix,[10] though some abolished the common dorter and refectory.

The behaviour of the inferior clergy was infinitely less satisfactory: the texts concerning them are too numerous and too explicit for any doubt to remain. In their ranks immorality was rife; and indeed how could it be otherwise? Parish priests were chosen carelessly, educated indifferently and forced to live by expedients. Some even argued that poverty entitled them to keep a concubine, for only a woman, they claimed, could stretch their miserable pittance to cover the expenses of a household.[11]

The monks endured sore trials, particularly at the end of the ninth century and the beginning of the tenth. They suffered more than anyone else from the incursions of Vikings and Magyars, for their wealth attracted the invader. Many of them must have fled, taking with them only a few valued possessions, above all the relics of saints. The wanderings of the brethren of Noirmoutier are famous; in 836 they left their is-

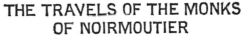

THE TRAVELS OF THE MONKS OF NOIRMOUTIER

land, and, bearing with them the body of their holy patron Philibert, they made for Dées, on the shore of the lake of Granlieu. But this was not far enough, for they were only twenty miles from the sea, and in 858 they moved far-ther east to Cunault, on the Loire, down-stream from Saumur. In 862 they set out again and settled well inland at Messay, in Poitou. In 872 or 873 they were off again to St.

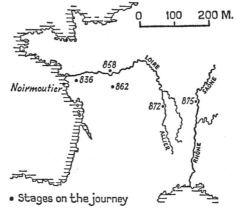

Pourçain in Auvergne, and at last in 875 they found a safe retreat in the walled town of Tournus on the Sâone.[12]

Not only were monastic domains ravaged by the invasions; they were also reduced by secularization. The patrons of abbeys – kings or feudal princes – thought nothing of alienating their holdings or dividing them into fiefs on which to settle their vassals.[13] They often bestowed the abbot's mitre on unworthy clerics, even on laymen, whose only interest in the house was its revenue. Sometimes they moved into the cloister with wife and children, servants, horses, dogs and hawks.[14] We may imagine the trials of houses governed by such superiors, without the minimum qualifications needed for a stable monastic life. It was inevitable that the reform of the Church should start in the monasteries, for it was with them and amongst the lower

109

clergy, about the year 900, that the need was greatest, and it was only here that a rapid recovery was possible.

Recovery was not long delayed: the Norman incursions had scarcely come to an end when reformers appeared in several parts of the Christian world. Their objects were limited: they were concerned only with those hardest hit by the troubles of the ninth century, the monastic houses, and their only ambition was to revive the traditional discipline. Yet without knowing it they were fostering a more radical

THE INTERRELATION OF MONASTIC RULES IN THE XTH. CENTURY

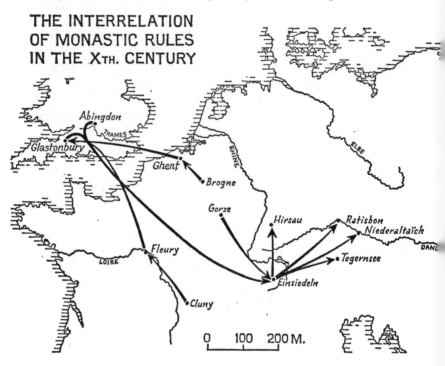

and far-reaching revival which was to spread swiftly through the whole Church and guide it firmly back to the straight and narrow path.

It is well-nigh impossible in a few pages to give the monastic history of the West from 900 to the middle of the eleventh century, a period during which reformers appeared everywhere, in Burgundy, Lorraine, England, Northern Italy and elsewhere. To begin with each of them followed his individual inspiration, and restricted himself to founding or restoring a single convent, but he was soon carried away by his own enthusiasm, and once his success became known he would be invited by bishops and princes to intervene elsewhere. Thus he would extend his field of action and soon cross into some other reformer's territory. Contacts were made, ideas exchanged, methods compared. Dunstan and Ethelwold for example were in close touch with St. Peter's in Ghent, which had just been reorganized by Gerard of Brogne, then with Fleury-sur-Loire, which derived its rule from that of Cluny. Out of these contacts was born the *Regularis concordia Anglicae nationis*, which the English monastic houses were required by a Council of the Church to observe.[15] Very soon afterwards an Englishman called Gregory carried this rule to Einsiedeln in Swabia, where it was combined with customs perhaps borrowed from the Lotharingian John of Gorze, to form an *Ordo* which became widespread in South Germany and Austria. In this way movements combined or influenced one another, or formed more tangled skeins which we cannot disentangle here. Nor can we enumerate the countless houses founded or reorganized in this spirit of emulation.[16] We must confine ourselves to those reformers who were most influential: Saint Berno at Cluny, the Lotharingians and, to a lesser degree, Saint Dunstan in England and Saint Romuald in Italy. Even in these instances we can only outline the essential features and trace the main lines of their evolution.

In Burgundy Berno, abbot of Baume and of Gigny, met William the Pious, Duke of Aquitaine and Count of Mâcon. The former was finding the large number of aspirants attracted to his two houses by their high reputation something of an embarrassment; the latter, like many of the magnates of the time, was prepared to devote part of his wealth to the establishment of a religious community which would intercede with God for himself and his issue in perpetuity. The two men came to an agreement, and on the 11th of September 909, in the presence of several bishops and a crowd of laymen, the foundations of the new monastery were laid at Cluny.[17]

The Rule of the new house was not original: it was practically speaking the Rule of Benedict of Nursia, as altered by Benedict of Aniane at the beginning of the ninth century.[18] It had been piously preserved at St. Savin sur Gartempe, near Poitiers, the foundation of one of the counsellors of the Emperor Louis the Pious; from there it had passed to St. Martin's abbey at Autun about 870, and thence, in 886 and 890 respectively, to Baume and Gigny. The successors of Berno introduced some modifications, dispensing the brethren from manual labour and enforcing rigorous silence in the cloister, but keeping, and indeed strengthening, the one essential and characteristic feature, its conception of the religious life. Communal prayer, the 'Opus Dei', was made the *raison d'être* of the monastic life, to such a degree as to upset the balance between prayer and work required by

111

the original customs of the Benedictines. The idea had been taken up by Cluny and pushed to the extreme: the praise of God was the sole object, exemplified in the chanting of the Office, now extended to such a length that any other activity became impossible,[19] in beauty of ceremonial, and in the 'splendour of the place wherein He dwells', for Cluny built the finest churches in Christendom.[20]

The principles and practices governing the relations of Benedict of Aniane's foundations with the world and with their spiritual father were adopted and logically developed by Cluny. From the ninth century experience had shown that a monastic house was certain to fall into decay when one of the magnates was its overlord and was consequently in a position to choose its abbot and squander its estates. Louis the Pious's counsellor had been aware of the danger and had tried to obviate it. He had not however demanded that the Council of Aix should apply what would have been the only efficacious remedy – to abolish the subordination of the monastic houses to feudal lordship. The outcry would have been too great. He had at least persuaded them to divide monastic property into two lots, of which one was to be outside the governance of the abbots and their possible dilapidations, and was to furnish the needs of the community, if necessary in spite of the abbot. For some houses he had contrived to obtain the privilege of electing their own head. This again was a precedent which Cluny exploited: William of Aquitaine 'ceded to the Holy Apostles Peter and Paul' the land on which the monastery was to be built. Thus it would belong to the first Vicar of Christ or to his successor, the Roman pontiff; no temporal power would have the right to intervene, above all in the appointment of an abbot, and none would have the effrontery to lay claim to its estates.

Nor could any authority apart from the Holy See interfere with the house. The Ordinary was no longer allowed access unless invited by the abbot, and the abbot was no longer obliged to apply to him rather than any other bishop to ordain his monks or give him a blessing. The Burgundian abbey had become the property of Saint Peter and owed allegiance to his heirs alone.[21]

Benedict of Aniane was also aware of the opposite danger of isolation and had reserved the right of inspection or visitation of those monastic houses he had founded or restored. Here again Cluny took up and extended the idea. In 910 Berno was already abbot of Baume and Gigny and when he founded Cluny he kept both those offices. Thus the three houses had the same superior and followed the same customs. For a century this unity was sanctified by usage alone;[22] the group of monasteries, linked only by a common head and common customs, grew closer to each other. However the *de facto* union gradually acquired legal status. Under Saint Odilo considerable power over the whole order was constitutionally vested in the abbot of Cluny, and a true religious order was now in being, the first in the history of the Church. The order was soon flourishing, and until decadence set in in the eleventh century it continued to spread and acquire riches. The reasons for its extraordinary success were several. First of all, its exceptional abbots: four out of five of them, Odo, Maieul, Odilo and Hugh, were true saints, and talented organizers, as well as being men of such astonishing toughness that they spent their long careers in ceaseless travels; the first of them lasted 16 years and the others 50, 55 and 60 years respectively. Secondly, there was the special attraction of a rule which from the start guaranteed its followers against lay interference, and which was gradually refined and elaborated into a complete and precise code of monastic life. Thirdly there was the support of the Holy See, particularly in opposition to some of the bishops who were loath to tolerate the establishment in their dioceses of houses exempt from their jurisdiction.[23] Fourth, there was the geographical situation of Cluny, at the centre of Christendom and at the crossroads of the great routes of commerce, not far from Champagne where all the merchants of the Christian world gathered. And so the total of priories founded by Cluny, and of houses, old and new, which attached themselves to the order, grew with great rapidity.[24] There were some in Aquitaine in Berno's day, then, in Odo's time, in Central France and in French-speaking Switzerland and Italy, finally in the early eleventh century in the Iberian peninsula, and towards the end of the century in England, Belgium and Germany.

Altogether at the end of the eleventh century the order comprised 1,450 houses scattered very unevenly over the whole of Western Europe; and round the order proper gravitated hundreds of houses which adopted the *Consuetudines cluniacenses* in whole or in part, but preserved their independence. Some of them multiplied in their turn: Fleury-sur-Loire spread its influence over the whole of France and into Lorraine and England; St. Benignus at Dijon was soon the centre of particularly vigorous congregations in Lombardy and Normandy; La Cava in Italy; Hirsau in Germany; the list is long.

In comparison with the success of the Burgundian house the achievements of the Lotharingian reforms seem modest enough.[25] They lacked the consistency which is so remarkable in the case of Cluny. Neither Gerard of Brogne nor his followers thought of founding an order; in any case they would have faced opposition from houses jealous of their autonomy. At the most they arrogated to themselves a certain authority over the houses they had reformed, but when the reformer died the monastery recovered its freedom of action, and for lack of a formal constitution many fell into decay again. For this reason Lorraine experienced several parallel or successive restoration movements.

In the houses of Lorraine the brethren's daily life was harder than at Cluny. At Gorze in particular, John of Vandières, who must have known the Italian hermits, and whose predecessor, Einold, was himself a former recluse, insisted on the duty of manual labour, and a multiplicity of fasts and vigils. The Lotharingians also adopted a more flexible attitude towards the outside world than Berno and his successors. Admittedly they attempted to mitigate the evil effects of lay patronage and to ensure that abbots were chosen from the regular clergy. They tried, too, to revive the temporal power of the abbots, but expediency made them accept the overriding power of kings and barons. They did not seek to evade episcopal authority, for most of the bishops were admirable prelates; in fact they sought their support and protection. In this way they created a system suited to the political and religious conditions of the region, an imperial monasticism. Some houses were particularly successful: Gorze, for example, influenced the whole of western and southern Germany, as far as Fulda, Ratisbon, Niederaltaïch and Einsiedeln.

The major interest of the reforms of Dunstan, Ethelwold and Oswald resides in their decisive influence on the hierarchy and the diocesan clergy of England.[26] These three not only rejuvenated English monasticism, which was at a low ebb in 945; they instilled a new and vital Christian spirit into the Anglo-Saxon world, to which the Scandinavian missions bear eloquent witness.[27] It is true that circumstances favoured this movement, particularly the protective attitude of King Edgar and his successor, Edward the Martyr, with the consequent elevation of Dunstan to the see of Canterbury, Aethelwold to Winchester and Oswald to York.[28]

Finally in Lombardy, Etruria and Tuscany we must note the rise of an original type of monasticism which aimed at combining anchoritism and cenobitism. From time immemorial the search for perfection, the longing for union with the Godhead and the will to mortification of the flesh have driven men to withdraw into the wilderness, but from the beginning the hermit's retreat was besieged by would-be disciples and imitators. This was particularly true in the eleventh century and it was not exceptional in the tenth, when hermits were to be found in many regions of Western Europe, and especially in Italy. One of them was Saint Romuald, a monk of St. Apollinarius in Ravenna, who found the discipline of his house too easy and left it to live for a time a life of solitude. Later he travelled from house to house until he met the superior of St. Michael of Cuxa in Catalonia and followed him to his convent. There he meditated on the lives of the desert Fathers and planned the foundation of anchorite communities, in which life in common would be limited to a few meals or pious exercises, and the remainder of the time would be spent in the solitude of small, separate cells. Soon after, the plan was put into practice, notably at Camaldoli, and somewhat later at Fonte Avellana.[29] The principle was to prove attractive to others: Romuald was the precursor of Bruno and, in general, tenth-century reforms prefigure those of the eleventh century.

Indeed, despite lacunae in the evidence we possess, we can say with certainty that the era of Norbert of Gennep and Robert of Molesme, of Peter Damian and Humbert of Silva Candida owed much to that of Odo of Cluny and John of Gorze.[30] Through the efforts of John and Romuald in particular monasticism acquired greater austerity, and, one might say, came closer to its original form. At the same time a reform of the secular clergy was set in train, for, although the regulars were not particularly interested in them, their example was none the less influential. Some of the regulars of course, and they were often the most eloquent, uttered violent denunciations of ecclesiastical depravity. Some again, both on the continent and in England, notably the Cluniacs, governed dioceses, choosing to forget Benedict of Aniane's ideal of segregation from the world, and accepting episcopal sees. Some of them were to rise to the pontificate. In the tenth century again, as in the ninth, it was found that, freedom from lay interference was better than example and exhortation as a means of leading prelates and priests to a worthier way of life and a deeper consciousness of their pastoral duties.[31] That method had borne fruit in the monasteries: it was natural that sooner or later it should be applied to the Church as a whole. Thus the Cluniac custom of making their houses the property of Saint Peter, of the Holy See, had the effect of increasing the authority of the Pope, giving him strongpoints all over Christendom and involving him actively in the work of reform. Without having any such intention the proponents of monastic revival were preparing the ground for a wider movement, the Gregorian Reform.

However, this influence was distant and indirect. The tenth-century reformers acted on their own initiative. They concentrated on the monasteries, following the ideals of Benedict of Aniane. They never explicitly condemned lay intervention in ecclesiastical matters; they laid down practical rules, not abstract principles. At no time did they insist on the primacy of Rome and the universality of its power; they made isolated decisions, and deduced no general theory from them. The Gregorian movement on the other hand was led by the Papacy and embraced the whole Church. It was intended not only to raise the moral level but, more important, to correct the unfortunate weaknesses of organization introduced, or at least confirmed, by the Carolingians. In other words, to put it positively, the intention was to organize the Church in accordance with the Divine will, unify it around the Holy See and set it above civil authority.

In what way then did the lead pass from individuals to the sovereign pontiff? How did the field of reform extend from the monastic houses to the clergy as a whole, and indeed to the whole of Christian society? Why was the original aim of going back to the norms of the ninth century completely reversed? And how did a pragmatic attitude become doctrinaire, a collection of scattered precedents become a system of clear-cut concepts? In spite of the assiduous research carried on over the past twenty years the answer to these questions remains uncertain. It will become clear only when we know more about the canon law collections compiled in Lorraine or those in use in Rome. In the present state of our knowledge we may suppose that the genesis of the movement could be described in the following terms.

In the middle of the eleventh century the Papacy was prompted by its own situation and preoccupations, as much as by the general current of ideas, to concentrate its attention on the notion of freedom. For in 1012 the Papacy had fallen once again under the domination of the Roman nobles, and, either spontaneously, or at the instigation of the Emperors, it reacted against this thraldom and set out to restore the dignity of the clergy at large and the Papacy in particular.[32] But this was not to be done so long as church appointments were made by laymen, as Carolingian and Cluniac experience had shown. In this movement the Papacy was ably served by the Lotharingians, in whose own country the distinction between the civil and ecclesiastical domain had always been emphasized, from Ratherius of Verona to Wazo of Liège.[33] The climate was one of renaissance and reform, casting back to the days when the Church was imbued with the spirit of its Founder and consequently untrammelled by worldly ties.[34] Symbolically the popes of the time took such names as Clement, Damasius, Victor; names which had been borne by the pontiffs of the earliest period of the Church's history but had been forgotten for some six or seven centuries.

It was in the person of a Lotharingian, Humbert of Moyenmoutier, cardinal bishop of Silva Candida, that these tendencies finally crystallized. The needs of the times coinciding with his own radical temperament brought him to formulate with new vigour and urgency the theory of ecclesiastical independence. In 1057 Victor II died. The Romans took advantage of Henry IV's minority to break the promise made to his father not to intervene in the election of the sovereign pontiff, and set on the throne of Saint Peter the Curia's favourite,

Stephen IX, who thus became Pope without the Emperor's intervention. He died after six months and the Roman nobles again made their own choice, naming Benedict X, but this time the Curia refused to sanction the election and set up their own candidate, Nicholas II. The Curia needed support to ensure victory for their nominee. Should they appeal for help to the Imperial court? Humbert was firmly opposed to such a move, and to justify his position he wrote his *Adversus simoniacos*, in which he condemned out of hand all lay interference in religious questions, even from the Emperor himself, not so much on the empirical grounds hitherto adduced as on fundamental principles of Christian society, requiring a clear separation of the spiritual and the temporal. The emphasis was moved from the moral sphere to the constitutional, from fact to law. The Gregorian movement was born.[35]

Humbert laid down two other long-standing principles, both of them given new force and pertinence by the spirit and needs of the time. The offensive launched against the Holy See by the Patriarch of Constantinople, Michael Cerularius, who in 1054 had confirmed the schismatic position of the Eastern Church, was made the occasion to proclaim more firmly than ever the primacy of the see of Rome. To confound the patriarch, who impudently set himself up as doctor of the universal Church, Humbert of Silva Candida demonstrated in his *Diversorum Patrum Sententiae*, with texts to support his thesis, that Peter's heir alone had authority over all the faithful.[36] Adducing arguments from the beginnings of the Christian church, particularly the views of Augustine and Gelasius on the functions of the priesthood,[37] and using the more recent precedent of Nicholas I, who profited by the weakness of Charlemagne's successors to proclaim himself supreme arbiter in the moral sphere and sole interpreter of the Divine will, Humbert arrived at a solemn affirmation of the superiority of the spiritual power over the temporal and a definition of 'Gregorian theocracy'.[38]

The pontiffs and their supporters expressed themselves clearly enough on principles, though they were less certain of their precise application. The basic text of their argument was the *Pasce oves* of Saint John, XXI, 15: the Papacy had been given the responsibility of the shepherd. It was accountable to God for all the actions of all Christians, for no action was morally indifferent. It had jurisdiction over princes as much as over the simple man, over public decisions as well as private transactions. It had a consequent right and obligation to censor the behaviour of emperors and kings, even in political matters, to warn them if they offended against morals or religious interests, and, should they turn a deaf ear to such criticism, to depose them and release their subjects from their oath of allegiance. So far there was no wavering. The question then arose: should papal authority go further, appointing temporal heads, giving them orders, building a Christian republic with the Pope at its head, or, in the terminology of the day, with monarchs as his vassals? Many thought so, amongst them Humbert, who said, 'At the head of the Church stands the Apostolic See, invested with full authority, divine and human, holding the reins of heaven and earth.' Gregory VII, who was to lend his name to the whole movement, was himself less radical. He believed he had authority at the most to confirm the choice of a ruler made by the notables or the people, to judge the suitability of the candidate, and either to refuse him, should he be deemed incapable of carrying out his duties, or to confer power upon him by consecration. Thus he did not claim direct power *'super reges et regna'*: if he concerned himself with politics, it would be indirectly, and from the ethical angle, by way of forestalling or censuring acts which were immoral; he would act *'ratione peccati'*, as it was put in later times, to anticipate or condemn an error. He did not consider himself the universal sovereign, sole holder of *'auctoritas'*, *'potestas'* and *'imperium'*, in short of every form of public power. It was only in the thirteenth century that certain political philosophers and some popes pushed theocracy to its final conclusion.

The programme was now complete: autonomy of the spiritual department, universal power for the pontiff, the right of ecclesiastical authority to censure civil authority whenever the affairs of God were at stake, and, from a more theological point of view, the organization of the Church under a Pope who was at once priest, sovereign monarch and judge, over all men and all deeds. In the *Dictatus Papae*, a kind of synopsis of the canons he intended to draw up, Gregory laid down the programme clearly enough.[39] It only remained to carry it out. A predecessor of Gregory, Nicholas II, namesake of the pontiff who had dictated his views to Charlemagne's successors, was able to mark up a success on the first point of the programme. His accession to the throne of Saint Peter had been a victory over the Emperor and the Roman patriciate, for he was elected by the Curia, without them or against their will; secure and confident, he decreed at the Easter Council of 1059 that the Pope would henceforth be chosen by the Cardinals.[40]

He was less successful in the case of the other ecclesiastical offices. At the same Council he forbade clerics 'to accept investiture from the hand of Emperor, king or any lay person'. But he remained unheard; so much so that in 1075 Gregory VII had to repeat and strengthen this prohibition.[41]

Immediately the inevitable battle began.[42] The pontifical decree had in fact grave political repercussions: from time immemorial kings and princes had made use of their right of nomination to high ecclesiastical offices, to appoint bishops and abbots devoted to their interests, and in this way to cover their kingdoms with valuable strongpoints. Now they were suddenly denied this right. How could they rely on prelates who were not to be recruited by themselves and who would become absorbed in pastoral duties? By forbidding them to appoint ecclesiastical dignitaries this decree struck at one of the foundations of their power. Its effects were more noticeable in Germany than elsewhere, for there, in the tenth century, many prelates had been entrusted with considerable political powers, and from that time on they had formed the surest bulwark of central authority against the pretensions of the nobles. If the Emperors were to renounce the right to nominate they would be delivered into the hands of the nobility. Henry IV, who was on the throne in 1075, could not give way to Rome in this matter; and so began the Investiture Controversy, which was to rend both Germany and Italy for fifty years.

To recount its vicissitudes in detail would be wearisome, for they were very complicated. The tables were turned a number of times. Early on, when Henry journeyed to Canossa and humbly begged the Pope to lift the anathema laid upon him, he came very close to defeat. Eight years later, at the death of Gregory, a resolute man and a saint, but a poor politician, he came near to victory. But in its turn the Papacy recovered, and in 1099, on the death of Urban II, who combined political subtlety with virtue and energy, it seemed the papal faction might carry the day. Pascal II however was too indecisive to exploit his predecessor's success.

In the end lassitude overcame both antagonists, and in 1122, to end the struggle, they arrived at an agreement. The solutions propounded by the Concordat of Worms to the problem of ecclesiastical offices, both high and low, were certainly in the nature of a compromise. The Gregorians of the eleventh century would never have agreed to dissociate the episcopal office from the lands attached to it. In their eyes these might well have been fiefs in the beginning, but they lost this character when they became a part of the Church's estates and the former lord had no power to take part in elections even in order to invest the new tenant with his fee. The pure Imperialists on the other side were equally strong in the defence of the indivisibility of the 'episcopatus'. In their view the office was an integral part of the fief and consequently the lord of the fief alone had the right to choose its holder. On this point the adversaries had to compound, and rallied to the principle traditionally attributed to Ivo of Chartres,[43] which had already been put into practice with some variations in France in 1098, and in England in 1107. It consisted in making a distinction between the ecclesiastical office with its spiritual prerogatives on the one hand, and the temporalities, with the political power they carried, on the other. The former was in the gift of the Church, the latter, of the secular lord. When there was a vacancy the bishop was to be elected canonically, '*a clero et populo*', then confirmed and consecrated by the metropolitan, who would give him ring and staff. Then he would take the oath to his lord, king or emperor, not feudal homage, but the oath of allegiance required of any vassal, and would receive by a symbolic touch of the sceptre his fief and the insignia of temporal authority. Such was the solution adopted by the signatories of the Concordat of Worms. The conditions of the agreement permitted the Emperor to take part in an election, 'without simony or violence', and to exert his authority in disputed cases, to support the better (*sanior*) party, though the exact nature of his intervention was not defined. Nor did the document say whether the Emperor might refuse to confer the temporalities *per sceptrum* on a bishop who had been duly appointed and consecrated. The door was left open to abuse and chicanery. Indeed in the later twelfth century Frederick Barbarossa and Henry VI were to take advantage of the ambiguities and the loopholes in the pact of 1122 to violate its spirit. It was only after 1200, with the decline of Imperial power that disputes ceased and the quarrel over lay investitures really came to an end.

Another question too was settled by a compromise. The sixth canon of the Council of 1059 had denounced lay control of preferment flatly, and without qualification. In 1080 Gregory VII had extended his decree of 1075 to cover 'inferior dignities'. Again in 1119 Calixtus II had tried to persuade the General Synod of Rheims to accept a decree prohibiting 'lay investiture to churches and ecclesiastical benefices', but faced with opposition in the assembly he was obliged to amend his text to a reference to episcopal sees and abbeys. As for parish churches, it was not found possible to withdraw them completely from secular patronage. The rights of patrons were gradually nibbled at to the point where they could do no more than make a nomination to the ordinary, in fact present the candidate for institution. The laity were emphatically and repeatedly ordered in the Lateran Councils of 1123 and 1139 to give, or restore, the churches to the clergy, with the revenues and particularly the tithes appurtenant to them. Many complied with the order; not that the incumbent, however, derived any material advantage from it, for the transfer was usually made to a bishop or a monastery. Many did not obey, and in some regions, such as Normandy, the majority of the churches remained in secular hands throughout the Middle Ages.[44] The Gregorian reformers then were not entirely successful in achieving the first point in their programme: the emancipation of the Church and in particular the freeing of ecclesiastical appointments. The sovereign pontiff was to be designated by the Curia, bishops by the clergy and the people, though in practice, in a growing proportion of cases, they were elected by cathedral chapters. The latter however were to come under strong pressure from the monarchy in France and England, and from the princes in the Empire, whilst many parish priests continued, practically speaking, to be designated by the lay patrons of their churches.

Their victory was absolute, however, on the second point. In accordance with the demands of the *Diversorum patrum Sententiae* and the *Dictatus Papae*, the heir of Saint Peter became a true 'universal bishop' and the Church a monarchy. Gregory VII promulgated decrees which were valid for all Christendom, dispatched legates everywhere and suspended and deposed prelates. From this time on centralization increased, resisted it is true by a few, but encouraged and accepted by the majority.[45] In the twelfth century the Papacy gradually supplanted the Archbishops as a court of appeal from the decisions of the ordinary and arrogated to itself the initiation of processes of canonization, to the detriment of the bishops.[46] From the thirteenth century Rome appointed many of the bishops, and other examples can be adduced to show that the Papacy was gradually coming closer to the Gregorian ideal.

On the last point of their constitutional reform programme, success was small. They pressed their demands in vain; they indeed scored some successes, but they could not make theocracy a reality.

From 1100 onward conflicts with princes and heresiarchs led the canonists and the pontiffs to enunciate even bolder theories. With the revival of Roman law the notion of the State, and its correlative, autonomy of the civil power, came into favour. Frederick Barbarossa, Frederick II and Philip the Fair declared that they held their authority from God alone and recognized no superior in temporal affairs; they thus claimed to rule all their subjects, clerics included. At the same time there was a sort of religious renaissance, a nostalgia for the earliest forms of Christianity, giving rise to movements like Waldensianism, which did not recognize any hierarchy. Combining with the Manichaean ideas brought into the Latin world by the Bogomils they gave rise to the redoubtable Albigensian heresy.[47] In the face of this dual threat it seemed indispensable to strengthen the Church by making the Papacy truly sovereign.

Innocent III, anxious for the freedom and unity of the Church, was compelled by events to take a more extreme position than the Gregorians.[48] He admitted the reality of the State and its mission. None the less he considered, as did all his contemporaries, that this mission was to help mankind towards salvation. Like his predecessors he concluded that he was bound to supervise the execution of this spiritual task and entitled to intervene indirectly in political matters, *ratione peccati*. But he went further than them in considering himself obliged if necessary to direct the enterprise, and therefore entitled to interfere in a direct and positive manner in politics, to choose kings and give them orders. Between 1198 and 1216 he chose one emperor, then dethroned him, enthroned one king, then crowned another, excommunicated a third and made several heads of states vassals of the Holy See. He exercised a true *auctoritas*, but he nevertheless believed that it was his duty to use it *casualiter*, when the case demanded exceptional measures.

In the thirteenth century, with Innocent IV, the adversary of Frederick II, the last reservations were swept away. In his eyes the separation of powers had no importance, for the Papacy was above such distinctions, having *plenitudinem potestatis* – absolute power. It was resorted to only when there was a direct threat to the interests of religion or of the Papacy itself. Only a reluctance to be defiled by contact with the material world impeded regular use of this power in all circumstances. The Papacy, and the Papacy alone, had true sovereignty. '*Nota papam imperatorem esse*', wrote a cardinal of the time; 'Observe that the Pope is Emperor'.

It remained to base theocracy on theological foundations rather than juridical or historical arguments, to make it in fact dogma. Boniface attempted it about 1300. He saw the unlimited authority of the Holy See as a *sine qua non* of the Church's unity and, as it were, an article of faith. Carried away by the heat of the argument and by the tendency of doctrines to become more extreme, Boniface propounded these views at precisely the moment when the reaction was setting in. The idea of the autonomous, parallel power had gathered strength and was on the point of winning the day. Even at the time of Canossa Gregorian ideas had not convinced everyone. There had always been some who invoked the precedent of Charlemagne to defend the Emperor's duty to lead Christendom. At the least they claimed that he held his authority directly from God and was accountable to none other. The juridical renaissance afforded strength and precision to this argument. Most of the canonists of the twelfth century acknowledged that the spiritual and temporal powers were distinct, that the latter was of Divine origin, so that it had not been conferred by the Pope and might not be withdrawn by him, and lastly, that certain acts of civil administration were quite outside pontifical jurisdiction.

In the thirteenth century some jurists developed this last point and held that civil authority had an ultimate spiritual object, but was free to choose the immediate object and the means towards it. Finally there were theorists in the fourteenth century who would do away with the very cornerstone of theocracy. From conceptions derived from Roman law they went on to take up Aristotle's ideas. For them the state had no spiritual function; it was a natural formation, a human society, created by the collectivity itself. It was based on the needs of the individual and took the common good as its only proper end. It followed that it was sufficient unto itself, it was not subject to outside surveillance and within its sphere it was sovereign. Only increasing strength could have enabled the Papacy to fight this rising tide, but it was weaker than ever. New conflicts with the Emperors, the extremism of Innocent IV and Boniface VIII, who assumed the character of universal monarch, and too often made use of their *auctoritas* to defend material interests, a degree of wealth in flagrant contrast with the ideals of poverty preached by twelfth- and thirteenth-century reformers, the development of the papal revenue system, the nepotism and venality of the Avignon court, the Great Schism itself, all these were elements which combined to undermine the power and the reputation of the Holy See. In conjunction with the rise of national monarchies they completed the ruin of the theocratic system dreamed of by the more radical amongst the Gregorians.

On the constitutional side they had achieved a partial but by no means contemptible success. Only occasionally did Pope outplay King, but the essential fact remained that the pontiff had become the head of a unified and relatively independent Church. On the moral side, too, considerable success had been achieved. The repeated exhortations of Peter Damian and others, the endless anathemas against clerics guilty of simony and concubinage, the careful selection of high ecclesiastical dignitaries made possible by the campaign against lay investiture, and above all the vigilant control exercised by Rome and her legates, all these factors certainly had their effect on the conduct of the great mass of the priesthood.[49] It was however limited and ephemeral. The lower clergy probably conducted themselves less scandalously in the later Middle Ages than in the tenth and eleventh centuries, but they were still poorly equipped for their task and remained ignorant, negligent and grasping.[50] To achieve a fundamental improvement there was only one sure remedy, and it was not till the very end of the Middle Ages that it was applied: lengthy training in special colleges. Without seminaries a real and lasting moral improvement was not possible.

The Carolingians had fallen into error not only in confusing the temporal and the spiritual, and thus subordinating Church to State, Pope to Emperor, and bishops to princes: in their work of reorganizing and unifying religious communities, both secular and regular, they had deviated seriously from sound principles or at any rate been

guilty of excessive tolerance. The Rule of Aix had authorized canons
to possess private property and to have private houses in the precincts.[51] The customs elaborated by Benedict of Aniane for the use of
monasteries had altered the spirit of Benedictinism by upsetting the
balance between prayer and work, emphasizing liturgical exercises
at the expense of manual labour. About the year 1000 this rule and
these customs continued to govern the majority of the religious communities of the former Empire; the principal reformers of the tenth
century drew their inspiration, as we saw in the case of Cluny, from
the ideas of the second Saint Benedict. The rigorists, the Gregorians
and their kind, might confidently feel that a return to primitive ideals
was called for in this field as well. Thence there were a series of
movements which claimed to recall canons and monks to a strict
observance of the precepts of Augustine, of Benedict of Nursia and
the Desert Fathers, or, to use the phrase of the time, the '*vita
apostolica*'.

We may ask whether these movements were in fact reforms, as is
often claimed today. If the term is taken to mean a return to a
primitive discipline, the answer is 'yes'. If it means stricter regulation
after a period of laxity, then the answer is 'no'. What was questioned
in the eleventh century was not the extent to which houses obeyed
their rule, but the tenor of the rule itself. This was no struggle between
order and disorder, but between two views of the religious life, the
one accepted for two hundred years, the other much older, and much
more demanding, but now buried in oblivion.

Shortly after 1000 the first reactions began against Benedict's code
of 816.[52] At Val de Castro in 1005 and Vallombrosa in 1038, under
the government of Romuald and John Gualbert respectively, and at
Saint Ruf in the diocese of Valence in 1039, clerics formed groups to
live 'regularly', that is to say as communities and in individual
poverty. This initiative was favoured by high ecclesiastical authorities,
the Bishop of Lucca, the Archbishop of Florence, the great reformer
Peter Damian and the future Gregory VII. At the Council of 1059,
where lay investiture was solemnly condemned for the first time,
Gregory denounced the retention of private property by canons as an
infringement of the 'usage of the primitive Church and the Holy
Fathers', and, as archdeacon of the Eternal City, he asked the Council
(which in fact refused his plea) to approve the true formula for the
vows which should bind Roman priests. Support at this level gave a
strong impetus to the new ideal. A number of existing chapters
amended the statutes of Aix so as to forbid the ownership of personal
property. Of those which were founded at this time many adopted
the new rules of Guy of Bobbio, or Ivo of Chartres, or those of Saint
Ruf or Marbach, which it is true were moderate enough, but which

Clasp from the Sutton Hoo treasure (England VIIth century).

Manuscript illumination from Charles the Bald's second Bible about 875 (f. 146 the word *Visio* at the beginning of the Book of Isaiah). Barbarian and Insular art, with geometrical and animal motifs.

West front of Trier Cathedral (XIth century) showing Early
Romanesque decoration.

Narthex at Tournus
(end of Xth century).

Nave at Vézelay (late XIth early XIIth century). Groin vaults
and vaults on transverse arches.

Cloister vaulting at Worcester (XIVth century) showing the rich decoration of English Gothic towards the end of the Middle Ages.

all condemned private possessions. Before 1100 there were Canons Regular everywhere in Western Europe, except England.[53]

At this point the movement changed; to be precise it split into two. Whilst the canons remained faithful to the reforming ideas of the eleventh century, others moved ahead towards greater asceticism. Under the attraction of eremitism, whose influence on the élite had constantly grown since the now far-off time of Romuald, they withdrew, alone or with a few companions to some out-of-the-way place to lead a life like that of the Desert Fathers. Such were Hermengard and Conon at Arrouaise in the Pas-de-Calais in 1090, William of Champeaux at St. Victor in Paris in 1108, Norbert of Magdeburg at Prémontré, near Laon, in 1120. But these men rapidly became known, disciples joined them and communities grew up around them. To ensure the stability of these groups their leaders were constrained to give them a Rule. They chose the Rule of Saint Augustine, at least as their basis. It was a severe one, requiring its followers to live in common and to observe individual poverty; they must recite the Office day and night, keep silence, carry out manual tasks; and austerity was required of them both in food and in clothing. They were scarcely distinguishable from monks, their houses were very like the abbeys and the congregations in which they were grouped looked like the regular religious orders. One difference there was, and that a basic one; the Canons did not shun ministry should the occasion arise, and the Premonstratensians in particular, almost from their foundation, took charge of rural parishes.

A growing anxiety to oppose any mitigation of austerity and to return to primitive zeal led the order of canons, now in full flower, to divide into a multiplicity of branches. In the final stage of their evolution there were side by side secular canons who remained loyal to the Rule of Aix, regulars like those of Saint Ruf who lived as a community and had no individual property, Augustinians of various observances, Victorines, and Premonstratensians, whose rule was particularly austere.

The same preoccupation, together with a desire to influence the laity, to instruct them, and thus obviate occasions of heresy,[54] instead of deliberately remaining apart from them, now led the monastic world into much the same paths. The unity so dear to the Carolingians gave way to a '*pulchra et decora diversorum ordinum ac professionum varietas*', in the laudatory words of a contemporary historian.[55]

Monks too then were attracted by the hermit's life, austere and propitious to meditation. Making anchoritism their ideal, like Romuald and Peter Damian, they left a cloister too full of comfort and human activity and made their way into the wilderness. The idea of founding new houses or new orders was far from their minds; a single idea drew them, to seek out the *'eremum'*, the wilderness, where, alone, without interruption, they might commune with God. But God often disposed otherwise, by sending disciples to them, and causing them to institute, for the strengthening of the weaker brethren, a superior, an organization and a body of statutes. So men whose dream was to mortify themselves in the bitter solitude of anchorites found themselves establishing congregations, with rules which came to terms with cenobitism.[56]

Some abandoned as little as they could of the hermit's austerity, in particular Saint Bruno of Cologne. A teacher of theology in the cathedral school at Rheims, he was dismissed by a proud archbishop, and retired to the high valleys of Dauphiné, and then to the forests of Calabria. He only demanded a minimum of conventual exercises of his fellows in the Charterhouses of Grenoble and Squillace: daily celebrations of matins and vespers, a weekly deliberation on community matters, meals in common on feastdays. The rest of their time was spent in prayer and study in a cell surrounded by a tiny garden. Total obedience was demanded of them, silence except on one day of the week, and their diet included no meat or fats.[57]

Greater concessions were made by some other proponents of the hermit life in drawing up their constitutions. Saint John Gualbert in Vallombrosa (1038), Saint Robert at Molesme (1075), and Cîteaux too (1098), adopted the Benedictine Rule, but they interpreted it in a more literal and hence more austere manner.[58] The Cistercians were to be especially noteworthy for setting their houses in remote, often marshy, valleys. They would not wear cloaks, hoods or shirts, since they are not mentioned in the Rule, but only a tunic of coarse, white wool, and a cowl or scapular of the same material. They had to sleep on a palliasse, habited and with their cord tied, without blanket or quilt, for Saint Benedict said nothing of bed-coverings. They might not eat meat, fats, fish, eggs, milk nor white bread, and from the fifteenth of September until Easter, might have only one meal a day. In the middle of the night they had to rise at the summons of the one bell the house possessed and sing matins in the most austere of churches. But the partisans of strict Benedictine observance were more concerned about poverty than corporal austerity; in their eyes, and those of many of the faithful in the eleventh century, poverty was the fundamental virtue from which all others stem. To accept wealth without mistrust, like Cluny, was to put a serious stumbling block in the path of perfection. The Cistercians therefore refused to accept gifts of churches, tithes or oblations. These they saw as properties and revenues fitted for clerics who 'served the altar' and might legitimately 'live by the altar'. They also refused the gift of manors, whose possession would put them on an equal footing with the lay world. They only had lands which they could cultivate '*propriis manibus*', in the intervals of celebrating a reasonably curtailed liturgy. This truly monastic poverty (soon abandoned in fact), much more than their asceticism, was the essence of the customs of the order laid down by Saint Robert,[59] and clearly formulated by Stephen Harding in 1119. About the same time a young man had joined the order who was destined to lay the foundations of its renown; he was Bernard of Clairvaux.[60]

The order was successful: by the year 1300 it had 694 houses. By its missionary zeal, its insistence on poverty, its Constitutions, which required the annual gathering of all the abbots in a general chapter, it pointed the way to the Mendicant Orders. Nevertheless the true ancestors of the Friars were not Robert of Molesme and his companions, but two contemporaries, Saint Stephen of Muret and Robert of Arbrissel, who were not content with a Rule which was a mere offshoot of others; they preferred the 'first and essential rule from which all others flow, like streams from a single spring, the Holy Gospel'. They wanted to 'cling to Christ as vine-shoots cling to the parent plant'. In Him Stephen of Muret saw 'one who chose poverty as the surest ladder to heaven'. He forbade his disciples in Grandmont to own land outside the boundaries of the monastery, or to keep cattle. They were to live by their work and by alms, and if they had nothing left, after two days fasting in their cells they were to 'beg from door to door at mills and houses, like any other beggars, and when they had enough to live for one day, with all their brethren, they must return to their house and share the proceeds, giving thanks to God'.[61] Robert was fascinated by the life of Christ in the world; like the Master he went barefoot through highways and byways, preaching the word of God, until he settled in Fontevrault with the men and women he had drawn to him.[62] Thus Stephen practised collective as well as individual poverty, Robert led an active public life for many years, and both developed a fidelity to the ways of the Gospel and the person of the Saviour which were to be the fundamental features of the Dominican and Franciscan orders.

At the end of the twelfth century the two orders marked in every respect the culmination of the great reform of monks and canons alike. They carried further than ever before Cluniac centralization, and that poverty, missionary zeal and imitation of Christ so dear to the eleventh and twelfth centuries. From the beginning the Dominicans[63] had a rigid organization; at the base the individual house, governed by a prior who was elected and advised by the community itself, sitting as a chapter; in the middle the province, governed by a provincial, chosen by conventual delegates to a provincial chapter;

and at the summit a master general appointed for life by the representatives of the provinces meeting in Rome. The Franciscans[64] took
longer to build their constitution but it was similar in form to that of
the Black Friars, and just as authoritarian. There was one more
intermediate level, the custody, between the convents and the
province, and there was greater independence for the general, who
appointed all office-holders, wardens, custodes and ministers provincial. The Dominicans refused to hold lands; the Franciscans insisted
on living on what they earned by their work or on public charity. The
former, who were regular canons, and the latter, a lay community
before they became a religious order, put great emphasis on public
activity. Far from fleeing to the wilderness or to the seclusion of a
cell, they sought contact with the world. They established their houses
in towns, formed Third Orders of laymen, disputed publicly with
heretics and preached to the people. They were strongly supported
by the Popes, and afforded them support in return. They had the rare
privilege of administering the sacraments wherever they wished.
Saint Dominic took as his only models Christ and his apostles. Saint
Francis too followed in his own life that of the Saviour, 'so that at
length accomplishing and perfecting, by the impression of the
Stigmata, that which He had begun, he was wholly changed into
Jesus'.[65]

The choice was wide: canons of Saint Ruf or Marbach, Victorines,
Premonstratensians, Carthusians, Cistercians, followers of Stephen
of Muret and Robert of Arbrissel, Black Friars and Grey Friars.
The wind of asceticism which rose in the South about the year 1000
and swept across Europe, scorching and irresistible, carried with it
not only clerks and laymen but women too. So much so that the
number of religious vocations gave rise to serious problems. There
was nowhere to house so many women, and no means of ensuring
proper spiritual guidance for them. Many solutions were put forward,
but none was wholly satisfactory when put to the test. The least
unsatisfactory was the system of *béguinages** which, during the early
years of the thirteenth century spread over the whole region between
Somme and Rhine.[66] There were too the congregations founded
everywhere to help the aged, the sick, blind men and lepers,[67] to
ransom prisoners or to redeem prostitutes: the Confraternity of the
Holy Ghost, founded in Montpellier about 1160, the Trinitarians of
John of Matha, licensed in 1198 by Innocent III, the Penitents of
Mary Magdalene, established in Hildesheim not long before 1227.
We must not forget the knights of the military orders, who unsheathed
the sword to defend the Holy Land, whole villages vowing themselves

Translator's note: Houses of lay sisters, leading a religious life, but
taking no vows.

to a common life of poverty,[68] generous but undisciplined movements in the towns which drifted into heresy.[69] It would seem that the whole Christian world from the eleventh century on was shaken by the wind of the Spirit.

In France and Italy, where the Church's decay had been most pronounced, and the subsequent reaction more vigorous, the general ferment had a profound influence on literature and the arts and indeed on the whole of civilization. Intellectual life was stimulated into activity. Moral and institutional reform deprived the clergy of temporal ambitions and sharpened their interest in speculative theology. The profusion of monastic houses entailed a profusion of centres of study. Even more important, the religious upheaval of the eleventh and twelfth centuries raised basic questions and prompted inquiry and polemic. On the one hand monks and canons reconsidered their status and tried to seek out the true traditions of the Church: what, for instance, was the real '*vita apostolica*', which they were attempting to revive, what was the Rule of St. Augustine, what was the true interpretation of the Rule of St. Benedict? On the other hand the Curia made it its business to show that the Pontiff held authority over all Christendom, western or eastern, in Spain or in Germany, and jurisdiction over all Christians, even Emperors. The controversies which set regular canons of the earlier kind, the Saint Rufians particularly, against the Augustinians (and especially the Premonstratensians),[70] and the White Monks of Cîteaux against the Black Monks of Cluny,[71] were a kind of echo of the quarrels between Gregorians and Imperialists.

Everywhere clerks were feverishly making compilations of the writings of the Fathers, the decretals of the Popes, the canons of the Councils, the commentaries of the Romanists. Unlike their Carolingian predecessors, however, who confined themselves to transcription and compilation, they considered their texts, dissected them, edited, collated and systematized them. The growing number of the congregations, like the desire to redirect the Church into its primitive path and mould the world to God's pattern, sharpened erudition and trained minds to reason, to analyse and synthesize.

Art too was enriched by the religious revival and the strength of the monastic movement. In architecture, the building of abbey churches was to Romanesque what the raising of the cathedrals was to be to Gothic in the period of urban expansion, affording them the opportunity to develop their strength and their character. Further, the diversity of ideals was reflected in a variety of styles. The predominance of the *Opus Dei* in the Rule of Berno and Odo explained and justified the splendour of Cluny or Jumièges. The asceticism of

Robert of Molesme and Bernard of Clairvaux left its mark on every stone of Fontenay in Burgundy and Thoronet in Provence. Those who have not seen these two austere masterpieces cannot imagine the beauty conveyed by a simple and moving line, the welcome offered by the play of light and shade.[72]

Here and there this influence was even stronger. The religious movements which followed on one another's heels from the tenth to the twelfth centuries worked on the very roots of civilization. After the failure of the Carolingian dynasty Western Europe was in danger of falling apart, its political unity irretrievably lost. Though the German Emperors claimed to be the heirs of Charlemagne they had no illusions about it. Otto III dreamed of a supra-national and truly universal Empire,[73] but it was no more than a dream. In 1124 when his successor Henry V attacked Louis VI, France was united behind the oriflamme of St. Denis, and so startling was this unity that Henry withdrew without giving battle. In these conditions unity of culture seemed condemned to disappear, as it would have done, had not religious unity survived to strengthen it. With Gregory VII the Papacy took firm hold of the government of Christendom. The Popes themselves were, turn and turn about, Italians, Germans, Frenchmen; their counsellors, the cardinals, were recruited from every land, their ambassadors, the legates, regularly increased in numbers, and not only had their powers been extended but their field of action spread as far as distant Ireland in 1101. In this way contact with the churches of every country was established and the links were constantly made closer. The common faith was strengthened by common rites and discipline: Rome's liturgy gradually supplanted national uses and her conception of the canon law was imposed on all Western Europe.[74] The great Orders working in concert with Rome used their influence towards the same ends: the Cluniacs from Castile to Westphalia and from Essex to Sicily, the Victorines from Naples to Nidaros obeyed the same constitutions and embodied the same spiritual attitudes. In spite of political divisions, then, the West remained one; strengthened by the Church's cohesion Christendom took over from the Empire.[75] A clear light is cast on this by the history of the Christian kingdoms of Spain at this period, Aragon, for example. In the tenth century she had broken away from the Marches of the Ebro, still nominally a fief of Western Francia. But scarcely had she broken the political bonds tying her to the lands across the Pyrenees than the religious links became stronger and closer. In 1032 monks trained in the Cluniac school settled at San Juan de Pena; from then on foundations multiplied and the Burgundian abbey set its seal more and more firmly on the country. In 1064 the Papacy stepped in and summoned all Christians to succour Aragon, weakened by a violent Muslim attack, and, heeding the appeal, troops began to move from Southern Italy, Aquitaine, Champagne and Normandy. Four years later the king, Sancho-Ramirez, made over his estates to 'God and Saint Peter' and became a vassal of the Holy See. Another three years and the Roman liturgy took the place of the Mozarabic Rite. Such facts are significant:[76] they prove that the cause of Western unity, lost by the last Carolingians, was saved in the tenth and eleventh centuries by the Church of the Gregorians and the monastic reformers; by the Church principally, but not by the Church alone. It was the first and greatest force set against political individualism and nascent nationalism, but not the only one, for the merchants were fighting at its side in this contest. From the tenth century onward in fact, commercial relations were increasing between all the Christian countries, the consequence of an ill-understood but significant phenomenon, the growth of population in the West.

Chapter 7

THE HUMAN FACTOR: POPULATION GROWTH AND ITS CONSEQUENCES

There is a close relation between demographic movement and the advance of civilization. A fall in the population level is a cause of stagnation and even regress in some fields. A violent upward movement may have dangerous consequences. A steady increase provides a stimulus and encourages progress.[1]

In spite of gaps in our knowledge and a paucity of research it appears undeniable that, perhaps at the end of the tenth century and certainly by the middle of the eleventh, population density in the West began to grow at a sustained rate. This was an important phenomenon which had far-reaching consequences. Two in particular deserve consideration, since they had a great effect on the subsequent history of the Middle Ages and their culture: the expansion of the Christian world, and the resumption of trade, with its corollary, the revival of urban activity.

In the study of demography there is only one form of proof – by statistics – and for the period in question we can scarcely avail ourselves of it. Tax rolls provide evidence for the development of the population of England and will support the not too hazardous statement that between 1086 and 1346 it rose from 1,100,000 to 3,700,000 souls.[2] On the continent records of this kind do not make their appearance until the thirteenth century, and in some places the fourteenth.[3] They would probably enable us to calculate the average number of children in a household and the variations of their number according to class, area and year; but such an inquiry is yet to be made. We are thus obliged, for lack of statistics, to rely on mere pointers, but there is no lack of these.

For three centuries the towns grew steadily, as can be seen by a regular extension of city walls, or a proliferation of churches. At the same time – and this is evidence that we are not concerned solely with an exodus of population or a concentration in certain areas – rural population was also on the increase. The *mansus*, which was originally, in principle, occupied by a single family, was in many regions divided into quarters, and these in their turn were broken into smaller parts. On the edges of the villages forest, waste and fallow gave way to cultivation. New centres of settlement sprang up everywhere, and in spite of the ceaseless extension of arable, land prices were increasing. These and other facts are not to be explained save by an increase of population.

Unfortunately we know no more than this; the evidence has been so little used that we know nothing of the details. As for the causes, we must suppose that they were technical; an improvement in agricultural techniques would increase yields, extend the variety of crops, and feed more people better than before.[4] But other factors may be responsible. The middle of the eleventh century is the date usually given as the beginning of the upward trend. However this cannot be true for Italy or Germany, or for Holland,[5] Flanders or Normandy. The end of the movement is variously given as 1300 or 1350.[6] Its degree is uncertain, and the expression 'demographic revolution' is difficult to support; the most generous estimates give an annual increase of 3·8 per cent for England, and 4·8 per cent for Germany, compared with 14 per cent and 11 per cent respectively for the period 1800 to 1850. Nor can we divide the trend into phases. All that we can affirm is that, from somewhere about the year 1000 until 1300 or perhaps 1350, the population of Western Europe increased steadily and continuously.

A first consequence was a vigorous expansion outward of the peoples of the West. As their numbers grew they overflowed the Carolingian frontiers and every kind of contact with their neighbours became more frequent.

It is true that the Christian West had never lived in a vacuum. In 953 John of Vandières, the Lotharingian reformer, was sent to the court of Cordoba by Otto I, and was guided on his journey by a merchant of Verdun '*gnarus partium Hispanorum*'. In 973 an Arab visiting Mainz found a variety of East Indian spices offered for sale there. Before 990 Bishop Gerard installed Greek monks at Toul. At the same time Hilduin, Count of Arcy in Champagne, endured the perils of the journey to Jerusalem, to expiate his cruelty and injustice. And these are but a few instances among many.[7]

However contacts were still individual and occasional; with Poland or Russia they were less frequent than with the frontier towns of the Elbe, and less common with the Orient than with its outposts in the

Venetian, Neapolitan, or Sicilian regions of Italy or in Muslim Spain. Some Westerners reached the Bosphorus and the Levant, particularly pilgrims and diplomats: it was an envoy who brought from Byzantium the Romance of Alexander which was to become so popular in medieval literature. But few ventured so far afield. Gerbert of Aurillac went off to Vich in Catalonia to complete his study of mathematics and astronomy, and it was by way of Salerno that Greek and Arab medicine made its way into the Latin and Germanic countries.[8]

In the eleventh century things changed. The West revived and made more and more contacts with Islam, the Middle East and Slavonia, some peaceful, some violent, but all fruitful.

The most important clashes with outside forces were Robert Guiscard's campaigns, the Reconquest in Spain, the Crusades, and the *Drang nach Osten*. In Italy, Spain, the Levant, or beyond the Elbe, the West either annexed new territories or recovered old ones.

At the end of the tenth century the Normans still kept their Viking restlessness and vitality; they still dreamed of conquests in distant lands. They were too fertile; for generations their families had been too large for the ancestral home. Demographic pressure, added to a taste for adventure, drove the descendants of Rollo and his men to emigrate. They were always ready to take service as mercenaries, and from 1009 onward many of them were hired by the princes who were fighting for the mastery of Southern Italy. They took advantage of the anarchy which reigned there, switching allegiance, and often enough conquering handsome domains of their own. About 1060 Robert Guiscard, one of the twelve sons of a poor squire who held a manor near Coutances, became one of their outstanding leaders. Helped by his brothers, he formed a fighting unit of his fellow Normans and for twenty years led them from one success to another. He drove the Byzantines out of Apulia and Calabria and the Arabs out of Sicily, subjugated the Lombards of Capua, Benevento and Salerno, and laid the foundations of a Norman Empire stretching from the Abruzzi to Syracuse. For a short time he had a foothold in Illyria and Epirus, threatening the Eastern Empire.[9]

At the same time the Christian kingdoms of Spain were enlarging their frontiers. The *Reconquista* was greatly aided by dissension amongst the Moors and by the support of crusading knights, summoned by the Pope in 1063 to combat the Infidel. Their military success was greatest in the high plateau, ideal for the *algarada*, their system of guerrilla attack, and as they conquered territory they consolidated their gains by setting up *castillos*, strongpoints. In 1085 King Alfonso VI of Castile brought off a master-stroke by capturing Toledo, one of the enemy capitals. Twice his position was endangered by the intervention of Muslims from Africa, the Almoravides and the

Almohades, but on both occasions the Christians recovered, maintained their positions and resumed their southward advance. In 1212 their victory at Las Navas de Tolosa finally opened up the Southern part of the peninsula, and soon only the Kingdom of Granada held out.[10]

In 1095 Urban II offered the ever-increasing battalions of feudal adventurers a still more glorious chance to display their valour in the service of God. He called on them to deliver the Holy Land out of the hands of the Infidel; a project which offered at one and the same time the opportunity to win salvation in a holy war, the hope of seeing in Jerusalem the second coming of Christ, the chance of distinguishing themselves in battle and the prospect of winning lands and wealth in the fabled Orient. Thousands answered the call:[11] in August 1096 four armies were on the march. In May 1097 they joined up in Constantinople and in June they lay before Nicaea. Then innumerable misfortunes befell them; there were quarrels among the leaders, a lack of supplies, the heat was intolerable and epidemics broke out. Of the 150,000 fighting men who had set out, no more than 15,000 remained in June 1099 before Jerusalem; but what they lacked in numbers they made up in ardour. On the 15th of July the city was carried and a Latin Kingdom proclaimed. Reinforced by fresh contingents, the Franks of Syria and Palestine widened their conquests and strengthened their hold. But this state of things was not destined to last long. They quarrelled among themselves, and real support from the West was not forthcoming; new crusades set out, but each with less enthusiasm and less prospect of success than the one before. The only achievement of the Fourth Crusade was an ephemeral Latin Empire in Constantinople.

In the middle of the twelfth century the *Drang nach Osten* entered a decisive phase. Two feudal princes, Henry the Lion and Albert the Bear, revived imperialist aims and struck out across the Elbe into Slav country towards the Baltic Sea and the Oder. Henry made Lübeck his base, founded Rostock, rebuilt Mecklenburg and brought Cistercian monks to Doberan. Albert's policy was to enlarge his margravate of Brandenburg, and his successors carried on this policy. A century later the Teutonic knights left the Holy Land for the Lower Vistula and laid the foundations of the other half of the future Prussia; they then established themselves along the Baltic coast, in Kurland, Livonia, Estonia, as far as Narwa.[13]

This military activity did not rule out peaceful, individual enterprise; on the contrary, armies reopened the old roads and built new ones, and soon pilgrims and missionaries were moving along them. From 1030 onwards devout Christians travelled in ever greater numbers to Jerusalem; in 1200 missionary brothers, particularly

THE *DRANG NACH OSTEN* ALONG BALTIC SHORES
XIITH., XIIITH. CENTURIES

ESTONIA

LIVONIA

KURLAND

PRUSSIA

•Narv

HOLS-
TEIN

BRANDENBURG

SILESIA

1. Lübeck
2. Mecklenburg
3. Doberan
4. Rostock

0   50   100 M.

Dominicans and Franciscans, embarked on the task of converting Asia and the Far East.[14] Scholars too were involved: during the eleventh century each generation acquired new scientific knowledge from the Arabs,[15] and early in the twelfth, Adelard of Bath, an Englishman educated in Laon and Tours, journeyed through Sicily, Cilicia and Syria, in quest of treatises on mathematics, astronomy and alchemy.[16] Artisans and even peasant farmers went to the East; Flemings and Walloons established settlements in Holstein, Brandenburg, Silesia and Hungary.[17] Last, but not least, there were the merchants; Christian conquest opened up new prospects for them and gave new impetus to international trade.

The commercial revival began in the ninth century, so that it probably preceded the population increase; the latter therefore was not its cause, but it must have facilitated its spread and enabled it to transform the West's way of living.[18] In the Carolingian period commerce expanded to a degree which, though modest, was significant and by no means as ephemeral as some have claimed. Under the second Frankish dynasty the area between the Loire and the Rhine emerged from the closed economy in which other countries were still stagnating. Wagoners and bargemen travelled its roads and rivers carrying cargoes of wine, grain, Flemish cloth and the products of Rhenish and Mosan metalworkers. In many of its cities licence was given by the lord to hold regular fairs;[19] along the main trade routes new cities sprang up, ancient cities awoke to new life, mints were set up to coin money. On the North Sea trade with England and Scandinavia brought wealth to Quentovic and Duurstede.[20] Insecurity, born of the decadence of the Empire and the Viking and Magyar invasions, checked this advance for a time; but only temporarily. In some places recovery began about 900, in others twenty-five or fifty years later; and something more than recovery, for commerce spread and increased. The growing population was driven to specialization; the supply of land was no longer sufficient to employ the labour available. The more enterprising merchants showed that trade led to riches faster than did agriculture.[21] As early as the tenth century in Northern Italy and Provence, in Ratisbon, Magdeburg, Hamburg and elsewhere, the number of merchants and artisans was on the increase and trade was developing.[22]

It was at this time in Spain, Sicily and the Orient that the Cross began to win decisive victories over the Crescent, and they were victories pregnant with economic consequences for Europe; as a result of them it gained control of the Mediterranean, easy access to raw materials essential for industry, and new outlets for manufactured goods. Italian merchants were not slow to see this: Venice, Genoa and Pisa enlarged their merchant fleets, fitted out expeditions and established trading posts everywhere from Catalonia to Egypt. They also built up their trade with the hinterland; in particular with the area between the Loire and the Rhine, where the commercial revival had begun exceptionally early, and above all with Flanders, famous for its textiles. The wool towns of the Low Countries and the ports of Italy came into ever closer contact, so that two centres developed, enriching each other and spreading their influence over the whole of Europe. The supremacy of agriculture was ended; industry and commerce became essential elements in the medieval scene.

This was a real revolution, with so many consequences, distant or immediate, widespread or limited, that they would be difficult to enumerate. In a general way commerce constituted a new and power-ful bond between Western European countries. Economic unity joined with religious and cultural unity to counteract the effects of political separatism. Commerce moreover strengthened cultural unity by fostering artistic and intellectual exchanges. In a special way economic progress influenced intellectual movements; it set new problems in the legal, moral and technical fields, and conferred a growing importance on such neglected fields as the law.[23] In the political and social sphere taxes on the movement of goods, and the profits from minting the coin needed for business transactions (in the absence of direct taxation) provided ample revenues for the royal exchequers, which had always been short of currency, and enabled kings to arm themselves with that essential weapon of authority, a large and well-trained civil service. At the same time devaluation, normal in an economy of commercial activity and plentiful money, considerably reduced the real value of quit-rents and thus improved the lot of the peasants, whilst sadly curtailing the principal income of the lesser nobility.[24] This new balance of political forces was accen-tuated in the towns: their burgesses opposed the feudal classes, whose turbulence was a danger to their prosperity, and gave their support to central authority in the form of financial aids and military levies. The revival of trade was thus accompanied by a remarkably vigorous urban growth.

Merchants and artisans, particularly those in a large way of business, could not remain isolated from one another. Even an itinerant merchant had to have a base where he could keep his stocks and take shelter in the slack season. Manifestly they could not safely remain scattered over the exposed open country, for their wealth was portable and the times were troubled. They therefore congregated in fortified places to protect themselves against attack, close to the trade routes, or, better still, where two routes crossed, so that their settle-ments were not mere refuges from danger but markets where buyer and seller came together. The artisans at the higher levels of industry used raw materials which often came from far away, and their pro-duction was more than the regional market could absorb. Only the large-scale '*negotiatores*' were in a position to ensure a regular supply of raw materials and carry their finished products to distant markets. The artisans and the merchants therefore were attracted to the same points,[25] and so industrial and commercial expansion created those organs of economic specialization, the towns.

So much for the causes of their foundation. The towns of the Middle Ages, particularly the important ones, grew up in places which were easy of access though easily defendable, but apart from these two invariables they developed in a number of different ways.

In those regions where urban life had flourished in Roman times merchants and artisans settled by preference in the ancient cities, which had survived as ecclesiastical centres; their ramparts had often been restored after the depredations of Vikings, Magyars or Saracens.[26] In the North-West on the other hand, where there had been few towns, they gathered in the shadow of fortified monasteries, round the castle of a great lord, or in new settlements founded by some far-seeing magnate.[27] Later, in the East European countries, merchants themselves built towns in the places they found most convenient.[28] However diverse the manner of their birth and development, the result was identical – Europe was gradually covered by townships, and its history was to be more and more influenced by them.

The town was the centre of social activity of every kind – political, economic, intellectual and artistic – and itself provided the motive power. From the middle of the twelfth century the prince resided within its walls, merchants did business, clerks sought learning, and master-builders, stone-carvers, glassworkers and jewellers carried on their trades. In the period from about 1125 to the end of the thirteenth century, which constitutes the peak of medieval achievement, their palaces and guildhalls, their market-halls and workshops, their schools and universities, their cathedrals and collegiate churches made the towns the focus of civilization in the widest sense. By concentrating every source of talent and energy within their walls they brought the spirit of the Middle Ages to full fruition. Later they were to be one of the most potent factors for change; in the fourteenth and fifteenth centuries, at the height of their power, now the equals of kings, they steered Europe into new paths.

Trade made the towns, and the towns made trade their leading preoccupation. The climate of the times was materialistic and spiritual values were often subordinate. The townsmen were jealous of their freedom and rejected the theocratic pretensions of the Church; they strove to circumscribe its field of action, to intervene in Church matters and weaken its influence. They moulded science, literature and the arts to their taste. Political theorists and certain theologians put forward democratic and egalitarian views. The experimental method became respectable. In literature the leading genres were social satire, didactic works, profane drama and somewhat uninspired lyric poetry. In sculpture, and then in painting, individualism and realism gained the upper hand. All these were the signs of bourgeois influence. Once materialism and secularism were in the ascendant, with a bourgeois ethic permeating literature and the arts, the end of the Middle Ages was at hand.

Immediately before this decline Christian Europe was to have its finest flowering. The East and the Arab world had provided contact with new sources of civilization. It was in the towns that these were grafted on to the older stock of the Carolingian Renaissance. But it was above all the increase of population which had both prompted closer contact with the East and led to the establishment of those towns; thus it was the motive force which raised medieval civilization to its greatest heights.

Chapter 8

MIND AND HEART: NOVA ET VETERA

The political and religious quarrels related in preceding chapters might well have had a fatal effect on cultural standards. Fortunately in some regions, in particular in Germany, they were composed quickly enough to save the situation. The Carolingian Renaissance survived; there was no real setback, it merely marked time for a while. The German Empire, and within it Saxony, Swabia, Lorraine and the Rhineland, preserved intact the Renaissance tradition, with its pedagogic system and methods, its literature and monuments, its ideas and spirit. Italy and France gave the movement new dynamism, by bringing to it elements borrowed from antiquity or from other cultures, so that in the eleventh century the seeds were sown for the great flowering of medieval civilization during the next two hundred years.

For the period which stretches from 875 to 1125 there are two main questions; first, in what places did the Carolingian Renaissance survive into the tenth century? Secondly, what further progress was there in the eleventh century? The answers will provide the subject matter of this chapter.

It was natural that in the earlier half of the tenth century the spiritual heritage of the Carolingians should be preserved most faithfully in the country where they were born, and which they had made the centre of their empire; the region where they had set up their best schools and their greatest monuments; where nobility, clergy and common people all kept alive the memory of the great Charlemagne himself, as the oldest *chansons de geste* bear witness, for example, the *Vita Caroli Magni* of Corvey or the *Gesta Caroli Magni* of St. Gallen. A glorious past, not altogether moribund, inspired the region between Loire and Rhine to continue into the tenth century this first renaissance. The territorial redistributions of 843 and 888, however, destroyed the unity of this area. Part of it became the Northern

141

section of what was to be France, other parts were absorbed in 923 or earlier into what would become in 962 the Empire of Germany. These events had not the vast importance that a contemporary mind might suppose, but they were not without consequence. Political divisions did not immediately entail a fragmentation of civilization, but did in fact create environments more or less favourable to its continued growth. The difference was one of quantity, of degree, no more, but none the less significant. New frontiers did not set barriers to the exchange of ideas, and the nationalism to which these boundaries later contributed was not to have a detrimental effect on culture before the fourteenth century. Until then Christendom, though divided into separate states, kept its basic unity. There is evidence enough to demonstrate this: the influence of Abbo of Fleury upon Hermann of Reichenau, the links between Chartres and Liège, the part played by Saint Anselm of Aosta, first at the Norman abbey of Bec and later as Archbishop of Canterbury, the visits of Baudry of Bourgueil to Rome and England. But from now on the atmosphere was no longer the same everywhere; in one place it had a stimulating effect on the artist and the thinker; elsewhere it might discourage them. In the tenth century, for instance, the cultural climate farther east was more favourable, so the Carolingian Renaissance was continued in the valleys of the Meuse, the Rhine and the Weser rather than on the banks of the Loire; that is to say, in the country governed by the Saxon kings and emperors.

The activity of the Ottonian dynasty was the essential factor; whilst France was hampered by feudal divisions, the Saxons maintained peace and unity in their states. They made judicious use of their right, which had become a monopoly, to appoint bishops, and they set over the German church zealous, and often learned, prelates who took more interest in the moral and intellectual conduct of their clergy than did their brethren in neighbouring countries. Without Eraclius the Saxon and Notger the Swabian, both appointed by the Ottonians, Liège would never have become the 'Athens of the North', as Gozechin called it. The political heirs of Charlemagne were determined to exploit their inheritance in the cultural domain as well. Otto I unified Germany, Italy and Lorraine and ruled half Western Europe; he was arbiter of dynastic conflicts in France and made the King of Burgundy a kind of vassal; he conquered the Magyars, contained the Slavs on the right bank of the Elbe and became the bulwark of Christendom; he founded an archbishopric in Magdeburg and a bishopric in Prague, and gave his support to the missionaries who were trying to move eastward from these bridgeheads; he freed the Papacy from the grasp of the Roman nobility, and was himself crowned with the Imperial crown by the Pope's hand in 962. All

CENTRES OF CULTURE
IN THE OTTONIAN AGE

------- Frontiers of Ottonian Germany

this was magnificent, but Otto was not content; he continued not only the foreign policy of his brilliant predecessor but also his cultural projects.[1] His court was a copy of Charlemagne's court at Aix and like his forerunner he learned reading, writing and Latin when he was over thirty. He started a school in his palace and gathered round him scholars and writers, Ratherius of Verona, Stephen of Novara, Liutprand of Cremona. His family joined in his efforts: his wife Adelaide, an intelligent and cultivated person, his brother Bruno, who, as Archbishop of Cologne, brought fame to the Schools of the city, and his niece Gerberga, whose pupil was Roswitha of Gandersheim. His son, carefully educated, married to a Byzantine princess, continued the paternal tradition when he came to the throne as Otto II. Otto III, who had as his tutor Gerbert of Aurillac, the most learned man of the time, was also a patron of letters and arts. The German civilization of the tenth century is justly called 'Ottonian'.[2] Like Swabia, Lorraine and the Rhineland, Saxony was one of the centres of this civilization, whose outstanding figures were Widukind, Roswitha and Bernward of Hildesheim. At Corvey, on the Weser, Widukind wrote, about 950, a *History of the Saxons* which had both documentary value and literary merit. At the same time, thirty miles away in Gandersheim, Roswitha, a nun, wrote six curious comedies imitated from Terence; his works were regarded as immoral and hers replaced them in monastic libraries.[3] Some decades later, between 992 and 1022, farther north, Bernward, Bishop of Hildesheim, gave patronage and encouragement to the lesser arts, manuscript illumination and metalwork; it was during his tenancy of the see that the great bronze doors were made, and the bronze column bearing scenes from the life of Christ.[4]

In Swabia, a country now partly in Germany and partly in Switzerland, the Abbey of St. Gallen continued the career which had begun in Carolingian times, with greater brilliance now than ever before. It had been practically untouched by the Magyar invasions and had kept intact one of the finest libraries in Europe. The librarian at the beginning of the tenth century was Notker Balbulus, who was also master of the oblates' school and a true poet. Amongst his vast and varied works forty sequences stand out, rhythmic poems serving as mnemonics for the modulations of the Alleluia in the Gradual.[5] Notker did not invent that highly successful genre, the sequence, but he is one of those who did most to develop and popularize it. The same remark is true, to a lesser degree, of another monk of St. Gallen, a generation or two later: Tutilo was not the inventor of the trope, a dramatization of a liturgical text, which contained the germ of religious drama, and consequently of the whole medieval theatre, but he contributed much to its success by composing such famous examples as the Easter trope '*Quem quaeritis in sepulcro*'.[6] The '*Waltharius*', the work of Ekkehard, a contemporary of Tutilo, is equally interesting; it takes its subject from ancient Germanic legend, showing that there was a growing relationship between literature in Latin and in the vernacular, one which was to develop and prove advantageous to both.[7] Finally, the German translations from Virgil, Cato, Terence, Boethius, Martianus Capella and Gregory the Great made by Notker Labeo, around the year 1000, constituted the first attempt on the continent to make the great writers of classical and Christian antiquity accessible to a wider public. Besides writers, St. Gallen had excellent illuminators, though its *scriptorium* was eclipsed about 960 by near-by Reichenau; the latter had had its most glorious epoch under the Carolingians, and some of its miniatures inspired the frescoes at Oberzell.[8] At the other end of the Empire Lorraine was becoming famous, thanks to Lobbes, on the Sambre. On the frontier St. Amand was one of the principal refuges of culture in the critical period from 875 to 925. Its titles to fame are many: illuminators rivalling those of Corbie, St. Vaast and Arras with a 'Franco-insular' style which contributed a great many elements to the eleventh century *scriptoria* of Flanders and Liège;[9] a library rich in classical works;[10] and above all its '*scholastici*', amongst them Hucbald, who revived the cathedral school of Rheims, glossed the *Isagoge* of Porphyry (thus becoming the first medieval commentator on Aristotle's logic), and acquired lasting fame as a musicologist by his *Harmonica institutio*.[11] At Liège, about 840 Bishop Hartgar had welcomed the poet Sedulius, and some fifty years later the next Bishop but one, Stephen, kept up a certain amount of cultural activity; it is true that he was more interested in music than literature, and if posterity remembers him, it is for his creations and innovations in the field of liturgy, of which the leading example is the introduction of the feast of the Trinity.[12] The question arises whether the monastery of Lobbes inherited more from St. Amand, or from the city of Liège. For, from 920 onwards, Lobbes produced a series of illustrious writers.[13] The first was Ratherius, a theologian whose difficult character caused him to lead the life of a wanderer, but whose works are remarkable for elegance of style, breadth of learning and orthodoxy of doctrine. Books III and IV of his *Praeloquia* have attracted special attention since they foreshadow the ideas of the Gregorian Reform: the independence of the episcopacy and the supremacy of Rome.[14] The next was an historian, Folcwin, brought up at St. Bertin in Flanders and raised to the abbacy of Lobbes in 965 by Bishop Eraclius of Liège. Like Flodoard's *Historia Remensis Ecclesiae*, his *Gesta abbatum Sitiensium* and his *Gesta abbatum Lobiensium* gave respectability to a new kind of work, the regional or local chronicle, based on archives and other reliable sources.[15] After Folcwin, round about the year 1000, we have a *scholasticus* of Liège, Heriger, too erudite to be original but none the less a gifted teacher. Among his pupils was Olbert of Gembloux, master and collaborator of Burchard of Worms and Wazo of Liège. The fame of Lobbes, however, should not make us forget other centres in Lorraine, such as Toul with its cathedral and its monastery, St. Evre. It was here that an unknown clerk wrote about 930 the *Ecbasis cuiusdam captivi*, an involved tale of a calf that escaped from the cow-byre, and forerunner of the animal epic of *Reynard the Fox*.[16] There was Metz, building its cathedral, making carvings in ivory; and above all Trier, where the abbot of St. Maxim in 906 compiled a '*De synodalibus causis et ecclesiasticis officiis*'; between 934 and 949 his successor built a double-towered front for the sanctuary, which was widely imitated, and there was a school of skilful goldsmiths there about 980.[17]

The schools of the Middle Rhine produced two works of considerable importance in ecclesiastical history. The so-called Romano-Germanic Pontifical was compiled about 950 in Mainz, which had become the seat of the primate of Germany and Gaul a few years before. Derived from a series of liturgical texts which had been preserved in the city, or near by, from the beginning of the century, notably the Fulda Sacramentary and the *Ordo romanus antiquus*, it was to be used everywhere in Western Europe from Hamburg to Amiens and Besançon, from England to Poland, and it provided the basis for the Roman Pontifical.[18] Sixty years later in Worms, Bishop Burchard compiled his *Decretum*, which was concerned largely with the problems of canon law; either in its original form or in recast versions it enjoyed wide currency in Germany, France and, later, Italy.[19]

At the beginning of the eleventh century this geographical distribution of culture suffered considerable modification. The Salians succeeded the Ottonians, and Saxony lost its importance. On its frontiers the abbey of Hersfeld alone kept up its cultural activity, supported by a fine library, producing, for example, in 1090 an anti-Gregorian treatise *De unitate ecclesiae*, whose moderate tone distinguishes it from the great mass of polemical writings inspired by the Investiture Controversy.[20] Other cultural centres, imbued with older traditions and closer to the ancient civilizations, were better able to preserve and even improve their reputation. Along the Rhine, in the cities which owed their birth and their riches to the river, German Romanesque raised the great cathedrals of Mainz, Speyer and Worms, and the unparalleled group of churches in Cologne. A little farther west the best example was the great monastery of Maria-Laach. At the end of the eleventh century the art of illumination flourished in Bingen and Wiesbaden.

In the south St. Gallen, Tegernsee, Reichenau and Ratisbon were equal in fame. At St. Gallen Ekkehard IV rewrote the '*Waltharius*', and under the title '*Casus Sancti Galli*' he related, with more zest than accuracy, the monastery's two hundred years of history. Tegernsee was the cradle of the '*Ruodlieb*', a younger brother of the '*Waltharius*', and the school which produced Othlon, glory of St. Emmeran in Ratisbon; a writer of distinction and an astute psychologist, his works are strewn with anecdotes and reflections which reveal the writer's personality in a way unusual in that period.[21] Reichenau was no longer the centre of German miniature; Ratisbon, Trier and Echternach had assumed the succession: but it could still boast Hermann of Reichenau, an invalid and cripple, unable to walk and well-nigh inarticulate, and yet an extraordinary man, musician and poet, historian and scholar, the last a rare thing in the Germany of that time. He wrote a treatise '*De musica*', composed the '*Alma redemptoris mater*', and possibly the '*Salve regina*', compiled an excellent universal chronicle, and wrote a number of valuable essays on mathematics and astronomy.[22]

Despite these men and their achievements, the Rhineland, Swabia and Bavaria compared unfavourably with Lorraine. From the time of Notger onwards the duchy of Lorraine passed through the most splendid period in all its history, a golden age of literature as well of the arts, both in the capital and in the monasteries surrounding it.[23] There were several schools in Liège, one in the shadow of the cathedral, others attached to its collegiate and abbatial churches, St. Bartholomew, St. Laurence and St. James. The cathedral school had a succession of famous masters, Wazo, trained by Heriger of Lobbes, Adelmann, the disciple of Fulbert of Chartres, Gozechin, and Franco. Though the other schools were less important, their teachers and pupils, Alger and Rupert among them, were of no mean calibre. The example set by Lobbes and Toul spread across the length and breadth of the country; many monasteries devoted themselves to humane studies: Gembloux, where Abbot Olbert, who had studied in Paris, Troyes and Chartres, gathered together a fine collection of manuscripts; Stavelot, reformed by the saintly Poppo, and enlivened by a scholasticus from Gembloux; St. Trond, St. Hubert and others. In all these centres, and more so in Liège, the horizon seemed wide; Lorraine cultivated every field of knowledge. Egbert wrote his treatise on grammar, in the medieval sense, the '*Fecunda ratis*', a 'vessel filled to the brim' with proverbs and quotations from the Bible, the Fathers and classical authors. Abbot Rudolph of St. Trond wrote a number of opuscula on musical theory, notably the '*Quaestiones in musica*'. Franco studied geometry. Anselm continued the *Gesta* of the bishops of Liège, which were started by Heriger, and turned them into an accurate chronicle, whilst an anonymous writer wrote a good history of the prelates of Cambrai. Rudolph of St. Trond and Lambert of St. Hubert each compiled a history of his house. Sigebert of Gembloux set out to tell the story of his abbey, and then widened his scope; he made a universal chronicle, marred by some errors and prejudices, but none the less one of the best of the Middle Ages. He assumed the task of continuing the '*De viris illustribus*' of Saint Jerome, Gennadius, Isidore of Seville and Ildefonso of Toledo, and succeeded in bringing it down to his own times. Alger of Liège intervened in the eucharistic controversy which had begun in Carolingian times and was fanned into flame again by Berengar of Tours; he wrote a '*De sacramento corporis et sanguinis Domini*', which overshadowed all other treatises on the subject. He devoted his '*De misericordia et justitia*' to canon law; a work of major interest, since in it he was not content with quoting texts, but attempted to interpret and reconcile them. In the middle of the twelfth century, Wibald of Stavelot's letters are those of an accomplished humanist. But this list only deals with literature in Latin. There might be much to add if we were better informed about the earliest writings in the vernacular. Reliable philologists have credited the abbey of Brogne, or St. Gerard, near Namur, with the composition of the '*Life of St. Leger*', and Stavelot with the '*Quatre Fils Aymon*', two of the earliest landmarks in French literature. These localizations remain problematical, but there is one which is less so: the placing of the '*Geste de Garin*' in Lorraine. There is nothing improbable in the theory that Lorraine guided and sustained French literature in its early steps, for it was in the Picard and Walloon area that its first infant cry was heard – the '*Cantilena of St. Eulalia*'.

The arts were equally flourishing.[24] Architecture dotted the country with buildings of austere beauty, St. Servais and Notre Dame at Maastricht, the abbey church of Lobbes, the collegiate church of Nivelles. In ivory-carving the Crucifixion of Tongres or the three Resurrections in Liège cathedral led the way, after a period of stiffness and gaucherie, to Notger's ivory book-cover and the one on the Bodleian gospel-book. In the field of calligraphy, the manuals copied in monasteries from the end of the tenth century, not without an eye to decorative effect, were the ancestors of the magnificent Bibles, psalters, gospel-books and sacramentaries prepared in the twelfth century for Lobbes, Stavelot, Hastière, St. Lambert and St. Laurence in Liège. In goldsmiths' craft the strength and nobility of the panels of St. Hadelin's shrine at Visé foreshadowed the reliquaries, portable altars and shrines of Godfrey of Huy and his fellow workers. In all the minor arts the style which the eleventh century was seeking emerged fully in the early twelfth. It had two characteristics: humanity and serenity. It was full of life and movement, even, for example, in the representation of the ground by a sinuous line; but they were expressed without confusion or fussiness. A calm pervades it, reminiscent of the great, slow-moving river which is the heart of Lorraine and has given it its character as well as its landscape. Between 1107 and 1118, Renier de Huy, the heir of generations of brass-founders, cast his masterpiece in this style, the baptismal font at St. Bartholomew's in Liège. 'In it there is something which men had not seen before in any work of art and which they would not see again before the Golden Age of Cathedrals: the flowering of the Christian spirit, the soul's ecstasy of love and adoration.'[25]

Lorraine was a clearing house of cultural exchanges: its most gifted sons completed their education in neighbouring countries; ideas converged here by way of the great routes which cross its soil, the Rhone-Meuse line and the road from Boulogne to Cologne.[26] Its school of illumination united the influences of Rheims, Reichenau, St. Amand, and, through Flanders, Winchester.[27] Lorraine's own influence spread all over Europe: countless strangers came to the Liège schools, countless Liègeois held ecclesiastical office in distant lands. In the first group we find Durand, scholasticus of Bamberg, Siegfried, abbot of Tegernsee, Günther, archbishop of Salzburg, Cosmas, the first Czech historian, Leofric, bishop of Exeter, Mauritius, archbishop of Rouen; in the second, Adelmann, scholasticus of St. Lambert, who was to be bishop of Brescia, Hucbald, scholasticus of Prague, Lieduin, bishop of Groszwardein, now Oradea in Rumania, Godfrey, bishop of Bath, Alexander, bishop of Plock in Poland, and his brother Walter, bishop of Breslau.

This cursory glance at the intellectual and artistic achievements of the Empire from 875 to 1125 shows their fundamental character; fidelity to tradition, a double tradition in fact, Carolingian and classical. In its cultural, as in its political aspect, the Empire clung to Carolingian traditions: its buildings had a central plan or a double apse and often even a double transept, scantily decorated and without vaulting; the lesser arts were particularly cultivated, especially goldsmith's work and ivory carving. Liturgy remained Carolingian in spirit, the Romano-Germanic Pontifical of Mainz particularly so. Canon law was equally conservative: Burchard's 'Decretum' drew its inspiration from the 'Dionyso-Hadriana', from the pseudo-Isidorian Decretals, probably fabricated in the region of Le Mans about 850, and from the 'Anselmo dedicata', compiled about 882 in North Italy. Literary composition, too, was traditional in both manner and matter, with a preference for history and particularly universal history, for while France was breaking up into principalities the Empire kept its wide horizons; there was a vogue for grammar and poetry, mark of a culture still scholastic in both form and subject, and a lack of interest in the '*quadrivium*', with the exception of music, the necessary accompaniment of liturgy.

But Germany's Carolingian heritage was combined with the inspiration of Rome and Byzantium. The imperial dignity which had fallen to the lot of the first Otto, and his son Otto II's marriage with a Greek princess, naturally orientated German culture towards the ancient capitals. In Saxony Rome inspired the comedies of Roswitha, Bernward's column in Hildesheim and the abbey-church of Hersfeld, whose continuous transept recalls certain palaeo-Christian basilicas. Either directly or through Italy's agency, Byzantium imparted some of its feeling for proportion and its knowledge of relief to frescoes and miniatures, ivories and metalwork.[28]

And so the Empire sought new material from alien sources, but blended it with its ninth-century inheritance and transformed it by its own touch of genius. Its architecture was quick to create new combinations of Carolingian elements, new effects, new juxtapositions of masses.[29] In this way it was to influence the whole movement of Western civilization; it has not been established, for lack of sufficient study, but it is not at all improbable that the master-masons of Germany influenced those of Normandy, and consequently the development of the Gothic style.[30] There seems to be no doubt that workers in bronze, ivory and enamel showed the way to the sculptors of Burgundy and the Île de France and that in a more general way, with others, they laid the foundation of the twelfth and thirteenth centuries' revelation of man, nature, creation and their immanent value.[31] The Empire then, was neither passive nor sterile, though it was more conservative than creative.

Other regions also passed on the Carolingian tradition to the greater centuries which followed. Lombardy, Northern France and Burgundy shared this honourable task with the Empire. Through every vicissitude the Lombards maintained secular schools, which educated such men as Liutprand of Cremona, the enthusiastic panegyrist of Otto I. In the North of France there were many schools, some of them distinguished ones, for example St. Amand, already mentioned, and St. Germain-des-Prés. Burgundy's role was greater; in that rich country, less ravaged than others by invasions, and firmly organized by its dukes, the Carolingian tradition was active. The monastery of St. Martin at Autun provided the transition from Benedict of Aniane to the Cluniac order; the abbey of St. Germain at Auxerre served the same purpose in matters of the intellect: Heiric (841–876) the pupil of Servatus Lupus and the Irishmen of Laon, was the teacher of Remigius (841–908) who reorganized the schools of Rheims and Paris. And it is perhaps permissible to see the influence of the cathedrals and abbey-churches of St. Rémy at Rheims, St. Riquier, Aix or Cologne in the earliest churches built in Burgundy, or by the Burgundians, Cluny II, Tournus, St. Benoît sur Loire, with their narthex, or double transept.[32]

The Empire continued the Carolingian Renaissance without changing its direction. In the eleventh century France, and Italy to a lesser degree, set it in new paths.

For a long period the ambience in western Francia was not favourable to culture, but slowly it altered, and about the year 1000 the situation was much less turbid. The invasions had ended and great principalities had been created whose heads, dukes of Normandy and Aquitaine, counts of Toulouse, supported the Church in maintaining peace, encouraged vernacular literature, protected monastic houses and, through them, sustained the arts. A powerful religious movement was born in Burgundy, developed quickly in Normandy and the Loire valley, and gave those regions monasteries whose teachers were as distinguished as their master-masons. The movement spread, engendered new Orders, stimulated communities of canons, reformed the episcopate and finally regenerated the whole Church. Trade developed; more and more regular merchants travelled the roads and sailed the rivers; soon they were to breathe new life into old cities and young towns. Monks, pilgrims, soldiers, clerks began, or began again, to take to the road. Fruitful contacts were made between Christendom and the Arab world, between France and Moorish Spain.

Sooner or later the same factors were at work in Italy: easy contact with other civilizations, particularly by way of Sicily, which was a crossroads of Muslim and Byzantine influences; an urban growth which was earlier and more vigorous than beyond the Alps; a religious reform which rejuvenated the monastic system and made Rome the centre of canon law studies, since it fell to the Roman curia to support by text and argument the Papacy's claims against the Empire. One thing alone was lacking and that was peace; the tenth-century conquerors, the Ottos, delivered Italy from the Magyars, but in spite of their strength they were powerless to unite her. The Salian Emperors in the eleventh century fared no better. On the contrary they drew Italy into their quarrels with the Popes, with Saxony and Bavaria, and forced her into intestine struggles, which grew worse as their authority weakened and ended by turning families against each other. Such instability in public affairs, and the attraction of French scholastic teaching drove many of the finest minds to cross the Alps: Fulbert, Lanfranc, Anselm and many another. Italy continuously enriched France in this way, and as a result her own intellectual level was always lower.

The development of the political, religious and economic atmosphere gave a stimulus to intellectual circles. The Italian and French schools displayed an admirable degree of activity throughout the late tenth and eleventh centuries. Several of them were outstanding, thanks to the initiative of a bishop or an abbot, Fulk in Rheims, Desiderius at Monte Cassino, or to the genius of some teacher, Lanfranc at Bec, Anselm at Laon. Co-operating with one another, exchanging masters and pupils, they constantly raised the level of teaching and brought talent to the surface. Monte Cassino in South Italy was deserted for 77 years because it was too exposed to Saracen attacks, but it was restored in 950 and endowed with a fine library by Desiderius, who became abbot in 1058.[33] Set as it was at the limit of the Latin world the abbey provided a link with Greek and Muslim art and science; its illuminators and mosaic-workers were inspired by Byzantine traditions, and one of the monks translated medical and other treatises from Greek and Arabic. Others devoted themselves to 'grammar' and brought another kind of fame to the house. Alberic was probably the author, at least in part, of the '*Liber dictaminum*', the first of those '*Artes*', or treatises on composition which were to enjoy great popularity among teachers; they were a substitute for the '*Auctores*', and by cutting off the student from direct contact with classical works they contributed to the decline of literature after 1225 or 1250.[34] John of Gaeta, who entered the pontifical chancery in 1088, codified for its use the laws of the '*cursus*', a literary form practically forgotten since the eighth century and brought into fashion again by the Monte Cassino writers.[35]

In the same part of Italy Salerno provided another point of contact between East and West. There, physicians who combined the teaching of Hippocrates and the Arabs had a great reputation as early as the tenth century and patients sought their help from as far away as France: Adalberon II, for example, bishop of Verdun, consulted them in 988, though without finding a cure for his disease.[36] The monastery at Salerno, daughter-house of Monte Cassino, had an illustrious abbot in the middle of the eleventh century, Alphanus, who translated the *De natura hominis* of Nemesius of Emesa, and wrote skilful poems in Latin metres.[37]

In Umbria in central Italy, the recently founded house of Fonte Avellana gave shelter in his old age to Guido of Arezzo. Born either in Arezzo or somewhere near Paris and probably educated in the abbey of St. Maur-les-Fossés, at the gates of Paris, he went next to the monastery of Pomposa, near Ferrara. Although this is disputed, he seems to have been one of the greatest theoreticians of music of the medieval period; he is credited with the invention, or at least the development, of solmization, and if he did not introduce the musical stave he certainly extended its currency.[38]

But it was in the north, in Lombardy, that intellectual life was most vigorous. In Faenza, Ravenna, Pavia, Parma, Milan and Bologna the traditional secular schools produced pupils who gained them great repute, for example Peter Damian. They cultivated grammar with particular enthusiasm as one of the classic branches of teaching, but the political and economic circumstances of the day caused them to develop a new speciality, which was to have great success. The growth of commerce brought in its train a multitude of law-suits which could not be adequately settled by customary law, which had grown out of a rural society. The rise of large cities set new problems of public and private law. Then the Investiture Controversy, which had wider repercussions in the field of ideas than in practical politics, had a great influence on juridical studies. Both parties were anxious to prove their case by recourse to texts. The Emperor naturally sought arguments in Roman imperial legislation. Copies of the Digest introduced into Italy by Justinian's officials were brought out and discussed in the schools. Some of them soon acquired great renown in this field – Ravenna, Pavia,[39] and, in the twelfth century, particularly Bologna, where the great master Irnerius taught. His fame rests mainly on having undertaken the establishment of the exact sense of the dispositions of the *Corpus*, by textual analysis, comparison of parallel passages, and the resolution of apparent contradictions. He is famous too for his pupils, the Four Doctors, Bulgarus, Hugo, Martinus, and Jacobus who carried on his work of reviving Roman law, and legal studies in general.[40]

The progress of Canon Law ran parallel with the revival of Justinian's Code. In Rome, or at least at the behest of the Roman Curia, new collections of canon law were made to justify the reforms of Nicholas II and Gregory VII.[41] The work of Humbert of Silva Candida (*c.* 1060), Anselm of Lucca (1083), of Cardinal Deusdedit (1085), of Bonizo of Sutri (1089) had the virtue of being both richer and more systematic than that of their predecessors. The Gregorians dug up many ancient texts which for them had greater authority than more recent ones, and they arranged them strictly under subjects. Bonizo went further; he was not content with bringing together the various, and sometimes contradictory, canons concerning one subject. Like Ivo of Chartres, the Spanish author of the *Collectio Caesaraugustana*, Alger of Liège, or Peter Abelard twenty years later, he sometimes tried to eliminate contradictions by making use of Roman law, its concepts, principles, solutions, and by applying the light of reason. The way was open for the Bolognese clerk

153

Gratian and his *Concordia discordantium canonum*, the corner-stone of medieval canon law.

Beyond the Alps the great centres of intellectual activity were the cathedral and abbey schools north of the Loire,[42] except as far as vernacular literature and medicine were concerned. Epic poetry throve in Northern France from the tenth century on;[43] its origins are obscure, but it is perhaps not too fanciful to suppose that the feudal lords helped it into the world, if only by affording shelter and protection to the precursors and companions of Turoldus, who composed the immortal Song of Roland. The distant sources of the southern lyric, Provence's courtly poetry, are equally mysterious. Whether it was a natural product of the environment, an Arab importation, an offshoot of Roman poetry, or a synthesis of several raw materials is difficult to say.[44] Its immediate origins were clear: the first poet was a duke of Aquitaine, Guillaume IX (1071–1127). The only secular schools in France were founded about 1100, in the same part of the country, at Montpellier. From near-by Muslim Spain they adopted the study of medicine which later made them famous. In all other disciplines it was the Church and Northern France which had a monopoly. The great centres for Latin literature and scholarship in the tenth century were Rheims and Fleury; in the eleventh and early twelfth, Chartres, Bec, Laon, Tours, Angers, Le Mans, Paris. The schools of Rheims were re-established at the instance of Archbishop Fulk by the two great men of the day, Remigius of Auxerre and Hucbald of St. Amand, and they acquired a great reputation in certain fields. Inferior to other schools in the *quadrivium*, they ranked higher than all the rest in dialectic: Hucbald was the first medieval commentator of Porphyry's introduction to Aristotelian logic. In 972 their reputation in this discipline attracted the young monk Gerbert, who was to bring them even greater fame. Educated at St. Géraud in Aurillac he had spent three years at Vich in Spain, where he had studied mathematics, then he had been in Rome. Better versed in arithmetic, geometry and astronomy than any of his contemporaries, he more than made up for the backwardness of the Rheims schools in these branches of study.[45] He even raised the level of study in their favourite field; thanks to the use of Boethius's treatises, which were either unknown or neglected before, he opened up wider perspectives and gave new depth to their studies of dialectic.[46]

His contemporary Abbo carried out a similar task at Fleury, a monastery on the middle Loire, reformed by Cluny, where he was scholasticus and later Abbot. He too had had a careful training, at Fleury, then at Rheims, Paris and Orleans, and he was able to teach a wide syllabus, expounding with equal ease dialectic, music, arithmetic and astronomy, and even tackling canon law. It may be that besides all this he had a hand in the encouragement and development of the taste for religious drama, previously cultivated, together with the new art of polyphony, at St. Martial in Limoges. A few years ago it seemed certain that Fleury was the 'metropolis of the liturgical drama', but this is now disputed.[47]

In the eleventh century the schools of Chartres carried off the palm.[48] They existed, it is true, before the year 1000 but they owed their fame to Bishop Fulbert. An Italian, educated at Rheims and Chartres itself, his teaching covered as wide a range as that of Abbo, or Gerbert, and even included medicine. He wrote little, and he was not an original thinker, but he was an excellent teacher, and had a host of pupils spanning two generations.

Some of them remained to teach in the schools where they had studied, and thus Chartres kept its prestige through the century. At the beginning of the twelfth century there was even a step forward when Bernard took over the direction of the schools. He was the first of a series of great masters which continued till 1150 and formed a homogeneous group characterized by its enthusiasm for antiquity. They admired classical writers for their power to form the student's taste and teach him composition, for their clarity and their insight into psychology; and they revered its philosophers, many of whose ideas were to be adopted by Christianity. They were united too in their tireless curiosity, which ranged over the whole of human knowledge and led to ever deeper scrutiny of man and nature. They were humanists, both in their devotion to classical culture and in the inquiring spirit they brought to bear on God's creation and the creature which is its centre; they thus played a leading part in paving the way for the literary renaissance and the new outlook on life which were to be the great features of the later twelfth century.

Some of Fulbert's pupils left him after a few years and gave a new impetus to other schools. Amongst them were Adelmann of Liège, Olbert of Gembloux, Raimbaud of Cologne, Raoul of Orleans, Lambert of Paris, Gerald of St. Wandrille, Bernard of Angers, and especially Berengar of Tours and Lanfranc of Pavia. Berengar (1010–1088) was a passionate dialectician who acquired an unfortunate reputation by his application of logic to theology; his treatises on the Eucharist in which he denied the real presence sparked off one of the great controversies of the century.[49] A more respectable title to fame is that he probably taught Hildebert of Le Mans (1056–1134), one of the best poets of the Middle Ages. Well-read in ancient literature, like every good Chartres student, he incorporated it, like his masters, into his Christian culture. In his verse, sometimes classical in form and sometimes rhythmical, humanism and Christian thought complement one another. Indeed, apart from a Prayer to the Trinity and the *De exilio suo*, an account of his tribulations, his masterpieces are two eulogies of Caesar's Rome and the Rome of Peter.[50]

Lanfranc (1005–1089), after teaching in Avranches, entered the Norman monastery of Bec in 1042, and three years later opened a school which was soon to have the reputation of being one of the best, if not the best, in the France of the day. Clerks, sons of noble-men, and even teachers from other schools came to him from far afield. Two men stand out from this crowd, Ivo, who was to go to Beauvais and end his career as bishop of Chartres, and Anselm, who succeeded his master, first at Bec and then in the archiepiscopal see of Canterbury. Ivo was given a solid grounding in law by Lanfranc, who had learned it in his native town of Pavia, and became one of the most famous of canonists. Anselm (1033–1109) had learned from the master a subtly worked-out doctrine of the relations between dialectic and theology; he perfected it, and his bold application of it constituted his life's work.

Credo ut intelligam. Fides quaerens intellectum. The formula is justly celebrated, for it does more than distil Anselm's thought; it characterizes the intellectual attitude of most medieval theologians and philosophers. It was not a question of understanding in order to believe, or before believing, but of believing first so as to compel one's mind to understand. In other terms, faith comes first, unaffected by controversy, and inspires speculation. The task of dialectic is not to provide a foundation for faith but to make it explicit and firm. Theology's role, as far as theology can be distinguished from philos-ophy, is to clarify by the use of reason what revelation has disclosed. To confirm faith is the task of philosophy, which will show that there is no discord between faith and reason, that the two, if they follow the right lines, will coincide. This is the way in which Anselm gave a rational demonstration of the existence of God. Extending his system with an audacity that was not shared by his successors, he claimed to be able to demonstrate that reason requires God to be three persons in one, and the second to be incarnate. On another point he differed from most of his followers: like Augustine, whose inspiration he followed closely, he mixed speculation with meditation. He set beside the reasoning mind the intellective heart, whilst most of his successors stood firmly on pure dialectic. They had not the literary talent which combined with a vigorous mind to produce in Anselm an authentic genius.[51]

Soon after the Master of Bec had evolved the method and given it authority, another Anselm (†1117) made a formal programme of it. In his teaching at Laon he ran through the whole gamut of the liberal arts, but he concentrated more and more, as his career advanced, on

156

the interpretation of Holy Scripture. He did not content himself with reading and glossing line by line; when his literal commentary touched on an important point of doctrine, he gathered up all that Scripture and the Fathers had to say on the question and made a complete exposition of it, a *Sententia*. The idea was that if either he or one of his pupils collected all these *sententiae*, delivered in the course of the readings, and arranged them systematically they would form a kind of inventory of revelation which could be examined in the light of reason. The *Book of Sentences* of Anselm of Laon,[52] first of a genre which was to flourish thereafter, 'marked out the road, by setting down the basic truths of the Faith, which Reason in its turn might follow'.[53]

Thus at Tours, Bec and Laon, dialectic had taken a leading place in the schools' programme of studies. In Paris it was to have its greatest triumph with Peter Abelard (1071–1142). Thanks to him, at the beginning of the twelfth century the Capetian capital became the capital of logic in France, and once the logical method had become general, and France had imposed her pattern of thought on neighbouring nations, she was destined to become the intellectual capital of Europe. Paris already had teachers and schools of note, both abbatial and capitular. In fact it was William of Champeaux's reputation as a teacher of dialectic which brought Peter Abelard from Brittany about 1100. With his exceptional gifts the newcomer was soon the equal of his teachers, William in rhetoric and logic, Anselm of Laon in theology. Then he began to teach these subjects himself on the Montagne Ste. Geneviève with a success explained by the clarity, vigour and originality of his thought. All these qualities subsist in his writings. The most interesting of them for the development of theological studies was the *Sic et non*, in which he set down the frequently contradictory opinions of the Fathers of the Church on a number of matters. Thus he set a series of problems, *quaestiones*, in the schoolmen's Latin, which the dialectician was to resolve. Texts in favour, texts against, and resolution by logical reasoning; already we have the scholastic method. Abelard noted moreover that many of the apparent contradictions were purely formal and might come from the use of the same word with different connotations by different writers. This observation is linked in a way with his solution of the problem of Universals, his chief title to fame. On the question whether the class, the species, has an independent existence, either within the individual or outside it, Abelard answers in the negative. The only universals are words, and even they are not of their essence universal, but only in so far as our minds give them meaning. This theory was important because it was original and others were often to echo it; also because the problem treated and the manner of treating it were strictly philosophical; the question was studied outside any theological context and its solution was arrived at by pure logic. It was important also in its consequences, since it provided a precedent for the science of logic to be 'set up as an independent study, free of all metaphysical presuppositions', since it took as its object not beings but words.[54] No one could do more for the advancement of dialectic.

Such indeed was the opinion of Saint Bernard, a bitter opponent of Peter Abelard. He would not use the contemptuous words of a Peter Damian to describe profane studies, and logic in particular, but for him the truth could only be arrived at through Christ. True wisdom consisted in seeking Him and following Him, and the science to be taught above all others in the schools was the knowledge of His love. Basically Bernard was a mystic, the mystic of the living God, the God made man, and His mother the Virgin Mary. He was in his time the foremost representative of mystical theology, which had a great following. Hugh of St. Victor bridged the gap between the two movements, between dialecticians and anti-dialecticians. He was a Saxon settled in Paris, in the abbey founded by William of Champeaux after his defeat at the hands of Abelard. He was a great master of spirituality, but he did not condemn profane studies, so long as they led, as they indeed can, to meditation and speculation.[55] *Omnia disce, videbis postea nihil esse superfluum.*

From 950 to 1125 Italian and French scholars, like their contemporaries in Germany, were faithful to Carolingian and Roman traditions. But they drew more profit from them. Greater curiosity, greater maturity and self-confidence enabled them to widen their horizons, refine their methods and give greater individuality to their writings. Their starting-point was still rooted in the past. The jurists for example went to Justinian's *Corpus* for the answers to their problems, nor would they think for a moment of criticizing, modifying or rejecting its dispositions. Teaching and research were still a matter of commentary on the classical authorities, on the one hand the Fathers, Plato and Aristotle, or what they thought were Plato and Aristotle, on the other the Digest, the Decretals, or Galen. But these writers were now better known than in previous centuries or in contemporary Germany; works previously unknown or little regarded, like the treatises of Boethius, were now the object of close study; Arabic scientific works were being translated. The contemporary stock of ideas and facts was enriched in more than one way and perspectives were proportionately widened.

From Gerbert and Abbo onwards the *scholastici* strengthened certain of the conventional disciplines and added new ones. They kept the old framework of the liberal arts, but felt themselves less and less at ease in it. The new conquests in logic, arithmetic, geometry and astronomy fell into place without any difficulty in the *trivium* and the *quadrivium*; but there was no place for law – canon, Roman or customary–or for medicine; and how could full justice be done to the expansion of theology? The time had come for a more up-to-date classification of the disciplines and more specialization among teachers. The solution was to be the twelfth-century university, with its four faculties.

The study of Boethius's treatises and the correlative development of logic led to another step forward – a belief in reason, and particularly reason as the chief instrument of scholarship. Berengar of Tours declared the rational faculty to be the 'honour of Man'. Anselm of Canterbury deemed it capable of confirming and renewing the truths of revelation. Bonizo of Sutri, Irnerius and Abelard required that it should reconcile and unify the branches of knowledge. In this way reason became the basis of a new intellectual technique. The teacher no longer merely 'glossed' the authorities, explaining the texts line by line. He quoted all the authorities on the question, and alone, or in discussion with his student, he would attempt to arrive at a synthesis by the operation of reason. Later all the glosses, all the *sententiae* of a master, might be collected systematically into an inventory of a field of knowledge which would be called a *Summa*.

The *Summa* would in time attract a commentary in its turn which would take the place of the authorities on which it was founded, just as in grammar *auctores* were replaced by *artes*. In short the thinker freed himself from the literal commentary; exegesis was no longer enough; he began to argue from the particular to the general, to induce from the application the principle which justified it and thus bring everything into a system.

Not only reason but also human problems and sentiments attracted attention; writers put more of themselves into their writings. French literature, then in its infancy, took its essential features from contemporary society; there is no better picture of feudal manners than the *chansons de geste*. Latin literature too came closer to the social environment; its language became suppler; less pure than in the Carolingian era, but more alive. It showed a predilection for new or refashioned forms which might be called medieval or at least Christian: rhymed prose and rhythmic verse, which lent themselves to lyric effusion.[56] A new genre developed in which the personal element was fundamental – the autobiography, for example the *De vita sua* of Guibert of Nogent, or Abelard's *Historia calamitatum mearum*.[57] The same orientation is noticeable in scholarship. The civilians had recourse to Roman law less perhaps to satisfy a love of speculation than to resolve concrete juridical problems. The theologians frequently set themselves moral problems whose solutions would necessitate a certain line of conduct: Peter Damian, Anselm of Canterbury, Hugh of St. Victor and their contemporaries were by no means pure theoreticians, and their writings were anything but academic exercises. Moralists tended to substitute the investigation of intention for the brutal application of a fixed scale of penances.[58] This interest in man was the last stage in the progress made by the intellectuals of Latin countries between 950 and 1200.

Admittedly these forward movements promised more than they actually accomplished. The horizon was vast but it was still empty. The scholastic method was defined, but its adversaries outnumbered its partisans and it was not fully exploited. An interest was developing in Man but Nature was still neglected. Writers and scholars had laid the foundations and created the tools for a movement which was to be greater than they knew.

Those concerned with the arts were more fortunate; they were already creating a style – the Romanesque, not only the first school of architecture in the West, but perhaps the finest, and certainly the one which makes the greatest appeal at the present time. Gothic has on its side technical perfection, constructive strength, boldness and height. The Romanesque has less formal beauty, but also less severity; all of it, even its occasional awkwardness, is alive, eloquent, moving. Though it has less grace, it has on the other hand an almost miraculous sense of volume and proportion. It distils an atmosphere which irresistibly calls the faithful to prayer. It shows the hand of man in its creation, it is built on the human scale, and it leads man directly to God. What building can compare with the calmly beautiful narthex at Vézelay, or the nave at Fontenay which is so conducive to worship? Whilst philosophers, theologians and jurists were still working out the itinerary which they would take over the last difficult bit of country, craftsmen had already reached the heights.[59]

But we must not exaggerate the contrast between intellectual life and artistic activity. For one thing there would be some risk of implying that Romanesque was completely original. It is incontestably so in its synthesis of various elements and the spirit which animates them, but not in the elements themselves. To scale the last heights architects and sculptors took the same route as the scholars. They started from the Carolingian level and moved gradually away from it with the help of ideas borrowed from neighbouring countries or from Antiquity. Romanesque was largely the art of the ninth century, altered by essential additions, some eastern or Muslim,[60] but the most important Roman. This fact should lead towards a solution of the fiercely debated problem of the origin of the new style. Logic would appear to require that the separate elements, being Arab,

Oriental or Roman, should make their first appearance in the South, which had direct contacts with the Muslim and Byzantine worlds and where a great many ancient monuments had been preserved. And indeed it is in the churches of this region that one finds the first examples: decorated bands and niches, characteristic of the 'first Romanesque manner' in Lombardy; monumental sculpture, belonging to the 'second manner', in Languedoc, Burgundy and Northern Spain; a vault covering the whole nave in St. Mary's church at Amer in Catalonia, and supporting arches in St. Peter's at Casserres, also in Catalonia.[61] One is tempted to argue that Romanesque was a creation of the South, but only if one forgets that a building is ground-plan and space as much as elevation and decoration. In fact Romanesque was born where tradition and innovation mingled; where the Carolingian conceptions of area and volume joined southern ideas of elevation and decoration to create great constructions, in the centre of France, in Burgundy, Touraine or Auvergne.[62]

The essential characteristics of the style, as far as they can be deduced from an infinite variety of types, are in fact the use of the vault to cover large areas and the development of exterior decoration.

The plan in itself was not modified; there were already examples in the ninth century of the ambulatory with chapels radiating from it, attached apses, with a choir between them and the nave, a definite transept, the simple or composite pier in place of the column of the classical basilica.[63] In the elevation on the other hand, the use of the vault was an innovation important not only *per se*, but also because of the consequences which flowed from it. The vault had two characteristics to begin with – it was constructed Roman-fashion as a continuous wagon-head roof whose weight was distributed equally along the full length of the side walls; it was built on a centring, and composed of a rubble of stoneblocks and mortar. Its weight was therefore enormous, and it exerted a formidable vertical and tangential thrust along the whole length of the walls, which threatened to crush them or push them outwards. To reduce this danger the architects first tried a number of expedients – limiting height, thickening the walls all the way along, backing them by tribunes or flanking towers, or reducing the openings. Later they invented a more advanced method, and threw a supporting arch across the vault between bays, resting on shafts or pilasters propped by buttresses, so that almost all the thrust was concentrated on their springing. Or better still, they replaced the tunnel vault by a groin-vault based on the intersection at a right angle of two tunnel vaults, which supported one another. In this way, the thrust was at last more effectively concentrated at a few points, at the four corners of the bay, which were solidly supported, so that the walls carried very little weight and there was no danger in making them thinner and less solid. Time and experience also showed how the vault itself could be constructed with less weight and more delicacy.

There were modifications too in ornament. Inside the church the emphasis shifted, and north of the Alps at least, painted interiors became almost universal, and mosaic, which was costly, nearly disappeared.[64] There was as yet no competition from stained glass, for in Romanesque churches the windows were too small for it to have proper scope. Painting, on the contrary, had ample surfaces for display, ideal for representing such majestic scenes as the Genesis

VAULTED NAVE WITH GALLERIES
ST SERNIN IN TOULOUSE

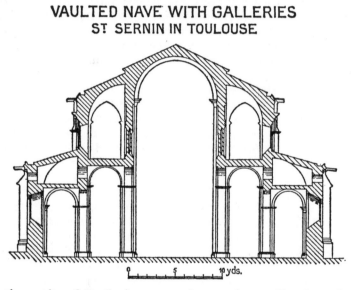

on the vaults of St. Savin or superhuman figures like the colossal Christ in the apse of the little chapel of Berzé-la-Ville; sometimes in brilliant, sometimes in duller colours, in the French-Byzantine tradition, inherited from the Carolingian epoch and reinforced by Ottonian and Italian illumination. Painting overflowed from walls and ceilings on to piers and pillars, covering them with geometrical patterns, or false marble, and when, belatedly, sculpture invaded the churches, carved capitals were enlivened with bright colours.

Exterior ornament underwent thoroughgoing changes. During the earliest period the walls were decorated with blind arcades and niches, with bands and geometrical patterns. Then in the second phase sculpture made its appearance, in the shape of figure sculpture in stone. The bold spirits who carried out this revival, in the early eleventh century, did not lack models and patterns: ancient carving, particularly on sarcophagi, and the contemporary work of gold-smiths, brassfounders and ivory-carvers. They found even wider sources of inspiration in miniatures, mosaics, frescoes and textiles. But the medium was difficult and progress slow. For a long time relief was shallow and clumsily executed. It was only very late in the eleventh century that figures stood out from the block and began to live.

From that moment the stone-carver became the valued ally of the mason, for sculpture was monumental, inseparable from architecture. Its mission was to beautify churches and cloisters, sometimes by covering the façade with statues and reliefs or stretching a broad frieze across it in the Roman manner, sometimes by concentrating on capitals and doors. The capitals might be decorated with foliage or geometrical motifs, with legendary creatures from oriental or barbarian art; they might relate in naïve terms episodes from the Bible, the life and miracles of a popular saint, or the incidents of the *psychomachia*, the battle between the virtues and the vices. Doors were enlivened with scenes and characters, set out first on the lintel and within the frame of the door jambs or the archivolts, then on the tympanum or the capital of a central pillar, and finally on lintel, central capital, tympanum, archivolt and jambs, thus creating the complete portal which was one of the marvels of medieval art.

This predilection for columns and arches explains a second characteristic, 'antirealism'. The master-sculptors could carry out their task successfully only by falsifying proportions, since the spaces the architect gave them to decorate were truncated cones or trapezoids on the capitals, segments and bands in tympanum or door jambs. Not only spatial requirements governed their distortions however but, more imperious aesthetic and spiritual demands: the need to be crystal-clear in representing the supernatural. The size and appearance of each personage or thing had to be a function of the part it played in the whole piece, and of its religious meaning. Christ was depicted on a larger scale than the apostles so that He should impress the observer. His index finger might be made larger than nature, as in the lintel of St. André de Sorrède, to show that He was 'the way, the truth and the life'. In their view, every object was a symbol, and therein lay its whole value. It was the reflection of the invisible world and a means of making it visible. Like his contemporaries, like the philosopher whose speculations were founded on faith, the sculptor of the eleventh and twelfth centuries did not limit himself to the natural plane; although he was not averse from direct observation he was not content with that. He saw symbols everywhere, which had to be interpreted, so he did not hesitate to fill his work with imaginary beings and nightmare animals, sirens, griffins and dragons. For this reason his art is not a mere pastiche of antiquity but a new creation.[65]

The substitution of vaults for ceilings and the development of decoration are general characteristics. Other, more detailed, features make it possible to allocate at least the greatest examples of Romanesque to individual schools, more or less homogeneous, whose great number is evidence of the vitality and variety of the art of the period. Precise limits cannot easily be assigned to these schools since their origin and development depended on many factors, on political frontiers, geological resources, artistic traditions, commercial relations or religious movements. Even those we think of as the most evidently regional can only be said to be *centred* on the regions whose names they bear. Some cannot be related at all to a single area: at Conques, Limoges, Nevers, Toulouse, Compostela there is a 'pilgrimage basilica' which is the most representative Romanesque building: it is characterized by a barrel vault on transverse arches, an ambulatory with radiating chapels, a transept with aisles and chapels, and galleries all round the building.

The most important schools of architecture were those of Burgundy, Normandy, Poitou and Aquitaine. The Burgundian school was no doubt the first to use the new principles of the earlier Romanesque manner, the vault and Lombardic decoration, in large buildings comparable with those of the Carolingian epoch: the leading example is Tournus. But the new synthesis was not expressed in the same way everywhere; in its full development in the twelfth century it had three styles: first, the church with a nave roofed by a tunnel vault, and aisles with rib-vaults; the nave was higher than the aisles and had three storeys, the arcades, the gallery and the clerestory, and thus had direct lighting; second, the type in which the nave is higher than the aisles, and like them had rib-vaults, but had no gallery; third, the type in which nave and aisles were practically equal in height and lit only through the bays of the side-aisles. The abbey church of Cluny, as it was rebuilt from 1088 onwards, represents the first type. The second type is exemplified in the church of the Magdalen at Vézelay, begun two years earlier. The third pattern was adopted at Fontenay and in many of the Cistercian churches, at Saint Bernard's direction; they were kept free of all unnecessary decoration, towers, sculpture, painting, patterned tiles and stained glass, and reached a high artistic level because of their very simplicity.[66]

The Norman churches, on the continent and in England, are characterized by the three storeys in which galleries usually replace the blind triforium arcade. Their great virtues are the balance of their design, the beauty of their proportions, their purity of line and sober decoration.

Excellent examples are the *Abbaye aux hommes*, begun in Caen about 1064, the eastern transept of Canterbury, whose first stones were laid in 1093, under Anselm, and the nave of St. Albans, dating from 1077–8.[67] The Norman style is also particularly interesting because of its preference for rib vaults as against tunnel vaults, which led its exponents both in England and France to look for ways of improving them, thus preparing the way for Gothic. Its influence is clearly to be seen in Tournai cathedral where the round-ended transepts and the four storeys, arcade, gallery, triforium and clerestory windows, show the transition to a new style. As for the schools of Poitou and Aquitaine, their characteristic marks are, in the former, an elevation consisting of a single order of tall arcades, and in the latter, an aisleless nave made up of a number of domed bays, for example Cahors cathedral, consecrated in 1119.[68]

Stone-carving is more easily divided into schools than architecture. The oldest is probably that of Languedoc, which was certainly related in some way to the workshops of Northern Spain.[69] Its essential characters, the product of a long period of development, are to be seen in St. Sernin at Toulouse and in Moissac: the dramatic intensity of the scenes displayed and the individuality of the figures. The Burgundian school is at its best in the capitals of Cluny III, the dating of which has given rise to violent controversy; it was probably built at the very end of the eleventh century or in the first years of the twelfth. It is distinguished by its richness and animation, its expressive strength, its exuberance and, particularly in the capitals and the statues, the formal beauty of its composition. It was probably the Burgundian school which gave its final form to the doorway which Gothic took over. The stone-carvers of Poitou made use of the entire façade of churches and, more than anyone else, subordinated their art to architectural requirements; they often treated capitals in a purely ornamental way and boldly adapted their subject to the shape of the coving it filled. Their contemporaries in Auvergne cultivated an archaic style full of simple, picturesque realism. As for the sculptors of Provence and their rivals or pupils in Lombardy, their work is full of classical references.[70]

Should the reader be surprised by the amount of space devoted to the French schools it must be said that Christian Spain, Northern Italy and France were the only really creative regions in the eleventh century, and in the twelfth both Spain and Italy had lost their original impulse and fallen under French influence. In the Romanesque period the foundation was laid for French dominance which remained unchallenged in the Gothic era. The first traces of the new style were already visible in Norman and English vaulting and in the doorways of Languedoc and Burgundy. Seen from this angle Romanesque is a transitional style; but it is also both a culmination and a new creation. It was a new creation in that it brought together a number of traditions – Carolingian, Roman, barbarian and oriental – and united them in a form which expressed their common spirit. Architectural elements dating from the ninth century were used to create homogeneous buildings,[71] and craftsmen ornamented them, under the close supervision of an overseer of works.[72] Unity in technical method gave unity of effect.

This unity was not merely a matter of organization and discipline. It grew out of the spirit; for not only the anti-naturalistic sculpture, but the whole church affirmed that only the supernatural was important, only the supernatural was real. Romanesque did not absolutely reject Nature, but it did not appreciate it and never hesitated to remodel and improve it in the interests of faith. It effected one of those fusions of antiquity and Christianity, or in a wider view, of the World and the Divine, which the West had sought to create since the days of Constantine. Thus it constituted the final materialization of centuries of effort and the perfect expression of one of the leitmotivs of the Middle Ages.

It was none the less only one form of expression, one mode, for another was already emerging in the Burgundian capitals, in the imperial goldsmiths' work, in the applications of dialectic, in the epic and in the earliest Provençal lyrics.

Chapter 9

SYNTHESIS: GOD AND NATURE

The period from 1125 to 1300 is one of brilliant achievement in every domain. It produced the *Prosae* and the *Sequences* of Adam of St. Victor, the lyrics of troubadours and goliards, the Legend of Tristan and Yseult, the *Roman de la Rose*, *Reynard the Fox*, the *Nibelungenlied*, the *Hymn to the Sun*, Bonaventure's mysticism, the *Concordia* of Gratian, the *Summa* of Saint Thomas, Chartres Cathedral, with its Royal Portal, its transept portals and its stained glass, the Sainte Chapelle, and Pérotin's motets.

It was the combination of a favourable environment and a new world-view that caused, or at least made possible, such a flowering of the arts. Before proceeding to analyse it we must consider its setting, the France of the Capetians. We shall have to cast back to the scattered remarks made in preceding chapters on the situation in that country, and on its links with the rest of Europe. We shall define and explain the attitude of the age to the universe. We shall then examine the principal literary, scientific and artistic works of the time; and finally, in outlining the general characteristics of the period, we shall draw attention to its basic unity, and detail the reasons for it.

The supremacy of France had been foreshadowed for many decades: from the time of Lanfranc of Bec, Anselm of Canterbury, Bernard of Chartres, Hildebert of Le Mans, Bernard of Clairvaux, Peter Abelard and Hugh of St. Victor, from the masons and stone-carvers of Cluny, Vézelay, Fontenay, Toulouse and Moissac. About 1125 it burst upon the world. During the next century and a half France was able to impose her influence on her neighbours, by the strength and creativeness of her art and thought. It was France who gave them their architecture and their sculpture, and guided their philosophical and theological speculations. In the study of law, civil and canon, she soon rivalled Bologna, and Montpellier had become the equal of Salerno as a school of medicine. The universal chronicles begun in

167

Germany and Lorraine were continued in France. In fact for a century and a half France and Europe meant almost the same thing.

Yet although the France of Saint Louis and Philip Augustus produced so many great works, they were not due entirely to the genius of the people or to the peculiarities of the political, social and economic structure. They owed a great deal to the fact that France was able to tap the reservoir of ideas of the surrounding countries, and attract their best brains.

During the period covered by this chapter France underwent a marked change of political structure; the policy of her kings was one of unification. In 1100 France was a mere collection of principalities, and when Latin was not being used the language of the court might be Norman, Picard, Champenois or Provençal. By 1300 she had become a monarchy.[1]

The consequences of this change were important from the cultural point of view; by uniting the country, and particularly by integrating Northern and Southern France, the Capetian monarchs encouraged interchanges between regions which were very different and almost foreign to one another. They made Paris a centre upon which the creative forces of France and Europe converged, where diverse manifestations of genius met and mingled; and it was there that medieval art and thought reached their zenith. By achieving unity the Capets avoided the internal quarrels which bedevilled Germany and Italy under Henry IV, and the recurrent political crises which characterized English politics from the death of the Conqueror until the accession of Edward I. A broad kingdom, made up of richly varied provinces, but peaceful, and centred on a great city – this was the ideal setting for a flourishing culture.

The religious situation was equally favourable. France stood outside the quarrels between Empire and Papacy; she experienced nothing like the conflict between the Plantagenets and the Church under Thomas à Becket and Stephen Langton. The Capetians did not hesitate to defend their independence against the claims of pontifical theocracy, but they contrived none the less to maintain a peaceful relationship with Rome and with the ecclesiastical power within the kingdom. Popular heresies, so vigorous in Lombardy, became powerful for a while in the South of France, and were supported by many among the nobility. Waldensianism was widespread at the end of the twelfth century, in Lyonnais, Dauphiné and Provence; Albigensianism was even stronger in Languedoc, and was tolerated by the Count of Toulouse himself. But neither heresy penetrated the North, and the Albigensians, who were the only serious threat to the Church, were wiped out in the most bloody manner, between 1208 and 1229. The new orders which were founded in France between 1075 and 1125,

Augustinians, Premonstratensians, Carthusians and Cistercians, lost nothing of their fervour in the following century; and in the thirteenth century two new orders appeared, Dominicans and Franciscans, who rapidly took a prominent place in the social life of the times, chiefly because they set up their communities in the towns.

The country as a whole, but particularly Northern France, took an active part in the revival of commerce. There were many merchant settlements which gave a vital impetus to society in general. They left no trace in the culture of the early thirteenth century; neither Gothic art, nor the courtly romance, nor even philosophical thought owed anything to their influence. It was only in the latter half of the century that they imposed their taste, their ideas and their spirit on artists and writers. But they supported them, devoting their wealth to building churches, and giving board and shelter to *scholastici* and pupils. They took the place of the monasteries in providing the basis for artistic and speculative activity.

The monasteries were buried in the countryside, and in any case they had practically abandoned teaching, as a profane activity. They distrusted the new dialectical method. For a time they were notable in certain disciplines – history, and theology of the positive, scriptural variety.[2] But everywhere they were being superseded by the town schools, attached to cathedrals, which in many cases became universities.

A last factor which favoured France was her geographical situation, between Spain and the Empire on the one hand, between England and Italy on the other. She was thus the crossroads of medieval Europe, ideally placed to create a synthesis of culture. And this was what happened in the period from 1125 to 1300; she borrowed, and repaid with interest, the ideas of her neighbours.

England stands high amongst the countries which gained from such exchanges, but then England was, from the cultural point of view, an appendix of France – conquered first in 1066 by the nobility and clergy of Normandy, and a second time in the twelfth century, with the accession of the Angevins and the arrival of Eleanor of Aquitaine.[3] Relations between the two countries were close and there was constant interchange. John of Salisbury was one of the last humanists of the Chartres school; the Lille poet Walter of Châtillon was one of Henry Plantagenet's chancery clerks; Walter Map, the story-teller, studied at the University of Paris, where John Garland, an Oxford scholar, was a popular teacher. The English and the French were in constant collaboration, to such an extent indeed that it is sometimes difficult to distinguish each country's contribution to their common civilization. There seems to be no way, for instance, of deciding where Gothic architecture originated. In some fields it is easier to draw a line: without Geoffrey of Monmouth and the Anglo-Norman tradition of the *Historia regum Britanniae*, the Celtic world of myth and mystery would never have had such an extraordinary influence on the literature of France, and the romance would not have begun its career so early.[4] Roger Bacon, who was teaching in Paris about 1245, may or may not have been responsible for introducing the *Physics* and *Metaphysics* of Aristotle to the University, but there is no doubt that he did much to make them known. England was by no means a passive recipient of culture, although she was more a province than a cultural centre in her own right, and France certainly gained by the association, more particularly since England, amongst other very individual characteristics, had a marked taste for experiment.

It may be that the germ of Gothic is to be found in Spain; in some Moorish domes the groin-vaults were strengthened by intersecting ribs.[5] Spain certainly gave France a number of teachers, like Peter of Lisbon, who died in Paris in 1277, after compiling the standard textbook of logic, the *Summulae logicales*. But her really important contribution was the vast number of translations done in Barcelona, Pamplona, Tarragona, Segovia and above all Toledo. It was in Toledo, under the direction of archbishop Raymond (1126–53), that teams of Christians, Moors and Jews, both natives and foreigners, worked assiduously to make accessible to Europeans the works of Greeks, Arabs and Jews – physicians, mathematicians, naturalists, geographers and philosophers.

Italy too took part in all this activity. Her northern ports maintained ever closer contact with the Levant. Sicily, under Norman domination, had a mixed population of Byzantines, Muslims and Jews, and was always hospitable to foreigners. The Pisans, and the scholars at the cosmopolitan court of Palermo, had the advantage over the Spaniards of translating directly from the Greek, instead of from inaccurate Arabic versions of Greek authors.[6] Burgundio of Pisa, for example, used original manuscripts in translating Galen, Hippocrates, Saint John of Damascus and the homilies of Saint John Chrysostom; and Aristippus of Catania did likewise for Euclid, Hero of Alexandria and Ptolemaeus.

The Italian scholars who came to France served her even better than the translators, for they were many and distinguished. Civilians and canonists from Bologna, theologians and philosophers, all were attracted by the political stability of France and by her intellectual prestige. Some of them, for example Peter Lombard and Thomas Aquinas, rank as the most famous scholars of their age. Many of them, it is true, were richer in promise than in attainment when they crossed the Alps, and it was only after completing their training in France that they made a name for themselves. This was true as well of the Englishmen, the Germans and Lotharingians, for example, the Archpoet, Nivard, Godfrey of Fontaine and Siger of Brabant. Most of the writers and scholars of the twelfth and thirteenth centuries only reached their full development after spending some time in France, just as many Renaissance painters only became full masters of their art after going to Italy.

Thus France borrowed men and ideas everywhere, to give them greater stature. Medieval civilization at its peak was essentially a French creation, not only because the kingdom of the Capets furnished most of the artisans and their material, but because it was what Innocent IV called 'a crucible in which the gold was refined', a forcing-ground for the most varied talents.

Political unity, the rise of commerce, religious fervour and contacts with the other peoples of Europe were external factors. There were other, deeper influences, which introduced a new world view into art and letters, and so gave them new vigour.[7]

First of all there was familiarity with the classical writers, read and re-read by the men behind the twelfth-century Renaissance, as it is often called.[8] Quotations from the classics and allusions to the ancient world continually flow from their pens – and not only from authors who wrote in Latin, but from Chrétien de Troyes, in his romances, Peter Cantor in his theological treatises, and Helinand of Froidmont in his sermons. The masters handed on their ideas and preoccupations to their followers. The works of Cicero and Seneca influenced moralists and political theorists towards natural doctrines, drawn from an analysis of man and society rather than from Christian teaching.[9] Plato's *Timaeus* encouraged the study of the 'macrocosm', the universe, and the 'microcosm', man, its counterpart, and their organization. Aristotle taught men to observe, analyse and classify, without regard to the presuppositions of religion.

The rising tide of Arab treatises swelled the current. Geographical works, which had gained in interest from the travels of missionaries in Asia, revealed the wealth and diversity of the world. Medical, botanical and zoological treatises drew attention to the laws of physics and physiology, to flora and fauna.

Religious feeling was changing in a comparable way, turning towards the evangelical life. The ideal was no longer imprisonment in a spiritual fortress, but rather acceptance of the world and its needs; lay virtues were encouraged – wisdom, strength, justice, well-doing. Christ and the Virgin Mary were the models, and the favourite devotional theme was the humanity of God and the womanly perfection of His mother. In this way religion acquired a more human reality.

A more important factor perhaps, in this Renaissance, though a less obvious one, was the fuller development of the European mentality in the direction indicated by Gerbert and Abbo of Fleury. Intellectual curiosity and self-confidence grew; clerks showed a passionate interest in 'the conformation of the globe, the nature of the elements, the positions of the stars, the nature of animals, the movement of the winds, the growth of plants and roots'. They had so much confidence and faith in the power of reason that they applied it universally: to law, substituting logical proof for formalism; to politics, jurists, philosophers and theologians together attempting to construct a theory of the state; to music, Léonin's freedom giving way to Pérotin's rules; to teaching methods – in fact to everything.

Technological progress too should be mentioned, based on the discovery that nature is governed by mechanical rules, the rise in population also, and the development of cities. Everywhere there was movement, expansion, new problems; the world seemed to be reborn, to be on the brink of a new Creation.

It seemed, in the famous words of William of Conches, one of the last of the Chartres school, that the world was an *'ordinata collectio creaturarum'*, no longer a formless, incomprehensible magma, subject to obscure, arbitrary forces and supernatural powers, but a coherent, harmonious unity, governed by laws, and consequently intelligible to human reason and even susceptible in some degree to man's control. The Universe and humanity, then, had intrinsic qualities, a validity of their own.

It was no longer necessary to deny it, to remould it into a form acceptable to religion. It was not for religion to reject or reform nature, but to discover her perfections and reveal their attributes, wisdom, goodness and beauty, as those of the *summus opifex*, so that they evoked feelings of admiration, gratitude and worship. This was what the Dominicans and Franciscans did. Called on to preach in order to crush heresy, defeat vice, teach the rules of faith and inculcate true morals in man, the Black Friars needed a solid academic grounding. In the course of their training they came into close contact with the intellectual movement and were soon its leaders. The best amongst them devoted themselves to reconciling revelation with experience and reason, in a theological system which kept up with the latest scientific knowledge. The Grey Friars welcomed all beings 'sentient and non-sentient', because, like the sun, they 'bear witness unto God', and because, like the stars, they are 'shaped by His hand, clear and precious and fair'. As the interpreters and guides of their time the two orders offered up to the Creator logic and science, men, animals, flowers, the elements – 'praising the Lord with all His creatures'.

Such ideas helped to strengthen culture and confirm its direction. The arts might depict creation, philosophy had to explain it. The twelfth century described man and his feelings, nature and her beauties; the thirteenth explained, clarified, rationalized, looked for common causes and principles.

The early writings of the period in fact were more artistic than philosophical, a literature in which, as in Gothic art, elegance tended to oust naturalism. For three-quarters of a century there was a series of works of this nature, in every literary genre, in Latin or in the vernacular, which suddenly came to an end about 1225, when the intrusion of reason stifled spontaneity, put an end to aesthetic considerations and did irreparable harm, to Latin literature at least.

Formal perfection is what most impresses in these writers; all of them are remarkable for their easy style, their clear composition, the richness of their vocabulary, and their feeling for rhythm. Some of the poets indeed concerned themselves largely or even exclusively with the form of their verse, and cared not at all whether they said anything personal or original. They would toy with a theme, find various permutations of its elements, and work them into a pattern of words and sounds.[10]

Most of these pieces however combine expressive phrase with sincerity of feeling. If the writers put themselves into their compositions they do not invent imaginary sentiments, and if they create characters they do not borrow their psychology from other and better writers. They are able to analyse feelings, and it is themselves and their contemporaries we see in their work.

The variety of their writings reflects geographical diversity as well as differences of temperament; contrast between North and South had resulted in the popularity of the epic in the one region and the lyric in the other; and it remained clear-cut, especially in the way love was treated, on the one hand as a brutal instinct, on the other as a refined sentiment. Eleanor of Aquitaine and her daughters, Alice of Blois and Marie of Champagne, were influential in the introduction of courtly conceptions into the North,[11] but if this transformed the epic into the romance it did not drive out all coarseness and realism, for they were expelled from the *chanson de geste* only to reappear in other forms, such as satire.

Each intellectual centre had its own speciality. The schools were already occupied with philosophy rather than letters – the works of the masters are *Summae, Quaestiones, Artes*, devoid of literary pretensions. But their pupils, especially at Orleans, were still given a solid humanist education, and trained to write well.[12] The monasteries no longer competed in speculative theology: they were a workshop for mystical treatises and devotional writings, which are amongst the finest and most attractive productions of the age. They never lost their liking for history, universal or local, sacred or profane, ancient or modern.[13] Many rulers too, anxious to transmit their fame to posterity, or simply to provide themselves with entertainment, encouraged writers and patronized chroniclers, translators and poets; for example Henry II in England, Roger, William I and Frederick II in Sicily. In France, where the Capetians were entirely taken up with politics and had no time for literary patronage, there were others who made up for this lack. The counts and viscounts in the South, and their ladies, were the patrons of the troubadours. In the North Marie of Champagne and her descendants gave encouragement to poets and romancers – indeed Thibaut IV, who died in 1256, was himself a lyric poet of some talent. Even such a minor figure amongst the nobility as the Count of Guines had his own historiographer, Lambert of Ardres, and had Latin works translated into French. Many royal and feudal courts, over a period of several generations, were in effect salons where vernacular literature was cultivated. The townspeople and merchant classes also provided a public for tales, satire, drama, so that every literary genre was now profitable. This is also the reason why there were now two streams of literature. Although vernacular literature maintained links with Latin literature and remained much longer under its influence than many have supposed, it now had equal status with it.[14]

Amongst Latin prose writings the most characteristic are two works by John of Salisbury, both dating from 1159, the *Polycraticus*, or Book of Government, an essay in political philosophy, and the *Metalogicon*, a defence of grammar and logic. He was the best humanist of the twelfth century and in these books he distilled the ideas of a brilliant mind in pure Ciceronian Latin.[15] Then there are letters; their number is an indication of the culture of the age; their content and form show the Atticism of writers and recipients. There were treatises on asceticism and mysticism, or collections of prayers, in the tradition of John of Fécamp (*c.* 1030), and Bernard of Clairvaux a century later, a tradition constantly rejuvenated by meditation on the life and death of Christ.[16] There were sermons which drew on the same springs of emotional fervour, and others in a newer vein, using dialectic, allegory and symbolism. Finally there was a great variety of historical works, hagiographic collections or legendaries, in which miracles played a large part; lives of saints and contemporary rulers which had a greater regard for truth; chronicles, whose authors quite often showed real critical sense and also knew how to tell a story. One of the best of them was a Bavarian, Otto of Freising, who compiled his *Chronicon* in the middle of the twelfth century, a work particularly interesting for its philosophic thread, which comes from Augustine's *City of God*, for its awareness of the place of the Empire in cultural history, and its respect for France – Otto had been a student in Paris. Otherwise most universal chronicles were written by Normans and Frenchmen: Ordericus Vitalis, whose *Historia ecclesiastica*, completed in 1141–2, was intended to relate the history of the monastery of St. Évroul, but in fact went far beyond this aim; Robert of Torigny, a monk of Bec, and afterwards abbot of Mont Saint Michel, who continued the *Chronographia* of Sigebert of Gembloux (†1186); Robert of Auxerre, whose *Chronologia* was to eclipse Sigebert's work (†1212); and Guy of Bazoches (†1103), cantor at Châlons, who was both chronicler and hymn-writer. In the writing of national history it was the English who excelled; the leading examples were William of Malmesbury in the later twelfth century, and Matthew Paris in the early thirteenth.[17]

In poetry an even richer vein was tapped. Continuing the tradition of preceding ages, the Carolingian period in particular, the poets of the twelfth and thirteenth centuries used verse for almost any subject, and they still used both classical metres and rhythmic scansion. The former naturally was used in works which borrowed their subject from antiquity: notable examples were the *Trojan War* of Joseph of Exeter, and the *Alexandreid* of Walter of Châtillon, written in 1182, in which his poetic genius gave new life to a well-worn theme. These metres were used too by authors recounting contemporary events, at least when they wished to write in the heroic manner; we have an example in the anonymous *Gesta Friderici I metrice* and the *Ligurinus*, which celebrated the exploits of the Emperor Frederick in 1152–62 and 1186–7. Latin prosody was used too in a vast number of didactic writings, many of them no more than versified manuals, but some works of art, like the *Anticlaudianus* of Alan of Lille, written in 1182–3. The subject of this last, the ways of educating man to take his place as the master of creation, and the allegorical manner in which it is treated, might have made its four thousand hexameters singularly wearisome, but Alan's imagination overcame this danger and enabled him to make it in its way a kind of forerunner of the *Divine Comedy*. In classical metre too were written what are sometimes called comedies, but, with more justice, Latin metrical tales, since it is highly improbable that these pieces were intended for the stage. Finally there are the animal epics, which poke fun at knights, satirize clerks, monks, bishops or cardinals. The *Speculum stultorum*, in which Nigel Wireker relates the misadventures of Burellus the donkey, and the *Isengrinus* of Nivard of Ghent, which is the source of some branches of the Reynard the Fox cycle, were the best of these satirical pieces, which were in any case more lively and natural than most of the

175

works in classical metres. Whatever the talent of their authors, they were too derivative in form, and often in matter, to be anything other than artificial.[18]

Rhythmic poetry was more original and spontaneous; versatile in form, it could be adapted to either tender feelings or violent passion. It could convey with equal felicity enthusiasm and despondency, joy and sadness, love and envy, pride and humility, intoxication and repentance. It was thus an ideal instrument for the goliards, celebrating Bacchus or Venus, and yet a suitable vehicle also for religious effusions.

Little enough is known of the goliards – a generic term covering rather haphazardly all the profane poets of the period. The origin of the word is doubtful, most of the pieces are anonymous, and when by some chance they can be attributed to a named author, he is most often someone of whom very little is known. The biographies of the two most famous goliardic poets are mere scraps of information: Hugh 'the Primate' was a canon of Orleans about 1140, and the Archpoet was the protégé of Archbishop Rainald of Dassel. But if the writers are unknown their works are not; they are brimming with vitality. Some are satires of unusual virulence, like the *Propter Sion non tacebo* by Walter of Châtillon, author of the *Alexandreid*, some are parodies, often of hymns, of the *Verbum bonum et suave*, for example, and most are simply about wine and women. J. A. Symonds, who translated some of the goliards into English, entitled his anthology *Wine, Women and Song*, and that this was their ideal is shown clearly enough by the Archpoet's famous *Confession*.[19]

At the opposite pole from this profane poetry, but just as natural, as varied and passionate, stood the religious lyric.[20] Before 1150 Peter Abelard was a brilliant exponent of it; the great teacher, the genius of dialectic, was also the poet of the *Planctus*.[21] Adam of St. Victor, doubtless a Breton, was equally remarkable in this genre in the later twelfth century: in hymns and sequences which admittedly smell of the lamp, but which are none the less admirably rhythmic, he conveys with a delicate touch all the feelings of the Christian soul. He celebrates the feasts of the Church, extols her joys, sighs over her sorrows, and tirelessly reiterates his love for the Mother of Christ.[22] The thirteenth century has no writer who can be compared with these two, but it has to its credit some isolated poems which count among the greatest examples of medieval literature: the *Veni sancte spiritus*, attributed to Stephen Langton, Archbishop of Canterbury; *Jesu dulcis memoria*, by an unknown author; the *Pange linguam*, by Philip de Grève, chancellor of the University of Paris; the *Dies irae*, attributed to Thomas of Celano; the *Stabat mater*, probably by the

Italian friar Jacopone da Todi; the *Philomena*, by an English Franciscan, John Peckham; and the *Lauda Sion*, by Saint Thomas. When the last of these hymns was being written Latin literature was dying. Soon after 1250 the progress of vernacular literature and the triumph of Reason had killed it.

The period from about 1150 into the early thirteenth century had been one of greatness for French and Romance literature, because it was the period of the vernacular romance and the Provençal lyric. In Toulouse, Carcassonne, Béziers, Narbonne and Montpellier the troubadours had brought their subtle art to perfection. In short pieces, richly worked, they were sometimes satirical, sometimes passionate. Sometimes they wrote of that love, which, in the words of Bernard Marti, is nothing but 'lies and lechery'; sometimes, as with Jaufrei Rudel, it was an ideal love, directed towards some far-away princess.[23] They brought woman into literature and made her the queen of their works. This was a real revolution and the results were important, particularly in Northern France, where these ideas were generally accepted by 1160 and had a decisive effect: they ended the career of the epic. We can scarcely give the name *chanson de geste* to poems in which the mainsprings of action were no longer the service of God or the king, the defence of one's homeland, loyalty to a feudal lord, friendship binding one to a brother-in-arms, or overweening pride, but desire for a woman, which had transformed the champions of old into faithful knights enslaved by their ladies. At the same time southern lyricism had spread its influence north of the Loire and, in combination with the subject matter and the spirit of Celtic lays and legends, gave rise to the romance proper. A great writer, Chrétien de Troyes, who was both a good stylist and a clever psychologist, created this genre, in which subtle analysis is combined with the freest imagination, reality is adorned with dream-like seduction, and love is the only true end. This provides an excellent example of the successful way in which medieval France used disparate foreign materials to produce something quite new: borrowing from courtly literature, from Celtic legend, from Christianity and antiquity, she created the romance, the most truly French of literary genres, and indeed the finest flower of French literature.[24] Lyric poetry and the great romances however – *Tristan, Érec, Cligès, Yvain, Perceval* – were not the only literary productions of Northern France between 1150 and 1225. There were also fables and tales, the first parts of the *Romance of Reynard the Fox*, written about 1170, allegorical and didactic pieces, the *Jeu d'Adam* and the *Miracle of Saint Nicholas*, the romances of Alexander, Thebes, Troy, Aeneas, and Villehardouin's *Conquest of Constantinople*.

In the early years of the thirteenth century the French language had won a firm footing in all branches of literature. From then on it gained ground, more particularly as it had now evolved sufficiently to treat any subject. It was the same in neighbouring countries: the various vernaculars acquired elegance and accuracy, and, sometimes in imitation of France in her various aspects,[25] sometimes by developing their own resources, they rapidly built up a national literature.

German literature for example around 1200 could boast of such remarkable works as the *Nibelungenlied*, the poems of Hartmann von Aue, the romances of Wolfram von Eschenbach, and the lyrical poems of the Minnesänger, Walther von der Vogelweide.[26] Everywhere in Europe Latin was now only the language of the Church and the theologians. Soon only one literary genre remained in which Latin might be used with any aesthetic pretensions: the religious lyric. For scholars after all cared little whether their dissertations were couched in elegant diction; it was enough that they should be clear, accurate and well-argued.

Intellectual progress was another reason for the decline of Latin literature, for there had been revolutionary changes in methods of teaching, and in the value accorded to its various branches. The thirteenth century became more and more an age of Reason. Abstraction by analysis, the deduction of universals and absolutes, these were its chief preoccupations. Teachers of grammar and rhetoric therefore abandoned the simple but rewarding method of teaching used since Charlemagne; they no longer gave readings, commenting on the text of orators and ancient writers, but dissected their works, extracting from them laws of good oratory, or good writing, which they then propounded. Some even went so far as to make grammar a philosophy of language '*qui assignat causas*'. They no longer set the models themselves before the pupil, but stuffed him with derived precepts. Not everything was bad in this movement – the ratiocinations of these *grammatici* led to a very desirable increase in clarity and precision in the use of language. Unfortunately the rules of composition have always had the effect of stifling rather than stimulating talent, and so it was in the thirteenth century. Taught by means of *Artes* – *Artes dictaminis, Artes poeticae*, even *Artes praedicandi*, writers of Latin were weighed down by artifice.[27] Their number decreased, for science was now the fashion. Students were interested in philosophy, law, medicine, and no longer learnt more than the minimum Latin necessary to make themselves understood in the language. The Faculty of Arts in a university was no more than an anteroom where the clerk waited as short a time as possible. The faculties, in any case, as we have already seen in the two literary branches of the *trivium*, were now concerned with speculative philosophy, and were anxious to turn out logicians rather than humanists.

The vernacular literatures too were naturally influenced by this change in teaching methods and in the intellectual climate. They too suffered from the disaffection of the university world and the growing disdain for classical models. Until then vernacular writers had been educated in the classical school. They too had now to bow to Reason. The great work of the first half of the thirteenth century, the first *Roman de la Rose*, codified courtly love into a sort of *Ars amatoria*, and pushed allegory to the limit, arriving in fact at abstraction. A little later, in Italy, the lady of the Provençal troubadours was dehumanized, in the *Dolce stil nuovo*, into a mere personification of Science, Poetry, Beauty or Virtue.

None the less the vernacular literatures had more powers of resistance than Latin literature. For one thing they were written in a living language, which was linked with reality and could not be entirely divorced from the concrete. And they not only held but enlarged their public; they kept the aristocratic public, and at the same time increasingly attracted the bourgeoisie and the lower orders.

The Crusade against the Albigensians in the early thirteenth century ruined the southern courts and made life difficult for writers who were not beneficed clergy, and could not live without patronage. But if courtly poetry was henceforth to languish in its native land, it remained vigorous in the great northern domains, in Champagne and Flanders or in frontier principalities like Hainaut. It was even more flourishing and brilliant in Italy. Many troubadours seeking a protector haunted the court of Frederick II or Charles of Anjou, and, together with the native poets, created the Sicilian school, one of whose masters, Sordello of Mantua, was immortalized by Dante.

The steady favour of the courts enabled the romance to continue its career, but in a lower key. The first part of the *Roman de la Rose* was written in 1236 and it was one of the high points of medieval literature. Guillaume de Lorris, who was a gifted poet, imparted a graceful reality to the allegories which crowd his poem. But it is questionable whether it is really a romance, rather than a kind of compendium of the literary tendencies of the time, the courtly, the romantic, the didactic, the satirical and the mystical. *Manekine*, the *Châtelaine de Vergy,* the *Châtelain de Coucy* are much nearer the conventional romance, but none of them will bear comparison with *Tristan* or *Lancelot*. This is also true of courtly poetry; there was a great deal written in the latter half of the thirteenth century, but at least in France it was very inferior to what had gone before.

Other literary genres were aimed rather at the bourgeoisie than the nobility, amongst them social satire, as pointed in the sequels of

Reynard the Fox as in the second part of the *Roman de la Rose,* or in *Martijn,* written by a Fleming, Jacob van Maerlant. It sometimes happened that the writer of satire was concerned to popularize the learning of the clerks among laymen: the continuer of the *Roman de la Rose* is a case in point. More often this concern inspired strictly didactic or encyclopedic works, like the *Livres dou Tresor* of Brunetto Latini, or van Maerlant's trilogy.[28] The first man to exploit the comic vein in the theatre was Adam de la Halle, a good poet and an excellent musician. Joinville developed an anecdotic style of biographical writing, simple, natural and delicately observant. Lastly in the big towns of Italy and the North of France, such as Florence and Arras, there emerged a popular lyric, connected with the Franciscan *Laudi;* about 1270 poor Rutebeuf in Paris was one of its most talented exponents.[29]

All this however was not strictly new; there were Latin and vernacular writers in the twelfth century who popularized the learning of the clerks, like the mysterious Honorius of Autun;[30] there were goliards, troubadours, playwrights, chroniclers. What was new was the importance assumed by these branches of literature, and in some of them the different spirit animating them: violence in satire, naturalism in poetry. Writers were writing for the new bourgeoisie and adopted their outlook in many ways; they exchanged grace and elegance for directness and vivacity. Their work would have lost nothing by the change had they exercised more restraint, had they not yielded to the fashionable taste for abstraction, and constantly given free rein to moralizing and didacticism. It was this lack of subtlety, of a certain sense of proportion, this slight pedantry which caused literature in general, and bourgeois literature in particular, to fall short of the standard of the earlier thirteenth century.

From the middle of the thirteenth century, then, Latin literature was decaying, and, apart from Italy, where Dante was already on the horizon, the national literatures were at a low ebb. Henceforward it was in the academic field that the most remarkable work was to be done.

The first advances of scientific study had preceded the decline of humanism. The movement begun by Anselm of Canterbury, Irnerius, Ivo of Chartres, Anselm of Laon, Peter Abelard and their colleagues did not slacken during the great renaissance of humanism in the twelfth century, and never swerved from its objective, the systematization of knowledge and its consequent division into distinct disciplines. The task was not easy, for it was generally not enough to gloss the ancient writers: as the eleventh-century masters had seen, a rigorous analysis of the authorities was called for, followed by an individual process of deduction and sometimes induction. But the difficulties did not dismay them, and gradually categories were constituted and defined: civil law, Roman and customary law, canon law, positive, moral and speculative theology, philosophy and natural sciences. These essential distinctions were personified in the universities; the work had been done by their members, and their several faculties bear witness to its successful accomplishment.

The teachers of Roman law had the great advantage of a ready-made field. The jurists of antiquity had created it and Justinian had completed the great work. They had only to take over the *Code*, the *Institutes*, the *Novellae* and the *Digest*. At the beginning of the twelfth century Irnerius had been able to isolate Roman law from other disciplines, particularly rhetoric, and define its method: the establishment of the precise meaning of the text and the reconciling of contradictions by a process of dialectical analysis.

After the master's death the study of the subject followed the lines he had laid down.[31] In Bologna the *glossatores* followed one after another until Accursius grouped and classified their commentaries in his *Glossa ordinaria* about 1250.[32] North of the Alps, scholars who had studied in the Italian school taught its achievements and its methods: Magister Vacarius taught in Canterbury about 1150, and Placentinus in Montpellier from 1160 onward.[33] However in England and France Roman law met opposition from the royal power, both Plantagenet and Capetian. Roman law recalled only too clearly an age when the Emperor was the supreme secular authority, and thus tended to strengthen the pretensions of the Hohenstaufen, self-styled successors of the Caesars, to the hegemony of Europe; and for this reason its study was soon prohibited in England. It was condemned in Paris too in 1219, but soon afterwards authorized in Orleans – a demonstration of the powerlessness of official prohibitions to dam the movement begun by Irnerius and his pupils.

Customary law benefited by the general revival of legal studies. It was now committed to writing, so that it should not be contaminated by Roman law. Then it was subjected to the same process: the division into logical sections, the analysis directed towards greater precision, and the deduction of general principles. A number of books bear witness to this process – the *Ancient Custumary of Normandy*, about 1200, the *Great Custumary of Normandy* of 1250, and the *Customs of Clermont en Beauvaisis*, codified by Philippe de Beaumanoir in 1280.[34] Glanvill's *Tractatus de legibus et consuetudinibus regni Angliae* (1187–9) and Bracton's *De legibus et consuetudinibus Angliae libri quinque* (between 1250 and 1260) are more remarkable and more important. They made a powerful contribution in fact to the formation of the Common Law, that national system which was developed by the

N 181

royal courts, and triumphed over local customary law.[35] As for the *Sachsenspiegel*, compiled by Eike von Repgow between 1220 and 1227, it was a manual of the law applied in the province of Anhalt to freemen and vassals – *Landrecht* and *Lehnrecht*.[36]

No doubt the interest in customary law had something to do with the foundation of the school of *Post-glossatores*, about 1280, by a former Toulouse professor, Jacques de Révigny. Their object was to give more flexibility to Roman law by borrowing elements from customary law, or, in other words, to improve, complete and give precision to customary law by following the example of Roman law. This is an attitude typical of the later thirteenth century, when scholars were independent and confident enough to dissent from authority from time to time, particularly when observation of reality appeared to support their heterodoxy. Roman law was admirable and should be followed as far as possible; but it was not perfectly adapted to medieval society, and had therefore to be modified as the social situation required. Similarly Aristotle might require correction when experience showed him to be in error. It was a positive position to take up: adopted by Bartoli in Italy (1316–57) it produced valuable results. Unfortunately, like all the scholars of the fourteenth century, the *Postglossatores* soon degenerated into the most arid dialecticians.[37]

Thanks to the work of canonists, theologians and civilians at the beginning of the twelfth century, especially Ivo of Chartres, Peter Abelard and Irnerius, ecclesiastical law earned the right to be deemed an independent discipline. As early as 1140 in Bologna Gratian codified it in his *Concordia discordantium canonum*, in which he brought together all the texts he could find – and he found more by far than previous compilers. He arranged them systematically, discussed their significance, established their application, reconciled those which were in conflict, and extracted their essence, substantially in the same way as Tribonian and his collaborators developed the *Digests*. They too had built up a logical system from a chaos of legislation, in which there was much that was obscure, outdated or contradictory. But they had had the advantage of being numerous, and of having a long and brilliant tradition behind them. Gratian was single-handed and he was dealing with a discipline that was practically new. For this reason his work was not perfect – there were considerable gaps in it, and he did not distinguish clearly between purely juridical questions and problems of morals and dogmatics; it was none the less a successful compilation, and provided the foundation of the canon law.[38]

Working in the same spirit as Gratian, and using the same methods, his successors, with papal support, completed his work. They collected texts which had escaped him or which were promulgated after the 1140s, in the *Decretals of Gregory IX*, the work of the Dominican

Raymond of Peñafort, completed in 1240, in the *Liber Sextus* of 1298 and the *Clementines* of 1317. With the *Concordia* and two subsequent compilations, the *Extravagantes* of John XXII and the *Extravagantes communes*, the new collections were to be brought together in the sixteenth century under the common title of *Corpus juris canonici*. At the same time the 'decretists' and the 'decretalists' defined their discipline more rigorously and completed the process of codification, whilst resisting the encroachments of Roman law.[39] Thus the thirteenth century had the advantage of a system of canon law distinct from other faculties, sacred or profane; it was complete, coherent and accepted by all Christendom. The importance of this seems even greater if we remember that canon law covered a vast field – *ratione personae* all matters touching clerics, and *ratione materiae* all causes touching the Church, its organization, its administration, properties, sacraments (especially marriage), wills and contracts.

The monumental work of Gratian was paralleled in exegesis and sacred history, and even more in theology. The *Historia scholastica* (*c*. 1170) by Petrus Comestor, chancellor of the School of Notre Dame in Paris, was a wide-ranging exposition of the Old and the New Testaments; he was a voracious reader and he gleaned with considerable penetration from his vast reading anything which served to support or clarify Holy Scripture.[40] Peter Lombard, another Parisian, wrote his *Quatuor libri sententiarum* in 1152, a systematic exposition of Christian doctrine. It was certainly a less original work than Gratian's; it is not so clearly the work of a master-mind and only defends traditional positions. Nevertheless both the object and the method were the same; the one to harmonize all knowledge within the field and reconcile contradictions, and the other the now legitimate use of dialectic in theology. The same virtues are discernible in both – vast documentation, clarity, confidence, completeness. The popularity of the Lombard's work was great, particularly in teaching, and it became the standard manual of theology, the more so as its impersonal style encouraged the teacher to develop his own thought freely, but on a solid and reliable foundation.[41]

Amongst his many commentators we must mention Peter Cantor and his English pupil, Cardinal Robert Curzon, for the interest shown by them in practical questions, which the Lombard had sacrificed to more theoretical aspects of doctrine. By complementing the work of the Magister Sententiarum in this way they laid the foundations of moral theology and casuistry.[42]

Some theologians paid less attention to authorities than Peter Lombard and his followers. Richard of St. Victor, in the fourth chapter of his remarkable *De Trinitate*, declared that he preferred reasoning to listing and collating the opinions of his predecessors. He resembled Anselm of Canterbury in the confidence he showed in human understanding, enlightened of course by divine wisdom, and in his mingling of meditation with speculation.[43] He was one of the great theorists of mysticism. A few decades later the author of the *Ars fidei* made great use of dialectic;[44] but the twelfth century generally confined itself to positive theology; these first essays in speculative theology were the prototypes of the great works which came in the thirteenth century after the rediscovery of Aristotle.[45]

The disciplines we have dealt with up to this point developed fairly quickly because they used materials which were already familiar to the medieval mind, or, if they were not, at least appeared to offer no threat to the doctrine of the Church. Speculative theology on the other hand, philosophy, mathematics, geography and natural science, in 1140, were still based on a very inadequate body of ideas and observations. It was only after the principal works of the Greek and Arab scholars were translated into Latin that these sciences began to develop. Mathematics made rapid progress: the *Liber abaci* (1202) was the first of a series of works of genius from the pen of the Pisan Leonardo Fibonacci.[46] Metaphysics developed more slowly because the ideas derived from pagan thought conflicted with the Christian vision of the universe, and could not be assimilated in their raw state by medieval philosophy, and also because they were heterogeneous and difficult to reconcile with each other.

The problem of the thirteenth century was to enrich Christian thought by the infusion of Aristotelianism without corrupting or mutilating it. By 1200 most of the Stagirite's works were accessible to the Latin world, so that from then on they could not be ignored. Their powerful appeal lay in a rigorous experimental method, leading to sound and far-reaching conclusions. On the other hand there was no question of blind acceptance, since these writings were 'conceived without any religious preoccupation, and did not recognize certain philosophical truths which lie at the foundation of all the great religions'.[47] So the Church at first reserved judgement; in 1210 the Paris professors were forbidden to expound the *Physics* and *Metaphysics*. This was a limited, local and, in practice, a temporary prohibition; it did not extend to private study of the two books, and it did not affect the *Logic* or the *Ethics*. Nor was it followed in other universities, Oxford, for example, or Toulouse. And it was gradually forgotten as Aristotelianism was absorbed by Christian philosophy: by 1225 it was no longer observed. This cautious approach had even more justification in the case of Aristotle's commentator Averroes, whose work became known in Europe between 1230 and 1240. He had seen the weaknesses of the master's metaphysics, and for that matter of his psychology, and he buttressed them by unorthodox

184

arguments, such as the eternity of the world, the negation of providence and monopsychism.

The great diversity of new ideas brought difficulties for the thinkers of the thirteenth century, since the translators working in Spain and Italy did not confine their attention to Aristotle; they also made known that later development of Greek philosophy, the neoplatonist school, both directly, by the translation of two of Proclus's treatises into Latin, and indirectly through Avicenna, whose writings were known and used by the Christian world before the turn of the century.[48] Like Averroes, anxious to supply deficiencies in Aristotle, Avicenna had made borrowings, unconsciously, from Plotinus and Proclus. As for Platonism proper, it was still little known, in spite of the translation of the *Phaedo* and the *Meno* about 1150. Faced with this variety of doctrine, the theologians and the philosophers were hesitant. The period of assimilation of ancient thought by Christian doctrine was thus one of eclecticism, and the final synthesis of ideas was slow in emerging.

From 1230 on, the influence of Greek and Arab thought resulted in a marked increase in theological speculation.[49] The authorities were not thrown overboard, and theology remained basically Augustinian, for the great Bishop of Hippo was the authority *par excellence* of the Roman Church, but at the same time truths revealed by reason were now considered worth scrutiny, and philosophy had become the handmaid of theology. A Paris professor, William of Auvergne, set his feet firmly in this path about 1230, and a number of masters followed him, notably two Franciscans, Alexander of Hales, an Englishman (1180-1245), and his Italian pupil, Saint Bonaventure (1221-74), who came to study in Paris and stayed to teach. Quite soon most authors of *Quaestiones, Treatises, Commentaries, Summae* brought philosophical elements into their theology. But until Saint Thomas (1225-74) no one had a complete, consistent system of philosophy on which to rely, not even Bonaventure, who worked out a remarkable synthesis of traditional theology, but in his philosophy did not go beyond the eclectic stage. It may well be that after he was called from his university chair in 1257 to the arduous duties of General of the Franciscan Order he no longer had the leisure to organize his ideas in this field. On the other hand it may be that, like the other thinkers of his Order, he did not believe it was possible to construct a philosophical system without the aid of theology.[50]

The 'angelic doctor' did not share this view. Thomas agreed that philosophy, on its own, was sure to fall into occasional error, and must be wrong if it contradicted dogma. He held too that it was inferior to theology and must be integrated into a theological system. Nevertheless, like Albertus Magnus (1206-80), whose pupil he had been in Cologne before coming to Paris, he insisted on the claim of philosophy to be an independent discipline, with the mission of resolving by observation and ratiocination the problems facing mankind. He had no hesitation therefore in setting out to construct a philosophical system, the first conceived by a Christian scholar.

It was authentically a *system* of philosophy, since he left nothing out; he did not, like so many of his predecessors in Paris, confine himself to logic and morals. He touched on every question and formulated, for instance, a system of politics. It was also a true philosophical system by reason of its originality. Saint Thomas borrowed widely from Aristotle, the intellectualist and abstractive theory of knowledge, for instance, which, in opposition to the 'illuminist' position, makes no appeal to a special intervention of God in order to explain the origin of ideas. He also drew upon other sources, ancient or Christian, in fact any which were accessible, provided they were not suspect, for he did not believe that human thought had made no progress since the days of the Portico, and he preferred to neglect nothing which might lead him to truth. None the less he showed complete independence of all his sources, even Aristotle, whose ideas he examined, criticized and corrected, and indeed supplemented with a metaphysical system which pruned out his naturalistic tendencies. His philosophical system was authentic too in that it was a unity, despite its amplitude and diversity; thanks to Thomas's unusual capacity for synthesis, all his material, whatever its source and whatever its nature, was worked into a harmonious whole.

In spite of its transcendent qualities Thomism met with harsh opposition in some quarters. In 1277, three years after his death, some of his propositions were condemned in Paris and Oxford. Another manifestation was seen in a new philosophical system, Scotism. Its creator, John Duns Scot (1266–1308), a Scottish Franciscan who taught in Oxford and later in Paris, found room in his system for 'Aristotelian novelties' but he made more use than the angelic doctor of those Augustinian principles so dear to his order: for example, in affirming the superiority of will over intelligence, in the field of action, and its complete independence of the latter. But the ideas he borrowed from Augustine, like those he took from his other predecessors, were examined with the same critical rigour as was to be applied by the fourteenth century schoolmen, particularly the English Franciscan, William Occam.

The thirteenth century knew other currents of philosophy older than Thomism. One, whose most notable representative was Siger of Brabant (*c.* 1240–84), was formulated in Paris between 1260 and 1265. As far as one can judge at this distance, it was marked by a complete devotion to Aristotle, that is to say to somewhat unorthodox principles, and some of its followers even professed an Averroistic variety of Aristotelianism still more foreign to Christian orthodoxy. The other, older, school was adorned by Oxonians, Robert Grosse-teste (1168?–1253) and Roger Bacon (c. 1210–92), and its most interesting characteristic was the importance given to mathematics and natural sciences, and to practical experiment as a method.[52]

It was not only the English who showed an interest in the natural sciences. The influx of Greek and Arab treatises on geography, astronomy and astrology, on physics, alchemy and medicine brought attention to bear on these disciplines, but at the same time inhibited progress by providing texts which were material for argument and by thus dispensing and discouraging the inquirer from personal research. When he undertook an inventory of the knowledge of his time, Albertus Magnus held in principle that 'natural science does not consist in ratifying what others have said, but in seeking out the causes of phenomena', and in fact he frequently corrected Aristotle in matters of physics, botany and zoology.[53] His compatriot and colleague, the German Dominican Theodore of Freiberg, devoted an excellent treatise to the rainbow. The Emperor Frederick II made interesting observations in falconry. Peter Pérégrin of Maricourt, a Picard, studied magnetism. The thirteenth century, then, was aware of the experimental method, which associates logic and mathematics with direct experience; it may in fact have perfected the method.[54] Thus a fertile field of research was opened, but it was scarcely exploited at the time. Most learned men did not think of verifying or completing by experiment the assertions of the ancients. Either they simply made compilations from them, like Vincent of Beauvais when he wrote his monumental encyclopedia, the *Speculum majus*, or else they commented on them and discussed them in the light of dialectic.[55] The critical sense was scarcely exercised at the time, except in the analysis of texts. The great technique of the time was deductive logic; applied to the positive sciences in the place of induction, it did little to further them. It is probably significant that in the universities there was no 'faculty of sciences'.

The universities were in fact a perfect mirror of the scientific movement. They encouraged its development by bringing together all the talents, and they made its progress manifest by their definitive organization. A strictly medieval creation, the *Universitas magistrorum et scholarium* was, as the phrase conveys, a corporation established in a particular form, enjoying privileges conceded by the civil and religious authorities: the exclusive right to organize studies, with exemptions in legislative, juridical, fiscal and military matters. It gave a collective organization to those who had licence to teach and made it their profession, and to those who, wherever they came from and whatever their personal status, desired instruction leading to an academic degree. It imposed on both a programme of lectures, sanctioned by examinations which conferred the *licentia docendi*, and enabled the student, one might say the apprentice, to enter the body of masters. Since the students were legion they were divided into 'nations', and since the subjects taught were now many they were divided into faculties – four of them at the most: arts, theology, law and medicine. The first was an inheritance from the Carolingian schools and formed an introduction to the three others; in theory it included the seven liberal arts, but in practice, without completely neglecting the other branches, it emphasized dialectic more and more, and starting from there, gradually annexed other philosophical fields, including the natural sciences, considered as a part thereof. Once he was received master of arts and equipped with a solid general culture, the student might embark on theology, law or medicine. Such were the essential features of that original institution, the university, as it was slowly developed in the twelfth century in Paris and Bologna, and extended in the thirteenth century – on the Paris model in the North, and the Bologna model in the South – to Oxford, Cambridge, Cologne, Toulouse, Montpellier, Pavia, Salamanca and other places. The number of students and the variety of lectures bear witness to the spread of intellectual ambitions in the medieval world, as much as to the extension and development of the domain of scholarship since the days of Abbo of Fleury and Gerbert of Aurillac.[56]

Those qualities which ornament the literary and scientific works of the years between 1150 and 1300 are to be seen even more clearly perhaps in the art of the period, the Gothic. Strength, audacity and energy in construction, order and clarity in composition, variety in means of expression, elegance and formal perfection – these are the essence of what was universally described at the time as *opus francigenum*. The expression is worthy of note since it casts some light on the origins of the new style. Technically speaking it grew out of the ogival vault, itself derived from the groin vault. Once architects thought of using the groin vault to cover large areas, central naves in particular, they were obliged to give it greater strength. Influenced probably by Armenia, and perhaps by Moorish Spain as well, they had the idea of running ribs along the groins of the vaults to support them.[57] They then thought of constructing these 'augives' (from Latin *augere*, to augment, increase) before the vault itself, combining them with archbands and formerets to form a skeleton which only had to be filled up by thin webs to cover the building; and in order to ensure the equilibrium of this skeleton they replaced the semi-circular arch by the pointed arch used in Burgundy. The resulting vault was light, and could be carried to considerable heights, so long as it was propped by flying buttresses, which carried the tangential thrust out far from the base of the construction. The vault was then borne entirely by the buttresses and columns, which carried its vertical thrust down to the ground; the walls no longer carried the weight and could be opened out or replaced by any material, glass, for instance. From this moment the edifice was no longer a solid mass, but an articulated unity, open, upsurging – in fact, Gothic.

The earlier stages of this process were worked out in Normandy and England; the later in the Île de France. It was in Normandy that architects went over definitely to the formula of the articulated construction, made up of a framework of arches and piers with an outer shell, and set the first groin vaults over the naves of their churches. It was there too, in the chapter-house of Jumièges, and in England, in the choir of Durham Cathedral, that they took the next step, about 1100, of introducing the pointed arch. But it was in the Capetian domain, prompted by aesthetic and mystic ideas, that they derived a whole new style from what was originally a method of roofing. They dreamed of working to mathematical principles which would reflect celestial harmony, and of letting in the light which they believed, with the neoplatonists and their kind at Chartres, provided a link between multiplicity and unity, between material and spiritual, created and Creator.[58] Therefore they sought to make their churches high and light, the two fundamental characteristics of Gothic. This was indeed an *opus francigenum*, a French achievement.

It was not the work of one man, nor of one generation. Beginning with the ambulatory of Morienval (Oise), which dates from about 1122, experiments continued for three-quarters of a century, in the country, then in the towns of the Île de France, that chosen country – seat of royalty, closely populated, centre on which roads and rivers converged – whose quarries provided a kind of stone resistant to weathering, but easy to cut. One after another the constituent elements of the new style appeared; at St. Denis, reconstructed by the great abbot Suger in 1132; or at Chartres, between 1145 and 1155, with its Royal Portal, beneath which the great figures of the Old Testament look down on the faithful and welcome them into Christ's fold, and its magical windows full of light and colour;[59] at Sens (*c.* 1140), with its three storeys, arcades, gallery and clerestory; at Senlis (*c.* 1155), where the life of the Blessed Virgin is carved in stone; at Laon (1155–60), there was the bold opening out of walls, in Paris (*c.* 1163), the upsurge of the nave towards heaven, and the design of the façade, inspired by the great Norman churches. By the end of the twelfth century Gothic existed as a style, its principles were clear and were now exemplified in a dazzling series of cathedrals.

Fundamentally they all had the same features. In plan there was a

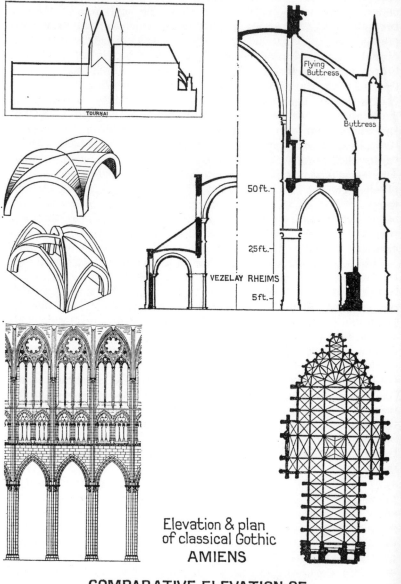

TOURNAI

Flying Buttress

Buttress

50 ft.

25 ft.

VEZELAY RHEIMS

5 ft.

Elevation & plan
of classical Gothic
AMIENS

COMPARATIVE ELEVATION OF
ROMANESQUE AND GOTHIC

choir almost as long as the nave, an ambulatory opening into radiating chapels, round or polygonal, and, in the later stages, side chapels between the buttresses. The elevation consisted of a great arcade with pointed arches, a gallery, often glazed, and tall, wide windows, divided by mullions, from about 1220 onwards, into two, and then four, vertical sections of lancet shape, crowned by a rose. Fascicular piers climbed up the three storeys, some of their elements stopping at the first storey to take the springing of the aisle vaults or the upper walls, whilst the rest shot straight up to support the main quadripartite vault. Outside were flying buttresses, standing out further and further from the bulk of the building, sometimes double or treble, strutted by colonnettes, and decorated with crockets, pinnacles or statues. The west front and the transepts were adorned with monumental porches, surmounted by one or two rows of statues, a rose window and a pair of towers. A spire raised above the transept crossing would ideally complete the set of towers; in fact it was not so completed anywhere, either at Chartres, Rheims or Amiens, the three classical examples of Gothic.[60]

These characteristics of the great cathedrals built in the first half of the thirteenth century subsist in what is customarily called the 'Rayonnant' style, infelicitously, for it is only a new variation on the old style. The architects kept to the general lines laid down by their predecessors, but they forced to their limit the technical possibilities already revealed. They opened up the structure more and more. In the Paris Sainte Chapelle they replaced walls by a skeleton of columns enclosing vast bays. In the choir of St. Urbain at Troyes (1262–6) they incorporated the gallery into the windows, which thus came down to within ten feet of the ground. The vaulting was carried to dizzy heights, 157 feet at Beauvais; piers and buttresses were thinned down; in short the architects were bent on showing their virtuosity, on accomplishing the impossible. Their buildings gained for a while in lightness, but after a time they became elegant solutions of theorems, and from 1300 on architecture was a matter of formulae and dry theory. Virtuosity was as fatal to it as to scholastic thought; philosophers and architects alike were drunk with their own brilliance and executed variations instead of composing themes.

In this period the other arts were still centred on architecture; less dominated by it than in the Romanesque era, but still not independent. Sculpture, for instance, no longer distorted its subject in order to fill the spaces assigned to it by an architect; it accentuated relief and slowly detached itself from the structure of the building, whilst remaining monumental; the stone-carver and the mason still worked together towards the one total effect.

The Gothic tradition in sculpture, developing out of the reliefs at

St. Denis and the portals of Chartres, where 'life is revealed discreetly beneath the folds of drapery and touches the smiling faces', may be defined in five words: naturalism, didacticism, calm, abundance and clarity. Imaginary beasts faded into the background with the fantastic fauna of the bestiaries and the whimsical flora of barbarian and oriental art. Models were now taken from life, and reproduced faithfully: the figuration of man was of real man, the plants were the plants of the fields and woods of the Île de France. This did not mean the end of idealism and symbolism; the new naturalism led to realism, but only by slow degrees, and for some time types rather than individuals were represented. Moreover, although distortion was no longer used as a means of conveying the supernatural, other means, the selection and disposition of subjects, were used to suggest it.

This selection and disposition were not governed by the inspiration and fantasy of the artist alone; they were to some extent dictated by the didactic object laid down by the clergy for sculptor and glassworker alike. The decoration of a Gothic cathedral was intended to teach sacred history: the Old Testament opened the way for the Messiah, and the Church triumphant, with its apostles, martyrs, confessors and virgins, pointed the way to the Last Judgement and to Paradise. It was intended to teach a moral doctrine, glorifying manual and intellectual work, encouraging virtue and recalling the struggle which had to be sustained against vice. It was also a compendium of theology in which all creation joined to magnify the Creator's might and exalt His goodness.[61]

The days of terror in fact were over; it is not Jehovah but Christ who reigns over Gothic statuary, and His mother shares His sovereignty. Innumerable cathedrals were dedicated to her; her life was endlessly related in their porches. Sculpture centred upon God made man, and on the most feminine of His creatures, must inevitably be instinct with love and tenderness.

Clarity of composition reinforced this impression of peace and serenity. For the Gothic image-makers, as for Saint Thomas, there was no beauty without order. They divided large areas into sections in which they set calm personages in orderly ranks. They kept the more prominent positions for important subjects; and they carved them in the round, on a large scale. Secondary scenes were treated on a lesser scale and in lower relief, on the plinths of the building.

The final characteristic of Gothic sculpture was that it overflowed from portals into porches, climbed to the pinnacles on the buttresses and the roof balustrades. It had lost the favourite field of the Romanesque sculptor, the capitals of columns: to adorn these with legends would break the flowing line of the column. In some places, Rheims, for instance, even the tympana were no longer used in this way. On the other hand the exterior was taken over entirely by sculpture. Interior decoration became the business of the stained-glass workers, and they acquitted themselves with considerable talent. By the time of Suger's reconstruction at St. Denis they were certainly equal in artistry to the architects and masons. In the great bays opened out by the architects they set out, in the lower part, round, square, lozenge-shaped or quatrefoil medallions, and above them large oblong surfaces. In the latter they placed figures as majestic and expressive as those in the porches; in the former they set jewel-like scenes analogous to the ones carved in stone on the plinths, inspired by scripture or the Golden Legend, and, like them, naturalistic and symbolic at the same time. In the cathedrals of Chartres, Bourges, Laon, Rouen or Rheims, in the Sainte Chapelle in Paris, in all the churches, there was a flood of dazzling colours, deep blues and gleaming reds, giving joy to the eye and exaltation to the soul.[62]

When the major arts are so vigorous they dictate to the minor. The goldsmiths of the Limousin made reliquaries in the shape of tiny churches, enlivened by the addition of small, carved figures and bright colours. The illuminators, who worked for the most part in Paris, borrowed many of their motifs from the stone-carvers, and their style was closely related to that of the stained-glass makers. Like the scholarly disciplines at the same period, the arts had clearly defined boundaries, but they were the handmaids of architecture just as those disciplines were the handmaids of theology.

On this organic unity, as we may call it, was superimposed another, more clearly recognizable than in the Romanesque period – geographical unity.[63] The style of the Île de France soon spread outside its original domain. Monks such as the Cistercians, Villard de Honnecourt and Étienne de Bonneuil carried the new style everywhere, from Christian Spain to Scandinavia, Poland and Hungary.[64] It was adapted to the resources, genius and traditions of the regions it entered. In Catalonia it was applied to an original plan, adopted by Southern France and exemplified particularly in the cathedral of Albi in the fourteenth century – the single nave with side chapels lodged between buttresses brought inside the building. The Low Countries restricted the upward surge of Gothic, made it more solid and robust. In Germany it was mixed with relics of Romanesque. In each country, however, it kept the same basic features.

Italy was more recalcitrant: the style was known and used in quite a number of thirteenth-century churches; but the true spirit was absent.[65] Her churches were spread out on the ground rather than thrust up towards the heavens; she sought to create a space rather than translate an aspiration. Decorative art went into church furniture rather than church exteriors – the best works of sculpture were pulpits, especially those made by the Pisani family, and the interiors were brightened more by frescoes than by stained glass. Mural painting was the most successful art of the Duecento, and it owed little to the France of Saint Louis. Its sources of inspiration were the Constantinople of the Macedonian emperors, the Umbria of Saint Francis and Constantine's Rome. The Tuscan Cimabue (c. 1240–1302) used the first two, and in this way tempered Byzantine rigidity with realism. The Roman Cavallini (c. 1250–1316) derived from the last the majesty of his work and his feeling for space. In this he was the forerunner of Giotto (1266–1337), the great interpreter of Franciscan piety, whose works, with their pathos and simplicity, achieve a realistic perspective, without losing their monumental character or their spiritual depth. At this turning point of the Middle Ages he marks the apogee of the Italian fresco.[66]

England was exceptional in a different way, not in reacting against the Gothic style, but in thinking it out differently, and less logically than the French. Romanesque survivals dominated Early English, which originated in Durham: square east end, duplication of transepts, horizontal emphasis in the elevation, decoration of mouldings and arcades, importance of the great lantern towers. Then, after a short period of geometricism and verticalism, a new style came in about 1270, with a predilection for luxuriant decoration, for curves and countercurves, inherited from Anglo-Saxons or Celts, and called Decorated or Curvilinear. The object was movement, and beauty of construction was sacrificed to it. The lines of the façade were lost in a profusion of blind arcades and statuary, the design of vaults was masked by multiplying liernes and tiercerons, so that bays were broken up into countless small curved surfaces, studded with carved bosses, corbels and cornerpieces. The stone-carvers moreover were not satisfied with the opportunities for display provided by the structure of their churches. They built a great number of sepulchral monuments and alabaster altar screens.[67]

Gothic, then, as it was conceived in the Île de France, was not imposed on the whole of Europe, though it dominated most of it. It became in fact an international style.

This unity, organic on the one hand, and geographical on the other, was not manifest in art alone. It was to be seen in every domain of civilization. There was not only a 'Western' art: there was a Western philosophy, a Western theology, worked out by French, Italian, English and German masters in Paris, and even a common Western literature, Latin literature first of all, in an international language, then French literature, whose forms and themes quickly attained international status. The lyric of Provence, the romance of antiquity, courtly romance, animal epic, satire, liturgical drama were cultivated throughout the Christian world. Everywhere, on the banks of the Rhine, along the North Sea coasts, on Mediterranean shores, poets sang of their love for a lady, told the exploits of Christian knights, and satirized the great ones of the earth. They were adapters rather than imitators, and they often found their themes in the legends and traditions of their own countries. The unity of literature was not absolute, any more than that of art, but it was just as real. There was a European civilization, independent of political frontiers, centred upon France, which performed a function of concentration, assimilation and transformation.

This unity, which might be called external, was complemented by a firm, internal unity, often based paradoxically on very heterogeneous elements. The Middle Ages were always encyclopedic, open to every kind of influence, more so in the twelfth and thirteenth centuries than at other periods. They found everything interesting and acceptable; they aimed at universal culture, and built it up from the most diverse sources – Christian or classical antiquity, Byzantium, Armenia, the Muslim and Celtic civilizations. Yet the opposite dangers of diffuseness and eclecticism were avoided. This was an age which had great constructive powers; it was equally strong in analysis and synthesis and it succeeded in creating piece by piece a completely original civilization.

The basic work of medieval man was to define the literary genres, the different art techniques, the scientific disciplines, to formulate their objects and their methods, and thus ensure unity. Starting from classical, Celtic and Provençal contributions, he created for example the romance, a psychological study of the sentiments of imaginary characters, particularly people in love. By resolutely detaching the statue from its block of stone, he made sculpture once again the art of relief. He distinguished theology, based on revelation, from philosophy, which proceeded by observation and ratiocination.

Next, the branches of literature were integrated into one general movement, the arts into one style centred upon architecture, and the academic disciplines into a system dominated by theology. Painters, for instance, made only frescoes and stained glass, so that they were auxiliaries of the stonemasons, and all philosophers were also, and first of all, theologians.

Then the Middle Ages imposed on this total system the same fundamental characteristics which made up the complex of civilization at its best, the will to order, clarity and harmony. There was a kind of effortless audacity, exemplified in Guillaume de Lorris, who made a great poem of a code of love, in which the personages were abstractions, in the builders of cathedrals, who raised vaults a hundred feet from the ground, in the masters who challenged Aristotle. There was a taste for life, for the realities of life, animated and colourful, combined fortunately with an enthusiasm for ideas and a sense of the universal. Humanity and nature were never excluded, even from mysticism; no one forgot them, though no one dwelt on them; everyone tried to discern the type behind the individual, the spirit behind matter, the eternal behind the contingent. Hence the ideal of beauty, not strictly plastic, nor intangible; the predilection for symbolism, in which the story entertained the reader, whilst encouraging him to discover the equally intriguing inner meaning; the feeling for greatness and nobility. In fact, to condense this into one word, equanimity, the happy mean between cowardice and arrogance, clumsiness and mannerism, puritanism and affectation, poverty and prodigality, dogmatism and scepticism, unworldly intellectualism and coarse materialism – this was where the medieval ethic lay.

Finally, at the summit, the binding principle of this unity, stood the Church, as vigorous and cohesive as it had ever been. Since Gregory VII it had been tightly organized behind the Papacy, and after 1200 this hold became even tighter, through the Mendicant Friars and the universities, and through the imposition of a unified, exclusive body of canon law. The Church was monarchic, and very strong; its power was already undermined, but not yet shaken. More than a thousand years old, it remained a live and positive force, integrating and moulding to its pattern the most varied new elements; it dictated its laws to the new urban economy,[68] maintained a monopoly of teaching, and controlled the nascent universities; in 1220 Montpellier, whose foundation had been outside the Church, was brought firmly into the fold, and in 1257 the secular masters of the University of Paris had to admit defeat at the Church's hands. Classical thought was incorporated in theology and classical beauty in sculpture. Even Provençal poetry and the Celtic romance were assimilated; the Virgin Mary became the Lady of the last of the troubadours, courtly love was transmuted into that 'love which is love alone' of the German mystics, and Lancelot led to the epic of the Grail.

It was the Church then which integrated European civilization: because the Church was supra-national, and because it provided the framework of civilization, it followed that culture had no frontiers. Without the Church it seems unlikely that France could easily have gathered together so much talent on her soil and influenced the rest of Europe to such an extent. It is significant that her sway did not reach beyond the countries which followed the Roman Church.

The Church also gave medieval culture its deeper unity and originality. It was she who gave artists and scholars alike their *Weltanschauung*, and enabled them to create something new by breathing a fresh spirit into their borrowings from the ancients. It was she who created the characteristic pattern in which everything fell into place in a whole conceived by God and revealed to man. This state of equilibrium, in which every being is at the same time himself and something else, has both a personal and a symbolic value. Augustinian exemplarism overflowed from theology: it is to be seen in the saints, the peasants, the flowers carved in Chartres or Notre Dame, and even in the enduring love binding Tristan and Yseult. Everything is the creation and the reflection of the Eternal.

In the heart of the Middle Ages unity of culture was no more absolute than at any time in history. There were irregular currents that the Church had difficulty in controlling, even in strictly religious matters; heresies were numerous and often deep-seated. In the later thirteenth century there were already signs of profound changes. The Church registered a weakening of her influence in cultural and in public life. Her grasp over the State was weakening; it had developed a stronger political and administrative structure and was backed by growing national feeling, and by towns whose citizens showed a vigorous independence. The Church recoiled from the increasing realism of writers and artists; she was becoming old and tired, and was living in the past.

But these were still no more than warning signs: at the beginning of the fourteenth century a work of genius completed the remarkable edifice of Christian civilization in Europe. It already had its *Summae* of art, but it lacked a poetic *Summa*. Dante gave it this in the *Divine Comedy*, in which scholarly poetry, derived from courtly literature, was joined with popular poetry, instinct with Franciscan sensibility, and in which the whole universe, all knowledge and all beauty were brought together in a grand system with God at its summit.[70]

PART III
DUSK

Change is the essence of history; whilst medieval civilization was still in the ascendant its decline was already inevitable. The Church, its vital core, was faced with increasingly powerful enemies. Monarchies grew stronger, towns prospered, new ambitious forces arose, impelled by political and economic considerations rather than moral or religious imperatives, and every step forward increased their appetite for independent power. Between them and a priesthood jealous of its universal authority no agreement was possible. Long before the end of the medieval period the conflict which was to be so disastrous to the Papacy broke out.

After a few skirmishes the decisive struggle was engaged about 1300. The outcome was not in doubt: on the one side were monarchies systematically increasing their strength in spite of temporary setbacks, and townsfolk whose influence was based on their wealth; on the other a Church weakened by its struggle to maintain and tighten its hold on Europe in the previous century, torn by quarrels and schisms, racked by heresy, and enfeebled by abuses it was unable to rectify. The adversaries were ill-matched: the Church did not capitulate, but retreated, step by step, perhaps, but irretrievably.

The civilization which the Church had engendered and to which she was so closely linked, kept in step with her. Its unity, its harmony, its spirit, everything which identified it and gave it value was gradually lost. Nationalism took root, scientific studies broke away from theology, sculpture and painting threw off the yoke of architecture, music separated from poetry, literary currents diverged more and more. In every field trends were exaggerated; scholars, artists, writers, moved towards dogmatic extremes: verbalism or scepticism, mysticism or empiricism, mannerism or the opposite extreme of realism. Though everyone still professed to be Christian, many, particularly some of the most brilliant writers, were no longer inspired by the faith, and their works were not imbued with it; they drew their ideals from antiquity and tried to build a new world on its foundations. They failed indeed, but there were to be others who would succeed. From 1300 to 1450 the shadows lengthened over medieval culture, but the dawn of the modern age was appearing.

However, we must not fix our eyes on the lightening sky, we must not consider positive factors as we have done in previous parts of this book, or concern ourselves with the first evidences of a new civilization; we must rather follow the decline of the old, and move, with the Middle Ages, into the gathering dusk.

Chapter 10

THE SETTING: THE SEARCH FOR STABILITY

Western Europe in the fourteenth and fifteenth centuries seemed to be a world which had rejected most of the principles by which it was governed, and was feverishly striving to find new political, economic and social foundations. Unrest had been quelled for a while by the combined action of prelates and kings, but now violence reigned supreme. Civil wars and rebellions of nobility against monarchy combined with national conflicts, and their consequent rapine and devastation, to create an atmosphere of misery and apprehension. The economy, which had been developing healthily up till 1300 began to be saturated, and, in self-defence, was subjected to restriction and regulation. This was only a palliative, for excessive planning leads to paralysis. Other troubles arose at the same time; political unrest, monetary instability, national calamities. From decade to decade disorder increased, and from time to time the working classes, who were the most sorely tried, broke into rebellion. The Middle Ages were ending in misery and confusion.

Underneath the ruins, however, the seeds of the modern world were taking root. The rulers of Europe, amid the crises caused by the weaknesses of some of them and the resistance of the old order, were pursuing the programme they had had more or less consciously in view since the twelfth century, which had been rationalized, extended and given legal form by the philosophers and jurists of the thirteenth century. In the big cities, particularly in Italy, men of business were perfecting commercial techniques. A new order of things was growing up based on absolute monarchy and merchant capitalism.

Culture was affected both by the disorganization and by the new political structure. This will be discussed at the end of the chapter after we have dealt in outline with the political and economic history of this difficult but fertile period.

Kings stand out from the mass of actors in the political drama. The plot centres on them and their plans, and often they direct the action. The basic datum, everywhere the same, was simple and at the same time very complex, namely the reconstruction of the State. The development of the story lay in the opposition to these plans by nobility and clergy, successful or otherwise according to locality.

About 1100 – and we must go thus far back, for it was then that efforts were first made to restore royal authority – monarchy still suffered more or less in different countries from weaknesses inherited from barbaric ages, and aggravated by the universal spread of feudalism. It was a personal monarchy, but without full liberty of action: the state was no stronger in the twelfth century than in the fifth or sixth. There was no 'full, round' authority, to use the image of a thirteenth-century jurist, no sovereign will which could monopolize essential powers, the legislature and the judicature, and delegate them temporarily to individuals according to exact dispositions. The King had no specific duties and was not chosen on strict constitutional principles; at least his prerogatives and his mode of accession to the throne were ill-defined, and governed by circumstances rather than by theory. There were no officials worthy of the name; no numerous body, devoted, skilful, capable of supporting his government, executing his decisions, giving continuity to his actions and, in case of need, covering his weakness. In his household he had three or four great officers of state whose personal power rendered them more dangerous than useful, and a *curia regis* whose prerogatives were as vague as they were extensive, recruited at his pleasure amongst his familiars and vassals; in the country there were the Counts, who for many years in France, and more recently in Germany, had ceased to be the agents of central power, and in England the Sheriffs, more reliable, but tending soon after their creation to make their office hereditary and consequently less dependent. Generally speaking there was no more than an embryo administration. The monarchy had not subjects, but lieges: the great ones of the land were vassals of the King and regarded him as their feudal lord. There were no taxes unless we count the English Danegeld; in exceptional circumstances the King received an *auxilium* from his vassals; normally he lived on his demesne and other properties. Finally, the King had no army to speak of, apart from feudal contingents, whose help could never be relied on, and whose service was in any case severely limited by custom. Moreover the King was hemmed in by his barons below and the Church above. The former took a part in the King's nomination, and, in virtue of an ancient principle which feudalism had adopted, they deliberated with him on the graver affairs of state; all important decisions were to be made with their advice and counsel. The Church – following Gregorian principles – claimed the right to exercise control over the use of a power which God had granted for the material and spiritual good of the people.

In these conditions a series of measures was clearly essential for any monarch. First of all he had to ensure that the crown passed by right to his son, or better (but only the Castilian rulers thought of this in the thirteenth century) lay down in detail rules of succession in order to obviate crises resulting from the failure of male heirs. Then, he should reserve certain fundamental rights, such as the issuing of edicts of general application and the hearing of all law-suits either at first instance or by way of appeal. It was necessary to suppress the great Court dignities or leave them vacant and develop a nucleus of central administration, by bringing in, besides the great vassals, officials of such modest origin as to ensure their loyalty, but with the capacity and training to carry out their duties. The court was split into specialized sections: political council, courts of law, exchequer. The next task was to strengthen local administration and entrust it to officers recruited from the lesser nobility, and later the merchant classes, who were subject to dismissal, were moved about to prevent collusion with inferiors, and were rewarded by a salary and not by a fief, for fiefs were hereditary and tended to make the office hereditary. Officials must be compelled to render account of their acts from time to time to the central administration, and go out as commissioners on tours of inspection. Wider use must be made in financial affairs of written documents which would be a better safeguard for the royal revenues and would permit a more rigorous check on their management; and the royal demesne must be extended, and extraordinary resources multiplied by increasing and generalizing feudal aids, in order to pay for a mercenary army. Lastly, the monarch must free himself from domination by the barons, and from the theocratic claims of the Papacy, and must even gain control over the clergy. This was the programme which the Ottonians and the Salians had adumbrated in Germany as early as the tenth century, and which, in the twelfth century, the successors of William in England, the Normans and the Hohenstaufen in Sicily, the Capetians, the Castilian kings and the later German princes strove to realize little by little, as circumstances permitted.[1]

It was no small project, and at its beginnings it was vague and empirical, but theorists were soon at work to transform it into a formal doctrine and reduce it to a few clear propositions. What one might call the royal prerogative had never disappeared completely in Germany and England. In the latter country for instance the King had always insisted, at long intervals admittedly, on calling a great council or parliament. Even in France at the height of the feudal period some clerics had not forgotten that the King was in theory the source of law and justice. The ceremony of consecration had moreover set the Capetian kings apart from even the greatest of their lieges. But it was not till mid-twelfth century that the notions of Sovereignty and State were given some force.[2] From Roman sources Irnerius and his colleagues resuscitated the idea of a *potestas publica*, a public authority above all others, which acknowledged no restraint except the general good, and conferred upon its holder the privilege of making laws and raising taxes. A hundred years later Aristotelians derived from the '*Politics*' the concept of the State, a collective entity born of man's nature, the perfect autonomous society. The ruler of this state then, in whom the *potestas publica* was vested, 'emperor in his kingdom' to use a phrase of the time, held as of right the widest authority conceivable, without any control or limitation except that of the *bonum commune*. Before the end of the thirteenth century the civilians, and some of the scholastics, had thus defined the essence and extent of royal power, and *ipso facto* they legalized the King's actions and assigned to them a clear object: not despotism, for Machiavelli and the 'reason of State' were not to appear until the late fifteenth century, but absolutism. The whole programme of monarchy could now be defined in this one word.

The realization of this grandiose plan met opposition from the Church and the nobility which continued through the fourteenth and fifteenth centuries.

For a long time the Church had been the faithful and valued auxiliary of royalty. More interested than any other institution in the maintenance of order, she had given liberally of her culture and authority, and had trained the best royal servants: chancellors, counsellors, ambassadors, prince-bishops. By consecrating kings and proclaiming the exceptional nature of their mission she had helped them to survive their worst difficulties without serious harm.

Yet from the moment when kings declared their pretensions to absolutism, the Church's attitude changed, and for obvious reasons. The Gregorian theory, in the eleventh century, had claimed for the Church the right to censure and even depose rulers, and in course of time the theory had hardened.[3] It had become more trenchant than ever in the fourteenth century in the works of Giles of Rome, James of Viterbo and Alvaro Pelayo. The Church, wrote Giles, without mincing words, has universal authority in temporal matters: '*Omnia temporalia sunt sub dominio et potestate Ecclesiae.*'[4] The others argued in the same categorical way: God is one; his unity is reflected in the unity of creation, and demands, first, the unity of humanity, and, consequently, the unity of the power which governs humanity. This unique power cannot be devolved upon a temporal ruler, like the Emperor, for temporal possessions are given to Man only for spiritual ends and their use must therefore be governed and controlled by spiritual authority. This universal monarch can only be the Pope and he has full authority in temporal affairs: '*Omnia temporalia sunt sub dominio Ecclesiae collocata, si non de facto, de jure tamen, et ex debito temporalia summo pontifici sunt subjecta.*'[5]

In the eleventh century, after a fierce struggle, the Church had attained freedom and unity, centred on Rome. She had no intention of giving up these conquests willingly, and allowing the setting-up of more or less national churches. Within the Christian kingdoms she had acquired a privileged position which she was by no means prepared to abandon: her clerks could only be brought before ecclesiastical courts, they enjoyed exemption from taxes, and thus formed a state within the State. Rulers who were determined to be strong, and indeed absolute, could not tolerate such privileges, such independence under the protection of a foreign power, nor even the claim to them. They felt obliged sooner or later to subject to their jurisdiction and their taxation these ecclesiastics, who were amongst their richest and most powerful subjects, and not only to shake off the yoke of the Church, but even to arrogate to themselves some constitutional authority within it, in order to make use of its considerable influence in every sphere of life.

Conflict was inevitable – it had broken out in the twelfth century and went on until the end of the Middle Ages. The first blows were struck in England where political and administrative organization was already well advanced. Moved by the undue encroachment of ecclesiastical courts during the war of the two Matildas, the remarkable ease with which they granted benefit of clergy and their lenient sentences, Henry II, in the Constitutions of Clarendon, 1164, proposed to bring back the Church in England to its 'ancient customs', and in particular to settle the matter of ecclesiastical jurisdiction over temporal offences.[6] Fifty years later John Lackland launched a fierce attack on the clergy, drove the Archbishop of York into exile because he declined an aid to the King, refused to recognize Innocent II's candidate Stephen Langton as Archbishop of Canterbury, and seized the temporal possessions of the English clergy. Neither king was entirely successful, indeed the only result of John's attack was that his kingdom became a fief of the Holy See.

The next episode, decisive for the history of theocracy, took place about 1300 in France, which the Capet kings had now made the strongest kingdom in Western Europe. The question at issue was again that of the fiscal and judicial immunity of the clergy, but the argument was not long confined to secondary matters – the antagonists fought over the whole problem of the relations of Church and

State.[7] In his celebrated Bulls Boniface VIII took up the Gregorian position and proclaimed that 'the temporal power must bow down before the spiritual' and that 'it is for the spiritual authority to appoint the temporal and to judge it, if necessary'.[8] Philip the Fair and his party appealed to Roman law and affirmed that the King had no superior in the temporal affairs of his kingdom. Then they took rapid action. The Pope was arrested at Anagni on the 7th of September 1303, his death, provoked or hastened by this violence, took place on the 11th of October, and his successor annulled the condemnation of the king in April and May 1304. Supported by his people, who were shocked by the wealth and greed of the clergy and prone to dynastic loyalty, if not nationalist feeling, even at this early date, the French king had little difficulty in defeating the Papacy, now weaker than at the time of Innocent III. Theocracy had had its day, and only defeats were in store for it. Even the Golden Bull of 1356 which settled the procedure for the election and coronation of the Emperor, made no reference whatever to the Pope.

Having won a victory in the matter of elections the kings were determined to have their way, too, on the questions of the privilege and independence of the clergy, and to bring them under the same law as the commonalty of subjects. They were even more anxious to limit the interference of Rome in church affairs in their kingdoms, particularly in presentations to livings, and, urged by certain jurists, they determined to gain some control in these matters. About 1302 the author of the '*Dispute of the clerk and the knight*' demanded for the civil power the right of overseeing the spiritual domain. In his *Defensor Pacis* written in 1324 Marsilius of Padua was clearer still: he made the Church an element in the State. With his Parisian colleague Jean de Jandun and the Oxonian William Occam, who was undermining the foundations of medieval culture in many fields, and whom we shall have occasion to mention often in the course of this exposition, he worked out a philosophical and juridical theory of gallicanism, anglicanism, and Hussism, in fact of all those movements which were to gain credit gradually and destroy the Gregorian work of unification.[9]

The struggle continued, but there were no more sensational incidents and no more decisive victories. The Assembly of Vincennes in 1329 which forbade clerics to sit as judges, and the drafting in England of the two *Statutes of Provisors* 1351 and 1390, and the first and second *Statutes of Praemunire* 1353 and 1393, which settled collation to benefices and appeals to the papal courts, had neither the importance nor the wide repercussions of the quarrel with Boniface. It was by a persistent, invisible process that the kings and their agents reduced the jurisdiction of the Official, compelled clerics to contribute to public revenue, and established their interest in ecclesiastical appointments.[10] They were not completely successful. Benefit of clergy was not abolished nor the right of the clergy to agree taxation, and after 1418 it was by Concordats, compromises in fact, that the delicate question of presentment to benefices was resolved.[11]

The nobility, another conservative force, pitted itself, like the Church, against monarchist innovations. In some regions it was independent within its demesne, and even within all its fiefs, and wished to remain so. In others the nobles at least held valuable privileges, particularly that of being consulted in all high matters of state, and refused to give them up. Therefore as soon as rulers showed clearly a tendency towards centralization and absolutism, a battle was engaged whose fortunes varied greatly from one kingdom to another. Paradoxically it was the English monarchy, the strongest of all in the twelfth century, which offered the least resistance to the attacks of the barons. Born of the Conquest of 1066, based on a happy combination of elements borrowed from Anglo-Saxon kingship and the feudal system, and rich in confiscated lands, the monarchy was at first very strong. It was in a position to curb the barons, to lay down their military obligations, limit their judicial privileges and restrict their building of castles. It gave England, a hundred years before France, a highly developed political and administrative system; at the centre a *curia regis* split into specialized organs, the Council, the Chancery, with the records, the Exchequer controlling finance, and the judicial bench; in the counties there were the sheriffs, royal officials under the control of the Court. But the very strength of English monarchy became a handicap, for it induced many a mediocre king to behave despotically, and consequently compelled the magnates, both laymen and ecclesiastics, to act in concert against him. As individuals they would never have been able to resist the King's power, but united they were often able to mate his moves. They took advantage of his mistakes and his constant lack of money, occasioned by repeated wars against Scotland, Ireland, Wales or France. They even won pitched battles against him. Gradually there grew out of their diplomatic and military victories a system which was not democratic, but at least constitutional, characterized at the end of the Middle Ages by the institution of Parliament. In the thirteenth century it was no more than a widened form of the *curia* whose principal activity was to be a high court of justice, in which the King's men held an important place. In the fourteenth century both its composition and its powers changed considerably: political questions now occupied it more than judicial decisions. In its regular and frequent sessions it judged political crimes, received complaints and petitions, promulgated laws, granted subsidies, the essential revenue of the monarchy, and fixed their rate and their incidence. At the same time the barons set themselves above the officials and formed a closed group of hereditary peers, supported by the great dignitaries of the Church. From 1327 the representatives of counties, cities and towns met regularly, and soon formed a House of Commons distinct from the Lords but closely dependent on them. The institution of Parliament thus took on gradually the form which is now familiar, and became an essential mechanism of government,[12] a transformation less dangerous to the crown than might at first appear. What was lost in scope was gained in stability, for Parliament by voting subsidies, ensured regular resources for the King, besides bringing him the valuable support of the people whom they represented. Thus kingship was firmly established and was able to weather the terrible civil war fought by the Yorkist and Lancastrian factions from 1450 to 1471.

In fourteenth- and fifteenth-century Spain, as in England, and indeed even more so, the nobles, enriched by the *Reconquista*, offered resistance to the crown; but by abusing their strength they hopelessly jeopardized their position. With the clergy and the delegates of the cities they controlled the royal power in the *Cortes*, the oldest representative assemblies in Europe. They flaunted their power with impunity in endless coalitions; but the troubles they stirred up, together with violent dynastic struggles, greatly weakened their position. The longer they continued, the more there awoke both in town and country a longing for a government capable of maintaining order. Imperceptibly the door was opening to authoritarian monarchy, even to absolutism. As the modern age dawned an absolute monarchy appeared – the *Reyes catolicos*, more repressive than the Tudors, and more long-lasting. The rout of the proud aristocrats of Spain was complete, as complete as that of the feudal lords on the other side of the Pyrenees, whose leaders, in these last medieval centuries, were as utterly lacking in political sense as the grandees. The French nobles had not lacked opportunities, but their disunity prevented their profiting from the initial difficulties of the monarchy, or the terrible crises it endured in the fourteenth and fifteenth centuries, and they suffered defeat.

About 1100 the Capetians were weak: they could not even control the Île de France. They had first of all to restore order, then to extend their domains, and it was only at the very end of the twelfth century that they could think of laying claim to sovereign rights and building an administration imitated from the English system. From this moment progress was rapid – so that in 1300 under Philip the Fair, France was held by all to be the most powerful kingdom in Christendom. The French monarchy remained vulnerable, however, because it was largely feudal. Its resources were to all intents and purposes only the revenues of the royal demesne, and the budget was frequently in deficit. For, although the royal demesne had grown considerably and commercial development before 1300 had greatly increased its product, expenditure too had grown even faster. Without taking into account the style of the court, and the pensions and favours distributed, there was now a great body of officials to support, fortifications to maintain, mercenaries to be paid, and an interminable war against England to be financed. It is true that for this last the King could call on the whole country to provide subsidies in view of the war. But these subsidies, derived from the feudal aids, remained exceptional, so difficult was it to substitute the idea of a state tax for the traditional ideas implanted in the mass of the people. It was not only subjects, however, who found it difficult to accept new ideas. Many of the kings, the Valois particularly, could not get away from personal and feudal conceptions of power and adopt the modern ideas of the jurists. They were unable to see their authority as *sui generis*, and consequently to devolve it in organized ways. They insisted on regarding the kingdom as a vast demesne or a fief of which they were the feudal lords, rather than a State of which they had the temporary governance, and they had no hesitation in cutting rich apanages out of them for their younger sons: a terrible blunder, heavy with consequences. This was one cause of the Hundred Years' War. It also permitted the creation of a new form of feudalism, more dangerous in its ambitions than the English. The feudal lords did not, however, succeed any better than the earlier nobles, since they were equally incapable of unity.

Unity, in fact, was what the French nobles lacked in their struggle with royalty. In the thirteenth century each one of its leaders was strong enough to pit his weight against the King's, and none of them felt the need for coalition. They always went into battle in open order and never managed to divest themselves of the habit; and so they never gained a decisive victory.

In any case rebellion, civil strife, and wars against foreign invaders, with their dreadful consequences, did less harm to the crown than to the nobles. They were themselves decimated, their finances, already seriously affected by devaluation, wasteful luxury and bad management, were weakened still more by wars, which at the same time awoke national sentiment and a desire for peace. In France, and elsewhere, disorders were of comparative advantage to the King. The Hundred Years' War led to the absolutism of Louis XI, just as the Wars of the Roses were followed by the authoritarian rule of the Tudors, and Castilian anarchy by that of Ferdinand and Isabella. In

France, England and Spain the Middle Ages ended with the defeat of feudalism, complete on the continent, only partial in England, where the House of Lords remained to the peers.

What was true of these great powers was also true of what had been the Empire. Centralization and authoritarianism scored a victory over the forces of fission and dispersion in the German principalities, and, with the Dukes of Burgundy and the 'tyrants', in the rich and powerful towns of the Low Countries and Italy.

Political disorder was matched by economic difficulties and social upsets, phenomena which proceeded largely from the same causes, but whose importance varied from region to region in proportion to the strength of the different factors involved.

From somewhere about the end of the tenth century until 1300 the European economy had steadily advanced, but after that it entered a period of stability, if not actual contraction. Although in subsequent years there were prosperous phases in this or that country, there were also economic crises which grew ever more serious. To establish the causes of these movements in the present state of knowledge is no easy matter.

At the root of the trouble it seems there lay a phenomenon of saturation whose effects were only aggravated by the false remedies applied. If production was not increased it was because in general it was becoming more difficult to find a market. One after another, areas became industrialized: centres of manufacture became greater in number and competition became fierce, whilst improvements in transport and commercial technique only served to make it fiercer still.[13] Outlets no longer increased, either in Western Europe, where population was stationary, or in the East where farmers were no longer making inroads into Slav lands and attracting merchants to the heart of Russia and the shores of the Black Sea. The horizon was not expanding either on land or sea.

What was the cause of this economic saturation? Guided by knowledge of the previous period we are tempted to answer: demographic variations. It was the rising tide of population which had given an impetus to the economy in the tenth century, and, as numbers increased, had pushed it higher and higher, further and further. Since about 1300 or 1325 the wave no longer advanced, even if it did not actually retreat. Here again, however, our only reliable and precise figures are for England, where the number of inhabitants, which had noticeably increased between 1086 and 1240, had only risen slowly from 1240 to 1348, and between this last date and 1430 it had dropped by half![14] We are less well informed about the continent. We only know, for example, that in 1789 France had scarcely any more households than in 1328: 4,806,183 against 4,398,750. But where there are no actual figures there are sufficiently clear indications: the slowing up, indeed the end of land clearance: the great period of the '*Roden*' the '*assarts*' or the '*artigues*' was closed, in many places areas of land and even whole farms were abandoned. Another sign was the diminution of the acreage under corn, or the end of the growth of towns, even the shrinkage of many: Toulouse, to cite one instance, lost half its inhabitants in a century.

It is not certain, however, that this movement holds the key to the enigma. It certainly provoked stabilization of demand, and consequently of supply. But it could only be taken as the true explanation of the economic malaise if it could be proved to have been caused by diminished vitality in Western Europe and if it had incontestably preceded the stagnation. Neither of these can be demonstrated.

It is possible, even probable, that the reversal of the demographic trend may have been due to a fall in the birth-rate, showing a drop in vitality, but it is not certain. Disasters on a large scale may have been the cause of the stationary or falling population. At no time were they worse than in the fourteenth century. Wars ravaged the countryside; armies of soldiers, and during intervals of truce, idle leaders and disbanded mercenaries, pillaged, slaughtered, and burned untiringly. There were social uprisings, just as costly in human lives, peasant revolts, prompted by terrible poverty, or the wild hope of destroying the seignorial system, riots of the common people of the big towns against capitalist exploitation. Famines too, one of which lasted from 1315 to 1317, and in six months carried off 15 per cent of the population of Ypres. Finally terrifying epidemics broke out: the famous Black Death of 1347–50, which in the Burgundian village of Givry, where the average annual death rate was 30 to 40, caused 650 deaths in 5 months, and carried off perhaps a third of the population in most Western countries, the weakest and least productive third it is true; the plague of 1360–3; other more localized outbreaks in 1371–4, 1381–4 and in 1400 in Italy. Never had Christian people suffered so much from the three great scourges of mankind – famine, pestilence and war.

It cannot be affirmed categorically then, that demographic stagnation preceded and occasioned economic stagnation, since we are not in a position to date the two phenomena. Possibly the opposite was the case; population stopped increasing as a defence mechanism, a useless one of course, more likely to worsen than to improve the state of affairs.

Another equally foolish reaction was the attempt to control the economy by official regulation. Public authorities tried to lessen the effects of competition by multiplying restrictive decrees. Some of them gave the legally constituted guilds a monopoly of production within the town and its outskirts, even in the surrounding country, as far as the town's jurisdiction extended.[15] Other ordinances, and they were many, laid down the distribution of raw materials, the maximum size of enterprises, rates of pay, hours of work and, in unusual detail, the methods of manufacture.[16] Some restricted the freedom of foreign merchants and forbade them, for instance, to trade directly among themselves. So the commerce of towns was hampered by severe restrictions, limited to traditional practices, and lacked any stimulus to initiative. Competition was limited, expansion of workshops closely controlled, technical progress forbidden. A day came when the workmen, the 'journeymen', were forced to give up hope of climbing the social ladder; the right to take the rank of master, which had been hereditary in some guilds, now tended to become hereditary in all.

Stagnation can be explained then by saturation of markets, levelling-off of the population curve, and excessive controls. But this does not explain the recurrent crises.[17] Other phenomena triggered them off, sometimes an imbalance of supply and demand. It could happen that supply was unusually low: a series of bad harvests, a resulting dearth of food, with a consequent rise in prices, and the consumer would cut down his consumption of less essential goods, thus upsetting the whole economy. Or an epidemic broke out, there was a shortage of labour and a marked increase in wages, a situation particularly damaging to the employer if the demands of the workers coincided with a drop in the price of manufactured goods. The only resort was the usual shifts, an appeal to authority to restrict either wages or production. Sometimes, but this was exceptional, the opposite situation arose in the industrial sphere: for some trifling reason such as a change in taste there might be overproduction in some sector, and, by a now only too familiar process, it would affect other sectors too. But most often wars were the disruptive element, the great wars of the fourteenth and fifteenth centuries, which upset the economy in a number of ways. They caused general insecurity, for the merchant hesitated to travel over roads infested by pillaging mercenaries. Financial instability resulted from their high cost, the consequent rise in taxation, and devaluation. Aids and subsidies were more frequent. New indirect taxes were imposed, customs tolls and excise levies. Money melted away: in France in the year 1421–2 the coinage lost ninety per cent of its value. This instability of prices was a basis for lucrative speculation for clever traders, and a cause of misery for others; it was thus the seed of great changes of fortune and of social conflict.

214

The diffusion of communistic doctrines helped to exacerbate these conflicts. For a long time intellectuals and heterodox spirits had criticized the established order and all the inequality which it embodied. The Fleming van Maerlant, for example, wrote in his *Wapene Martijn* 'There are two dreadful words in the world, Mine and Thine. If we could suppress them peace and concord would reign everywhere. Men and women would all be free; there would be no more slaves. All things would be in common, corn and wine. Wealth is abundant; it should be enjoyed in common and given to those who are poor. Then all war would cease, and souls would be washed and purified of sin.'[18] In some countries, England particularly, these theories were given wide currency by the disasters of the day, and became part of the doctrine of certain religious sects. In the fourteenth century they infected whole layers of the population and encouraged them to rebel against the propertied classes. Of all the countries of Europe France was the one most affected by every kind of ill,[19] except social upheavals. The support given by royalty to the burghers of the towns prevented the rebellions which set the 'thin' against the 'fat', as the Italians put it, and the only serious peasant revolt, the Jacquerie of 1358, was too localized and too easily suppressed to inflict serious damage on the country. From the time of Philip the Fair, France suffered greatly from monetary manipulation; and after the succession of the Valois kings she was the theatre of an unprecedented calamity, the Hundred Years' War, in which hordes of paid-off mercenaries, who were no better than armed bandits, completed the work of murder and pillage done by the regular armies.[20] What was worse, the insecurity born of these troubles, and the development of navigation, turned away from France the currents of trade which had brought prosperity in the thirteenth century. Communication between Italy and Flanders, the two poles of European commerce, was now made by sea and not as heretofore through the fairs of Champagne.

The situation in England was similar. There too urban rebellions were unknown, but in 1381 there was an important peasant revolt led by Wat Tyler, which lasted several weeks, and the kingdom also suffered from its involvement in the Hundred Years' War. The country was not ruined directly by military operations, but just as certainly by crushing taxation, currency devaluations, and a civil war caused by defeats in France and general distress. It is true that in the same period, encouraged by Edward III, England was developing her commercial and industrial possibilities; raw wool was no longer exported as such, but was now woven and sold as cloth. The English also discovered the sea and began to use it as a means of expanding trade, but in these promising directions they were only taking their first steps. The great economic strongholds at the end of the Middle Ages were still the towns of the Low Countries, Italy and the Baltic.

The towns of the Netherlands were at grips with serious problems.[21] Their basic industry was weaving, in which competition was more bitter in this last part of the medieval period than in any other trade. Everywhere there were new or expanding centres of production, some in the towns and villages of Flanders, others in East Anglia, Northern Italy, Normandy and elsewhere. Restricted by regulations which it insisted on maintaining and even tightening up, the old Flemish cloth trade had difficulty in competing with younger rivals with more freedom of action and more capacity to adapt to changes of taste. The supply of raw materials was a great anxiety too. Several times England, the traditional source of supply, had halted delivery for political reasons. Worse still, the English began to manufacture cloth themselves. There were other sources, Spain, in particular, but their wool was a shorter and rougher type and required alterations in the mode of manufacture. The country weavers adapted themselves to it, but the big towns objected: the lack of enterprise of their citizens handicapped them. Of old their merchants had travelled by land and sea to find outlets for their wares, but now they sat at home and waited for custom. Lastly, economic difficulties were increased by class struggles of unwonted violence. The artisans rose against oppressive capitalists who had a monopoly of commerce and public administration, and, once victorious, they quarrelled among themselves for years.

Because of these conditions the great Flemish cities declined. One of them, Ypres, was in a poor way in 1300. Ghent was more resistant and up to the end of the Middle Ages was one of the most active towns of Europe; her artisans had acquired such skill and reputation that their rivals needed many years in which to catch up. Ghent had also the advantage of being close to Bruges, which provided an excellent outlet for her, as for the younger towns of Brabant. Far from regressing, the town on the Zwyn was at its most prosperous in the fourteenth century. It was the natural centre for maritime commerce, which was displacing land commerce, an obligatory port of call for Mediterranean galleys and Scandinavian 'Kogges', and thus the great market place of the period. And about 1450, when Bruges too was paralysed by restrictions, victim of her own outdated and troublesome protectionism, and began to decline, the neighbouring port of Antwerp, which had grown up during the last century of the Middle Ages, in comparative freedom from restrictions, took over. Modern Antwerp usurped the trade of medieval Bruges, just as the '*nieuwe draperie*' of the countryside made great strides in comparison

ITALIAN TRADING COLONIES IN THE LEVANT & THE ADVANCE OF THE TURKS

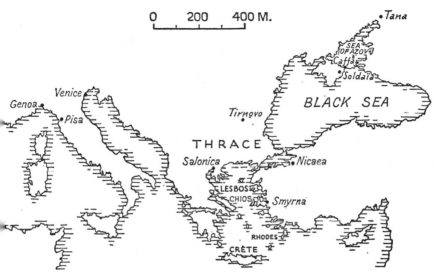

with the old guild industry of the cities. Prosperity was not to desert the Low Countries.

The great Italian cities, in spite of their constant quarrels, which were economic rather than political in origin, maintained their lead over the rest of Europe better than the Flemings.[22] Venice and Genoa tightened up their monopoly of commerce with the East and opened new trading posts in the Greek Islands, at Chios and Lesbos, on the Black Sea, at Caffa and Soldaia, and even in the distant Sea of Azov at Tana. Venice developed new resources by starting the manufacture of silks and glassware, whilst Genoa founded the Casa di San Giorgio, ancestor of modern banking. But the great industrial and financial centre of the peninsula was Florence, with her cloth trade, which, at the end of the fourteenth century, was comparable to that of Flanders, and her companies, the most celebrated being that of the Medici family. By utilizing and improving on thirteenth-century innovations, written records and accountancy, merchants were able to stay at home and conduct their business through correspondents, instead of continually travelling, thus greatly increasing their efficiency; and these powerful family firms, with branches in every important commercial centre, engaged in a number of profitable activities, trade, money-lending, exchange, marine insurance, tax-farming. So long as they were not drawn by speculation into risky

217

operations they reaped rich profits. Italy was the essential intermediary between East and West, well supplied with capital, and cleverer than anyone at investing it. She retained in the fourteenth and fifteenth centuries an unchallenged supremacy in commerce.

But circumstances were already conspiring to destroy her. Whole states were organizing their economy and were soon in a position to compete successfully with isolated cities. Even more important was the advance of the Turks, who reached Smyrna in 1320, Nicaea in 1331, Thrace in 1362, Tirnovo in 1393, Salonica in 1430. The old trade route with the East was closed. Then in 1434 Portuguese navigators reached Cape Bojador, in 1437 the Azores, in 1482 the mouth of the Congo, in 1485 the Cape of Good Hope and in 1497 Calicut. A new route was now open but it started from Portugal; it opened a new era, the era of the Atlantic, not the Mediterranean.

The towns of the German Hansa suffered a similar fate, brought on by their quarrels among themselves, their conservatism, and the rise of the Scandinavian states. Until the fifteenth century the Hansa towns had control of the Northern seas, but by the sixteenth they had lost it. They were losing ground, too, to the cities of South Germany, which were stimulated to activity by the proximity of Venice, their position between the Adriatic and the Baltic, and the exploitation of the Central European mines.[23] Thus while absolutism was triumphant, the essential features of a modern economy were appearing, with its trend towards liberal capitalism, its improved methods of credit, its new axes: Antwerp, England, the Atlantic. But the movement was slow: until the middle of the fifteenth century Florence and Bruges remained the commercial poles of Europe, but over-regulation of trade discouraged initiative and aggravated the ills it was intended to cure. The end of the Middle Ages was a gloomy period of political struggles, economic difficulties and social conflicts.

Cultural life could not but be influenced by these changes. They were reflected in the quantity, quality and source of its achievements.

A devastated and impoverished France no longer led western civilization towards new horizons. In spite of the enlightened patronage of the Valois kings her influence faded and her place was taken by Italy and the Netherlands, both of them rich countries, full of prosperous towns, whose prosperity was sufficiently long-standing for their citizens to have time for other activities than money-making.[24] There is always an interval between economic success and the intellectual and artistic activity which it makes possible. When a town is founded its inhabitants for some time think only of amassing wealth. It is only after several generations that they conceive more noble ambitions and aspire to enrich their lives with art and learning.

This evolution was observed in Florence between 1250 and 1300 by two contemporaries, Dante and Villani. Thanks to it, the initiative of a few literary men, and the patronage of the Medici family Florence became the cradle of humanism. The towns of the Netherlands, which had also been prosperous for a long period, disputed the crown with Italy, not, it is true in the revival of classical antiquity, which had left no trace there, but in civil architecture. They began to build enthusiastically in mid-thirteenth century, and after 1300 endowed their towns with belfries, market halls and guildhalls. At the end of the fourteenth century and in the early fifteenth, under the patronage of the Dukes of Burgundy, Sluter's achievements in sculpture, the Van Eycks' in painting and Dufay's in music were outstanding.

But whatever the activity of these towns, and their smaller neighbours, the number of scholarly and literary works was smaller after 1300 than before. Masterpieces were certainly more rare. The total for the fourteenth and fifteenth centuries is meagre compared with that of the two preceding centuries. To a great extent this is the effect of the falling population and the gravity and persistence of political and economic troubles.[25]

These troubles not only put a brake on cultural development; they also left their mark on it in the pessimism of some writers and the predilection of others for scenes of pathos. We can surely attribute to the misfortunes of the age the lack of that balance which was such a marked characteristic of the previous era.

Universality, that typically medieval characteristic, was also compromised by the general environment. The efforts of kings to create states and the battles that ensued, aroused or strengthened national sentiment. Each country's inhabitants became conscious of their common patrimony, language, material interests, or a glorious past. The importance of towns which had become, in their prosperity, centres of social life, gave a new value to their citizens' particular characteristics. Europe in the fifteenth century tended to split up into religious and cultural entities. In England protest was vehement against inducting foreigners into benefices. The reforms of religious orders were carried out by national congregations. The Huss heresy was a Czech matter.[26] The philosopher and scholar Nicole Oresme wrote in French, the historians Villani and Lopez de Ayala in Italian and Spanish, the mystic Suso in German, his contemporary Ruysbroeck in Dutch, the political theorist John Fortescue in English. In their works there is often more than a language difference, there is a national difference. In the monk of Groenendael for instance, a mystic who reached the summits of contemplation without losing his sense of the concrete, we see the ancestor of those

219

Flemish artists who painted reality with minute exactitude whilst distilling the essence of spirituality. Distinct civilizations began to take the place of the universal civilization of the thirteenth century; perhaps it would be truer to say that there are national variations on the same theme.

There was another, more fundamental, cause acting in this direction – the decline of the Church's authority, which had given unity to medieval culture. Now both kings and city corporations were making onslaughts on it. They were all anxious to bring clerks under the common law in judicial and fiscal matters, and the city authorities in particular wanted to carry out the duties entrusted to them by their fellow citizens – public administration, justice, charity and education – without outside interference. In order to limit the clergy's influence and prevent too much property being immobilized in their hands they also laid down conditions for the acquisition of houses and lands *intra muros* by religious institutions, or forbade it altogether. The Church's prestige was weakened by these measures, but it was more seriously undermined by its own policy in this final era of the Middle Ages, during which it brought disruption and discredit upon itself.

Chapter 11

SPIRIT: CHURCH AND PAPACY IN PERIL

In 1291 the Mamelukes captured Acre, the last stronghold of the Crusaders' descendants. The Ottoman Turks, their blood-brothers, captured the Byzantine citadels of Asia Minor – Bursa in 1326, Nicaea in 1329, Nicomedia in 1337. About 1350 they crossed the Straits and began the conquest of the Balkans. The Holy See appealed to the faithful time and time again, first to recapture the Holy Land, then to resist the advancing infidel. Only the marches of Christendom answered the appeal, Hungary, Bosnia, Serbia and Albania, for they were directly menaced by the Turk. Elsewhere, except in 1396, there was no response, or at least it was barely perceptible. The time of Urban II was gone, and the crusading spirit of Saint Louis's day. Europe was now divided by intestine quarrels which took up all its energy and prevented it making a united effort on a large scale. By reason of the growing power of monarchy and town, politics and trade took precedence over spiritual matters; national and commercial interest spoke louder than religion. At this juncture Church and Papacy were squandering the vast authority they had built up. Weaker and weaker, more and more discredited, they were no longer able to impose their will and carry Europe along in their wake.

During the fourteenth and fifteenth centuries, in fact, both Church and Papacy passed through a new crisis, more complex, and in many ways more serious, than that of the tenth and eleventh centuries. The abuses which had weakened them and lost them credit even with the most devout, were now accompanied by grave dissensions. The exile of the Popes to Avignon, where they fell under French influence, furnished arguments to the proponents of freedom for national churches, as against papal authority. With the return of the pontiffs to Rome in 1378 the Great Schism opened. For forty years it divided Europe and provided an opportunity for believers in the superiority of Council over Pope to elaborate their doctrine, and pass from words to deeds. The Inquisition was powerless to prevent the birth

221

and diffusion of ever more dangerous heresies, which threatened soon to divide Christendom.

At the beginning of the fourteenth century, in his letter announcing an oecumenical council to be held at Vienne in 1311, Clement V included in the agenda the reform of morals, those of the clergy in particular, and invited the bishops to give him their views on this matter. In deference to this command Guillaume Lemaire, Bishop of Angers, listed, in a lengthy report, a series of abuses which he thought it urgent to correct, and ended by demanding, in terms fashionable at the time, a general reform of the Church, 'in its head as in its members'. Twenty or thirty years later the Franciscan Alvaro Pelayo, John XXII's confessor, remarked with some bitterness, in the Prologue of his *De statu et planctu Ecclesiae*, Book II, that the Church had lost much of its purity and holiness. Later in the fourteenth century Saint Catherine of Siena declaimed vehemently against priests 'who spend holy days in hunting, debauchery and carousing with the creatures of the Devil'. The Council of Constance, 1417–18, found it necessary to issue edicts on the 'morals and good living of clerks'.[1] Thus complaints about the clergy's way of life were many. Let us see what in fact was alleged against them.

First, their immorality. Certainly it was rife; the result of bad recruitment, inadequate training, and the influence of secular society, for immorality was general, particularly amongst the ruling class. There was no lack of clerics who were guilty of gaming, tippling or keeping concubines, but only detailed research could tell us whether they formed a majority. The answer might well be that the life of the clerk in this period was lacking in dignity rather than violently unprincipled.[2]

A more serious matter was the neglect of pastoral duties.[3] This was not a weakness of the sovereign pontiffs, either those of Rome or of Avignon: they had their faults, but this was not one of them. Many bishops, however, bastards or younger sons of the nobility, who had entered the Church in pursuit of wealth or power, and acquired their benefices with the support of some prince, gave all their attention to politics and worldly matters.[4] They delegated spiritual duties to subordinates, rarely visited their bishoprics, and took no trouble to direct their clergy and assemble them in synods, nor to perambulate their dioceses, so as to make contact with their flock and ensure that their spiritual diet was adequate. Many canons, recruited in a similar way, showed less interest in the divine office than in the profits of their prebend. With the best will in the world some of them could not have assumed the duties of all the benefices they had cumulated; it was quite impossible to be at one and the same time in Utrecht, Antwerp,

Louvain, Brussels and Maubeuge. Parish priests of doubtful vocation, selected without discernment by their presentors, and left to their own devices by their superiors, carried out their duties badly; their standard of preaching was low, and they often absented themselves from their parishes, or employed a vicar by way of replacement, to whom they gave a pitiful proportion of their living. Barely educated themselves, they had scarcely enough knowledge of doctrine to impart it to their parishioners. As late as 1569 Fray Lorenço de Villavicencio wrote to Philip II: 'In Your Majesty's Low Countries the parsons of the towns and villages are ignorant and mercenary. They do not know what doctrine is Catholic and what heretical, so that they cannot impart true doctrine to their charges.'[5] Thus in spite of some efforts by the regular clergy in particular, and some diffusion of books and pious images, religious ignorance was widespread, a situation which facilitated the reforming preachers' task; their enthusiasm was in contrast with the apathy of the priesthood generally.

What most degraded the clergy and alienated their flock was their cupidity: at every level of the hierarchy there was a scramble for money and a life of luxury and ease. At the top the Avignon popes introduced, or at least generalized, the system of multiple taxes, gathered in the most grasping manner by their collectors. At a lower level cardinals, bishops, prelates, canons fought for benefices, and some contrived to cumulate eight, ten, twelve or more. One pluralist cardinal in the fourteenth century held twenty-three; another in the fifteenth century was titular of four bishoprics, five abbeys and three priories in France alone, apart from his Italian benefices.

On the lowest rung of the ladder clustered a multitude of rectors whose parishes had been ruined by war and famine, curates reduced to a *portio congruens*, and altarists dependent on an endowment, an ecclesiastical proletariat scrambling for crusts at the feast. In their case cupidity was sharpened by real poverty.

Church authority was by no means indifferent to such grave and patent ills, but lacked the strength and the energy necessary to remedy them. In the middle of the fourteenth century Innocent VI commanded his court to follow a life of austerity, setting an example himself, and solemnly prohibited two of the most baneful practices of the time: plurality of benefices and the concession of abbacies *in commendam*.[6] However he was unable to make these prohibitions effective. Two generations later the Councils of Constance and Basle, which were expected to propose a great reform of the Church, promulgated a few decrees on the conduct of the clergy, but did not dare to meddle in these two crucial questions because, as one of those attending the Councils remarked, too many powerful personages, clerics and princes, were interested parties: *'quia multos tangebat, nunquam prohiberi potuit.'*[7]

The regular clergy too suffered a decline, but were quicker to initiate a reform movement.

In the thirteenth century and more generally in the fourteenth many houses had mitigated the severity of their rule, particularly in the matter of poverty. Their income was converted into prebends and private possessions were legitimized, even in the orders which, in the Gregorian period, had been based on absolute individual poverty and total community of possessions, like the Cistercians and the Premonstratensians,[8] or the younger Mendicant Orders, in which even collective property had been forbidden. Since about 1350 a good many French Dominican houses had shared out their revenues amongst the members of the community, and assigned to them, or indeed farmed out to the highest bidder, districts in which they might preach and collect alms.[9] As for the Franciscans, they had split after their founder's death, one faction, the 'Observants', fiercely defending the ideals of the *'Poverello'*, and the others, the 'Conventuals', claiming they were unrealizable, or at least not compatible with a life of teaching and preaching. After a long struggle, which shook the whole Church, the latter were victorious, with the result that many houses of Minors about 1350, though not exactly owning property, at least had the enjoyment of houses and incomes which brought them a good deal more than the 'strict essentials'.

There was some excuse for this relaxation of the old rules: often enough, in the older orders particularly, the Superiors, instead of being elected by the community amongst themselves, were outsiders appointed by Rome, frequently under pressure from secular powers, and their authority was as frail as their piety. They could not easily rule men to whom they were strangers and who had had no say in their election. Many of them, moreover, were highly placed ecclesiastics or younger sons of powerful families who were only interested in the income of the benefice which they held *in commendam*, and did not even reside in the house they governed. Religious houses had multiplied with the increase in the population, and now that it was stationary or regressing there were too many of them. It was common in the fourteenth century to find houses with less than a dozen members, too few for a proper conventual life to flourish. Political and economic disturbances were particularly harmful to institutions which depended on a settled society and stable incomes.

Yet although the life of the regular clergy was affected it was not made impossible. This is shown by the fact that, although the general situation did not improve after 1350, there was a noticeable improvement in the monastic world. There were many reform movements, encouraged by popes and princes, varying in their scope but identical in intention. Whether they were local or national, they all aimed to return to what were thought to be the primitive customs of the order, and to tighten the links between the different houses in order to prevent backsliding. It was thus that, soon after 1354, Paolo Trinci founded the Observant reform amongst the Italian Franciscans, and in 1406 Saint Colette founded the Poor Clares. Generals, provincials and simple brethren, all worked to reform the Dominicans – Raymond of Capua, Conrad of Prussia, Giovanni Dominici and Barthélemy Texier. In 1442 many Carmelites joined in the congregation of Mantua, the Spanish Cistercians in that of Mount Sion, the old Benedictine abbeys regrouped round a number of centres, Kastl in the Palatinate in 1404, St. Justine in Padua in 1408, Melk on the Danube in 1418, Bursfeld, near Göttingen, in 1439, Valladolid in 1450, and Monte Cassino in 1504.

At the same time new religious families were founded: the Alexians in the Netherlands in 1348, the Italian Jesuates in 1360, the Hieronymites in Spain in 1370 and 1380. Saint Brigid of Sweden founded the Order of the Holy Saviour and His Blessed Mother in 1346, Gerard Groot the Brothers of the Common Life about 1380, Florent Radewijns the Canons Regular of Windesheim in 1387, and Saint Francis of Paola the Minims in 1435. None of these spread in the way that Cluny and Cîteaux had done in earlier times. There were far more religious houses in the fourteenth century than at the beginning of the tenth or even at the end of the twelfth, and the population had now stopped increasing. Nevertheless the Brigittines counted some eighty convents in Scandinavia at the end of the Middle Ages, the Windesheim congregation had about 115 in Germany and the Low Countries, and the Minims about 450, largely in Latin countries.

Unfortunately the new foundations only served to increase the great diversity of regular orders, and the reforms in the end had the same effect. They were by no means able to bring about changes in all the monasteries and convents of Europe, and like the reforms of the tenth and eleventh centuries they caused many scissions within the older orders. The Dominicans were able to preserve their unity, but the Franciscans, by the end of the fifteenth century had split into Conventuals, Observants (or Friars of the Regular Observance), divided into two congregations, Recollects (or Friars of the Stricter Observance) and Alcantarines (or Discalced Friars).

As the Middle Ages declined disunity grew, and the traditional bickering between orders became universal. In the thirteenth century the secular clergy had been in dispute with the Mendicants, whom they accused of encroaching on their recognized domain, and now, on top of this, there were internal quarrels between lax and reformed sections of the same order.

These divisions and dissensions, however, were not the gravest danger to the Church; arguments over the powers of the Holy See, and the multiplication of heresies were both much more dangerous.

For the Papacy, keystone of the Church, the last phase of the Middle Ages was truly critical. Whilst the claim to be set above secular princes had crumbled away, as we have seen, the spiritual authority of the Church was now shaken by the exile to Avignon, the development of religious nationalism, the Great Schism, and the elaboration and practical application of conciliary doctrines.

Bernard de Got, Archbishop of Bordeaux, who was raised to the Pontificate in 1305, did not set off immediately for Rome. It may be that by remaining in France for a time he hoped to arbitrate in the conflict between Capets and Plantagenets, which was the prelude to the Hundred Years' War. There is no doubt that he also feared that, once he crossed the Alps, he would become the prisoner or puppet of the factions which for centuries had disturbed the peace of Italy and the Eternal City. Of his thirteen immediate predecessors on the throne of Saint Peter, ten had died far from Rome, and between 1085 and 1304 popes had been forced thirty-three times to flee the turmoil on Tiber's banks. Clement V, then, prolonged his stay in the marches of France and the Empire; he was crowned in Lyons, held a council in Vienne and arrived in Avignon. He had no intention of remaining there; he still hoped to reach Italy one day; but, without wishing to do so, he settled the fate of the Papacy for the next sixty years and initiated one of the most controversial periods of its history.

These supposedly exiled Popes, 'captive in Avignon', have been roundly condemned for centuries. The most recent studies, free of the nationalist passion which vitiated earlier views, do greater justice to these pontiffs.[10] They were indeed superior to many, both before and after, who sat upon the papal throne. For one thing they gave encouragement to the missions to Asia.[11] In fact, the only reproaches to be made against them are their fiscal policy and their nominations;[12] and the first of these was largely forced on them by circumstances.

The financial burdens they had to bear were considerable, and most of them irreducible. Although the pomp of the pontifical court was largely superfluous, the military expeditions dispatched to maintain the authority of the Holy See in its domains in Central Italy were unavoidable expenses. So were subsidies to missions, and the salaries of Curial officials. Since the Gregorian period the Pope's powers within the Church had constantly grown, with the inevitable result that a large centralized administration had developed. By creating, or reorganizing, a whole series of specialized services, the Avignon Popes were only taking the last, indispensable step in a process which had been going on for a century.

To balance this massive budget it was essential to find new ways of raising money, or to use ones which had not been generally practised. Clement V's successors raised a quantity of taxes by methods which were far from gentle. There was the *census*, payable by vassal states, exempt monasteries, archbishops on receiving the pallium, and by bishops on the occasion of their visit *ad limina*; the *servitia communia*, payable by new bishops and abbots; annates, imposed on holders of benefices, and equivalent to the income from the first year of possession; and extraordinary subsidies, *procurationes, jus spolii*, etc. At the same time they increased the number of their 'reserves', cases in which the Pope himself might nominate to a benefice; there was a double advantage in this: in addition to being able to appoint his own man, he took the revenues so long as the office was vacant.

Their nominations were often dictated, alas, by personal convenience. The immediate entourage of the Pope and his own compatriots received special consideration. Figures for the Sacred College of Cardinals are easy to establish and make the situation abundantly clear: of 134 cardinals created between 1305 and 1375, 113 were Frenchmen, 13 Italians, 5 Spaniards, 2 Englishmen and one a Swiss.

This was a dangerous tendency, for it gave the Holy See the appearance of a financial power in the service of the Capetian monarchy, rather than a universal, spiritual power. It was also unfortunate because it coincided with the awakening of national sentiment and encouraged it to cross the frontier between politics and religion. Englishmen and Italians were indignant because the popes gave them so small a place in the Curia, appointed foreigners to their benefices and drained away their money by taxation. There was consequently a demand to restrict papal power and give more freedom to the national churches, a demand which was made by the French as well, after the return of the popes to Rome. Two of the most illustrious theologians, Pierre d'Ailly and Jean Gerson, advocated a general decentralization of the Church,[13] and in 1438, at a meeting of the French clergy at Bourges, an attempt was made to effect this, but without success. Late in the fifteenth century the Papacy succeeded in silencing the Gallican movement, but not in destroying it.

The trend towards national churches had done no more than threaten the authority of the Holy See and the unity of the Church. The Great Schism, on the other hand, seriously weakened papal authority and destroyed the unity of the Church for more than a generation.[14] It began in 1378 when the College of Cardinals elected a successor to Gregory XI, who had brought the Papacy back to Rome. This was Bartolommeo Prignano, who took the name of Urban VI. After the election the majority of the cardinals, disappointed in him, changed their minds; alleging that the Roman people had put pressure on them, they declared the election null and void, and, on the 20th of September, gave the tiara to one of their number, Robert of Geneva, Clement VII.

The schism had now begun: there were two popes, one in Rome and one in Avignon, two popes under whom Christendom was divided into two parties on a basis of political preference. Each pope was prepared to make concessions in such matters as ecclesiastical appointments, if by doing so he might bring this or that ruling prince into his camp. Each laid his anathema on the other. Each was convinced of the justice of his cause, and had no intention of retreating from his position. It was a tragic situation for the Holy See and for the Church as a whole, and it continued for twenty years.

It was in vain that men of good will made every effort to reconcile the antagonists. They tried to get one of the rivals, or even both, to resign, but with no result. They tried to force abdication on them by refusing obedience, again unsuccessfully. Finally there remained one way only of returning to normality; by convoking a council to depose the two adversaries and designate a new pope.

This was an extreme solution and entailed serious risks for the Papacy, since it postulated that the Pope was not supreme, for over him was set the Council. This was indeed the doctrine propounded by an increasing number of theorists.[15] As far back as the beginning of the fourteenth century Jean de Paris had claimed that, although the Pope's authority was greater than that of any other Christian, it was inferior to that of the totality of Christians. Marsilius of Padua had maintained that in religious, as in civil, society, full power resided in the people, and that in consequence the Church should have as its prime organ of government a sort of regular parliament, made up not only of bishops, but also of delegates of the lower clergy and the laity, which would give its mandate to the Pope. During the first years of the Great Schism several theologians and canonists – Conrad of Gelnhausen, Henry of Langenstein, Pierre d'Ailly, Jean Gerson, Francesco Zabarella – propounded theories no less radical. Zabarella found an apt sentence which summed up the general attitude: '*Potestas est in universitate tamquam in fundamento, et in Papa tamquam in principali ministro.*'[16]

In view of the situation and the pressures from powerful clerics, a council had to be convened. Cardinals, bishops, abbots, delegates of chapters, and doctors of theology met at Pisa in 1409. They dismissed both popes and elected a third, Alexander V; it proved a sovereign

228

way of increasing confusion, for the dismissed popes had much support, and now there were three rivals instead of two. Therefore a new council was held at Constance; but this time simple priests and even laymen sat with the great dignitaries of the Church and the universities, and this time the delegates sat and voted as nations. The meeting was a success; on the 11th of November 1414 it elected a pope who was recognized by all Christendom, Martin V. The schism was at an end.

It was the Council that had ended it, but there was serious danger that in so doing it had given Rome an empty victory, for the Council had been *de facto* the supreme organ of Church government for some years, and had come very close to being supreme *de jure*. On the 9th of October 1417, by the decree '*Frequens*', the Council of Constance decided to meet every ten years. The Papacy, it might seem, had only been reunited at the expense of its freedom.

Martin's energetic successor, Eugenius IV, however, delivered the Holy See from this peril. Eugenius put up strong resistance to the council which met at Basle in 1431, in conformity with the decree '*Frequens*'. He resisted when the delegates proposed to limit appeals to Rome, regulate themselves the operation of excommunication and interdict, suppress annates, control papal finances, and conduct negotiations with the Greek Church, and above all when they attempted to make a dogma of the Council's primacy over the Holy See. Moreover the Anti-Pope put up by some members of the Council was a very moderate success. When Eugenius died, in 1447, he had saved the papal cause.

The Papacy had won a victory over the Council, and it was to win another against Gallicanism. The College of Cardinals, which had made one attempt in Avignon, and others later, to check the Pope by imposing capitulations, also suffered defeat; and the Pope's subjects in Central Italy, rebellious for years, were now cowed into submission. Victory, in fact, on every front; but still only a qualified victory, for Europe was by no means purged of ideas hostile to Roman centralization and absolutism; and a costly victory, for in the struggle the Papacy had spent much of its strength, and lost much of its prestige. It had made many enemies and granted many unwise concessions to princes. At the moment when the Middle Ages were drawing to a close the Papacy was once again the undivided power which governed the Church, and in his *Summa Ecclesiae*, written in 1448 and 1449, Juan de Torquemada reaffirmed with vigour its supreme and universal authority.[17] And yet it was a far cry to the power, authority and glory of earlier times.

A last cause of weakness and disunity in the Church was heresy. The climate was favourable to its growth, for the abuses which it attacked and proposed to remedy, like the apathy and incapacity of the authorities whom it intended to replace or abolish, were only too flagrant. For two centuries heresies flourished; as one flagged another appeared to take its place, whilst the Inquisition strove in vain to repress them.

The wind of reform which blew through the eleventh century raised a swarm of sects in Northern Italy and the South of France.[18] They appealed to laymen, aiming to lead them back to primitive Christianity, for such was the ideal of the time. They called on men to practise the poverty of the Gospels and to read the Scriptures with assiduity; and to that end they disseminated translations in the vernacular. Since they had developed outside the hierarchy, and beyond its control, they soon drifted towards heresy. They made the Bible the sole source of doctrine, they denied this or that dogma of the Church, the existence of Purgatory or the Communion of Saints; they condemned devotional practices, or some of them, such as the cult of relics; they held that all the faithful had the right to administer the sacraments, or at least to preach; they attacked the clergy, whom they considered useless, and in any case corrupted by riches, and demanded that they be suppressed or replaced by others, under the surveillance of the faithful. One sect, Waldensianism, founded in 1176 by Peter Waldès, a merchant of Lyons, established itself over a wide area. In course of time it reached Italy, Germany, Austria and Hungary, and settled firmly in Bohemia and Moravia. In the fourteenth century its followers were still numerous in those countries.[19] Other, more localized sects, competed for the favour of the poorer classes. In Germany various groups of obscure origin, bearing the generic name of Brethren of the Free Spirit, were distinguished by their radicalism; they professed pantheism and claimed complete freedom from all restraints for the man who had accepted God; *ubi spiritus Domini, ibi libertas.* In Italy the prophecies of Joachim de Flora, who had predicted a 'Kingdom of the Holy Spirit', to begin about 1260, troubled many souls, and encouraged the foundation of several more or less heterodox movements like the *Fraticelli*, whose first members were misguided Franciscans.[20] Some of the Observants, who were hostile to the Papacy, which supported their Conventual rivals, had come under the influence of the Calabrian abbot, and were in open revolt against the Church, its hierarchy, its liturgy, and some points of its dogma.

Up to the end of the Middle Ages these sects survived the terrors of the Inquisition, but they gradually lost impetus, to such an extent that by mid-fifteenth century they were no longer a danger to the Church. By that time the last of them had disappeared, but in the meantime most of their ideas had been taken up and developed by intellectuals. And so new heresies arose which constituted a greater danger to the Church, because their more coherent philosophy attracted followers in the most influential ranks of society, not only among the common people.

John Wyclif, a professor of theology at Oxford, was the most impressive among these intellectuals.[21] Like many of his contemporaries, he attacked the wealth of the clergy and pontifical taxation, and affirmed the right of secular rulers to seize possessions which the Church used for wrong ends. Emboldened by success and encouraged by the Great Schism in the Church he became more radical. He rejected Catholic tradition, and based his theology solely on his close study of the Scriptures. He denied the supremacy of Rome, identified the Pope with Antichrist, and denounced cardinals, bishops, monks and clerks as mere tools of the devil; he moved towards absolute predestination, rejected confession, confirmation and extreme unction, condemned indulgences and the cult of saints, and finally cast doubt on transubstantiation. His doctrines were bold, but he enjoyed so much authority and had so much support that he suffered no serious restraint. His trial in 1378 and the condemnation of his teaching by the Council of London in 1382 did not prevent his ending his days in peaceful retirement. It was only twenty years later, with the Lancastrian succession, that his followers, the Lollards, were persecuted systematically. Their numbers were quickly reduced.

Wyclif's ideas soon affected Central Europe, which was linked both politically and culturally with England by Richard II's marriage with Anne of Bohemia. There they combined with the very similar theories of the Czech Janov, and with the ideas of the Waldensians, brought in by Nicholas of Dresden, to form the basis of the Hussite movement; it was characterized by a rejection of tradition, a free interpretation of Scripture, a belief in predestination and salvation by faith, and by impatience with priests and the trappings of organized religion.[22] The people of Bohemia were greatly attracted by this doctrine, for, amongst other things, it set them apart from the Germans, whose imperialism they regarded as a threat. Confronted with the orthodoxy of their political opponents, they adopted the novel views of Huss as a Czech national religion.

The consequences for the Hussites were harsh. The martyrdom of John Huss, who was burnt at the stake in Constance in 1415, did not cow his compatriots. On the contrary: for twenty years the struggle continued, and finally the Church was forced to accept a compromise. The Compacts of Prague, which the majority of the Hussites accepted in 1433, were ratified in the following years by the Council of Basle.[23] The Holy See first accepted them, and then tried in vain to get them rejected in 1462; after further strife they were finally accepted in 1483 by the Catholics of Bohemia. Although the Compacts served to safeguard the unity of the faith, they had a destructive effect on liturgy and discipline. The Hussites had compromised on some basic points, but had nevertheless obtained satisfaction on others. The Compacts had been drafted largely by the Utraquists, the moderate party, whose main demand had been for communion in both kinds (*sub utraque specie*), but there were other Hussites closer to the spirit of the founder, who kept his influence alive in Bohemia until the coming of the Reformation.

What is true of the Hussites is true, to a lesser extent perhaps, of most of the heresies which flourished in the last phase of the Middle Ages. Rome was able to check them, but not to root them out down to the last man, and even less to erase all traces of their doctrines. In the middle of the fifteenth century there were still Waldensians, Brothers of the Free Spirit and Lollards, and the sixteenth century did not forget the critical attacks made in the fourteenth and fifteenth centuries on the Church, its doctrines and its institutions.

For two hundred years the Church had found obstacles strewn in its path, but it was strong with the accumulated strength of centuries and was able to surmount them. Heresies were vanquished and schisms patched up; and although the secular clergy was never reformed, a vigorous improvement was effected amongst the regulars from 1350 onwards. These successes were admittedly limited and temporary, but they were considerable and significant; the effective power of the Church was evident until the very end of the Middle Ages.

In the fourteenth and fifteenth centuries the Church was no longer identified with Western Europe. The scandals which had ravaged her were so grave and so flagrant, the conflicts which rent her were so many, so prolonged and so acrimonious, that much of her prestige and her enterprise had left her, and she could no longer impress her stamp on men's minds. For many there was a gulf between religion and life, or between Christianity and Catholicism. The great majority of politicians, merchants, scholars and artists kept their religious belief, but many no longer felt it as the mainspring of their actions, and others forged their own individual faith. Amongst the common people piety was still strong, but was now less dependent on the sacraments and on public worship, presided over by discredited clerics, and more on devotional practices such as the Way of the Cross.[24] All classes were casting off the yoke of the Church to some degree, and were less willing to accept its hierarchy and its tradition. Henceforward the unity of Western civilization had gone, since its one solid foundation had been the Church. There were men who had still hoped at the beginning of the fourteenth century to make the Empire what it had never been since the time of Charlemagne, a supra-kingdom whose effective power would extend over the whole of Christendom. This was only a dream, and events had shown its unreality. As early as 1312 the emperor Henry VII's attempt to make King Robert of Naples recognize his authority had been a failure, both in word and in deed. Henry had failed to move his antagonist, and his manœuvres had prompted Clement V to promulgate the Bull *Pastoralis cura*, by which the sovereign pontiff formally denied the Emperor any rights *extra districtum imperii*, that is to say, *in regem*.[25] So much so that, in 1356, the Empire was reduced to a mere German kingdom. It is true that in spite of the protectionism practised by the towns, and sometimes by states, merchants still travelled the roads and rivers of Europe, but these commercial relations could only maintain a certain cosmopolitanism, not a true common civilization. It was the Church which had welded together the medieval West in the Middle Ages. As her influence weakened, cultural unity broke up. The structure could not remain when the cornerstone was crumbling.

Chapter 12

CULTURE: COMPLEXITY AND STAGNATION: RENAISSANCE AND RENEWAL

The Middle Ages derived from Saint Augustine their noblest ambition: to order the cities of this world like the City of God and so achieve unity and stability. After centuries of unremitting toil it seemed at one moment that this ideal was about to be realized, in the achievements of Thomas Aquinas, Dante and the master-masons of Amiens.

But there was a certain falling-off in enthusiasm and effort after 1300, still more in the second half of the century. A growing number of scholars, artists and writers began to rebel against the discipline that such an ideal imposed, and preferred individual freedom. Some felt that previous generations had been wrong to devote themselves to trying to achieve what must be an illusion of unity; such an attempt had in any case failed, and sense and experience both advised against following the same road. But many of their contemporaries were so impressed by what had been accomplished that they insisted on continuing along the same lines, with only slight variations, because they were afraid of a change of direction. Yet another group took up and developed in an exaggerated way the new belief in nature and gave it an absolute value. Medieval culture was threatened by the number of divergent, even contradictory tendencies that it contained. The political, economic and religious evolution which gave rise to them also began to undermine its foundations.

Intellectual and artistic life began to lose the buoyant universality it had enjoyed in the thirteenth century. Other towns and other countries began to challenge France's supremacy in the West; Paris and its university, the cathedrals and the culture of the Capetian kingdom, France's peculiar literary themes and styles now had rivals. Traditional disciplines went overboard: scholars threw off theology's yoke, painters and sculptors were no longer limited to serving architecture, musicians were no longer poetry's servants; they all wanted to rule their own empire and enjoy independent mastery of a science or an artistic skill.

Inspiration began to dry up; with less boldness and real creativeness, there was a tendency to lose sight of the whole in the parts, and to be satisfied with mere virtuosity. It was particularly evident in theology and courtly poetry, which the Church and the nobility had encouraged; they faded as their patrons' power dwindled. Other art-forms, less dependent on the clerical or aristocratic world, did not undergo this ageing process, but they lost their medieval idealism, and in the hurly-burly of town life they were themselves transformed. This duality in Western European culture – evolution side by side with stagnation – was a pointer to future developments, which the Renaissance was to exploit fully.

France had succeeded in welding all Christendom's various talents into a new synthesis, the zenith of medieval achievement. Epic poems, songs, stories, the mystery play, the '*Summa*' of philosophy or theology, the art of the cathedrals – all found their most original expression in France. In the twelfth and thirteenth centuries France was the heart and centre which any culture needs in order to grow. As such she had enjoyed a position of unrivalled authority in Western Europe.

She was still in the forefront after 1300. The university of Paris played an important part in religious controversies. Inquiring spirits felt at home there: as well as being a sanctuary for scholars, it soon became one of the Occamist strongholds, and the most remarkable fruits of this English doctrine were produced by teachers and pupils there. Students of many nations flocked to Paris, and left as teachers to staff other schools: Eckhart, the great German mystic, rubbed shoulders with the Dutchman Groot, who was the father of the Modern Devotion, and the newly founded universities at Heidelberg and Vienna persuaded Parisian scholars to come and be their first rectors. The *opus francigenum* still inspired most Christian mastercraftsmen. Jean Pucelle and the other miniaturists who worked in the Seine valley were preparing the way for the Flemish primitives.[1] The revival, one is almost tempted to say the creation, of the art of music was largely the work of French composers and theorists under the early Valois kings.[2] The literature of Central France was widely influential. In every sphere, in fact, France took the lead.

But political troubles and economic difficulties began to undermine its vitality and prestige. Soon the newest ideas and developments began to spring from other soil. Prague University was founded in 1347, and, with Oxford, it began to put Reformation ideas into men's minds. 'Modern' mysticism was born in the rich Low Countries; it was there, too, that the new music and polyphony were given a definite shape, and that painting and sculpture turned towards realism. A flourishing Italy undertook the task of bringing back to life the literature, the arts, the very spirit of the classical age of antiquity. As the modern world became more complex a bankrupt France found its outlets restricted by such rivals: it had probably identified itself too closely with the Middle Ages. The enterprise and initiative of these regions carried all before them, and by the fifteenth century they were the leaders of the West. In these circumstances cultural links on a geographical basis began to weaken. They did not wholly disappear because the growing number of centres which now contributed to intellectual and artistic life kept in close contact with one another.[3] In this connection Jerome of Prague's travels are significant: after studying at the university in his native city he went to Paris, Oxford, Cologne, Heidelberg, before staying for a time in Austria, Hungary, Poland, and going as far as Lithuania. Many characteristics were still common to the whole of Western Europe; fourteenth-century painting, for example, can justly be called international. But without a focal point dominant enough to assimilate and transmute what it received, the forces of cohesion were much weaker than when French ideas set the standard in Christian art and thought.

The organic unity of culture was destined to break up even more easily. In the twelfth and thirteenth centuries, under the aegis of the Church, intellectual studies had all centred on theology, and artistic techniques on architecture; the Church was the inspiration of intellectual and artistic endeavour. All this was rejected by the fourteenth and fifteenth centuries; analysis appealed to them more than synthesis, and they cherished liberty more than discipline; they were more critical and more individualist. All scholarship, whether social, philosophical, experimental or religious, became self-governing. The different branches were not only clearly distinguished, they were now independent of theology, and no longer subsidiary to it. As early as the beginning of the thirteenth century Accursius, who was recognized as the leading legal authority until the end of the Middle Ages, declared roundly that the law was sufficient unto itself, and its code was not beholden to Holy Scripture. Political theorists, too, ruled out moral or religious considerations, and the acknowledged aim of politics was power for the ruler and wealth for the ruled.

Averroistic Aristotelians, who were the descendants of the purist Aristotelians of the thirteenth century, were relatively numerous, especially in Padua; they maintained that there were two truths, one based on faith and one on Averroes, and the two did not coincide. Among orthodox thinkers there was not much support left for Anselm of Canterbury's proposition that all dogmas should be confirmed by dialectic; but the aim of reconciling conclusions based on faith and reason was still dear to the hearts of many, and the great success of Thomism had been in achieving such a synthesis. Duns Scotus, like the angelic doctor, was preoccupied with the threat that the success of Graeco-Arabic thought implied for Christian doctrines, and with the desire to reconcile the two; however, between 1290 and 1308 his works only underlined the weakness of human understanding and its inability to give clear proof of such fundamental truths as Providence or divine uniqueness. At the beginning of the fourteenth century another Oxford Franciscan, William Occam (c. 1300–49) took up the question in a spirit of penetrating inquiry and produced more radical results. In his view the world was controlled by the divine will; abstract reason was therefore powerless to explain it; it could only be done by revelation. This amounted to saying that theology could not expect any essential support from philosophy, and encouraged thinkers in either discipline to go their separate ways.[4] It also tended to favour experiment rather than speculation, and experiment not tied to dogmatism. In other words, it gave an impetus to what were later called the natural sciences, and freed them from theology's yoke. Mysticism itself developed independently of theology.[5] The greatest fourteenth-century mystic, Meister Eckhart, thought that the soul must seek to unite itself to God 'until they are one and the same', and would do so by casting off everything, especially the thoughts, images and outward appearances that encumbered it.[6] A hundred years later the Dutchmen who were the pioneers of the Modern Devotion, best expressed in the 'Imitation', declined to 'discuss things veiled or obscure', and advocated asceticism, like a number of Italian and Spanish religious writers.[7] At the very end of the Middle Ages Nicolas of Cusa made an abortive attempt to elaborate a new synthesis of Christian dogma, incorporating fourteenth- and early fifteenth-century discoveries.[8] It had very little success and aroused little or no interest. The breach was final. The principle that every intellectual discipline was '*Ancilla theologiae*' was too narrowly medieval and had had its day. The struggle which Abbo and Gerbert had initiated to constitute the sciences as separate disciplines was thus wholly successful.

If one continued the investigation and looked closely into each discipline one would uncover many contradictions. In philosophy, for example, there had always been conflicting schools of thought; but now the differences were accentuated. While Thomism and Scotism pursued their separate ways and Averroism turned inwards, a new theory was evolved which, as Étienne Gilson rightly says, gave rise to 'a true philosophical and theological schism'. Occamism, by denying that universals had any reality, even in the Godhead, went a stage further than its predecessors, and soon acrimonious arguments broke out between its supporters, the *'Moderni'*, and its opponents, the *'Antiqui'*.

Architecture shared the same fate as theology: the ancillary arts broke away. Sculptors were too highly skilled to content themselves with putting finishing touches to masonry, carving a doorway or shaping a pinnacle. They began to fashion memorials and tombs, statues, and domestic and ecclesiastical furniture. They were not only less dependent on architecture in a material sense, but it also had less influence on their style; their work became more individual and realistic, and not so monumental. Painting followed the same path. It was no longer confined to sanctuary walls; artists worked on wooden panels or canvases, painting pictures, not frescoes. They were more concerned to represent real life in vivid terms than to depict the grandiose.

Even here, a more detailed inquiry would reveal many divergent, and perhaps opposing trends in the art of painting, sometimes in a single work. *'Quattrocento'* painters are, after all, grouped into numerous schools, and in a flamboyant Gothic cathedral there is a marked contrast between the simplicity of its lines and its exuberant decoration.

The Middle Ages came to an end in an atmosphere of confusion. It was as if they had grown too old and feeble to be able to encompass all the new cultural manifestations. Science and the arts had known a new birth and had grown to maturity, so that they felt confident enough to make their own rules and go their own ways. They had thrown off the yoke of tutelage.

Such rebellious tendencies were not general. Considerable numbers of scholars, writers and artists remained faithful to medieval concepts; too much so, in fact, since their loyalty prevented them producing anything really new or outstanding. With a few exceptions their scientific and artistic achievements were lacking in vigour and originality. In the sciences work was sophisticated but shallow. Their art was often graceful and delicate, but the energy, sanity and power that had been the glory of earlier masters were gone. Both art and science were a mirror of the society which produced them or for which they were intended; they reflected an established Church which was being seduced by earthly pleasures and the trappings of a life of ease, and was too weak to take itself in hand. They reflected a nobility crushed between the monarchy and the bourgeoisie, kept on a tight leash by kings and supplanted in royal councils by lawyers of humbler birth, defeated on the battlefield by foot-soldiers, ruined financially by the rise of an urban, monetary economy. In other words, the nobles were shorn of their political, military and economic functions, had nothing to fall back on, and in their enforced idleness it was only their cunning which enabled them to survive.

Scholars who consciously continued medieval traditions usually ended by becoming wordy and narrow-mindedly dogmatic. They respected the authority of earlier writers so much that they made no material alterations to their work, and were content with composing commentaries or making minor additions. In so doing they followed the system which had already been evolved; they were perfectly familiar with it. They even became too adept, and sometimes lost sight of the object of their studies in an obsession with techniques of research, and became unjustifiably self-important; they debated merely for the sake of argument, and thought that they had achieved something when they had displayed their skill in dialectic. This was typical of the canon law 'decretalists' after Jean André's death in 1348. Bartoli died in 1357, and subsequently Roman and civil law experts suffered the same decline; apart from the '*Somme rural*' by Jean Boutillier,[9] the Tournai magistrate (and even that was not as scholarly as Beaumanoir's 'Customs') their books were a hotchpotch of quotations and syllogisms. Schoolmen who lost their way in labyrinths of logic and battles of words, Thomists tied hand and foot to the angelic doctor's teachings, Scotists who revelled in 'subtleties', and even many Occamists – they were all tarred with the same brush.

Like the two branches of law, like philosophy and theology, medieval literary forms still had devotees in the fourteenth and fifteenth centuries, writers who produced epic poetry, courtly songs and stories, *fabliaux* and didactic poems. They were prolific, but masterpieces were very rare. About 1350 appeared the '*Canzoniere*', which raised the Provençal type of lyric to its highest level. Then, three generations later, an exile 'looking towards the land of France' from the cliffs of Dover, wrote '*Ballades*' and '*Complaintes*': he would have been a great poet if he had had just a little more fire and passion.[10] But one Petrarch and one Charles d'Orléans could not make up for the large number of writers who could neither feel deeply nor express themselves simply, whose works were artificial and affected. There were too many rhetoricians, accomplished craftsmen but poor artists, who could turn a verse as easily as contemporary scholars could turn an argument, though the one lacked inspiration and the other originality: too many unashamed moralizers and pedants.

Many works of art show the same tendencies, namely, weakness of line and an over-elaborate style. Architecture set the tone; it was no longer mindful of basic precepts, and the flamboyant style aimed at showy elegance rather than real beauty and grandeur.[11] The master-builders' technique, like that of their literary contemporaries, was irreproachable, but they laid too much stress on it. They exhausted all its possibilities, so that their buildings were lifeless and unimaginative; their over-all lines were simpler but too slender and delicate. The extreme simplicity of the structure was cancelled out by a profusion of complicated decorative work: traceries with flowing curves divided windows, liernes and tiercerons broke the smooth line of an arch, keystones, gables, balustrades and galleries abounded, ornamented wherever possible. In painting Giotto's genius inspired few followers. The 'international' school which grew up in the fourteenth century was more influenced by illuminators working in Paris, Flemish 'primitives' and, in particular, the Siennese school, than by him. Its interest in the individual did pave the way for realism; but it was its extravagance, its enjoyment of luxury and refinement, that were most characteristic. Even the Van Eycks' realism only triumphed for a short time; in the second half of the fifteenth century painting would abandon realism and once more languish. Stained glass design became over-elaborate; colours became soft and subtle, lines less angular, depth was suggested, so that the fullest virtues of the medium were not developed, and windows became merely pictures. Music, too, grew complicated; polyphonic works were as mechanical and involved as flamboyant Gothic architecture, and much monodic music is reminiscent of contemporary lyrics. Guillaume de Machault's Coronation Mass (he lived in Champagne c. 1300–77) had all the grandeur and integrity of a Gothic cathedral, but his ballads and virelays were as mannered and well-bred as his poetry.[12]

The signs that medieval culture was on the wane were now clear – inspiration was giving way to an obsession with technical skill, strength and vigour to delicate, languid grace; even ideas and emotions were no longer being expressed in simple, direct terms. But in certain respects this was a foreshadowing of future lines of development. From the angle of the past it might seem that things were deteriorating, but with the hindsight of the future we can see that progress was being made. Civil and religious disputations trained men's minds in logical argument, and disputations were increasingly used in all branches of study. Vernacular languages were enriched and made more expressive as a result of translations of classical works on law and philosophy, and by the virtuosity and skill in the use of words displayed by rhetoricians. Language was better equipped to express subtleties of thought and feeling, and new modes of expression and new poetic forms were developed. Architects and painters made fuller use of line and colour in their search for striking effects, and polyphonists at last discovered the potentialities of their instruments and the latent possibilities of rhythm, so that music, as we know it, can be said to date from the fourteenth century. What was even more significant was that this insistence on elegance and grace stimulated artists to seek beauty for its own sake, beauty of form as much as of idea: a sign of things to come.

A new spirit was stirring, even in works of art firmly rooted in the Middle Ages. It was still more obviously at work in those which to some extent departed from the medieval pattern.

We have just discussed the work of a few scholars and artists; amongst their contemporaries, sharing the same medieval outlook, there were some who were destined to change it radically. They represented movements like critical rationalism, and an intense emotional realism, which had existed in the thirteenth century but had not been developed. Now the great men of the time, men like Occam, Oresme, Sluter and Van Eyck, Boccaccio, Chaucer and Villon set free these latent trends, and there was a great upsurge of original creations; they were, each one of them, a kind of latter-day Boethius, contributing to the modernization of Western Europe.

A critical, inquiring mentality was not new in the fourteenth century. Thomas Aquinas had questioned Aristotle, the Post-Glossators had criticized the Code; but now there was more edge to it. William Occam, one of the most impressive medieval philosophers, demanded logical thought of himself and of the 'authorities'.[13] He resolved not to accept any proposition which was not either self-evident or directly derived from such a proposition. Other scholars had laid down this principle before, but he applied it with exceptional stringency and consistency. As a result he maintained that the genus and the species had no existence in reality. In his view only individual objects, which could be identified experimentally or by the senses, could be said to exist; otherwise there was nothing, nothing but 'terms' and conventional 'signs' which were accepted by people in general and found a place in their language. It was empiricism rather than scepticism. Occam did not claim that the human mind was incapable of discovering truth, for he recognized the value of perception. Even so, his ideas undermined traditional metaphysics by asserting that only the individual had a real existence. Earlier philosophical systems which had been based on a sort of reality in universals, at least at the divine level, were also overturned. In a sense he condemned the Middle Ages as a whole, with their striving towards the universal.

On scholarship, however, he had a revitalizing effect. It had been stagnating because of the cramping influence of authority. Scholars had edited texts, commented on them, at best discussed them in accordance with the rules. Their reasoning had been based less on observable facts than on the written word. Occam put dogmatism in

241

the dock, and stressed the value of direct experience. He encouraged his followers to observe closely and to experiment, and some of them made remarkable discoveries.[14] Jean Buridan (†1366?) who was a secular teacher in the faculty of arts in Paris studied the problem of gravity, and indicated the way in which it was to be resolved. Another Frenchman, a theologian this time, Nicolas Oresme (†1382) continued the research and carried it a step further by clarifying the effects of time and space factors in the theory of falling objects. It was he who found weighty arguments to support the theory of the earth's diurnal movement, and advocated that co-ordinates should be widely used in scientific work. Such men as these could not achieve definitive results, they lacked the necessary instruments and experimental techniques, but at least they could formulate problems and pave the way for their solution by men like Copernicus.

This late medieval period also witnessed a flowering of the social sciences; it was due to a wider use of the same experimental method, a keener critical spirit and significant changes in the environment. Political theorists were installed in many princely courts, and, following the example of Aristotle, reinforced by Marsilius of Padua and William Occam, they based their very positive theories on observation of actual situations. The schoolmen, and that scholar in a more modern mould, Nicolas Oresme, whom we have just mentioned, tackled economic problems which had been particularly troublesome since the tenth-century revival of trade. Schoolmen argued about the concept of value, contracts and money-lending.[15] Nicolas Oresme wrote a famous treatise on money.[16] Pierre d'Ailly, in his *Imago mundi*, included geographical discoveries which traders and travellers like Marco Polo had made.[17] Before long Lorenzo Valla (1407–57) was to create textual criticism; his method was an insistence on textual exactness, followed by searching interpretation of the texts, enlivened by studying the milieu which produced them.[18]

The interest in what was individual and tangible was not confined to scientific circles. In the fourteenth and fifteenth centuries there was a widespread preference for the concrete and definite, and an interest in nature; it was the inevitable result of the evolution which was taking place in Western Europe. Political and economic forces, as embodied in towns and states, were rapidly gaining strength. New social classes, the bourgeoisie and the common people, were becoming increasingly important; neither of them had any natural aptitude for abstract logic. Religious fervour was on the decline as far as the privileged classes were concerned; and amongst the lower orders it was radically affected by their changed attitude. Christianity itself was becoming, in a way, less abstract. At the beginning of the thirteenth century, with Saint Francis of Assisi, religious zeal had known a new resurgence; he had emphasized the oneness of the Creator and His creation, and fostered fervent devotion to Christ and His sufferings on the Cross. His kind of emotional mysticism, epitomized in the stigmata and the *Hymn to the Sun*, was likely to appeal to the man in the street, and it had a special appeal in a century torn by war, plague and famine. Its influence gradually spread, concentrating devotion on the human, physical personality of the Son of God. It was not surprising that the artists and writers of such a time should pay more attention to the things of this world and be more inclined to realistic treatment of them than their predecessors.[19]

Realism first appeared in sculpture. Quite early, stonemasons and carvers tired of the grandiose impersonality that had prevailed in low reliefs and statuary; canopied tombs with mortuary figures began to replace flat, largely plain stones, and expressiveness and movement were the order of the day. Sculptors tried to achieve a real likeness. The change was most marked in Italy, which produced Donatello (1386–1466), and in the Low Countries, where Adrien Beauneveu of Valenciennes (†1406) and Hennequin of Liège were the forerunners of Claus Sluter. This Brussels-trained Dutchman's carvings – the Chartreuse of Champmol portico, the 'Well of Moses', the procession of weepers on the sides of Philip the Bold's tomb – are all full of vitality. His characters, their expressions and their clothing are all drawn direct from life. His work is deeply felt, and, in technique and impact, in advance of its time; it is powerful as well as beautiful, and very moving. Sluter is of outstanding importance in the history of sculpture.

Painting, with its two dimensions only, had to limit itself to depicting expression, light and colour. There was less scope for realism. In the fourteenth century artists were painting within the restrictive limits of a courtly, mannered style. Even so, realism gradually tinged primitive retables, triptychs and diptychs, as it did Jean Pucelle's and Jaquemart de Hesdin's miniatures and those of their followers. With each new generation it grew in strength. Facial expressions became more true to life, human physiology was better understood and draperies were more flowingly rendered. Backgrounds became more naturalistic; oil was widely used, and good, quick-drying varnishes were produced, making possible more shades of colour and greater variations of light; instead of the traditional gold background more or less imaginary landscapes appeared, giving an impression of depth and distance. So much so, that by the fifteenth century realism was in the ascendant. In Italy, a hundred years after Giotto's death, Masaccio's painting reflected the same qualities – power of suggestion, expressiveness, feeling for size and space, calm and serene splendour, and a balanced, mature outlook. In France there were Fouquet's portraits (c. 1415– 80), Nicolas Froment's 'Burning Bush', and the contemporary Avignon 'Pietà' which epitomized the mysticism of a tortured time, when the Sacred Heart, Sacred Blood and Virgin of the Sorrows were the chief objects of devotion. But its most important expression was in the Low Countries, where the Van Eycks (Jan †1441) produced masterpieces of technical brilliance; Roger van der Weyden (c. 1399–1464) was more sensitive to beauty of line, had more feeling for movement, and found inspiration in touching scenes; Hugo van der Goes (†1482) had a masterly touch in seizing and recording fleeting impressions. In them the Flemish school reached its zenith. It created traditions destined to endure: a passionate delight in colour, technical virtuosity, and, more particularly, a love of life which was tempered by deep religious feeling, so that physical loveliness became a reflection of the soul's beauty.

As in the arts, so in literature there was an increasing vogue for observations on everyday life, and for the new literary forms which had come into existence to satisfy bourgeois and popular taste. A fourteenth-century 'fabliau' tended to be heavy-handed, and satire was often excessively savage. But they were jointly responsible for the short story, which was the great success of the period. All classes of society were depicted in it, wriggling on the hook; the emphasis was on their eccentricities or vices rather than their virtues, but there was little malice in it. Nor was there much evidence of reforming zeal; the chief object was to amuse and entertain. The masters of this genre were Boccaccio in Italy (1313–75), Juan Ruiz in Spain († c. 1350), and Chaucer (c. 1340–1400) in England.[20]

Froissart (1338–1404) was very close to them in style, though he started out with a different object;[21] he was much better at telling a story than at chronicling events. It is true that he was an intelligent man who had seen a great deal, and he had been assisted by reliable informants. His writings are indispensable to anyone interested in the period; but he is too lacking in the critical faculty to be called a true historian. On the other hand, he has no rival in drawing characters in the round, bringing events to life, making crowds move, and giving everything a touch of glamour. The fourteenth century was the age of the great story-tellers.

In the fifteenth, they still had worthy successors, keen-eyed and quick-witted; Chastellain (1415–75) for example,[22] was a better historian and, when he shed his rhetorical manner, as good a raconteur as Froissart. Antoine de la Salle (1388–c.1462) in his *Quinze joies du mariage* shows himself to be a subtle psychologist, and his *Petit Jehan de Saintré* was the first psychological prose novel.[23] The theatre was even more lively.[24] The preceding hundred years, during which it had enjoyed uninterrupted public favour, had seen the emergence of new dramatic forms: the allegorical type of morality play which originated in the Liège district, the Flemish 'abelspel' which was romantic in style, and, most important, the mystery play. It may have come from the Rhineland to begin with; for the first time Christ himself was one of the characters, a living, suffering, dying Man-God, the object of popular piety. So far this form had borne few notable fruits, but after 1400 there appeared the *Condamnation de Banquet*, the *Franc archer de Bagnolet*, and particularly *Master Pathelin's Farce* (1464) which still makes people laugh, and Arnould Gréban's *Passion* (*c.* 1450) which has many movingly tender passages, and some acid ones, interspersed between tedious '*longueurs*'.[25]

Fifteenth-century literature has another claim to fame in the work of the first, perhaps the greatest, French poet, François Villon (*c.* 1431–65),[26] whose forerunner had been Rutebeuf. Lyric poetry, whether bourgeois or popular, was undistinguished and ephemeral until Villon's wonderful talent suddenly burgeoned. In the technical perfection of his art he rivals the Flemish painters in theirs; the tragic element in his poems is of the same quality as the *Pietà* or 'Danses Macabres'. He is patently sincere and grippingly realistic; he lays bare the human heart, and describes it as searchingly as La Belle Heaulmière's body or a corpse swinging on the gallows. The most striking and original aspect of his poetry is the prominence he gives to beggars and reprobates. The scoundrel, whose legacy was rags, whose boon companions were poor clerks, prostitutes and ne'er-do-wells, understood better than anyone human frailty and distress. He presents, even to us today, a faithful record of those poor, wretched victims of nature and society, and pleads eloquently for them. In his *Lais* and *Testament* we have the whole drama of fallen mankind – fallen but redeemed, sinning yet saved. In the midst of their degradation and disorder Villon and his wild friends cherish in their inmost hearts the hope of Redemption.

In science the blinkers were off, art and literature were looking straight at life: it is clear that medieval attitudes were shifting, but they were not revolutionized. Philosophy was tending towards rationalism and empiricism, but it was still profoundly influenced by theology, and far from ready to threaten or attack it. Artists may have scrutinized the world intently: they also meditated upon it. To the Flemings, and many others, the physical world was the 'sign' of a deeper, spiritual reality. Villon is not like a free-thinker of modern times; he has the sensuality, and fits of remorse of the thirteenth-century goliards. Criticism ranged only within limits laid down by the Faculty. Nature was not a law unto herself. Men's lives and works still breathed Christianity.

Classical Greece and Rome had to be rediscovered before Christianity would loosen its hold, criticism break the barricades, and Nature become a law unto herself.

Antiquity was indeed reborn. In France, and especially in Italy, interest in classical studies, which had never flagged since the Dark Ages, increased in the fourteenth century and was intensified in the fifteenth.[27] At first it was centred on the early Fathers as much as on classical authors, but gradually the emphasis changed.[28] Humanists studied pagan works of literature more closely. They began to understand them and their implications more clearly. Through them they discovered classical Greece and Rome, not as the Middle Ages had distorted them and imagined them to be, but as they had really been. Fired with enthusiasm, they decided to recreate them, building a new civilization on their foundations, borrowing not merely the raw materials but the very breath of life. It was at that moment that Catholicism and culture began to draw apart; the Middle Ages were indeed moribund.

It was a zealous scholasticism and, paradoxically, concern for a religious revival, which accounted for the renewed interest in Greece and Rome in late fourteenth-century France. Dialectic had invaded the country about 1150, as we have seen, and came to dominate intellectual life. The universities succumbed to it and it held sway over all the best brains; anything which did not fit in with deductive methods was relegated to the background. Positive theology had to make way for the speculative brand, mysticism for philosophy, literature for scholarship, and experimental research was rejected in favour of syllogisms. But from 1300 or 1350 this tyranny seemed to be weakening. Too much time was spent in pointless exercises and turgid ratiocination. Dialectic began to fall from favour, and the mental disciplines which had been ousted by it came back into vogue. The change took place with only slight disruption because there had always been devoted followers of mystical and positive theology, especially in the monasteries; and a need was felt for a more emotional, less dryly academic approach to hold the mass of the population, whose faith had been renewed just as the privileged classes were losing theirs. So there was a return to the early Fathers' writings, and to grammatical and rhetorical studies, even in the University of Paris. This direction led eventually to those classical writers who had inspired Saint Jerome, Saint Ambrose or Saint Augustine, and revealed the subtleties of fine writing and the art of persuasion.

In Italy the return to the classical past was effected more rapidly and completely.[29] Already in the middle of the 'Trecento' Petrarch (1304–74) was engaged in special pleading on behalf of Latin literature:[30] it was so much more beautiful than 'barbarous' medieval writings. It was Italian too, and had more call on his fellow Italians' attention than the 'French' works of earlier centuries. It had formed the main education of Christian authorities, especially Saint Augustine, the greatest thinker in the Western Church. So, the heirs of Constantine's Rome and pagan Rome had every reason to encourage and support Latin studies. At the end of the century Leonardo Bruni opened windows on a wider view. He encouraged interest in the Eastern Fathers and Greek writers; his initiative was taken up, and others followed his example.[31] Classes were held in Greek, which had been almost forgotten for a thousand years, manuscripts were unearthed or brought from Byzantium; Bruni had translated Plato into Latin, and translations of Demosthenes, Homer and Xenophon followed. After the Council of Constance attempts to reconcile Catholicism and the Orthodox Church led to more frequent contact with the Eastern Empire, where many Greek masterpieces had been preserved; the result was a greater impetus to the renaissance. The capture of Constantinople by the Turks in 1453 and the flight from the city reinforced it. Devotees of Greek and Latin literature were growing in numbers in many Italian towns, especially Florence and, a little later, Rome.

It was they who uncovered the real essence of the classical world. They first scanned all classical writings, sacred and profane, and after sifting them, concentrated on the best. To begin with they embraced them enthusiastically but uncritically; the next step, however, was to study the texts closely, intensively, even scientifically. Thus they finally reached the heart of the matter. A civilization was revealed based firmly on the natural world, man and reason.

'Quattrocentro' artists were just as stimulated by classical achievements.[32] There was large-scale borrowing of architectural ideas, especially by Brunellesco (1377–1446) and Alberti (1406–70); octagonal, Greek-cross and basilical ground plans, semi-circular vaulting and ceilings, two-tier façades, triumphal arches and porticos, entastic pillars, classical orders and medallions were all put to use again. Donatello and his school revived favourite 'genres' in sculpture – busts, medallions, equestrian statues and even nudes. They were anxious to discover the classical rules governing their art. They tried to work out a system of ideal proportions from the theories and practice of Vitruvius and others. They followed his example, concerning themselves with calculating mathematical laws of aesthetics; they even looked at things through his eyes. His ideals of nobility in architecture, a naturalistic style of sculpture which revelled in beauty of form and was inspired by the human face and body, were theirs entirely.

247

The Renaissance and the Middle Ages met on common ground at several points during these last decades: there was a more lively interest in the individual and the material world, the critical spirit was gaining on the narrowly dogmatic, idealism and symbolism were being pushed out by realism, and beauty was cherished for its own sake. But the Renaissance pushed all these tendencies to extremes and thus drained them of any Christian content. It exulted in the splendour of created beings and almost forgot their Creator. It exalted man and his intelligence, his strength, beauty and freedom – heady stuff indeed. Nature was divorced from the supernatural, set free from God's control, and endowed with absolute value.[33] The very foundations of medieval civilization were overturned.

The profound changes that took place in the arts, sciences and literature had their counterpart in the political, economic and religious spheres. During the fourteenth and fifteenth centuries the development of central government, the growing importance of industry and commerce, and the setback to the Church weakened the cornerstones on which Western Europe had been rebuilt after the Germanic invasions; they opened the way to a world divided by nationalism, dominated by individualism, and chiefly interested in the material world. By about 1450 the Middle Ages were under sentence of death.

Yet, once more, in the Mystery plays the medieval ideal of oneness in God was clothed in reality again. All the arts were pressed into the great task of recounting their Redeemer's life to His faithful flock. Architecture provided the setting, painting enhanced the décor, music helped to keep up the audience's interest. The words were a patchwork of theology and literature, rational and emotional elements, satire and lyricism, farce and drama. A whole town would be involved in performances, and all other activities and occupations ceased for the time being. France was again the favoured milieu for this medieval swan-song, in which all human gifts and endeavours were brought together to minister to religion; and individual souls were united in one faith, one devotion. It would not happen again. The shadows cast by the towers of Notre Dame were already darkening the rough stage as the Confraternity of the Passion spoke their last words; the evening breeze carried them away; but it was not only the end of a Mystery play by Arnould Gréban or Jean Michel, it was the final curtain of the Middle Ages. The sun would rise next morning on a new world.

CONCLUSION:
THE LASTING LEGACY OF THE MIDDLE AGES

Periods of history follow one another, but never cancel what has gone before. Each is the heir of its predecessor: none destroys all the work of its forebears. The modern age took the place of the Middle Ages, but did not relegate them to utter oblivion.

Between the two ages there was no clean break, but rather a modification of perspectives, a change in the scale of values, a different approach, all of which had already begun in the thirteenth century, and even earlier in some parts of Europe. The main action became subsidiary; what had been fundamental became accessory. Yet the factors changed very little: political frontiers; national languages whose variety reflected different aspects of the same human species; absolutism in government, more or less tempered, according to the region and its traditions, by the subjects' participation; a money economy, free, and based on the towns; commercial methods, notably recourse to credit and the use of double-entry book-keeping, which simplified business relations and encouraged capitalism; literary forms like the theatre or the ballad; the technique of oil-painting, musical notation by stave and bar; universities, where different scientific disciplines jostled one another; the autonomy, within its sphere, of reason led by logic and informed by experiment; a bourgeoisie which provided a bridge between social classes; woman's primacy in social life; Roman Catholicism, ruled over by the Papacy, and served by a number of religious orders; evangelical Christianity stemming from the popular heresies of Gregorian times; all these elements, without which the modern age would be inconceivable, date from the Middle Ages.[1] They were forged into something new by gradual modifications in emphasis and general arrangement during the fourteenth and fifteenth centuries; thus medievalism was in some sort integrated and perpetuated in modern times, a sort of survival after death.

It survived too in works which our age has often scorned, but which, for those of us who are still Christians and Europeans, have taken on a new lease of life, and glow with the same colours as of old.

At the end of our work we may summon up a living multitude of medieval figures: the glorious cohort of missionaries, founders of orders, ascetics and mystics, led by Gregory the Great and Boniface, Benedict of Nursia and Benedict of Aniane, Odo of Cluny, Robert of Molesme, Norbert of Xanten, Francis of Assisi, Dominic of Osma, Romuald, Peter Damian, Bernard of Clairvaux, Richard of St. Victor, Master Eckhart and Ruysbroeck; the glittering procession of princes, builders of political unity and defenders of peace; the feudal nobility, symbols of fidelity, and, when the Church had enlisted their aid in crusading expeditions, of chivalrous generosity; the brilliant phalanx of scholars, theologians and philosophers, jurists, historians, mathematicians and physicists, led by John Scotus Erigena, Ratherius of Verona, Anselm of Canterbury, Rupert of Deutz, Peter Abelard, Peter Lombard, Thomas Aquinas, Duns Scotus and William Occam, Burchard of Worms, Irnerius, Gratian, Bracton, Jacques de Révigny, Bartoli and Accursius, the Venerable Bede and Sigebert of Gembloux, Gerbert of Aurillac, Leonardo Fibonacci, Jean Buridan and Nicolas Oresme; the motley troop of writers, led by Servatus Lupus, Hildebert of Lavardin, Adam of St. Victor, the Archpoet, Walter of Châtillon, Chrétien de Troyes, John of Salisbury, William of Aquitaine, Guillaume de Lorris, Dante, Petrarch, Villon and Arnould Gréban; the countless legion of metalworkers in the Rhineland and Lorraine, the masons and sculptors of Aix, Germigny-sur-Loire, Cluny, Vézelay, Toulouse, Moissac, Caen, Chartres, Paris, Amiens, Rheims and Champmol, the painters and miniaturists of Auxerre, Oberzell, Berzé-la-Ville, St. Savin, of Italy and the Netherlands, the stained-glass makers of St. Denis and Chartres, the first musicians, from Hermann of Reichenau to Guillaume de Machault; the army, the vast army of those who, under God's watchful eye, served the cause of the good, the true and the beautiful for a thousand years.

As we leave the age, often brutal but always creative, we should remember its imperishable achievements, the Benedictine Rule, the Utrecht Psalter, the Chanson de Roland, the font of St. Bartholomew's church in Liège, the ambo of Klosterneuburg, the Romanesque abbeys and the Gothic cathedrals, the Royal Portal of Chartres and the Tympanum of the Blessed Virgin at St. Denis, the Legend of Tristan and Yseult, the religious hymns and the songs of the goliards and troubadours, the theological and philosophical *Summae*, the stained glass of the Sainte Chapelle in Paris, the sacred motets, the *Divine Comedy*, the *Canzoniere*, the *Messe du Sacre*, the Well of Moses, the Adoration of the Lamb, the Testament, the Mysteries, and the Pietà of Avignon. They were the creations of Europe, which gave them birth, and the Church, which inspired them; and they were made possible because the Carolingians united Europe and the Saints gave it the Church. Thanks to them the Middle Ages have not died; nor will they die so long as there remain, somewhere, to understand and love them, without slavishly imitating them, men who feel themselves heirs of that European heritage and members of that Church.

So long as there is a Western Culture, and a Christian Church, the Middle Ages, which created the one and were nurtured by the other, will not die.

NOTES

INTRODUCTION

1. G. L. Burr, *How the Middle Ages got their name*, in *American Historical Review*, XVIII, pp. 710–26 and XX, p. 813.

2. H. Schmalenbach, *Das Mittelalter, sein Begriff und Wesen*, pp. 11–16, Leipzig, 1926. A. Pauphilet, *Le legs du moyen âge*, p. 32, etc., Melun, 1950, notes that this contemptuous attitude was an error of the Renaissance, and that as early as the seventeenth century the Middle Ages were regarded with sympathetic interest by some writers.

3. We have done no more than outline the leading theories; we shall expound and criticize them later, particularly in Chapters I, II and III. Seventeenth- and eighteenth-century writers identify the Middle Ages with the later Empire, and this is sufficient to explain their choice of the foundation of Constantinople as the beginning, and its fall in 1453 as the end of the Middle Ages. Contemporary historians who opt for the same date, 330, rely on a less narrow and superficial view of the evidence; they emphasize the rapid regression of classical civilization after A.D. 250 and show that this regression, more pronounced in the West than in the East, inevitably caused the division of the Empire. See G. I. Bratianu, *Une nouvelle histoire de l'Europe au moyen âge; la fin du monde antique et le triomphe de l'avenir*, in *Revue belge de philologie et d'histoire*, XVIII, 1939, pp. 252–66.

4. A synopsis of the theories of the nineteenth-century historians is to be found in the introduction to A. Dopsch, *Wirtschaftliche und soziale Grundlagen der Europäischen Kulturentwicklung aus der Zeit von Cäsar bis auf Karl den Grossen*, 2. ed., Vienna, 1923.

5. H. Pirenne, *Mahomet et Charlemagne*, Paris, 1937.

6. E. Gilson, *Héloïse et Abélard*, Paris, 1938, underlines the continuity of the Middle Ages into the Renaissance, which we shall mention again in Part III. More recently A. Sapori, *Moyen âge et renaissance vus d'Italie*, in *Annales, Économies, Sociétés, Civilisations*, XI, 1956, pp. 433–57, proposes a new division of periods: Middle Ages, third to eleventh century; Renaissance, twelfth to fifteenth century inclusive. But P. Francastel, reviewing E. R. Labande, *La Renaissance italienne*, in *Annales*, IX, 1954, p. 562, argues the retention of a clear frontier between the periods and warns against attributing Quattrocento thought and sensibility to the thirteenth and fourteenth centuries.

7. E. Lousse, *Facteurs de civilisation à l'époque moderne*, in *Les Études classiques*, IV, 1935, p. 411.

8. Weber's theories of the influence of Protestantism on the rise of capitalism have been fiercely opposed; see E. Sayous, *Calvinisme et capitalisme. L'expérience genevoise,* in *Annales d'histoire économique et sociale,* VII, 1935, p. 225, etc., and J. Lejeune, *Religion, morale et capitalisme dans la société liégeoise du XVIIme siècle,* in *Revue belge de philologie et d'histoire,* XXII, 1943, p. 109, etc.

9. V. M. Godinho, *Les grandes découvertes,* in *Bulletin des études portugaises,* N.S., XVI, 1952, pp. 3–54.

10. W. K. Ferguson, *The Renaissance in historical thought,* Boston, 1948.

PART 1: DAWN

1. G. de Reynold, *La formation de l'Europe.* I: *Qu'est-ce que l'Europe?* p. 33, Fribourg, 1944.

CHAPTER I

1. In this chapter, and, generally speaking, throughout the book, by *East* we mean the Eastern Empire, and by *North* those regions of Europe to the North of the Loire and the Alps.

2. F. Cumont, *Les religions orientales dans le paganisme romain,* 3. ed., Paris, 1929 and E. Griffe, *La Gaule chrétienne à l'époque romaine,* vol. I, Paris, 1947.

3. P. Lambrechts, *La composition du sénat romain de Septime Sévère a Dioclétien (193–284),* in *Dissertationes Pannonicae,* ser. I, fasc. 8. Budapest, 1937.

4. Chapter IX of A. Piganiol, *Histoire de Rome,* in *Clio,* vol. III, 2. ed., Paris, 1946, gives a short account of this crisis period; fuller details are in the *Cambridge Ancient History,* vol. XII. *The Imperial Crisis and Recovery (193–324),* Cambridge, 1939. For Gaul in particular see C. Jullian, *Histoire de la Gaule,* vol. VIII, pp. 180–241, Paris, 1926.

5. The sequel of the crisis is set out in F. Lot, *La fin du monde antique et les débuts du moyen âge,* new ed., Paris, 1951, and H. Dannebauer, *Die Entstehung Europas,* vol. I, Stuttgart, 1959.

6. The article by H. van de Weerd, *Het economisch Bloeitijdperk van Noordgallië in den Romeinschen tijd,* in *Mededeelingen van de K. Vlaamse Academie voor Wetenschappen, Klasse der Letteren,* no. 4, 1940, illustrates this point.

7. M. Lombard, *L'évolution urbaine pendant le haut moyen âge,* in *Annales, Économies, Sociétés, Civilisations,* XII, 1957, pp. 7–28 sketches the comparative history of the towns in the two zones of the Empire; Chapters X and XI of M. Rostovtzeff, *Social and Economic History of the Roman Empire,* Oxford, 1926, describe the decline of the towns of the Western Empire; M. Garaud, *Note sur la cité de Poitiers àl' époque mérovingienne,* in *Mélanges Halphen,* pp. 271–9, analyses one instance.

8. C. Diehl, *Les grands problèmes de l'histoire de Byzance,* Paris, 1943, and *Byzantium. An introduction to East Roman Civilization,* a volume of essays edited by N. H. Baynes and H. S. L. B. Moss, Oxford, new ed.,

1949, summarize the history of Byzantine civilization. References are given in them to more extensive works.

9. A study of the origins and the position in the fourth century of the peoples who took part in the great invasions, Germans, Asiatic nomads and Slavs, takes up the greater part of vol. V, *Frühes Mittelalter*, of the *Historia Mundi*, Berne, 1956. In French there is R. Grousset, *Histoire de l'Asie*, 3. ed., Paris, 1942, on the Asiatic hordes.

10. F. Lot, *Les invasions germaniques. La pénétration mutuelle du monde barbare et du monde romain*, Paris, 1935; E. Demongeot, *De l'unité à la division de l'Empire romain*, 395–410, Paris, 1951; R. Latouche, *Les grandes invasions et la crise de l'occident au Ve siècle*, Paris, 1946; R. G. Collingwood and J. N. L. Myres, *Roman Britain and the English Settlements*, 2. ed., Oxford, 1937.

11. For the lack of effective imperial authority over the barbarian kings see P. Goubert, *Byzance avant l'Islam*, vol. II. i. *Byzance et les Francs*, Paris, 1956.

12. The effect of the Germanic invasions on Western institutions will be examined at length in Chapter II. As for Eastern institutions an outline will be found in L. Bréhier, *Le monde byzantin. II. Les institutions byzantines*, Paris, 1949.

13. H. Pirenne, *Histoire de l'Europe des invasions au XVIe siècle*, p. 7, Paris, 1936.

14. Greek, which was not in any case a general language of communication in the West at the beginning of the Christian era (C. Mohrmann, *die Rolle des Lateins in der Kirche des Westens*, in *Theologische Revue*, LII, 1956, col. 1–18) was forgotten as early as the fifth century in Spain, England and Ireland. It disappeared in North Africa with the Vandal conquest, and although it was still known in Southern Gaul and Italy in the sixth century it was only amongst the higher nobility (P. Courcelle, *Les lettres grecques en occident de Macrobe à Cassiodore* 2. ed. Paris, 1948) and perhaps by some groups of merchants (G. S. M. Walker, *On the Use of Greek words in the writings of St. Columbanus of Luxeuil*, in *Bulletin du Cange*, XXI, 1951, p. 117). Conversely, from the fourth century on, Latin was despised by the Byzantines, who called it a barbaric tongue (G. Bardy, *La question des langues dans l'Église ancienne*, vol. I, Paris, 1948), and the Roman theologians were quite unknown in Constantinople from the fifth to the ninth century (B. Altauer, *Augustinus in der griechischen Kirche bis auf Photius*, in *Historisches Jahrbuch*, LXXI, 1952, pp. 37–76).

15. C. Diehl, *Manuel d'art byzantin*, 2. ed., Paris 1925–6; P. Lemerle, *Le style byzantin*, Paris, 1943.

16. G. Labuda, *Die Einwanderungen der Slaven auf den Balkan im 6–7 Jahrhundert*, in *XIe Congrès international des sciences historiques, Stockholm, 1960. Communications*, pp. 80–2, suggests a pattern of Slav penetration into the Balkans; G. Ostrogorsky, *The Byzantine Empire in the World of the Seventh Century*, in *Dumbarton Oaks Papers*, XIII, 1959, pp. 1–21, underlines its importance.

17. R. Draguet, *Histoire du dogme catholique*, Paris, 1941.

18. L. Bréhier, op. cit. and, in a more limited field, R. Haacke, in his contribution to A. Grillmeier and H. Bacht, *Das Konzil von Chalkedon*, vol. II. *Entscheidung um Chalkedon*, Würzburg, 1953, define with exactitude the religious policy of Constantine's successors and warn us of the danger of the oversimplification involved in the concept of 'Caesaro-Papacy'.

19. In a study of Canon 28 of the Council of Chalcedon, in the volume referred to in note 18, E. Herman shows that, contrary to accepted opinion, this celebrated text does not lay down as a principle the equality of Pope and Patriarch; it was not directed against Rome and her supremacy, but against the ecclesiastical hierarchy of the Eastern Church, which set Constantinople below Alexandria, Antioch and Jerusalem.

20. M. Jugié, *Le schisme byzantin. Aperçu historique et doctrinal*, Paris, 1941.

21. P. Bognetti, *I rapporti etico-politici fra Oriente ed Occidente dal sec. V al sec. VIII*, in *X Congresso internazionale di scienze storiche. Relazioni*, III, Rome, 1955, emphasizes the importance of these religious dissensions in the rupture between East and West.

22. C. Diehl, *Justinien et la civilisation byzantine au VIᵉ siècle*, Paris, 1901. B. Rubin is writing a monumental work under the title *Das Zeitalter Justinians*. The first volume appeared in Berlin, 1960.

23. On Islam and the Islamic conquests see H. Massé, *L'Islam*, 3. ed., Paris, 1940.

24. H. Pirenne, *Mahomet et Charlemagne*, Paris, 1937.

25. Amongst the historians who still see Islamic expansion as the factor which ended Antiquity and introduced the Middle Ages, we may mention R. Buchner, *Die Provence in merowingischer Zeit*, Stuttgart, 1933, and H. Dannenbauer, *Die Entstehung Europas*, in *Grundlagen der mittelalterlichen Welt*, p. 11, etc., Stuttgart, 1958. Some scholars defend the same position but on different arguments, sometimes even contradictory arguments, notably A. R. Lewis, *Naval Power and Trade in the Mediterranean, A.D. 500–1100*, Princeton, 1951; for him it was not the Arabs but the Byzantines who interrupted Western trade by sea; after a temporary setback at the hands of the Arabs, the Byzantines created a fleet, blockaded the Muslims and turned the Mediterranean into a dead sea.

26. R. Boutruche, *Seigneurie et féodalité. Le premier âge des liens d'homme à homme*, Paris, 1959, p. 31, etc. He summarizes the controversy opened by Pirenne's theories and notes the present state of opinion.

27. C. Courtois, *Les Vandales et l'Afrique*, Paris, 1955, questions the traditional view of the thorough Romanization of North Africa.

28. N. K. Chadwick, *Poetry and Letters in Early Christian Gaul*, London, 1955; A. Loyen, *Sidoine Apollinaire*, in *I Goti in Occidente*, pp. 265–84, Spoleto, 1956. There were perhaps still schools in Rheims in the fifth century where Saint Remigius could have been trained in oratory.

29. Research is still going on into the position of Christianity in Northern Gaul and the Rhineland immediately after the great invasions. Christianity certainly survived in the towns, in Bonn, Trier, Toul,

Verdun (E. Ewig, *Trier im Merowingerreich*, Trier, 1954). It may have subsisted in the countryside: mortars of Christian origin which probably date from 425 or 450 have been found in several cemeteries (J. Breuer and H. Roosens, *Le cimetière franc de Haillot*, in *Annales de la Sociét archéologique de Namur*, XLVI, 1956, particularly p. 243, etc.). But here and there it seems to have retreated: the episcopal lists of some cities, like Cologne and Mainz, break off in the fifth century. Signs of paganism became more frequent in the burials of the period (E. Salin, *Le haut moyen âge en Lorraine d'après le mobilier funéraire*, p. 304, Paris, 1939).

30. Their vitality is shown by the rise in population. Excavations in Alamannic cemeteries prove, according to J. Werner and other specialists, that the population increased tenfold between the sixth and the eighth centuries.

31. L. Genicot, *Aux origines de la civilisation occidentale. Nord et sud de la Gaule*, in *Miscellanea historica L. van der Essen*, p. 81, etc.

32. A map of royal villas and treasuries under the Merovingians, and of Carolingian estates, made by A. Bergengruen, *Adel und Grundherrschaft im Merowingerreich*, Wiesbaden, 1958, shows that the first Frankish dynasty settled in the Seine basin and the second in the north-eastern part of Gaul.

33. A number of German scholars, the most recent E. Ewig, *L'Aquitaine et les pays rhénans au haut moyen âge*, vol. I, 1958, pp. 37–54, have drawn attention to the political, cultural and religious relations between Austrasia and Aquitaine, both public and private. They were lively in the sixth century but became less frequent towards the middle of the seventh.

34. A. Dasnoy, *Les sculptures mérovingiennes de Glons,* in *Revue belge d'archéologie et d'histoire de l'art*, XXII, 1953, p. 137, etc.

35. E. Sabbe, *Les relations économiques entre l'Angleterre et le Continent au haut moyen âge*, in *Le Moyen Âge*, LVI, 1950, p. 169, etc.; A. R. Lewis, *The Northern Seas*, p. 110, etc., Princeton, 1958.

36. Below, Chap. II, p. 35. This is evidence of the relatively happy situation in Italy in the fifth century; up to 536 Roman churches were being rebuilt or embellished (R. Vieilliard, *Recherches sur les origines de la Rome chrétienne*, Mâcon, 1941).

37. A van de Vyver, *Cassiodore et son œuvre*, in *Speculum*, VI, 1931, p. 278.

38. Below, Chap. II, p. 40.

39. E. Lévi-Provençal, *Histoire de l'Espagne musulmane*, I, new ed., Paris, 1950.

40. F. Udina Martorell, *Consideraciones acerca de los inicios del medioevo hispanico y la alta reconquista*, in *Hispania*, XI, 1951, pp. 211–34, shows that the Middle Ages began in Spain with the Arab conquest.

41. A. D. von den Brincken, *Studien zur lateinischen Weltchronistik bis in das Zeitalter Ottos von Freising,* Düsseldorf, 1957.

42. A. van de Vyver, *Les étapes du développement philosophique du haut moyen âge*, in *Revue belge de philologie et d'histoire*, VIII, 1929, p. 443. For Boethius see below, p. 35.

43. For architecture and its auxiliary arts, E. Mâle, *La fin du paganisme en Gaule et les plus anciennes basiliques chrétiennes*, Paris, 1950; and for the minor arts, N. Åberg, *The Occident and the Orient in the art of the seventh century*, 3 vol., in *Kungl. Vitterhets Historie och Antikvitets Akademiens Handlingar*, LVI, 1943–7.

44. E. Sabbe, *L'importation des tissus orientaux en Europe occidentale au haut moyen âge (IXe–XIe siècles)*, in *Revue belge de philologie et d'histoire*, XIV, 1935, p. 811, etc. and 1261, etc.

45. G. Schreiber, *Gemeinschaften des Mittelalters*, Münster, 1948, emphasizes the influence of the East on spiritual movements and religious foundations, including hospitals, in Western Europe in the eleventh and twelfth centuries.

CHAPTER II

1. H. Mitteis, *Der Staat des hohen Mittelalters*, 4. ed., Weimar, 1953.

2. *Das Königtum. Seine geistigen und rechtlichen Grundlagen*, Lindau, 1956. I have analysed this collective work in *Revue belge de philologie et d'histoire*, XXXVII, 1959, pp. 162–7.

3. L. Genicot, *La noblesse au moyen âge dans l'ancienne 'Francie'*, in *Annales, E.S.C.*, XVII, 1962, pp. 1–22 summarizes the theories on the origins of the nobility. There is no doubt we must distinguish regions, particularly 'Inner' Germany, untouched by the Roman Empire and the Germanic invasions, where the nobility doubtless derives from the *principes* of Tacitus, the area between Loire and Rhine where it grew up, or perhaps was reconstituted, around the Frankish kings, and the Mediterranean countries, where it appears to owe much to the senatorial families.

4. The king was chosen by the nobility from amongst the members of the royal family. The Germans call this combination of hereditary and elective systems *Geblütsrecht*.

5. K. Bosl, *Staat, Gesellschaft, Wirtschaft im deutschen Mittelalter*, in *Handbuch der deutschen Geschichte*, I, 8. ed., p. 589, etc., Stuttgart, 1954; P. W. A. Immink, *At the roots of medieval society*, Oslo, 1958, a new and persuasive study of the political and social structure of the barbarian kingdoms, but a little controversial.

6. K. Bosl, *Die Reichsministerialität der Salier und Staufer*, p. 8, etc., Stuttgart, 1950, emphasizes the seriousness of the problem in Germany.

7. E. Ewig, *Das Fortleben römischer Institutionen in Gallien und Germanien*, in *X Congresso internazionale di scienze storiche, Roma, 1955, Relazioni*, VI, pp. 561–98.

8. H. Dannenbauer, *Adel, Burg und Herrschaft bei der Germanen*, in *Historisches Jahrbuch*, LXI, 1941, p. 1, etc., or in *Grundlagen des mittelalterlichen Welt*, p. 121, etc., Stuttgart, 1958.

9. Tacitus, *Germania*, edited and translated by J. Perret in *Collection des Universités de France*, Chapters 13 and 14. The origins of feudalism are complex and subject to much discussion. For F. L. Ganshof whose book *Qu'est-ce que la féodalité*, 3. ed., Brussels, 1937, examines the

machinery of the phenomenon and for R. Boutruche, *Seigneurie et féodalité*, p. 150, etc., who sets it in its context, the origins are to be found in the late Empire as much as in Germanic antiquity. In *Medieval feudalism*, Ithaca, 1952, G. Stephenson distinguishes feudalism derived from the Germanic *comitatus*, and the lordship which came from Roman *commendatio*. The latter was not based on a duty of armed service and did not establish any sort of social equality between the contracting parties. The distinction seems valid, and it seems too for reasons too complicated to set out here that feudalism is more German than Roman. Other views, more concerned with the fief than with personal vassal relationships are in C. Sanchez-Albornoz, *El stipendium hispano-godo y los origenes del beneficio prefeudal*, Buenos Aires, 1947, and P. W. A. Immink, op. cit., p. 54, etc.

10. Tacitus, *Germania*, Chapter 19. On the *Sippe* see H. Conrad, *Deutsche Rechtsgeschichte*, I, p. 47, etc., Karlsruhe, 1954.

11. M. Bloch, *La société féodale*. I. *La formation des liens de dépendance*, p. 191, etc., Paris, 1939; R. Grand, *L'agriculture au moyen âge*, pp. 162 and 191, Paris, 1950.

12. A. Latreille, E. Delaruelle and J. R. Palanque, *Histoire du catholicisme en France*, p. 204, Paris, 1957.

13. F. L. Ganshof, *Histoire des relations internationales*. I. *Le moyen âge*, p. 17, Paris, 1953.

14. J. Balon, *Le droit des obligations*, in *Anciens pays et Assemblées d'États*, XIV, 1957, p. 12.

15. *Recueils de la Société Jean Bodin*. IV. *Le domaine*, Wetteren, 1949; M. Bloch, *Les caractères originaux de l'histoire rurale française*, I, Paris, 1931, II, Paris, 1955; W. Schlesinger, *Die Entstehung der Landesherrschaft*, Dresden, 1941.

16. F. Lot, *Nouvelles recherches sur l'impôt foncier et la capitation personnelle sous le Bas-Empire*, in *Bibliothèque de l'École des Hautes Études. Sciences historiques et philologiques*, fasc. 304, Paris, 1955, in Chapter V deals with the vexed question of the origin of the mansus; C. E. Perrin, *Observations sur le manse dans la région parisienne au début du XIe siècle*, in *Annales d'histoire sociale*, VIII, 1945, p. 39, etc., emphasizes the diversity of *mansi*.

17. The origin of lordship and seignorial privilege are the subject of lively discussion: the personal immunity which the nobility enjoyed, according to most German historians, particularly O. von Dungern, *Adelsherrschaft im Mittelalter*, Munich, 1927; the needs of the demesne and its human community by certain French-speaking historians, notably L. Verriest, *Institutions médiévales*, Mons, 1946; the appropriation of seignorial rights by others, led by C. E. Perrin, *Recherches sur la seigneurie rurale en Lorraine d'après les plus anciens censiers (IXe–XIIe siècles)*, Paris, 1935.

18. J. Babelon, *L'orfèvrerie française*, Paris, 1946.

19. P. Spitaels, *Les fibules émaillées gallo-romaines en Belgique*, in *Fédération archéologique et historique de Belgique, 36e Congrès, Gand*, 1953, pp. 33–59; *The Mildenhall Treasure*, London, 1947.

20. The influence of local traditions in decoration and even in the techniques used is shown by E. Salin, *La civilisation mérovingienne d'après les sépultures, les textes et le laboratoire*. 3me partie: *Les techniques*, Paris, 1957, and T. D. Kendrick, *Anglo-Saxon Art to A.D. 900*, London, 1938.

21. J. Babelon, op. cit., p. 14, etc., summarizes the theories put forward on the origins of this 'Iranian' art; J. Baum, *La sculpture figurale en Europe à l'époque mérovingienne*, Paris, 1937, traces its diffusion into the barbarian kingdoms. However for some authors, like W. Holmqvist, *Germanic Art during the first Millennium A.D.*, Stockholm, 1955, this animal style was not brought in by German peoples, but was an internal development of Scandinavian or Anglo-Saxon Art; but it is difficult to accept this view after seeing the collections in the Historical Museum in Stockholm: they show clearly that this artistic tradition was initially figurative, became geometrical with the Germans, then animal with, and only with, the Goths, originally neighbours of the Scyths and Sarmatians.

22. J. B. Ward-Perkins, *The Italian element in late Roman and early mediaeval architecture*, in *Proceedings of the British Academy, XXXIII,* 1949.

23. J. Hubert, *L'art préroman*, Paris, 1938; A. W. Clapham, *English Romanesque Architecture before the Conquest*, p. 55, etc., Oxford, 1930.

24. This poem, in which Roman influence is already perceptible, survives in a West Saxon version of the tenth century, edited by F. Klaeber, *Beowulf and the Fight at Finnsburg*, 3. ed., London, 1936; the problems it presents are examined by R. W. Chambers, *Beowulf, an Introduction to the Story of the Poem*, 3. ed., Cambridge, 1959. Eginhard, *Vita Karoli Magni Imperatoris*, Chapter 29, edited by L. Halphen, in the *Classiques de l'histoire de France au moyen âge*, Paris, 1923. J. van Mierlo jun., *Geschiedenis van de oud- en middelnederlandse letterkunde*, p. 7, Anvers, 1938.

25. The origins of the French epics have been the object of many theories; they are summarized in I. Siciliano, *Les origines des chansons de geste. Théories et discussions*, Paris, 1951; there is also a review by R. Lejeune of a Slovak monograph by A. Vantuch, *Le poète Saxon et les chants épiques français*, in *Le Moyen Âge*, LXVII, 1961, pp. 137–47. We do not insist that the *chansons de geste* are derivatives or transpositions of the *Heldenlieder* but that the Germanic spirit had something to do with their origins. In the case of the Spanish epic the same position is taken by R. Menéndez Pidal, *Los Godos y la origen de la epopeya espanola*, in *I Goti in Occidente*, pp. 285–322, Spoleto, 1956.

26. An inventory of the Greek philosophical writings known to the early Middle Ages has been made by M. De Wulf, *Histoire de la philosophie médiévale*, 6. ed., I, p. 64, etc., Louvain, 1934.

27. R. R. Bolgar, *The Classical Heritage and its beneficiaries*, Cambridge, 1954. The work contains valuable appendices, amongst them a census of the translations of Greek and Latin classics into the vernacular before 1600.

28. On the sources of Isidore of Seville, J. Fontaine, *Isidore de Séville et la culture classique dans l'Espagne wisigothique*, Paris, 1959; on

medieval libraries J. de Ghellinck, *En marge des catalogues des biblio-thèques médiévales*, in *Miscellanea Fr. Ehrle*, V, pp. 331–61, Rome, 1924; for a reconstruction of a Carolingian scriptorium, see E. K. Rand, *A survey of the Manuscripts of Tours*, I, p. 81, etc., Cambridge, Mass., 1929. The *scriptorium* was the place where monks wrote, copied or compiled, and, by extension, those manuscripts kept in the place; the room or the piece of furniture where they were deposited might also be called an *armarium*.

29. R. M. Martin, *Arts libéraux* (*sept*), in *Dictionnaire d'histoire et de géographie ecclésiastiques*, IV, 1930, col. 827–43.

30. But not as well as was thought from *a priori* argument, as J. de Ghellinck remarks, *Patristique et moyen âge*, II, p. 3, etc., Paris, 1947.

31. For the ancient Latin translations of Greek authors see M. Schanz, *Geschichte der römischen Literatur*, III, 3. ed. by C. Hosius and G. Kruger, pp. 441–58, Munich, 1932, and IV, pt. 1, 2. ed., pp. 415–57 and 482, Munich, 1914.

32. H. I. Marrou, *Saint Augustin et la fin de la culture antique*, new ed., Paris, 1949. We shall return to the influence of Augustine on pp. 37, 38, 64.

33. The civilization of Italy under the Ostrogoths, as of Visigothic Spain, is studied in the symposium *I Goti in Occidente*, Spoleto, 1956.

34. G. Bardy and A. Bocognano, *Boèce*, in *Le christianisme et l'Occi-dent barbare*, p. 229, etc., Paris, 1945, and A. Viscardi, *Boezio e la conservazione e trasmissione dell'eredità del pensiero antico*, in *I Goti in Occidente*, pp. 323–44, Spoleto, 1956.

35. An edition of *De Consolatione philosophiae* by L. Bieler is in *Corpus christianorum*, XCIV, 1957.

36. H. R. Patch, *The Tradition of Boethius. A study of his importance in mediaeval culture*, New York, 1935.

37. A. van de Vyver, *Les étapes du développement philosophique du haut moyen âge*, in *Revue belge de philologie et d'histoire*, VIII, 1929, p. 44, etc.

38. Above, Chap. I, p. 23.

39. F. Novati and A. Monteverdi, *Storia letteraria d'Italia. I. Le origini*, p. 57, etc., Milan, 1926.

40. For the continuity of pagan and Christian art see the first four chapters of A. Fabre, *Manuel d'art chrétien*, Paris, 1930.

41. H. I. Marrou, *Histoire de l'éducation dans l'antiquité*, 2. ed., p. 349, etc., Paris, 1950.

42. M. van Assche, '*Divinae vacari lectioni*', in *Sacris erudiri*, I, 1948, p. 13, etc., on the rôle of Saint Benedict in the creation of an intellectual vocation in Western monasticism.

43. G. Bardy, *Les origines des écoles monastiques en Occident*, in *Sacris erudiri*, VIII, 1953, pp. 86–104, concludes from the examination of literary sources that at least until the middle of the fifth century monks were not interested in classical authors.

44. J. Leclercq, *L'amour des lettres et le désir de Dieu*, p. 25, etc., Paris, 1957, rejects, with justice, it would seem, the current view of

Cassiodorus as the source of the intellectual traditions of monasticism and particularly Benedictine monasticism.

45. P. Lehmann, *The Benedictine Order and the Transmission of the Literature of Ancient Rome in the Middle Ages*, in *Downside Review*, LXXI, 1953, pp. 407–21.

46. This attitude was not a principle imposed by the Church (M. W. Laistner, *Christianity and the Pagan Culture*, Ithaca, N.Y., 1951) and permits personal interpretation (B. Blumenkrantz, *Siliquae porcorum*, in *Mélanges Halphen*, pp. 11–17).

47. *Patrologia latina*, C, col. 501.

48. A. W. Clapham, *English Romanesque Architecture before the Conquest*, p. 33, Oxford, 1930.

49. D. Tardi, *Fortunat*, Paris, 1928.

50. For Rome as a literary and artistic market, see Novati and Monteverdi, op. cit., p. 66, etc.

51. H. Riche, *La survivance des écoles publiques en Gaule au Ve siècle*, in *Le Moyen Âge*, LXIII, 1957, pp. 421–36.

52. E. Lesne, *La contribution des églises et monastères de l'ancienne Gaule au sauvetage des lettres antiques*, in *Revue d'histoire de l'Église de France* XXIII, 1937, p. 476, etc. C. Charlier, *Note sur les origines de l'écriture dite de Luxeuil*, in *Revue bénédictine*, LVIII, 1948, pp. 149–57, thinks that the *scriptoria* of the South-East of France were active at least until the Arab invasions.

53. L. Bréhier, *L'art en France des invasions barbares à l'époque romane*, Paris, 1930.

54. J. Hubert, *L'art préroman*, Paris, 1938.

55. R. Lantier and J. Hubert, *Les origines de l'art français*, p. 178, Paris, 1947.

56. M. Aubert, *Le Vitrail en France*, p. 7, Paris, 1946.

57. D. Fossard, *Les chapiteaux de marbre du VIIe siècle en Gaule*, in *Cahiers archéologiques*, II, 1947, p. 70, etc.

58. A. W. Clapham, op. cit., p. 41, etc.

59. *I Goti in Occidente*, Spoleto, 1956.

60. J. Fontaine, *Isidore de Séville et la culture classique dans l'Espagne wisigothique*, Paris, 1959.

61. A. Michel, *Tolède (Conciles de)*, in *Dictionnaire de Théologie catholique*, XV, col. 1176–1208, Paris, 1946.

62. P. Palol de Salellas, *Esencia del arte hispánico de época visigoda*, in *I Goti in Occidente*, pp. 65–126, Spoleto, 1956; E. Lambert, *La tradition wisigothique en Occident et dans l'art omeiyade d'Espagne*, in *Art musulman et art chrétien dans la péninsule ibérique*, Paris, 1958. L. Torres-Balba, *Arte hispano-musulmán hasta la caida del califato de Córdoba*, in *Historia de España* de R. Menéndez Pidal, V, Madrid, 1957, finds Visigothic art thin and awkward and holds that Spain picked up the great Roman traditions only at the end of the eighth century, with the Mosque of Cordoba.

63. Above, Chap. I, p. 23.

64. The diffusion of the writings of Isidore of Seville is studied by

C. H. Beeson, *Isidor Studien*, in *Quellen und Untersuchungen zur lateini-schen Philologie des Mittelalters*, IV, Munich, 1913. Their influence on law is noted by J. Tardif, *Un abrégé juridique des Étymologies d'Isidore de Séville*, in *Mélanges J. Havet*, p. 659, etc., Paris, 1901, and on ecclesiastical history by L. Ott, *Das Konzil von Chalkedon in der Frühscholastik*, in A. Grillmeier and H. Bacht, *Das Konzil von Chalkedon*, II, p. 874, Würz-burg, 1953.

65. F. M. Stenton, *Anglo-Saxon England*, p. 191, etc., Oxford, 1943.

66. The part played by the Irish in the genesis of European civilization is a subject of controversy. The evidence, and proposed solutions of the problem will be found in M. Cappuyns, *Jean Scot Érigène*, p. 16, etc., Louvain, 1933, whose conclusions we have adopted, and in L. Bieler, *The Island of Scholars*, in *Revue du moyen âge latin*, VIII, 1952, pp. 213–31, who attributes a major importance to the Scots; for the arts, see F. Henry, *Les Débuts de la miniature irlandaise*, in *Gazette des Beaux-arts*, 1950, pp. 5–34, who defends the importance of Irish influence on the English miniature, and T. D. Kendrick, *Anglo-Saxon Art to A.D. 900*, London, 1938; also F. Masai, *Le monachisme irlandais dans ses rapports avec le continent* (*art*), in *Il monachesimo nell'alto medioevo*, pp. 139–84, Spoleto, 1957, who claims that this school of miniature was an original production, or at least derived from Romano-British antiquity, from Scandinavia or from Italy.

67. M. L. W. Laistner, *Thought and Letters in Western Europe, A.D. 500–900*, p. 151, etc., 2. ed., London, 1957.

68. J. D. A. Ogilvy, *Books known to Anglo-Latin writers from Aldhelm to Alcuin, 670–804*, in *Medieval Academy of America: Studies and Docu-ments*, no. 2, Cambridge, Mass., 1956.

69. *Bede, his Life, Time and Writings. Essays edited by* A. Hamilton Thompson, Oxford, 1935.

70. This work has been published with notes by C. Plummer, Oxford, 1896; the questions it raises are discussed concisely by P. Hunter-Blair, *Bede's Ecclesiastical History and its importance today*, Jarrow, 1959.

71. M. L. W. Laistner and H. H. King, *A Handlist of Bede Manu-scripts*, Ithaca, N.Y., 1943.

72. T. D. Kendrick, op. cit., p. 111, etc. For illumination see plates 37 to 42 *in fine*.

73. A. W. Clapham, op. cit. (note 48), p. 76, etc. and G. Webb, *Archi-tecture in Britain. The Middle Ages,* p. 14, etc., London, 1956.

74. S. Corbin, *L'Église à la conquête de sa musique*, Paris, 1960.

CHAPTER III

1. *La Cité de Dieu,* with introduction and notes, translated by G. Bardy and G. Combes, in *Bibliothèque augustinienne: section textes.* Paris, 1959. *Le Christianisme et la fin du monde antique*, Lyon, 1943, gives typical extracts from the *Gouvernement de Dieu*, of which the most recent edition is to be found in *Monumenta Germaniae Historica, Auctores antiquissimi,* I, 1, 1877.

2. *Germain d'Auxerre et son temps*, Auxerre, 1951.

3. P. Courcelle, *Sur quelques textes littéraires relatifs aux grandes invasions*, in *Revue belge de philologie et d'histoire*, XXXI, 1953, pp. 23–37, illustrates the contradictory feelings of the Christians in barbarian times.

4. E. de Moreau, *Histoire de l'Eglise en Belgique*, I, 2. ed., p. 79, etc., Brussels.

5. L. Gougaud, *Les surnuméraires de l'émigration scottique*, in *Revue bénédictine*, XLIII, 1931, p. 269, shows that the number of Irish missionaries (as indeed that of the Aquitainians) has been exaggerated. Even when corrected it is still considerable.

6. L. Genicot, *Aux origines de la civilisation occidentale*, p. 53.

7. *Il monachesimo nell'alto medioevo,* Spoleto, 1957; a map of the monasteries of Europe in the period from 300 to 600 will be found in *Atlas of the Early Christian World* by F. van der Meer and C. Mohrmann, Amsterdam, 1958.

8. R. Louis, *Le séjour de Saint Patrice à Auxerre*, in *Mélanges Halphen*, p. 447, puts forward the theory that the future Saint Germain founded a monastery at Auxerre before 418.

9. L. Bieler, *The Life and Legend of Saint Patrick*, Dublin, 1949, summarizes the present state of knowledge on the life and activity of Patrick; L. Gougaud, *Christianity in Celtic Lands*, p. 221, London, 1932, emphasizes the preponderance of monasteries in the Irish Church.

10. *Mélanges colombaniens. Actes du Congrès de Luxeuil, 1950*. Paris, n.d.

11. Perez de Urbel, *Los monjes españoles en la edad media*, Madrid, 1933–4.

12. Saint Benedict's work was not very original. He made great use of a Rule by an unknown author (F. Masai, *La Règle de saint Benoît et la 'Regula magistri'*, in *Latomus*, VI, 1947, p. 207, etc.). His secondary inspiration came from other conceptions such as the Gaulish monasticism of the fifth century (B. Steidle, *Das Inselkloster Lérins und die Regel Sankt Benedikts*, in *Benediktinische Monatsschrift*, XXVII, 1951, pp. 376–87). It was however Benedict who ensured the wide diffusion of this Rule and these ideas. There is an edition of the Benedictine Rule by P. Schmitz, *Sancti Benedicti Regula monachorum*, Maredsous, 1946.

13. The practices of the Irish monasteries, which disputed the field for a time with Benedictine usage, particularly in Northern Gaul (E. de Moreau, op. cit., p. 169), succumbed in the end because of their lack of moderation and practical sense; they went far in austerity (L. Gougaud, *Dévotions et pratiques ascétiques du moyen âge*, p. 143, etc., Paris, 1925) but did not lay down with sufficient precision the organization of the monastery and the duties of the brethren (J. Gaudemet, *Les aspects canoniques de la Règle de Saint Colomban*, in *Mélanges colombaniens*, pp. 165–78).

14. It is generally agreed that the Visigoths adopted Arianism before they entered the Empire. But E. A. Thompson, *The Date of the Conversion of the Visigoths*, in *Journal of Ecclesiastical History*, VII, 1956, pp. 1–11, puts their conversion as late as 382–95.

15. H. von Schubert, *Geschichte der Christlichen Kirche im Frühmittelalter*, p. 21, etc., Tübingen, 1921, a study of Germanic Arianism.

16. The conversion of Clovis has been the subject of lively controversies amongst scholars. We accept here the views of A. van de Vyver, *La victoire contre les Alamans et la conversion de Clovis*, in *Revue belge de philologie et d'histoire*, XV, 1936, p. 859, XVI, 1937, p. 35, etc., and XVII, 1938, p. 793, and *La chronologie du règne de Clovis d'après la légende et d'après l'histoire*, in *Le Moyen Âge*, LIII, 1947, p. 177, etc. These views are not shared by many historians, for example R. Barbaroux, *Saint Rémi et la mission de Reims*, Paris, 1947. The bibliography of the question will be found in these authors and in the article 'Reims' of the *Dictionnaire d'archéologie chrétienne et de liturgie*, Paris, 1947.

17. E. de Moreau, op. cit., p. 59.

18. E. Salin and A. France-Lanord, *Traditions et art mérovingiens*. I. *Le cimetière de Varangéville*, in *Gallia*, IV, 1946, p. 199, etc.

19. The preponderant role of Frankish officials and missionaries in the conversion of Germany is emphasized by H. Feurstein, *Zur ältesten Missions -und Patroziniumskunde im alemannischen Raum*, in *Zeitschrift für die Geschichte des Oberrheins*, XCVIII, 1949, p. 1, etc. and by I. Zibermayr, *Noricum, Bayern und Oesterreich*, 2. ed., Horn, 1956.

20. *Bedae opera historica*, ed. C. Plummer, I, p. 45.

21. The tradition referred to here rests on the Venerable Bede and the *Libellus responsionum* which reports the answers of Gregory to the questions of his envoy. It is rejected by S. Brechter, *Die Quellen zur Angelsachsenmission Gregors des Grossen*, in *Beiträge zur Geschichte des alten Mönchtums und des Benediktiner Ordens*, XXII, 1941. But the critical examination of this work by P. Meyvaert, *Les 'Responsiones' de S. Grégoire le Grand*, in *Revue d'histoire ecclésiastique*, LIV, 1959, pp. 879–94, reveals certain weaknesses in the argument. The question remains open.

22. Above, Chap. II, p. 42.

23. For Roman Catholics tradition is another source of doctrine.

24. W. Baetke, *Die Aufnahme des Christentums durch die Germanen*, Darmstadt, 1959, notes the weaknesses of the work of conversion of the German peoples; R. Sullivan, *Early mediaeval missionary activity; a comparative study of Eastern and Western methods*, in *Church History*, XXIII, 1954, pp. 17–35, which emphasizes the difference between East and West.

25. This is not certain. The example of the Byzantine East, where Pagan survivals, magical practices and belief in the efficacy of relics were as widespread as in the West, if not more so, (L. Bréhier, *Le monde byzantin*. III. *La civilisation byzantine*, p. 278, etc., Paris, 1950), would lead us to answer in the negative. The case of modern Mexico on the other hand (G. Escarpit, *Au Mexique: christianisme et religions indigènes*, in *Annales, Économies, Sociétés, Civilisations*, III, 1948, p. 317, etc.) inclines one to a positive answer.

26. For the southern part of ancient Gaul, E. Griffe, *Les paroisses*

rurales de la Gaule, in *La Maison-Dieu*, no. 36, 1953, pp. 33–62, and for the North, E. de Moreau, op cit., p. 282.

27. J. R. Palanque and E. Delaruelle, *Le rôle temporel de l'Église du IVe au VIIe siècle*, in *Inspiration religieuse et structures temporelles*, pp. 77–106, Paris, 1948.

28. *Le chiese nei regni dell'Europa occidentale e i loro rapporti con Roma fino all'800*, Spoleto, 1960; M. Pacaut, *La théocratie. L'Eglise et le Pouvoir au moyen âge*, Paris, 1957.

29. E. Magnin, *L'Église wisigothique au VIIe siècle*, I, p. 79, Paris, 1912.

30. Above, Chap. II, p. 28.

31. Above, Chap. II, p. 33.

32. W. F. Volbach, *Mosaïques chrétiennes primitives du IVe au VIIe siècle*, Rome, 1943.

33. Above, Chap. III, p. 52.

34. E. Amann, *L'adoptianisme espagnol du VIIIe siècle*, in *Revue des sciences religieuses*, XVI, 1936, p. 281, etc.

35. G. de Plinval has devoted to *Pélage, ses écrits, sa vie et sa réforme*, Lausanne, 1943, a work in which he idealizes the figure of his hero.

36. E. Amann, *L'époque carolingienne*, p. 303, etc., in *Histoire de l'Église* by Fliche and Martin, VI, Paris 1937.

37. Above, Chap III, p. 51.

38. E. Magnin, op. cit., pp. 30–1 and 58–9.

39. See the articles '*Origène*' and '*Origénisme*' by G. Bardy and G. Fritz respectively in *Dictionnaire de théologie catholique*, XI, col. 1489, etc., Paris, 1932.

40. H. van Schubert, op. cit., p. 161, etc.

41. H. F. Dudden, *Gregory the Great, his place in history and thought*, London, 1905; P. Batiffol, *Saint Grégoire le Grand*, Paris, 1928.

42. These works are published in Migne, *Patrologia latina*, XXXV–XXXIX. The former was translated into French in 1928, by J. Boutet.

43. Above, Chap. III, p. 51.

44. A letter of Agobard of Lyons, in *Monumenta Germaniae Historica, Epistolae*, V, p. 158.

CHAPTER IV

1. L. Halphen, *Charlemagne et l'Empire carolingien*, 2. ed., Paris, 1949.

2. R. Sprandel. *Der merowingische Adel und die Gebiete östlich des Rheins*, in *Forschungen zur oberrheinischen Landesgeschichte*, V, notes that the expansion of the Merovingians was more the work of the nobility than of the kings, who were confined to the Paris area.

3. *Translatio Sancti Huberti*, in *Monumenta Germaniae Historica, Scriptores*, XV, I, p. 234.

4. W. Levison, *England and the Continent in the Eighth Century*, Oxford, 1946 and A. W. Clapham, op. cit., p. 76, etc.

5. F. Rousseau, *La Meuse et le pays mosan*, in *Annales de la Société archéologique de Namur*, XXXIX, 1930, p. 45, etc.

6. The antecedents of the coronation of Charlemagne at Christmas 800 and the intentions of those who took part in it are the object of differing theories. In the most recent article devoted to these questions, *Das Römische Reich und der Westen vom Tode Justinians bis zum Tode Karls des Grossen*, in *Grundlagen der mittelalterlichen Welt*, pp. 44–93, Stuttgart, 1958, H. Dannenbauer maintains that the coronation of Charlemagne was only an expedient imagined by the Pope to avoid arraignment before the only existing emperor, the Basileus. The bibliography of the subject is to be found in this article and in R. Folz, *L'idée d'empire en Occident du V*ᵉ *au XIV*ᵉ *siècle*, Paris, 1953, and H. Beumann, *Nomen imperatoris*, in *Historische Zeitschrift*, CLXXXV, 1958, pp. 515–49

7. H. Loewe, *Die Karolingische Reichsgründung und der Südosten*, p. 150, etc., Stuttgart, 1937.

8. E. Ewig, *Zum christlichen Königsgedanken im Frühmittelalter*, in *Das Königtum. Seine geistigen und rechtlichen Grundlagen*, Konstanz, 1956, pp. 69 and 76 particularly, insists that the Carolingian Empire was more Christian than Roman.

9. W. Levison, op. cit., p. 132, etc.

10. In *La spiritualité médiévale*, Paris, 1958, I have given a biography of Boniface, translated some of his more revealing letters and noted the recent works devoted to him.

11. M. Tangl, *Epistolae selectae. I. Sancti Bonifatii et Lulli Epistolae*, p. 4, in *Monumenta Germaniae Historica in usum scholarum*, Berlin, 1916.

12. A. Kleinclausz, *Alcuin*, Paris, 1948, and L. Wallach, *Alcuin and Charlemagne. Studies in Carolingian History and literature*, Ithaca, N.Y., 1959.

13. On these Italian manuscripts see E. Lesne, *Histoire de la propriété ecclésiastique en France, IV. Les livres. Scriptoria et bibliothèques du commencement du VIII*ᵉ *à la fin du XI*ᵉ *siècle*, p. 66, etc., Paris, 1938.

14. The Greek influence in the Carolingian Renaissance is described in the early pages of J. Théry, *Études dionysiennes*, I, Paris, 1932, and established in a particular instance by N. Haring, *The Character and Range of the Influence of St. Cyril of Alexandria on Latin Theology, 430–1260*, in *Mediaeval Studies*, XII, 1950, pp. 1–19.

15. R. Lantier and J. Hubert, *Les origines de l'art français*, p. 158, Paris, 1947.

16. Admittedly certain Dutch historians, amongst them P. C. Boeren, *Sint Willibrord, apostel van Brabant*, Tilburg, 1939, maintain that he was the evangelist of Brabant rather than of Frisia. J. F. Niermeyer, *La Meuse et l'expansion franque vers le Nord (VII*ᵉ*-VIII*ᵉ *siècles)*, in *Mélanges F. Rousseau*, p. 461, Brussels, 1958, points out with justice that although Willibrord had little success north of the Lower Rhine that was none the less his chosen field.

17. Above, Chap. III, p. 49. M. Coens, *Saint Boniface et sa mission*

historique d'après quelques auteurs récents, in *Analecta Bollandiana*, LXXIII, 1955, pp. 462–95.

18. H. Verbist, *A l'aube des Pays-Bas. Saint Willibrord*. Brussels, 1953.

19. J. Leclercq, *Saint Liutger, un témoin de l'évangélisme au VIIIe siècle*, in *La vie spirituelle*, 1960, pp. 143–160.

20. A. Hauck, *Kirchengeschichte Deutschlands*, II, 5 ed., p. 371, etc., Leipzig, 1935 and E. Müller, *Entstehungsgeschichte der sächsischen Bistümer*, Berlin, 1938.

21. The activity of the Anglo-Saxon missionaries in Moravia before the arrival of Cyril and Methodius has been confirmed by a series of excavations which are reported in condensed form in *25 ans d'historiographie tchécoslovaque, 1936–1960*, p. 141, etc., Prague, 1960.

22. For the creation of parishes see above, p. 52. For the exceptional importance laid on preaching since the Carolingian period, see Schnürer, op. cit., I, p. 547, and the recommendations of the Councils of Attigny, in 822, and Aix, in 836, in *Monumenta Germaniae Historica, Concilia*, II, pp. 471 and 711–12.

23. E. Amann, op. cit., p. 71 etc.

24. F. L. Ganshof, *Observations sur le synode de Francfort de 794*, in *Miscellanea historica in honorem A. de Meyer*, I, p. 306, etc., Louvain, 1946.

25. L. Halphen, op. cit., p. 208, etc., is of the opinion that Charlemagne was inspired more by the Bible than by the *City of God*. The contributions of E. Ewig and R. Buchner in *Das Königtum*, op. cit. demonstrate the correctness of this theory. The influence of the Old Testament in this and other spheres and the fact that it overshadowed the New until the twelfth century set an interesting problem, which historians had scarcely touched until recently. E. Delaruelle, *Charlemagne et l'Église*, in *Revue d'histoire de l'Église de France*, XXXIX, 1953, pp. 165–99 and *Jonas d'Orléans et le moralisme carolingien*, in *Bulletin de littérature ecclésiastique*, 1954, pp. 129–43 and 221–8, as well as P. Rousset, *L'idée de Croisade chez les chroniqueurs d'Occident*, in *X Congresso internazionale di scienze storiche, Roma, 1955. Relazioni*. III, p. 556, etc., have considered it and found a partial solution.

26. H. X. Arquillière, *L'Augustinisme politique*, 2 ed., Paris, 1955.

27. R. Doehaerd, *Le monnayage des Carolingiens*, in *Annales, Économies, Sociétés, Civilisations*, VII, 1952, pp. 13–20 and R. Latouche, *Les origines de l'économie occidentale*, pp. 154 and 169, Paris, 1956, note that the movement from gold to silver began under the Merovingians. According to Doehaerd the movement was speeded up under the Carolingians with the object of easing relations with the Muslim world, which generally used silver coinage; we cannot avoid pointing out however that no Arab coins have been found within the confines of the Carolingian Empire, whereas thousands have been excavated in Northern Europe. A. R. Lewis regards the change as the culmination of a redirection of trade towards Scandinavia which had begun in the sixth century. (*The Northern Seas*, p. 110, etc., Princeton, 1958.) R. Lopez, *Moneta e scambi nel alto medioevo*, p. 723, etc., Spoleto, 1961, sees the essential

motive as a wish to unify the monetary systems of the *regnum* and to put to good use silver mines either newly discovered or reopened.

28. It was Louis the Pious or rather his adviser Agobard of Lyons who had the idea of imposing one Law on the whole of the Empire and thus achieving juridical unity. In a letter to the Emperor Agobard set out the reasons which appeared to him to warrant this reform (*Patrologia Latina*, CIV, col. 16).

29. In spite of setting up Counts all over the Empire administrative unity was not achieved. The conquered lands were divided into many counties, but no boundaries were laid down. In other words beyond the Rhine the county was not an administrative unit, but a strongpoint placed at a nerve centre, consisting of fortifications surrounded by royal domains cultivated by royal freemen, half farmers, half soldiers. This is the view expounded in particular by W. Schlesinger, *Die Entstehung der Landesherrschaft*, Dresden, 1941, and adopted today by most German historians.

30. This immunity meant that Imperial officials might not enter the estates of these princes of the Church. The beneficed cleric thus took the place of the count. This aspect of Carolingian policy is the first stage of the 'Imperial Church'.

31. This description comes from F. L. Ganshof, *L'échec de Charlemagne*, in *Compte rendu des séances de l'Académie des Inscriptions et Belles-Lettres*, 1947, p. 251. In *Charlemagne et l'usage de l'écrit en matière administrative*, in *Le Moyen Âge*, LVII, 1951, p. 1, etc., the same scholar shows how imperfect was the use of the written document. Moreover A. Dumas, *La parole et l'écriture dans les capitulaires carolingiens*, in *Mélanges Halphen*, p. 209, etc., Paris 1951, establishes that the document did not take the place of verbal relations; it was a memorandum and it was still the spoken word which had binding force.

32. M. Bloch, *Les rois thaumaturges*, Strasbourg, 1924.

33. F. L. Ganshof, *Charlemagne et le serment*, in the same *Mélanges*, p. 259, etc.

34. C. E. Odegaard, *Vassi and fideles in the Carolingian Empire*, Cambridge, Mass., 1945. The extension of vassality was much more the work of Charles the Bald than of his grandfather Charlemagne.

35. F. L. Ganshof, *Qu'est-ce que la féodalité?* 3. ed., p. 95, Brussels, 1957.

36. Pragmatism, characteristic feature of all Charlemagne's activity, both political and religious, by contrast with the radicalism of Louis the Pious and his counsellors, is emphasized by H. Fichtenau, *Das Karolingische Imperium*, Zürich, 1949.

37. F. L. Ganshof, *Louis the Pious reconsidered*, in *History*, XLII, 1957.

38. Above, Chap. IV, p. 61.

39. Charles Martel was succeeded, as mayors of the palace, by his two legitimate sons, the elder, Carloman, in Austrasia, the other, Pépin, in Neustria. In 747 the former retired into an Italian monastery, and the latter became sole mayor of Francia.

40. A. Werminghoff, *Monumenta Germaniae Historica, Legum sectio III, Concilia aevi Karolini*, pp. 2, 4 and 33.

41. We have enclosed the word *reform* in parentheses. So far as the diocesan clergy are concerned it is questionable whether this was really a reform, although this is the usual view. Priests and deacons recruited amongst the Franks before 742 were not likely to rise to a sufficient level of either culture or purity of living. It is quite probable that there was no process of decay and reform but simply such slow progress that until Carolingian times canonical rules were not observed.

42. The metropolitan's dignity derives from the see: that of the archbishop is personal, conferred by the Pope, and its material symbol is the pallium, sign of pontifical delegacy.

43. In particular the *Admonitio generalis* of 789, edited by A. Boretius, *Monumenta Germaniae Historica, Legum sectio II, Capitularia regum Francorum*, I, p. 53.

44. The Carolingian plan to create archdeaconries and deaneries, intermediate between the ever more numerous parishes and the diocese, was not put into effect until the tenth and eleventh centuries (J. F. Lemarignier, *Le sacerdoce et la société chrétienne de la fin du IXe siècle au milieu du XIIe*, in *Prêtres d'hier et d'aujourd'hui*, Paris, 1954).

45. E. Griffe, *Aux origines de la liturgie gallicane*, in *Bulletin de littérature ecclésiastique*, LII, 1951, pp. 17–43.

46. E. Bishop and A. Wilmart, *La réforme liturgique de Charlemagne*, in *Ephemerides liturgicae*, XLV, 1931, p. 186, etc. On sacramentaries there is a clear and concise exposition in V. Leroquais, *Les sacramentaires et les missels manuscrits des bibliothèques publiques de France*, I, p. xi, etc., Paris, 1924. For the *ordines*, which are the complement of the sacramentaries, see part III of M. Andrieu, *Les ordines romani du haut moyen âge*, Louvain, 1931. For the breviary there is P. Batiffol, *Histoire du bréviaire romain*, 8. ed., Paris, 1911.

47. To use modern terms the Sacramentary contains the words of the Mass without the rubrics, not only the words recited by the celebrant (excluding therefore what is read by the deacon and the subdeacon, or sung by the choir, to be found respectively in the *Evangelistary*, the *Epistolary* and the *Gradual*) but also those accompanying the administration of the sacraments, baptism for instance, and other important liturgical functions such as exorcism. The *Ordinal* on the other hand gives the rubrics alone, without the formulae. It lays down the rites to be observed in the celebration of various ceremonies. The office or *Cursus* is shared out between a number of liturgical books: Psalter, Hymnal, Antiphoner, and so on. Like the player in an orchestra each executant has his own part written for him, separately from all the others.

48. G. Ellard, *Alcuin, liturgist; a partner of our piety*, Chicago, 1956.

49. P. Fournier and G. le Bras, *Histoire des collections canoniques en Occident*, I. p. 91, etc., Paris, 1931.

50. A. Werminghoff, *Monumenta Germaniae Historica, Legum Sectio III, Concilia aevi Karolini*, p. 321, etc.

51. C. Dereine, *Chanoines*, in *Dictionnaire d'histoire et de géographie ecclésiastiques*, XII, 1951, col. 369.

52. B. Albers, *Consuetudines Monasticae*, III, p. 115, etc., Monte Cassino, 1907.

53. P. Schmitz, *L'influence de Saint Benoît d'Aniane dans l'histoire de l'ordre de Saint Benoît*, in *Il monachesimo nell'alto medioevo*, pp. 401–16, Spoleto, 1957.

54. For the political role of the Frankish episcopate, especially after 829, see E. Delaruelle, *En relisant le De institutione regia de Jonas d'Orléans*, in *Mélanges Halphen*, p. 185, etc.

55. With Charles Martel the Carolingians began to practise 'secularization', that is to appropriate large portions of ecclesiastical domains and give them to their vassals. For want of any other means of rewarding their military men for their services they continued this practice as late as the eleventh century. The pernicious effects which resulted are illustrated by the example of Bavaria studied in P. Dollinger, *L'évolution des classes rurales en Bavière depuis la fin de l'époque carolingienne jusqu'au milieu du XIIIᵉ siècle*, p. 38, Paris, 1949.

56. *Epistola de litteris colendis, 780–800*, in A. Boretius, op. cit., p. 79.

57. *Admonitio generalis, 789*, in ibid., p. 53.

58. '*Quamobrem hortamur vos litterarum studia non solum non negligere, verum etiam discere . . .*' (*Epistola de litteris colendis*, loco cit.). '*Ad pernoscenda studia liberalium artium nostro etiam quos possumus invitamus exemplo.* (*Epistola generalis, 786–800*, in A. Boretius, op. cit., p. 80).

59. *Capitula ecclesiastica ad Salz data, 803–804* and *Capitula de causis diversis*, in A. Boretius, op. cit. pp. 119 and 135.

60. E. Lesne, op. cit., IV, p. 28, etc.

61. F. Masai, *Essai sur les origines de la miniature dite irlandaise*, Brussels, 1947, remarks on the influence of Anglo-Saxon miniature centred on Echternach. A. Boutemy, *Le style franco-saxon, style de Saint Amand*, in *Scriptorium*, III, 1949, pp. 260–64, points to the importance of Saint Amand as a centre of diffusion of this style.

62. E. Lesne, op. cit., V. *Les écoles de la fin du VIIIᵉ siècle à la fin du XIIᵉ*, p. 44, etc., Lille, 1940.

63. As E. Lesne shows, op. cit., V, p. 34, etc., the palace was less a school in the strict sense than an intellectual centre.

64. K. J. Conant, *Carolingian and Romanesque Architecture, 800 to 1200*, p. 11, etc., London, 1959; R. Lantier and J. Hubert, *Les origines de l'art français*, p. 158, etc., Paris, 1947.

65. C. R. Morey, *Lecture Notes on Carolingian Illuminated Manuscripts*, New York.

66. G. Haseloff, *Der Tassilo-Kelch*, Munich, 1951.

67. On these controversies see E. Amann, op. cit., p. 107, etc.; on the participants, A. Freeman, *Theodulf of Orleans and the 'Libri carolini'*, in *Speculum*, XXXII, 1957, pp. 663–705.

68. The poems of Theodulf have been published, with the rest of his works, in Migne, *Patrologia Latina*, CV, the *Historia Langobardorum* in

Monumenta Germaniae Historica, Scriptores rerum langobardicarum.
Theodulf is studied by H. Liebeschütz, *Theodulf of Orleans and the
Problem of the Carolingian Renaissance,* in *Memorial Essays for Fritz
Saxl,* pp. 77–92, London, 1957; Peter the Deacon is the subject of several
of the essays collected under the title *I Problemi della civiltà carolingia,*
Spoleto, 1954.

69. This is not certain. Recent excavations, at Souillac for example,
have brought to light hitherto unknown buildings which appear to
belong to the first generation of Carolingians.

70. The figure 8 symbolized eternal life; a building with eight sides
could symbolize Paradise.

71. Excavations carried out in Belgium in the last twenty years,
notably those of J. Mertens (see, e.g. *De oudheidkundige opgravingen in
de St. Lambertuskerke te Muizen,* in *Bulletin de la Commission Royale des
monuments et des sites,* II, 1950, p. 113–95) demonstrate that the central
plan was commoner than had been thought.

72. The origins of this Western block, often called by its German
name Westbau or Westwerk, are the subject of discussion. In a monograph long regarded as a classic, H. Reinhardt and E. Fels, *Étude sur les
églises-porches carolingiennes et leur survivance dans l'art roman,* in *Bulletin
monumental,* XCII, 1933, p. 331, etc., and XCVI, 1937, p. 426, etc., treat
it as a variation, a development or an improvement of the double choir,
known since the beginning of the Middle Ages. Many scholars today
reject this view, notably P. Francastel, *A propos des églises-porches;
du carolingien au roman,* in *Mélanges Halphen,* p. 247, etc. He holds that
this type of church originated in the joining up of two sanctuaries,
each of which had its liturgical function, for example devotion to the
relics of a martyr on the one hand and the worship of the Saviour on the
other.

As for the use to which this block was put opinions are still more
varied. For some it served to accommodate an altar to Christ the
Saviour, one of the principal devotions of the time. According to others
it was an imperial lodge, a *Gastkirche* for the sovereign and his suite.
Recently E. Stengel, *Über Ursprung, Zweck und Bedeutung der Karo-
lingischen Westwerke,* in *Festschrift A. Hofmeister,* pp. 283–311, Halle,
1955, gives it a military, defensive function.

73. Excavations conducted after the last war have shown that the
cathedral had indeed two choirs, but not two transepts as had been
thought. This and other discoveries have led L. Grodecki, *Sur l'origine
du plan d'église à transept double,* in *Urbanisme et architecture, études
écrites et publiées en l'honneur de Pierre Lavedan,* pp. 153–60, Paris,
1954, to push forward to the end of the tenth century the double
transept plan, a natural development of the double apse or the double
choir.

74. For one example see A. Boutemy, *Le scriptorium et la bibliothèque
de Saint-Amand,* in *Scriptorium,* I, 1946–7, p. 6, etc.

75. A. van de Vyver, *L'évolution scientifique du haut moyen âge,* in
Archeion, XIX, 1937, pp. 12–20, notes that Carolingian education was

almost entirely devoted to the *trivium*; outside this it cultivated astronomy and computation.

76. The work has been published in the *Patrologia Latina*, CXX. There is a monograph by H. Peltier, *Paschase Radbert, abbé de Corbie*, Amiens, 1938.

77. Dom M. Cappuyns, *Jean Scot Érigène, sa vie, son oeuvre, sa pensée*, Louvain, 1933.

78. *Hortulus* has been translated into French by A. Thérive, *Le jardinet de Gaufroy le louche*, Abbeville, n.d. (1925).

79. The works of Sedulius, Gottschalk and Wandalbert have been published in *Monumenta Germaniae Historica, Poetae Latini*, III, pp. 151, etc., 707, etc. and II, p. 569, etc.

80. L. Halphen, who has edited the *Vita* in the *Classiques de l'histoire de France au moyen âge*, refuses to allow it any historical value, but it is difficult to accept his view.

81. The *Vita* and the *Liber* are in the *Monumenta*, the first in the *Scriptores*, II, p. 604, etc., and the other in the *Scriptores rerum langobardicarum*.

82. This correspondence has been published by L. Levillain in *Les classiques de l'histoire de France au moyen âge*, Paris, 1927. The Latin in which it is written is the subject of C. Snyders, *Het Latijn der brieven van Lupus van Ferrières*, Amsterdam, 1943.

83. J. de Ghellinck, *Le mouvement théologique du XIIe siècle*, 2. ed., p. 29, etc., Bruges, 1948.

84. R. Rey, *L'art roman et ses origines*, p. 109, etc., Paris, 1945.

85. P. Deschamps and M. Thibout, *La peinture murale en France*, I, Paris, 1951.

86. R. Rey, op. cit., p. 134, has established a close relationship between the doors at Aix and those at Hildesheim or the font of Saint Bartholomew's church in Liège; the texts collected by F. Rousseau, *La Meuse et le pays mosan*, op. cit., p. 196, etc., show the truth of these views.

87. R. Crozet, *Les survivances de la pensée et de l'art antiques dans la peinture carolingienne*, in *Mélanges Halphen*, p. 165, etc.

88. S. Corbin, *L'Église à la conquête de sa musique*, Paris, 1960.

89. V. Lamperez, *Historia de la arquitectura cristiana española en la edad media*, I. 2. ed., p. 289, etc., Madrid, 1930.

90. F. M. Stenton, op. cit., p. 268, etc. and 436, etc. and P. Grierson, *Grimbald of St. Bertin's*, in *English Historical Review*, LV, 1940, p. 529, etc.

91. J. Seznec, *The survival of the Pagan Gods*, New York, 1954, draws attention to the fidelity with which Carolingian manuscripts reproduce the ancient Gods, who gradually become almost unrecognizable in later ages.

NOTES ON PART TWO

1. F. L. Ganshof, *L'échec de Charlemagne*, op. cit., p. 253; J. Calmette, *L'effondrement d'un Empire et la naissance d'une Europe*, Paris, 1942.

2. On the political activity of Louis the Pious see L. Halphen, op. cit., p. 221, etc. On his failures in the management of the royal fisc, see J. Dhondt, *Étude sur la naissance des principautés territoriales en France*, p. 13, Bruges, 1948. This latter writer alleges a maladjustment between political and economic organization as the basic cause of the fall of the Carolingian Empire; the economy was a land economy and 'an economy based on the soil cannot be reconciled with a great centralized state'. Agreed that the lack of commercial relations holding together the different regions of Western Europe and the absence of economic unity contributed to the break-up of the Empire; it is difficult to admit these as the main cause. We prefer to follow H. Mitteis, *Formen der Adelherrschaft im Mittelalter*, in *Festschrift F. Schulz*, II, p. 234, etc., Weimar, 1951, who regards the Germanic tradition of weak kings and an independent nobility as the real cause of political disintegration.

3. The question has never been resolved whether this first division of the Empire was caused, or at least hastened, by the birth of nationalism amongst the *Germani* and the *Franci*, as they were named by the historian of Louis the Pious. See E. Zoellner, *Die politische Stellung der Völker im Frankenreich*, Wien, 1950, for the affirmative case; W. Mohr, *Die begriffliche Absonderung des ostfränkischen Gebietes in westfränkischen Quellen des 9. und 10. Jahrhunderts*, in *Archivum latinitatis medii aevi*, XXIV, 1954, p. 19–41, is more circumspect; J. Dienemann, *Der Kult des heiligen Kilian im 8. und 9. Jahrhundert*, Würzburg, 1955, has discovered a phenomenon which strongly supports the first view: the appearance of patron saints of Eastern Francia, the kingdom of Louis the German, in the middle of the ninth century.

4. This quotation from Odo's *Collationes* is given in the translation by A. Fliche, *L'Europe occidentale de 888 à 1125*, in G. Glotz, *Histoire générale. Moyen Âge*, II, p. 591, Paris, 1941.

CHAPTER V

1. These three texts are respectively the Preamble and paragraph 30 of the 'law' given to the serfs of the chapter of St. Peter at Worms by Bishop Burchard; two passages from the *Liber historiarum* of Radulfus Glaber, a monk of Dijon and later Cluny; and finally some phrases from the life of Bishop John of Thérouanne by Walter of Thérouanne. They have been published in *Monumenta Germaniae Historica, Legum sectio IV, Constitutiones et acta publica*, I, p. 639, etc.: Migne, *Patrologia Latina*, CXLII, or M. Prou, *Raoul Glaber, les cinq livres de ses histoires*, in *Collection de textes pour servir à l'étude et l'enseignement de l'histoire*,

Paris, 1886, Bk. IV, Ch. V; *Monumenta Germaniae Historica, Scriptores,* XV, p. 1146.

2. L. Verriest, *Institutions médiévales,* op. cit., *passim,* attacks the exaggerated views which are current on this question.

3. L. Musset, *Relations et échanges d'influences dans l'Europe du Nord-Ouest* (*Xe-XIe siècles*), in *Cahiers de civilisation médiévale,* I, 1958, pp. 63–82.

4. G. Fasoli, *Points de vue sur les incursions hongroises en Europe au Xe siècle,* in *Ib.,* II, 1959, pp. 17–36: a general exposition, somewhat open to criticism.

5. M. Bloch, *La société féodale,* I, p. 64, etc., Paris, 1939, insists on the importance of these economic and political changes.

6. Below, Chap. VII, p. 134.

7. Below, Chap. VI, p. 114.

8. T. D. Kendrick, *Late Saxon and Viking Art,* London, 1949; D. Talbot-Rice, *English Art, 871–1100,* Oxford, 1952.

9. There was no longer any public for vernacular literature at the court or in those circles which took their lead from the court.

10. R. Bezzola, *Les origines et la formation de la littérature courtoise en Occident, 500–1200,* I, p. 239, etc., Paris, 1944, and A. Boutemy, *Autour de Godefroid de Reims,* in *Latomus,* VI, 1947, p. 231, etc.

11. K. F. Werner, *Untersuchungen zur Frühzeit des französischen Fürstentums, 9–10 Jh.,* in *Die Welt als Geschichte,* 1958, p. 261, etc.

12. W. Kienast, *Untertaneneid und Treuvorbehalt in Frankreich und England,* p. 23, Weimar, 1952.

13. Did the existence within the Carolingian Empire of 'peoples' or 'races' favour the rise of these political organisms? J. Dhondt, op. cit., answers in the affirmative for France and H. Mitteis, *Der Staat des hohen Mittelalters,* 4. ed., p. 110, Weimar, 1953, likewise for Germany. The most recent work, summarized by H. Sproemberg, *La Naissance d'un état allemand au moyen âge,* in *Le Moyen Âge,* LXIV, 1958, pp. 213–48, shows that the national or ethnic character of the duchies has been exaggerated and that they were essentially creations of the dukes.

14. The kingdom could not go on being divided; after three or four generations partition between all the sons of the king had to be abandoned, and it may well have been practical necessity which forced on the whole of Western Europe at that time the principle of indivisibility. This view appears to derive confirmation from the fact that partition was given up under the last Merovingians, only to be taken up again for a hundred years once the kingdom had been unified again by the Carolingians.

15. Quoted in E. Amann and A. Dumas, *L'Église au pouvoir des laïques,* p. 486, in *Histoire de l'Église* by Fliche and Martin, Paris, 1948.

16. *Gesta episcoporum Cameracensium,* in *Monumenta Germaniae Historica, Scriptores,* VII, p. 474.

17. Below, Chap. VII, p. 135.

18. The Kingdom of Burgundy became part of the Empire in 1034.

19. E. N. Johnson, *The Secular Activities of the Germanic Episcopate, 919–1024*, Chicago, 1931.

20. The origins of this official class and the stages of its social and legal elevation are a matter of controversy: A. Bosl, *Die Reichsministerialität der Salier und Staufer*, Stuttgart, 1950–1, summarizes the present state of knowledge in its early pages. In a review published in *Historische Zeitschrift*, 1960, p. 353, Bosl gives a slightly different colour to current views on Henry IV's policy towards this class; he holds that Henry did not place his reliance only on them but at the same time attempted to win over the nobility by conceding them lands and official positions.

21. Quotations from Bosl, op. cit.

22. On the Concordat of Worms and its political effects see below, p. 119. On the attitude of the Staufen towards the towns see H. Sproemberg, *Contribution à l'histoire de l'idée d'Empire au moyen âge*, in *Revue belge de philologie et d'histoire*, XXXIX, 1961, p. 322, etc., who has a different opinion from us; for him the successors of Henry IV broke the alliance which he had made with the cities; Frederick in particular valued the support of princes more than that of burgesses, and to gain the former he sacrificed the latter.

23. R. Folz, *L'idée d'Empire en Occident, du Vᵉ au XIVᵉ siècle*, Paris, 1953, and F. Kempf, *Das mittelalterliche Kaisertum*, in *Das Königtum: seine geistigen und rechtlichen Grundlagen*, p. 225–43, Lindau, 1956, analyse the notion of Empire and its incarnations; although the basic conception did not change, least of all with Frederick I (for him the Emperor remained the *summus ecclesiae defensor* as he was defined in the time of Louis the Pious) it was refined in minor ways by the different theorists who considered it at various times.

As for the association of universal monarchy with the German monarchy, it had both advantages and disadvantages for the latter: H. Mitteis, op. cit., p. 122, remarks that it helped to unite Germany by engaging her in tasks common to all; H. Sproemberg, loco cit., emphasizes that it prevented Otto I and his successors from giving a national character to their rule.

24. Frederick II's concessions to the German princes are examined by E. Klingelhoefer, *Die Reichsgesetze von 1220, 1231–32 und 1235*, Weimar, 1955. The destruction of political unity, given constitutional form by these laws, did not entail the disappearance of every trace of communal feeling. As H. Sproemberg has shown (*Die Hanse in europäischer Sicht*, in *Dancwerc: Festschrift D.Th. Enklaar*, 1959, p. 148), at the end of the Middle Ages the merchants, in particular the Hanseatic merchants, and the ruling classes in the towns were conscious of belonging to a German entity.

25. Dante, *Paradiso*, VI. 110.

26. R. Fawtier, *Les Capétiens et la France*, Paris, 1942.

27. Above, Chap. IV, p. 67

28. J. F. Lemarignier, *Les fidèles du Roi de France*, in *Recueil Clovis Brunel*, p. 161, Paris, 1955.

29. The whole of the work carried out in recent years comes to the

conclusion that the fragmentation of France was not a sudden pheno-menon of the ninth century, but a gradual process; see J. F. Lemarig-nier's review of G. Duby, *La société aux XIe et XIIe siècles dans la région mâconnaise*, in *Le Moyen Âge*, LXII, 1956, p. 169, etc. P. Feuchère, *Essai sur l'évolution territoriale des principautés françaises, X^e-XIIe siècles*, in *Le Moyen Âge*, LVIII, 1952, pp. 85–117, is able to show that its extent depended on such factors as the personal character of the ruler, the strength of the administration, commercial activity, the size and geographical configuration of the country.

For the region of Toulouse, where fragmentation reached its maximum about A.D. 1000 see A. Dupont, *Les cités de la Narbonnaise première*, p. 448, etc., Nîmes, 1942. For Provence see R. Aubenas, *Les châteaux forts des Xe et XIe siècles*, in *Revue historique de droit français et étranger*, LXII, 1938, p. 548, etc. For the Lyonnais see L. de Neufbourg, *Puissance relative du comte et des seigneurs en Forez au XIIIe siècle*, in *Le Moyen Âge*, LXI, 1955, p. 407. For Anjou see J. Boussard, *La Vie en Anjou aux XIe et XIIe siècles*, in ibid., LVI, 1950, p. 32, etc. For Burgundy see G. Duby, op. cit., p. 161.

30. R. Bezzola, *De Roland à Raoul de Cambrai*, in *Mélanges Ernest Hoepffner*, pp. 195–213, Paris, 1949.

31. L. Genicot, *L'économie rurale namuroise au bas moyen âge*. II, *Les hommes. La noblesse*, p. 6, Louvain, 1960.

32. G. Duby, *Recherches sur l'évolution des institutions judiciaires pendant le Xe et le XIe siècles dans le sud de la Bourgogne*, in *Le Moyen Âge*, LIII, 1947, p. 20, etc.; Y. Bongert, *Recherches sur les cours laïques du Xe au XIIIe siècle*, p. 71, Paris, 1948.

33. *Garin le Loherain*, transl. by P. Paris, p. 62.

34. *Chronicon Afflighemense*, in *Monumenta Germaniae Historica, Scriptores*, IX, p. 408.

35. F. L. Ganshof, *La Flandre sous les premiers comtes*, 2. ed., p. 104, Brussels, 1944.

36. For examples see G. Duby, *La société* (op. cit., note 29), p. 195.

37. Below, Chap. VI, p. 115.

38. R. Bonnaud-Delamare, *Le fondement des institutions de paix au XIe siècle*, in *Mélanges Halphen*, p. 19, etc., emphasizes that the pro-moters of the 'Peace' or 'Truce of God' were not immediately and uniquely concerned with putting an end to private wars and restoring peace among men, but with establishing the Divine order and the peace of Christ in the world, and their attack on all forms of disorder was directed to this end. Their object was really the same as that of the Gregorians. See p. 115.

39. Above, Chap. III, p. 51.

40. Lecoy de la Marche, *La chaire française au moyen âge*, Paris, 1886, notes that there was a Renaissance of preaching in the twelfth century.

41. This text, taken from a prayer for the blessing of the sword, which dates from the later tenth century, is printed in C. Erdmann, *Die Entstehung des Kreuzzugsgedankens*, p. 330, Stuttgart, 1936. Many passages in this book deal with the development of the ideal of chivalry.

42. Below, Chap. VII.

43. P. Rousset, *Les origines et les caractères de la première croisade*, Neuchâtel, 1945.

44. For examples see F. L. Ganshof, op. cit., for Flanders, J. Boussard, op. cit., for Anjou, and J. Richard, *Les ducs de Bourgogne et la formation du duché du XIe au XIVe siècle*, Paris, 1954.

45. R. Foreville, *Aux origines de la renaissance juridique*, in *Le Moyen Âge*, LVIII, 1952, p. 46.

46. J. Yver, *Contribution à l'étude du développement de la compétence ducale en Normandie*, in *Annales de Normandie*, année 8, 1958, pp. 139–83 and *Notes sur la justice seigneuriale en Normandie au XIIIe siècle*, in *Revue historique de droit français et étranger*, 1959, p. 272.

47. L. Genicot, *Noblesse et principautés en Lotharingie*, in *Scrinium Lovaniense. Études historiques E. van Cauwenbergh*, Louvain, 1961.

48. J. F. Lemarignier, *Autour de la royauté française du IXe au XIIIe siècle*, in *Bibliothèque de l'École des Chartes*, CXIII, 1955, pp. 5–36, defines the religious nature of the royal power.

49. This expression is borrowed from Ordericus Vitalis, *Historiae ecclesiasticae libri XIII*, ed. by A. Le Prévost, IV, p. 360, Paris, 1852. Y. Bongert, op. cit., quotes texts which prove the prestige of royalty in the eyes of the great feudal nobility.

50. On the royal domain before the Capetians see J. Dhondt, op. cit., p. 259, etc.: for the later history see W. N. Newman, *Le domaine royal sous les premiers Capétiens*, Paris, 1937.

51. J. Dhondt, *Quelques aspects du règne d'Henri I, roi de France,* in *Mélanges Halphen*, p. 199, etc.

52. *Vies de Louis VI et de Louis VII*, ed. by H. Waquet, in *Les classiques de l'histoire de France au moyen âge*, Paris, 1929.

53. W. Kienast, op. cit., p. 133; A. Dessau, *L'idée de la trahison au moyen âge*, in *Cahiers de civilisation médiévale*, III, 1960, p. 25, notes a change in this respect in the second half of the twelfth century: *chansons de geste* before this date allow the vassal to attack an unworthy lord; versions later than about 1150 deny him the right to attack his lord for any reason whatever; the author does not make it clear whether the rule applies to all, or only to the king; his examples are all royal.

54. G. Duby, op. cit., pp. 558–9. Compare this policy with that of the Carolingians, p. 66 above, and that of Frederick I, p. 95.

55. W. Kienast, op. cit., *passim*.

56. Y. Bongert, op. cit., p. 137, etc., describes the part played by the kings in the field of justice; L. Buisson, *König Ludwig IX, der Heilige, und das Recht*, Fribourg, n.d., deals with the activities of Saint Louis in this respect.

57. Research continues on Catharism and particularly on its origins (spontaneous genesis like the popular heresies of the time, Oriental influence, direct or secondary), on its doctrine (uncertain, for lack of texts) and its real content (religious or, in whole or in part, social). On these questions see A. Borst, *Die Katharer*, in *Schriften der Monumenta*

Germaniae Historica, XII, Stuttgart, 1953; C. Thouzellier, *Hérésie et croisade au XIIe siècle,* in *Revue d'histoire ecclésiastique,* XLIX, 1954, pp. 855–72; R. R. Betts and others, *Movimenti religiosi popolari ed eresie del medioevo,* in *X Congresso internazionale di scienze storiche, Roma, 1955. Relazioni,* III; and finally a somewhat tendentious work, which however is useful in that it employs the results of research in the Slavonic countries, E. Werner and M. Erbstoesser, *Sozial-religiöse Bewegungen im Mittelalter,* in *Wissenschaftliche Zeitschrift der Karl Marx Universität Leipzig. Gesellschafts- und Sprachwissenschaftliche Reihe,* Heft 3.

58. P. Belperron, *La croisade contre les Albigeois et l'union du Languedoc à la France,* Paris, 1942.

CHAPTER VI

1. Examples are to be found, for the regular clergy in the earlier pages of E. Sackur, *Die Cluniazenser,* I, Halle, 1892, and for the secular clergy in A. Fliche, *La réforme grégorienne,* I, Louvain, 1924.

2. E. Amann and A. Dumas, *L'Église au pouvoir des laïques,* in *Histoire de l'Église* by Fliche and Martin, Paris, 1948.

3. There is a traditional identification of political or simoniacal nomination to benefices with negligence of pastoral duties. There are many monographs which demonstrate the falsity of this opinion. A. Fliche, *Premiers résultats d'une enquête sur la Réforme grégorienne dans les diocèses français,* in *Comptes rendus des séances de l'Académie des Inscriptions et Belles-Lettres,* 1944, p. 162, etc., emphasizes that prelates who were elected for temporal reasons or by the use of bribes did not necessarily conduct themselves ill, and D. C. Douglas, *The Norman Episcopate before the Norman Conquest,* in *Cambridge Historical Journal,* XIII, 1957, p. 101–15, shows that bishops might lead a life most unsuitable to their office and yet be capable of good ecclesiastical government.

4. J. Choux, *Recherches sur le diocèse de Toul au temps de la réforme grégorienne: l'épiscopat de Pibon, 1069–1107,* p. 110, Nancy, 1952.

5. L. Duchesne, *Les premiers temps de l'État pontifical,* 2. ed., Paris, 1911.

6. The words of Gerbert of Aurillac at the Council of Basle, in 991 (*Patrologia Latina,* CXXXIX, p. 314).

7. H. W. Klewitz, *Königtum, Hofkapelle und Domkapitel im 10. und 11. Jahrhundert,* in *Archiv für Urkundenforschung,* XVI, 1939, p. 102, etc.

8. E. de Moreau, *Histoire de l'Église en Belgique,* 2. ed., II, p. 25, etc., Brussels, 1945.

9. Anselm, *Gesta episcoporum Leodensium,* in *Monumenta Germaniae Historica, Scriptores,* VII, pp. 224 and 225.

10. For the Rule of Aix, see above, p. 71; for its survival see C. Dereine, *Clercs et moines au diocèse de Liège, du Xe au XIIe siècle,* in *Annales de la Société archéologique de Namur,* XLV, 1950, p. 183–203.

11. Peter Damian, who was strongly opposed to clerical concubinage and marriage, reports this claim in his *Opusculum contra intemperantes clericos* (in *Patrologia Latina,* CXLV, col. 393).

12. M. Bloch, *La Société féodale*, I, pp. 36–7, Paris, 1939.

13. To give examples, A. Verhulst, *De Sint-Baafsabdij te Gent en haar grondbezit (VIIe-XIVe eeuw)*, in *Verhandelingen van de Koninklijke Vlaamse Academie voor Wetenschapen, Letteren en Schone Kunsten van België. Klasse der Letteren*. nr. 30, p. 58, etc. (p. 596 of the résumé in French) notes that the secularizations at Saint Bavo in Ghent continued until 1040.

14. J. Choux, *Décadence et réforme monastique dans la province de Trèves, 855–959*, in *Revue bénédictine*, LXX, 1960, p. 205, etc.

15. E. John, *The sources of English reformation*, in *Revue bénédictine*, LXX, p. 197, etc., differs resolutely from current views on the reform of English monasteries in the tenth century. For him the reform did not begin at Glastonbury, and Saint Dunstan did not establish any regular observance there; Saint Ethelwold was the principal reformer, but the reform had nothing very original about it; through Fleury it was influenced by Cluniac conceptions.

16. There is a picture of the monastic movements of the period in P. Schmitz, *Histoire de l'ordre de Saint-Benoît*, I, p. 127, etc., Maredsous, 1942 and a statement of the problems connected with them will be found in K. Hallinger, *Progressi e probleme delle ricerche sulla riforma pre-gregoriana*, in *Il monachesimo nell'alto medioevo*, pp. 257–92, Spoleto, 1957.

17. The main works on Cluny are listed in *À Cluny, Congrès scientifique*, Dijon, 1950, and in the introduction by G. Tellenbach to *Neue Forschungen über Cluny und die Cluniacenser*, Freiburg, 1959.

18. S. Hilpisch, *Günther und das Mönchtum seiner Zeit*, in *1000 Jahre St. Günther*, pp. 57–61, Köln, 1955 and K. Hallinger, *Le climat spirituel des premiers temps de Cluny*, in *Revue Mabillon*, XLVI, 1956, pp. 117–40 insist on an opposition between a purely religious monasticism and the cultural monasticism of the Empire; J. Leclercq, *Cluny fut-il ennemi de la culture?* in ibid., XLVII, 1957, pp. 173–82, sees little justification for this antithesis.

19. P. Cousin, *Précis d'histoire monastique*, p. 251, Paris, 1956, gives the time-table for the day at Cluny.

20. R. Rey, *Un précurseur de l'art des cloîtres: saint Benoît d'Aniane*, in *Annales publiées par la Faculté des Lettres de Toulouse*, I, 1953, p. 141–56, shows how Benedict of Aniane's buildings heralded those of Cluny; the latter are studied in K. J. Conant, *Carolingian and Romanesque Architecture, 800 to 1200*, London, 1959.

21. J. F. Lemarignier, *L'exemption monastique et les origines de la réforme grégorienne*, in *À Cluny*, p. 228, etc., digests and supplements the traditional views on the origins of the exemption which removed a monastery from the bishop's authority and made it an independent enclave within the diocese. W. Schwarz, *Jurisdictio et condicio, eine Untersuchung zu den Privilegia libertatis der Klöster*, in *Zeitschrift der Savigny-Stiftung für Rechtsgeschichte, Kanonistische Abteilung*, XLV, 1959, pp. 34–98, attacks these views on several points.

22. J. Hourlier, *Cluny et la notion d'ordre religieux*, in *À Cluny*, pp.

219–28, maintains that there was an institutional link between the houses which followed the Cluniac Rule. J. F. Lemarignier on the other hand thinks it is anachronistic to speak of a Cluniac order before 1027.

23. H. Diener, *Das Verhältnis Clunys zu den Bischöfen, vor allem in der Zeit seines Abtes Hugo,* in *Neue Forschungen,* pp. 219–352, differs slightly from current positions on this point; he holds that Cluny generally maintained good relations with the bishops and sometimes disagreed with the Papacy on the best means of improving the state of religion.

24. S. Berthellier, *L'expansion de l'ordre de Cluny et ses rapports avec l'histoire politique et économique du Xe au XIIe siècle,* in *Revue archéologique,* VI, 1938, p. 319, etc.

25. *Gérard de Brogne et son oeuvre réformatrice,* in *Revue bénédictine,* LXX, pp. 1–240; J. Choux, op. cit.; K. Hallinger, *Gorze-Kluny,* Rome, 1950–1; H. Dauphin, *Le bienheureux Richard, abbé de Saint-Vanne de Verdun,* Louvain, 1946. Hallinger picks out the differences between Cluny and the houses of Lorraine, but makes too much of them. Contacts were quite frequent between members of the two movements and quite a number of abbeys in Lorraine were influenced by the Burgundian monastery.

26. Above, note 15.

27. L. Musset, *Les peuples scandinaves au moyen âge,* p. 127, etc., Paris, 1951.

28. D. Knowles, *The monastic order in England: a history of its development from the time of St. Dunstan to the fourth Lateran Council,* Cambridge, 1940.

29. J. Leclercq, *Saint Pierre Damien, ermite et homme d'église,* Rome, 1960, has something on Romuald, p. 22, etc. Authors like M. della Santa, *Ricerche sull'idea monastica di San Pier Damiano,* Arezzo, 1961, rightly attack the current view that the foundations of Romuald, or some of them at least, contained both cenobites, the younger and stronger members, and hermits.

30. One work on these links between the tenth and the eleventh century is Th. Schieffer, *Cluny et la Querelle des Investitures,* in *Revue historique,* CCXXV, 1961, pp. 47–72.

31. The idea of cleansing the Church by freeing it from lay interference was formulated and applied in the Carolingian period, as the following authors have observed: H. Fichtenau, *Das karolingische Imperium,* pp. 231–2, Zürich, 1949; G. Mollat, *La restitution des églises privées au patrimoine ecclésiastique en France, du IXe au XIe siècle,* in *Revue historique de droit français et étranger,* 1949, pp. 399, etc.; J. F. Lemarignier, op. cit., p. 295.

32. See above, p. 107. On the activity of the Emperors, particularly Henry III, at the beginning of the movement, see the first chapters of C. Violante, *La Pataria milanese e la riforma ecclesiastica,* I, Roma, 1955.

33. In the work referred to in note 1 and in *La Querelle des Investitures,* Paris, 1946, A. Fliche makes Lorraine the cradle of the Gregorian movement. C. Dereine, *L'école canonique liégeoise et la réforme gré-*

gorienne, in *Fédération archéologique et historique de Belgique. Annales du XXXIIIe Congrès, Tournai*, 1949, II, pp. 79–94, gives a more modest place to the clerics of Liège: they took a conservative position, preferring collaboration and a balance of power as between Pope and Emperor, and except for Humbert of Silva Candida, never manifested the radicalism characteristic of the Gregorians.

34. R. Folz, *L'idée d'Empire en Occident*, p. 88, Paris, 1953.

35. G. Tellenbach, *Libertas. Kirche und Weltordnung im Zeitalter des Investiturstreites*, Stuttgart, 1936. An English translation of this book, by R. F. Bennet, has appeared under the title *Church, State and Christian Society at the time of the Investiture Contest*, Oxford, 1940; some of the original appendices are omitted but there are two new ones, particularly one on Gregory's aims. *Adversus simoniacos* has been published by F. Thaner in *Monumenta Germaniae Historica, Libelli de lite imperatorum et pontificum*, I, p. 100, etc.

36. The *Diversorum patrum sententiae* or 'Collection in 74 titles' have been attributed to Humbert by A. Michel, *Die Sentenzen des Kardinals Humbert, das erste Rechtsbuch der päpstlichen Reform*, Leipzig, 1943. S. Runciman, *The Eastern Schism: a study on the Papacy and the Eastern Churches during the XIth and XIIth centuries*, Oxford, 1955, insists that the break was not complete before the first crusade or perhaps even the fourth.

37. Above, Chap. III, p. 53.

38. Two recent works trace the origin and development of medieval theocracy: W. Ullman, *The Growth of Papal Government in the Middle Ages*, London 1955 and M. Pacaut, *La théocratie. L'Eglise et le pouvoir au moyen âge*, Paris, 1957. Both have been the object of adverse cirticism; on the first see particularly notices by R. Folz, in *Le Moyen Âge*, LXII, 1956, pp. 185–92 and A. Stickler, *Concerning the political theories of the medieval canonists*, in *Traditio*, VII, 1949–51, pp. 450–63.

39. The *Dictatus Papae* in the letters of Gregory VII have been published by E. Caspar in *Monumenta Germaniae Historica. Epistolae selectae. Das Registrum Gregors VII.*, 2 vol., 1920–3. On their origins see G. B. Borino, *Un ipotesi sul 'Dictatus Papae' di Gregorio VII*, in *Archivio della Regia Deputazione Romana di Storia Patria*, N.S., X, 1944, p. 240, etc.

40. The decrees of 1059 are in *Monumenta Germaniae Historica. Constitutiones et acta publica*, I, p. 539, etc. They required that the choice of new cardinals should be submitted to the people for approval and gave the Emperor, in very vague terms, a sort of watching brief. In 1060 the decrees were promulgated again and this time they mentioned neither people nor Emperor; see A. Michel, *Das Papstwahlpactum von 1059*, in *Historisches Jahrbuch*, LIX, 1939, p. 291, etc.

41. G. B. Borino, *L'investitura laica dal decreto di Nicolo II al decreto di Gregorio VII*, in *Studi gregoriani*, V, p. 345–59, Roma, 1956, compares the decrees of Nicholas II and those of Gregory VII and shows that the latter were more severe.

42. As Z. N. Brooke observes in *Lay investiture and its relation to the*

conflict of Empire and Papacy, in *Proceedings of the British Academy*, XXV, 1939, p. 217, etc., negotiations between Pope and Emperor followed the second promulgation of the sixth canon of 1059. We are not persuaded that it was the question of choosing a new archbishop of Milan, in December 1075, which caused the breakdown. Henry IV may have wished to reach agreement, but it seems more probable that he was only temporizing until he was sure of the submission of Saxony.

43. N. F. Cantor, *Church, Kingship and Lay Investiture in England, 1089–1135*, Princeton, 1958, observes that the distinction between investiture and homage, ecclesiastical dignity and lay fief, existed as early as the eleventh century in England.

44. G. Mollat, *Le droit de patronage en Normandie du XIᵉ au XVᵉ siècle*, in *Revue d'histoire ecclésiastique*, XXXIII, 1937, p. 463, etc.

45. Some churches, like those of Trier or Ravenna, and some individuals, Saint Bernard, for instance (*De consideratione*, in *Patrologia Latina*, CLXXXII, col. 727, etc.), strongly condemned this tendency. Many bishops, on the other hand, fostered it by referring very minor decisions to Rome. See A. Fliche, *Innocent III et la réforme de l'Église*, in *Revue d'histoire ecclésiastique*, XLIV, 1949, p. 98, etc.

46. The right of canonization, which was claimed as a prerogative of the Papacy from the time of Alexander III (1159–81), became in fact its exclusive right after the Decretals of Gregory IX (1234). See E. W. Kemp, *Canonization and Authority in the Western Church*, London, 1948.

47. Above, Chap. V, p. 103.

48. The studies of A. Fliche, op. cit., note 45 above, of F. Kempf, *Papsttum und Kaisertum bei Innocenz III*, Rome, 1954, and H. Tillmann, *Papst Innocenz III*, Bonn, 1954, have thrown new light on this figure, generally taken, quite wrongly, as the incarnation of theocracy.

49. B. Blégny, *L'Église et les ordres religieux dans le royaume de Bourgogne aux XIᵉ et XIIᵉ siècles*, Paris, 1960, gives details; bishops and canons were more influenced by remonstrance than the parish clergy.

50. For the continuance of grave errors in the recruitment of the lower clergy see O. Dobiache-Rojdesvensky, *La vie paroissiale en France au XIIIᵉ siècle d'après les actes épiscopaux*, Paris, 1911. For the behaviour of the lower clergy in this period see G. de Lagarde, *La naissance de l'esprit laïque au déclin du moyen âge*, I, 3. ed., p. 83, Paris, 1956, and below, p. 222.

51. Although canons might own their own houses they were required by the Rule of Aix to have dormitory and refectory in common.

52. C. Dereine, *Chanoines*, in *Dictionnaire d'histoire et de géographie ecclésiastiques*, XII, 1951, col. 375, etc.

53. The first community of Canons Regular of any importance in England dates from 1104. See J. C. Dickinson, *The origins of the Austin Canons and their introduction into England*, London, 1950.

54. M. D. Chenu, *Moines, clercs et laïques au carrefour de la vie évangélique*, in *Revue d'histoire ecclésiastique*, XLIX, 1954, pp. 59–89, deals with the aspirations which turned an increasing number of men

away from traditional monasticism and its detachment from the world. For the heresies of the Middle Ages see below, pp. 168 and 230.

55. *Sigeberti Chronographiae Continuatio Praemonstratensis, anno 1131,* in *Monumenta Germaniae Historica, Scriptores,* VI, p. 450.

56. H. Grundmann, *Religiöse Bewegungen im Mittelalter,* in *Historische Studien,* Heft 267, Berlin, 1935, and P. Mandonnet, *Saint Dominique.* II. *Perspectives,* Paris, 1937.

57. B. Blégny, *Les premiers Chartreux et la pauvreté,* in *Le Moyen Âge,* LVII, 1951, pp. 27–60, compares the spiritual life of the Carthusians with that of their contemporaries; A. de Meyer and J. M. de Smet, *Guido's 'Consuetudines' van de eerste Kartuizers,* in *Mededeelingen van de Koninklijke Vlaamse Academie voor Wetenschappen, Letteren en Schone Kunsten van België,* 1951, analyse the Constitutions of the Order.

58. Cistercian literalism was not uniquely caused by the common aspiration of the time to return to primitive perfection and by a consequent attachment to the precise wording of texts (an example of which is to be seen in Robert of Arbrissel's foundation of double, male-female, religious houses under an abbess, which he derived from the words of Christ on the Cross: 'Woman, behold thy son!'). P. Salmon, *L'ascèse monastique et les origines de Cîteaux,* in *Mélanges Saint-Bernard,* pp. 268–83, Dijon, 1955, shows that another motive was reaction against the spiritually dangerous distinction made at Cluny between immutable observances and variable usage.

59. Several articles, notably those of J. A. Lefèvre, the latest being *Que savons-nous du Cîteaux primitif?* in *Revue d'histoire ecclésiastique,* LI, 1956, pp. 5–41, cast doubt on the accepted theories of the origin of the Cistercian foundation, whilst others, like Dereine's *La fondation de Cîteaux d'après l'Exordium Cistercii et l'Exordium parvum,* in *Cîteaux in de Nederlanden,* X, 1959, pp. 125–93, defend the traditional view. It is interesting to note that before Saint Robert other eleventh-century monks interpreted the Benedictine Rule in a rather similar way, for example Herluin, founder of the Norman abbey of Bec in 1034, who governed his monks '*arctissime*' and set an example of manual labour in the gardens and fields of the monastery (*Patrologia Latina,* CL, col. 702).

60. *Bernard de Clairvaux,* Paris, 1953 and *Mélanges Saint-Bernard,* Dijon, 1955.

61. L. Genicot, *Présentation d'Étienne de Muret et de la pauvreté,* in *Revue nouvelle,* XIX, 1954, pp. 579–89; J. Becquet, *Les institutions de l'ordre de Grandmont au moyen âge,* in *Revue Mabillon,* XLII, 1952, pp. 31–42.

62. The *Vita Roberti* is in *Patrologia Latina,* CLXII.

63. M. H. Vicaire, *Histoire de Saint Dominique,* 2 vol., Paris, 1957.

64. L. Salvatorelli, *Movimento francescano e gioachimismo* and E. Delaruelle, *L'influence de saint François d'Assise sur la piété populaire,* in *X Congresso internazionale di scienze storiche, Roma, 1955. Relazioni,* III, pp. 403–66, provide a good introduction to Franciscanism and its problems.

65. These words of the Pseudo-Bonaventure are taken from F. Vernet, *La spiritualité médiévale*, p. 199, Paris, n.d. (1928). The Dutch review *Sint Franciscus* published a number of articles on the spiritual aspects of Franciscanism, in vols. LVIII and LIX (1956, 1957), which show clearly that Francis was 'playing the part of Christ'. L. Génicot, *La spiritualité médiévale*, pp. 73–84, Paris, 1958, expounds the part played by Dominicans and Franciscans in the discovery of the material world as a witness of the Creator's hand. See also below, p. 172.

66. A. Mens, *Oorsprong en betekenis van de Nederlandse begijnen- en begardenbeweging*, in *Verhandelingen van de Koninklijke Vlaamse Academie voor Wetenschappen, Letteren en Schone Kunsten van België. Klasse der Letteren*, IX, 7, 1947; E. McDonnel, *The Beguines and Beghards in medieval Culture*, New Brunswick, 1954; H. Grundmann, *Il beghinismo*, in *X Congresso*, pp. 467–84; according to D. Phillips, *Beguines in Medieval Strasburg*, Stanford, 1941, Strasburg must have had 300 beguines out of a total of 20,000 inhabitants, a figure which helps us to understand the importance of the problem.

67. J. H. Mundy, *Hospitals and leprosaries in Toulouse*, in *Essays in honor of A. P. Evans*, New York, 1955, is able to show that 13 hospitals and 7 lazarettos were founded in Toulouse between the end of the eleventh and the middle of the thirteenth centuries.

68. The *Chronicon* of Bernold of Constance speaks of the great multitude of German laymen who were leading some kind of community life at the end of the eleventh century. It is published in *Monumenta Germaniae Historica. Scriptores*, V, p. 453. G. G. Meersseman and E. Adda, *Pénitents communautaires en Italie au XIIᵉ siècle*, in *Revue d'histoire ecclésiastique*, XLIX, 1954, pp. 343–490, study the movement in Italy, where it was less ephemeral.

69. Ilarino da Milano, *Le eresie popolari del secolo XI nell'Europa occidentale*, in *Studi gregoriani*, II, p. 43, etc., Roma, 1947; also above, Chap. V, p. 103 and below, Chap. XI, p. 230.

70. C. Dereine, *Le premier ordo de Prémontré*, in *Revue Bénédictine*, LVIII, 1948, p. 84, etc.

71. See for example the *Dialogus duorum monachorum* published by Martène and Durand, *Thesaurus novus anecdotorum*, V, col. 1593.

72. It is difficult to discover whether Cistercian asceticism influenced their architecture from the start. The existing churches, none of which is earlier than 1145, cannot resolve the problem. But the documents, particularly the admirable Stephen Harding MSS. in the Municipal Library of Dijon, would lead us to give a negative answer; it seems that only after several decades was it decided to practise strict austerity.

73. For Otto III's political ideas, see R. Folz, op. cit., p. 69, etc.

74. G. Tellenbach, *Die Bedeutung des Reformpapsttums für die Einigung des Abendlandes*, in *Studi gregoriani*, II, p. 125, etc.

75. F. Kempf, *Imperium und Nationen in ihrem Bezug zur Christianitas-Idee*, in *X Congresso. Riassunti delle communicazioni*, VII, pp. 202–5.

76. For the influence on Spain of the French monastic orders, Cluny,

Cîteaux and the congregations of Canons, like Saint Ruf, see M. Defourneaux, *Les Français en Espagne aux XIe et XIIe siècles*, p. 17, etc., Paris, 1949; C. Higounet, *Une carte des relations monastiques transpyrénéennes au moyen âge*, in *Revue de Comminges*. LXIV, 1951, p. 129, etc.; C. Dereine, op. cit., col. 289. For the abolition of the Mozarabic Rite, see P. David, *Études historiques sur la Galice et le Portugal du VIe au XIIe siècle*, p. 350, etc., Lisbon, 1947, and R. B. Donovan, *The Liturgical Drama in Medieval Spain*, pp. 20–9, Toronto, 1958.

CHAPTER VII

1. A. Sauvy, *Théorie générale de la population*. II. *Biologie sociale*, Paris, 1954.

2. J. C. Russell, *British Mediaeval Population*, p. 235, etc., Albuquerque, 1948. 1086 is the date of the first surviving document, Domesday Book; thus it cannot be shown that the increase of population only began at the end of the eleventh century. Growth was especially rapid up to 1240; after that date it continued at a slower rate.

3. L. Genicot, *Sur les témoignages d'accroissement de la population en Occident, du XIe au XIIIe siècle*, in *Cahiers d'histoire mondiale*, I, 1953, pp. 446–62, explains the methods which have made it possible to write the demographic prehistory of medieval Europe, gives examples and a bibliography.

4. G. Duby, *Histoire de la civilisation française*, p. 77, Paris, 1958, claims that the most important advance was the use of iron ploughshares which cut a deeper furrow than their wooden predecessors; L. White, *The vitality of the tenth century*, in *Mediaevalia et Humanistica*, IX, 1955, pp. 26–9, lays emphasis on the generalization of the three-year rotation of crops and the related development of nitrogenous crops. J. N. Oller, *La contribución de los historiadores catalanes a la historia demográfica general*, in *XIe Congrès international des Sciences historiques, Stockholm, 1960, Communications*, p. 42, reports that, according to a study of skulls found in the Jewish cemeteries of Catalonia, longevity must have increased in the thirteenth century; it must be remembered that, on E. Salin's showing, the expectation of life at the beginning of the Middle Ages was 19 to 23 years (*La civilisation mérovingienne*. II. *Les sépultures*, Paris, 1952).

5. H. van der Linden, *De Cope*, Assen, 1955, has established that the great clearings began in Holland under Didrik I, who reigned from 993 to 1039.

6. Below, Chap. X, p. 212.

7. J. Ebersolt, *Orient et Occident. Recherches sur les influences byzantine et orientale en France avant les Croisades*, 2 vol., Paris, 1928, 1929; E. Sabbe, *L'importation des tissus orientaux en Europe occidentale au haut moyen âge (IXe et Xe siècles)*, in *Revue belge de philologie et d'histoire*, XIV, 1935, p. 811, etc.; G. Schreiber, *Gesammelte Abhandlungen. I. Gemeinschaften des Mittelalters*, p. 3, etc., Münster, 1948.

8. The different versions of the Romance of Alexander have been published under the title: *The medieval French 'Roman d'Alexandre'*, Princeton, 5 vol., 1937–49. The first scientific contacts between the Moors of Spain and the Latin world are examined in A. van de Vyver, *Les premières traductions latines (X^e-XIe siècles) de traités arabes sur l'astrolabe,* in Ier *Congrès international de géographie historique.* II. *Mémoires,* p. 266, etc., Brussels, 1931. Gerbert and Salerno are mentioned again in Chap. VIII, pp. 152, 154.

9. F. Chalandon, *Histoire de la domination normande en Italie et en Sicile,* 2 vol., Paris, 1907.

10. For the *Reconquista,* see R. Menéndez-Pidal, *La España del Cid,* 2 vol., Madrid, 1929, and E. Lévi Provençal, *Islam d'Occident. Études d'histoire médiévale,* p. 111, etc., Paris, 1948. For foreign participation, which was largely French, see M. Defourneaux, *Les Français en Espagne aux XIe et XIIe siècles,* Paris, 1949. For the Almoravid Empire (1050–1140) and the Almohads (1140–1200) see J. D. Fage, *An Atlas of African History,* Maps 9 and 10, London, 1958.

11. For the Crusades in general see H. E. Mayer, *Bibliographie zur Geschichte der Kreuzzüge,* Hanover, 1960; on the principles, motives and general character of the Crusades see C. Cahen and others, *L'idée de Croisade,* in *X Congresso internazionale di scienze storiche, Roma, 1955.* III, pp. 544–652; for the different Crusades see S. Runciman, *A History of the Crusades,* 3 vol., Cambridge, 1951–4 and P. Rousset, *Histoire des Croisades,* Paris, 1957; for the Franks in the Holy Land see J. Richard, *Le royaume latin de Jérusalem,* 1953; for the decline of the movement and its causes see P. A. Throop, *Criticism of the Crusade,* Amsterdam, 1940.

12. K. Hampe, *Der Zug nach Osten,* 3. ed., Leipzig, 1935.

13. E. R.Labande, *Recherches sur les pèlerins dans l'Europe des XIe et XIIe siècles,* in *Cahiers de civilisation médiévale,* I, 1958, p. 165.

14. L. Olschki, *Marco Polo's Precursors,* Baltimore, 1943.

15. Above, note 8.

16. J. de Ghellinck, *L'essor de la littérature latine au XIIe siècle,* pp. 61–2, Paris, 1946.

17. R. Doehaerd, *L'expansion économique belge au moyen âge,* p. 33, etc., Brussels, 1946.

18. The best exposition of the revival of commerce remains that of Henri Pirenne, referred to in our general bibliography. It has some serious failings. R. Latouche has made some criticisms in *Les origines de l'économie occidentale, IVe-XIe siècles,* p. 271, etc., Paris, 1956. We shall make some below, note 27.

19. F. Lyna, *Aperçu historique sur les origines urbaines dans le comté de Looz,* in *Bulletin de l'Institut archéologique liégeois,* LV, 1931.

20. R. Doehaerd, op. cit., p. 16, etc. and E. Sabbe, *Les relations économiques entre l'Angleterre et le Continent au haut moyen âge,* in *Le Moyen Âge,* LVI, 1950, p. 179, etc.

21. J. Lestocquoy, *Les villes de Flandre et d'Italie sous le gouvernement des patriciens (XIe-XVe siècles),* Paris, 1952, emphasizes the part played by individual men of business in the revival of commerce.

22. R. S. Lopez, *Some Tenth Century Towns,* in *Mediaevalia et Humanistica,* IX, 1955, pp. 4–6 and *La città dell'Europa postcarolingia,* in *I problemi communi dell'Europa postcarolingia,* Spoleto, 1955.

23. Below, Chap. VIII, p. 153.

24. Until the thirteenth century the immense majority of lands were leased in perpetuity and the rent fixed at the moment of the grant could not be modified. If they consisted of a money payment they suffered the effect of all devaluations and were no longer worth much. In the Namur region in the thirteenth century 'censal lands' paid 2 to 8 deniers per *'bonnier'* per annum, whilst the current hiring value was 99 deniers. The bonnier varied from 1½ to 3 acres. See L. Genicot, *L'économie rurale namuroise,* I, pp. 245–6.

25. H. van Werveke has analysed the process of industrial concentration in the towns in the *Introduction historique* to G. de Poerck, *La draperie médiévale en Flandre et en Artois. Technique et terminologie,* p. 20, Bruges, 1951 and in *Landelijke en stedelijke nijverheid,* in *Verslag van de algemene vergadering van het Historisch Genootschap,* Utrecht, 1960, pp. 37–51. In the second of these papers he notes that this concentration was not only called for by the needs of the artisans but also by those of the entrepreneur merchants, who, in the eleventh century, could not have carried on a business dispersed over the countryside.

26. For examples see G. Duby, *Les villes du Sud-est de la Gaule du VIIIᵉ au XIᵉ siècle,* in *La città nell'alto medioevo,* pp. 231–58, Spoleto, 1959.

27. Pirenne's theories on the origins of the towns of Northwest Europe are well known. They are open to discussion in many respects. First of all the assumption that all traces of commercial activity in the area were wiped out by the Vikings and that the towns thus date from the tenth century: in fact these invasions constituted a brief interlude and most of the towns were Carolingian in origin (L. Genicot, *Aux origines de la civilisation occidentale,* in *Miscellanea L. van der Essen,* p. 91). Then there is his view that the foundation of the towns can be attributed exclusively to merchants from outside: it can be shown that the nucleus of the urban population consisted of people from the immediate district (J. Lestocquoy, *Les villes et la population urbaine. L'exemple d'Arras,* in *Cahiers de civilisation médiévale,* I, 1958, pp. 55–62). Thirdly he gives a decisive importance to the renewal of contact between Europe and the Orient, whereas R. Grand, *Les paix d'Aurillac,* Paris, 1945, is able to show that this merely accelerated a process which sprang from the internal evolution of the economy.

The great mistake made by Pirenne and others was to attempt to work out a unitary theory to fit all cases. The Town owes its origin principally to two factors which might assume varied forms and appear in differing combinations: the defensive element, Roman or medieval, secular or ecclesiastic, and the trading element, Carolingian *'portus',* Germanic *'wick'* or market under the protection of a great lord. See E. Ennen, *Les différents types de formation de villes européennes,* in *Le Moyen Âge,*

LXII, 1956, pp. 397–412 and *Die Bedeutung der Maasstädte im Stadtwerdungsprozess des Mittelalters*, in *Mélanges F. Rousseau*, pp. 293–308, Brussels, 1958: the second article contains references almost entirely absent from the first. See also the collection of essays in *Studien zu den Anfängen des europäischen Städtewesens*, Lindau, 1958.

28. *La Ville. Première partie. Institutions administratives et judiciaires. Deuxième partie. Institutions économiques et sociales*, in *Recueils de la Société Jean Bodin,* VI and VII, a collection of essays on the structure of medieval cities.

CHAPTER VIII

1. This was not true of the first years of the reign, during which Otto remained no more than a rough soldier; intellectual ambitions came later in his life, encouraged by members of his court and particularly of the royal chapel. See R. Folz, op. cit., p. 48, etc.

2. H. Naumann, *Karolingische und Ottonische Renaissance*, Freiburg, 1926; H. Jantzen, *Ottonische Kunst*, Hamburg, 1959; *Karolingische und Ottonische Kunst. Werden, Wesen, Wirkung*, Wiesbaden, 1957.

3. Widukind's works have been published in *Monumenta Germaniae Historica. Scriptores rerum Germanicarum in usum scholarum.* 4. ed., 1904, and the comedies of Roswitha in the same series, in 1902.

4. F. J. Tschan, *Saint Bernward of Hildesheim*, Notre Dame, (Indiana) 3 vol., 1942–52.

5. An article by W. von den Steinen, *Die Anfänge der Sequenzdichtung*, in *Revue d'histoire ecclésiastique suisse*, XL, 1946, pp. 190–212 and 241–68, and XLI, pp. 19–49 and 122–62, points to the northern parts of Carolingian Francia as the cradle of this genre and the period round about 830 as the date of the earliest specimens. More recently he has edited the forty genuine sequences by Notker, with a study of his poetry, in *Notker der Dichter und seine geistige Welt*, 2 vol., Bern, 1948. Rhythmical poetry is defined below, notes 35 and 56.

6. G. Cohen, *Le théâtre en France au moyen âge*, Paris, 1948; G. Frank, *The Medieval French Drama*, Oxford, 1954.

7. There is a text of the *Waltharius* in *Monumenta Germaniae Historica. Poetae latini medii aevi*, VI, fasc. 1. Both the place and the date of composition are a matter of controversy: it is usually placed in the ninth century now rather than in the tenth.

8. For the scriptorium of St. Gallen at this period see A. Bruckner, *Scriptoria medii aevi Helvetica*, III, Genève, 1938. The author detects signs of decadence at the beginning of the tenth century.

9. For miniature in Belgium from the tenth to the twelfth century see A. Boutemy, in E. de Moreau, *Histoire de l'Église en Belgique*, II, 2. ed., 1945, p. 311, etc.

10. A. Boutemy, *Le Scriptorium et la bibliothèque de Saint-Amand*, in *Scriptorium*, I, 1946–7, p. 6, etc.

11. A. van de Vyver, *Hucbald de Saint-Amand, écolâtre, et l'invention*

du Nombre d'or, in *Mélanges A. Pelzer,* pp. 61–79, Louvain, 1947. This article controverts the views of W. Apel in *The Notation of Polyphonic Music 900–1600,* 2. ed., Cambridge, Mass., 1940, according to which Hucbald was the author of the *Musica enchiriadis* and the father of medieval polyphony and modern musical notation.

12. F. Cabrol, *Deux initiatives belges dans le domaine de la liturgie,* in *Bulletin paroissial liturgique,* 1926, p. 173.

13. E. de Moreau, op. cit., p. 249, etc.

14. The *Praeloquia* have been published, with the rest of the works of Ratherius, in *Patrologia Latinia,* CXXXVI, col. 143, etc.

15. These *Gesta* have been published in the *Monumenta Germaniae Historica. Scriptores,* XIII, pp. 600–73, and IV, pp. 52–74.

16. Published by E. Voigt, *Ecbasis captivi,* Strasburg, 1875.

17. The best edition is that of F. G. Wasserschleben, *Reginonis abbatis Prumiensis libri duo,* Leipzig, 1840.

18. For the origins and diffusion of this Pontifical see B. Luyckx, *Liturgie in donkere tijden,* in *Tijdschrift voor Liturgie,* XXXI, 1947, p. 14, etc.

19. See P. Fournier and G. Le Bras, op. cit., p. 364, etc., and the studies by F. Pelster and C. G. Mohr in *Studi gregoriani,* I, pp. 197, etc., and 321, etc., Rome, 1947.

20. The text of the *De Unitate* has been published by W. Schwenkenbecher in *Monumenta Germaniae Historica. Libelli de lite,* II, p. 173, etc.

21. The *Casus* and the surviving fragments of the *Ruodlieb* have been published in *Monumenta Germaniae Historica. Scriptores,* II, p. 75, etc., and by F. Seiler, Halle, 1882, respectively.

22. For the personality of Herman see W. Wattenbach, *Deutschlands Geschichtsquellen im Mittelalter. Deutsche Kaiserzeit,* new ed., I, p. 232, etc., Berlin, 1939.

23. L. Genicot and others, *Le milieu liégeois aux XIe et XIIe siècles,* in *Fédération archéologique et historique de Belgique, Annales du XXXIIIe Congrès, Tournai, 1949,* II, pp. 73–213.

24. *L'art mosan,* in *Bibliothèque générale de l'École des Hautes études, 6e section,* Paris, 1953; S. Collon-Gevaert, J. Lejeune and J. Stiennon, *Art mosan aux XIe et XIIe siècles,* Brussels, 1961.

25. M. Laurent, *Aspects de l'art mosan dans les fonts de Saint-Barthélemy de Liège,* in *Fédération archéologique et historique de Belgique, Congrès de Namur 1938,* p. 143. J. Lejeune, *Renier, l'orfèvre, et les fonts de Notre-Dame,* in *Anciens pays et assemblées d'États,* III, 1952, pp. 3–27, casts doubt on the attribution of the font to Renier.

26. M. Lombard, *La route de la Meuse et les relations lointaines des pays mosans entre le VIIIe et le XIe siècle,* in *L'art mosan,* pp. 9–28.

27. F. Rousseau, *La Meuse et le pays mosan,* in *Annales de la Société archéologique de Namur,* XXXIX, 1930, p. 149, etc.

28. J. Philippe, *L'évangéliaire de Notger et la chronologie de l'art mosan des époques préromane et romane,* in *Mémoires de l'Académie royale de Belgique. Classe des Beaux-Arts,* Brussels, 1956, considers the problem

of Byzantine influences; J. Lejeune, *A propos de l'art mosan et des ivoires liégeois*, in *Anciens pays et assemblées d'États*, VIII, 1955, pp. 91–157, suggests a different chronology.

29. L. Grodecki, *Au seuil de l'art roman. L'architecture ottonienne*, Paris, 1958.

30. P. Héliot, *Les antécédents et les débuts des coursières anglo-normandes rhénanes*, in *Cahiers de civilisation médiévale*, II, 1959, pp. 429–43.

31. For the many pieces of jewellery from the Meuse region which are preserved in French museums see J. de Borchgrave d'Altena, *A propos d'orfèvreries mosanes conservées en France. L'ancien pays de Liège vers 1150*, in *Bulletin de la Société royale d'archéologie de Bruxelles*, 1950, pp. 47–63.

32. The transmission of Carolingian traditions in the tenth and eleventh centuries was not the only feature common to the Saône valley and the Empire, particularly its western marches, the Rhineland and Lorraine: They all took part in developing the early Romanesque style (below, Chap. VIII, p. 160) which F. Deshoulières, *Le premier art roman*, in *Bulletin de la Société nationale des Antiquaires de France*, 1943–4, p. 146, etc., would prefer to call the Lotharingian style. Whether this artistic affinity was caused by religious connections, by the incorporation of these lands in the *Francia Media* of Lothar I, or by commercial connections based on the Rhine–Mediterranean route by way of Meuse or Moselle, Verdun or Toul, Langres, Dijon and the Rhône, is very much a subject of conjecture.

33. W. Holtzmann, *Laurentius von Amalfi, ein Lehrer Hildebrands*, in *Studi gregoriani*, I, pp. 207–36, Rome, 1947, casts some doubt on the current tendency to emphasize the importance of Desiderius: Laurence, a notable scholar, was a monk of Monte Cassino before Desiderius became abbot.

34. Alberic's work has been published by L. Rockinger, *Briefsteller und Formelbücher des XI. bis XIV. Jahrh.*, in *Quellen und Erörterungen zur bayerischen und Deutschen Geschichte*, IX, 1863.

35. The *cursus* is a literary trick which consists in contriving a certain number of unaccented syllables between the stressed syllables in the last words of a sentence or subordinate clause in order to create a rhythm. It is not to be confused with rhymed prose in which the last syllable of a sense group is made to rhyme.

36. For Salerno see F. R. Packard, *The School of Salerno*, New York, 1920. For the case of Adalberon see F. Vercauteren, *Les médecins dans les principautés de la Belgique et du Nord de la France, du VIIIe au XIIIe siècle*, in *Le Moyen Âge*, LVII, 1951, p. 71.

37. Alphanus's religious poems, the most interesting of his works, have been published in *Patrologia Latina*, CXLVII, col. 1219, etc.

38. The chief work of Guido of Arezzo, the *Micrologus*, has been edited by Dom Amelli, Rome, 1904. For the man himself and his importance see J. Chailley, *Histoire musicale du moyen âge*, p. 85, etc., Paris, 1950.

39. G. Mengozzi, *Ricerche sull'attività della Scuola di Pavia nell'alto medioevo*, Pavia, 1924.

40. A. Sorbelli, *Storia dell'Università di Bologna*, I, Bologna, 1940.

41. P. Fournier and G. Le Bras, op. cit., II.

42. E. Lesne, *Histoire de la propriété ecclésiastique en France*. V. *Les écoles*, Lille, 1940; A. Forest, F. van Steenberghen and M. de Gandillac, *Le mouvement doctrinal du XIe au XIVe siècle*, in *Histoire de l'Église*, by Fliche and Martin, XIII, Paris, 1951.

43. Above, Chap. II, p. 33; P. Acbischer, *La Chanson de Roland dans le 'désert littéraire' du XIe siècle*, in *Revue belge de philologie et d'histoire*, XXXVIII, 1960, pp. 718-49.

44. I. Cluzel, *Quelques réflexions à propos des origines de la poésie lyrique des troubadours*, in *Cahiers de civilisation médiévale*, IV, 1961, pp. 179-88, a summary of the present state of knowledge.

45. J. Leflon, *Gerbert. Humanisme et chrétienté au Xe siècle*, Saint-Wandrille, 1946; H. Lattin, *Astronomy: our views and theirs*, in *Medievalia et Humanistica*, IX, 1955, pp. 13-17.

46. A. van de Vyver, *L'évolution scientifique du haut moyen âge*, in *Archeion*, XIX, 1937, p. 17.

47. A. van de Vyver, *Les oeuvres inédites d'Abbon de Fleury*, in *Revue bénédictine*, XLVII, 1935, p. 125, etc.; P. Cousin, *Abbon de Fleury-sur-Loire*, Paris, 1954; R. D. Donovan, *The Liturgical Drama in Medieval Spain*, Toronto, 1958, casts doubt on the traditional view of the part played by the great Benedictine abbeys in the invention and spread of the liturgical drama.

48. A. Clerval, *Les écoles de Chartres au moyen âge*, Paris, 1895. L. C. Mackinney, *Bishop Fulbert and Education at the School of Chartres*, Notre Dame, 1957, reduces, quite rightly though perhaps excessively, the importance usually attributed to Fulbert and his teaching in eleventh-century culture.

49. M. Cappuyns, *Bérenger de Tours*, in *Dictionnaire d'histoire et de géographie ecclésiastiques*, VIII, col. 385, Paris, 1935.

50. *Patrologia Latina*, CLXXI.

51. C. Filliatre, *La Philosophie de saint Anselme*, Paris, 1920. Anselm's *Opera omnia* have been published by Dom F. S. Schmitt, Edinburgh, 1948-61.

52. For Anselm of Laon, his work and his background, see the bibliography in P. Anciaux, *La théologie du sacrement de pénitence au XIIe siècle*, p. 58, etc., Louvain, 1949. Dom A. Lottin, *Aux origines de l'école théologique d'Anselme de Laon*, in *Recherches de théologie ancienne et médiévale*, X, 1938, p. 101, etc., has established that the *Sententiae Anselmi* are the work of a pupil, whereas the *Sententiae Atrebatenses* were written by Anselm himself. H. Cloes, *La systématisation théologique pendant la première moitié du XIIe siècle*, in *Ephemerides theologicae Lovanienses*, XXXIV, 1958, pp. 277-329, points out that the works of the School of Laon are still not true *Summae*.

53. E. Gilson, *La philosophie au moyen âge*, p. 251.

54. Ibid., p. 288; J. G. Sikes, *Peter Abailard*, Cambridge, 1932.

55. F. Vernet, *Hugues de Saint-Victor*, in *Dictionnaire de théologie catholique*, VII, col. 240, etc., Paris, 1922.

56. Whereas the basis of classical poetry was syllabic quantity, rhythmical poetry is based on the stress accent. The lines consist of an alternating set of stressed and unstressed syllables. They are grouped in pairs, threes or greater numbers and corresponding lines count the same number of syllables and end with the same sound. The fundamental features of French poetry are already present. The origins of the rhythmic kind of verse have often been the subject of discussion; for the most recent example see D. Norberg, *Introduction à l'étude de la versification latine médiévale*, Stockholm, 1958.

The number of syllables is left to the taste of the writer: he may make it lesser or greater, thus speeding or slowing the measure and consequently giving intensity to the feeling conveyed. An extract from a twelfth-century sequence published in G. M. Dreves and C. Blume, *Ein Jahrtausend Lateinischer Hymnendichtung*, II, p. 21, demonstrates the flexibility of this poetry:

> Per hanc matrem venit laetitia,
> Qua deletur Evae tristitia,
> Osculatur pacem justitia,
> Terra dedit promissa gaudia.
> > Nutu patris
> > Vis amoris
> > Hortum matris
> > Inflammavit.
> > Tellus rorem,
> > Stella solem,
> > Virga florem
> > Germinavit . . .
> Hic in sole collocavit suum tabernaculum,
> Visitavit ambulantem lux in nocte populum.

57. Guibert's works have been published by G. Bourgin, in the *Collection de textes pour servir à l'étude et l'enseignement de l'histoire*, XL, 1907: Abelard's *Historia* in *Patrologia Latina*, CLXXVIII.

58. R. Blomme, *La doctrine du péché dans les écoles théologiques de la première moitié du XIIᵉ siècle*, Louvain, 1958.

59. P. Francastel, *L'humanisme roman. Critique des Théories sur l'art du XIᵉ siècle en France*, Rodez, 1942; L. Lefrançois-Pillion, *L'art roman*, Paris, n.d. (1949).

60. P. Francastel, op. cit., p. 161, etc., discusses the much worked-over problem of the contribution of the Orient to Romanesque art; E. Lambert, *Art musulman et art chrétien dans la péninsule ibérique*, Paris, 1958, shows what elements Romanesque art may have borrowed from Moorish art and thus indirectly from the East: the dome, the squinch, certain forms of arch and some decorative motifs.

61. The expressions 'first' and 'second Romanesque manner' were

invented by Puig I Cadafalch, *Le premier art roman*, Paris, 1929, and *Géographie et origines du premier art roman*, Paris, 1935.

62. The last of many monographs devoted to this question, A. Gybal, *L'Auvergne, berceau de l'art roman*, Clermont, 1957, gives Auvergne as the answer.

63. Above, Chap. IV, p. 77.

64. P. Deschamps and M. Thibout, *La peinture murale en France. Le haut moyen âge et l'époque romane*, Paris, 1951. In this way as in many others, for example, the subordination of sculpture to architecture, Italy was an exception: mosaic continued to be common there. We must point out with regard to painting, that a completely false impression is given by Romanesque churches as they are today, with their scoured and naked stonework. Fidelity to one's materials, a taste for the natural appearance of stone inside buildings is a modern feeling; it was certainly not the ideal of the eleventh and twelfth centuries.

65. P. Deschamps, *La sculpture française à l'époque romane*, Florence, 1930, and *La sculpture française: époque romane*, Paris, 1947; H. Focillon, *Recherches récentes sur la sculpture romane en France au XIe siècle*, in *Bulletin monumental*, XCVII, 1938, pp. 49–72.

66. C. Oursel, *L'art roman de Bourgogne*, Dijon, 1928; K. J. Conant, *Carolingian and Romanesque Architecture, 800–1200*, p. 107, etc, London, 1959; F. Salet, *La Madeleine de Vézelay*, Melun, 1948; M. Aubert, *L'architecture cistercienne en France*, 2 vol., Paris, 1943.

67. M. Anfray, *L'architecture normande*, Paris, 1939; G. Grigson, *English Cathedrals*, London, 1950.

68. R. Crozet, *L'art roman en Poitou*, Paris, 1948; R. Rey, *La cathédrale de Cahors et les origines de l'architecture à coupoles d'Aquitaine*, Paris, 1925.

69. C. Bernouilli, *Die Skulpturen der Abtei Conques-en-Rouergue*, p. 88, etc., Basel, 1956, considers Spanish influences and the question whether Languedoc or Burgundy can claim priority.

70. All the most important examples of Romanesque sculpture are reproduced with a commentary in L. Réau, *L'art religieux du moyen âge*, Paris, 1946.

71. This is one of the leading ideas of that excellent book *L'humanisme roman* (note 59, above): the Carolingian church was a complex of juxtaposed parts, whereas the Romanesque church is a unity made up of separate elements which have been successfully integrated; thus there is a greater difference than has been generally admitted, one of spirit. The conclusion, if not the premisses, would seem to be debatable: we should remark that what is especially characteristic of Romanesque architecture, its sense of volume, of mass and of equilibrium, is inherited from the Carolingian period.

72. L. Lefrançois-Pillion, *Maîtres d'oeuvres et tailleurs de pierre des cathédrales*, p. 114, Paris, 1949, lays stress on this subordination of all techniques to the creation of an overall effect. Churches like the one at Issoire, where the columns painted in horizontal zigzags break the general vertical line of the architecture, would lead one however to

modify this attitude somewhat: Romanesque decoration is monumental, but its elements do not all contribute all the time to a unitary effect.

CHAPTER IX

1. Unity does not mean uniformity. The essays in F. Lot and R. Fawtier, *Histoire des institutions françaises au moyen âge*, I, Paris, 1957, show that uniting territories does not necessarily entail unification of institutions; the principalities which made up the kingdom kept their own political institutions.

2. M. D. Chenu, *La théologie au XIIᵉ siècle*, Paris, 1957; P. Delhaye, *L'organisation scolaire au XIIᵉ siècle*, in *Traditio*, V, 1947, pp. 211–68. The foundation by the Cistercians of the Collège Saint-Bernard in Paris (E. Kwanten, *Le Collège Saint-Bernard à Paris. Sa fondation et ses débuts*, in *Revue d'histoire ecclésiastique*, XLIII, 1948, p. 443, etc.) shows how the abbey schools were falling behind the rival cathedral schools; if the monasteries were to keep up with the scientific movement they had to send their members to study at the universities.

According to J. Leclercq, *Saint Bernard et la théologie monastique au XIIᵉ siècle*, in *Analecta sacri ordinis Cisterciensis*, IX, 1953, pp. 7–23, there were two distinct theological currents in the twelfth century, differing in their object, their methods and their sources: the one, monastic, derived from spiritual experience, based on the Bible and the Christian Fathers, enriching religious life; the other, scholastic, speculative and theoretical, based on reason and aiming at a systematic exposition of Christian doctrine. In fact, although the first is to be discerned clear and undiluted in some writers of the time, it is none the less often combined with the second in others, some of them writers of merit, amongst the Victorines for instance.

3. R. Foreville, *L'école du Bec et le 'studium' de Cantorbéry aux XIᵉ et XIIᵉ siècles*, in *Bulletin philologique et historique du comité des travaux historiques et scientifiques*, 1957, pp. 357–74, shows the intellectual influence of the continental monks; J. C. Dickinson, *English Regular Canons and the Continent in the XIIth century*, in *Transactions of the Royal Historical Society*, ser. 5, I, 1951, pp. 71–89, shows how the French Canons Regular swarmed in England as much as the monks.

4. J. Marx, *La littérature celtique*, Paris, 1958 and P. Rickard, *Britain in Medieval French Literature, 1100–1500*, Cambridge, 1956. In a review of the former work, in *Le Moyen Âge*, LXVI, 1960, p. 424, M. Hanoset claims that the book's fundamental thesis, the Celtic origin of the great body of Arthurian and related legend, is unsupported by evidence.

5. E. Lambert, *Art musulman et art chrétien dans la péninsule ibérique*, pp. 44, 188, 206, 207, Paris, 1958.

6. The case of the Almagest of Ptolemy, reported in R. W. Southern, *The Making of the Middle Ages*, p. 65, London, 1958, proves that, although further from the original, the translations made by Spanish scholars were preferred to those made by Italians.

7. M. D. Chenu, *L'homme et la nature. Perspectives sur la Renaissance*

du XIIe siècle, in *Archives d'histoire doctrinale et littéraire du moyen âge*, XXVII, 1952, pp. 39–66.

8. C. H. Haskins, *The Renaissance of the XIIth Century*, Cambridge, Mass., 1927.

9. The influence of pagan thought on twelfth-century moralists has been established in several essays by P. Delhaye, notably *L'enseignement de la philosophie morale au XIIe siècle*, in *Mediaeval Studies*, XI, 1949, pp. 77–99.

10. R. Guiette, *D'une poésie formelle au moyen âge*, in *Revue des sciences humaines*, new ser., 54, 1949, pp. 61–8; P. Zumthor, *Recherches sur les topiques dans la poésie lyrique des XIIe et XIIIe siècles*, in *Cahiers de civilisation médiévale*, II, 1959, pp. 409–27.

11. R. Lejeune, *Rôle littéraire de la famille d'Aliénor d'Aquitaine*, in ibid., pp. 319–37.

12. G. Paré and P. Tremblay, *La Renaissance du XIIe siècle. Les écoles et l'enseignement*, Paris, 1933.

13. J. Leclercq, *L'amour des lettres et le désir de Dieu*, Paris, 1957.

14. E. R. Curtius, *Europäische Literatur und lateinisches Mittelalter*, Bern, 1954; French translation under the title *La littérature européenne et le moyen âge latin*, Paris, 1956.

15. For this literature in Latin, see J. de Ghellinck, *L'essor de la littérature latine au XIIe siècle*, 2 vol., Brussels, 1946, which contains a bibliography. John of Salisbury's works have been edited by C. Webb, Oxford, 1909, 1929; on the man and his ideas there is H. Leibeschütz, *Mediaeval Humanism in the Life and Writings of John of Salisbury*, London, 1950.

16. J. Leclercq and J. P. Bonnes, *Un maître de la vie spirituelle au XIe siècle, Jean de Fécamp*, Paris, 1946.

17. For the texts of the works mentioned here see as follows: for Otto of Freising, *Scriptores rerum germanicarum in usum scholarum*, 1912; for Ordericus Vitalis, the edition by A. le Prévost, B. Guérard and L. Delisle, Paris, 1838–55; for Robert of Torigny, Robert of Auxerre and Guy of Bazoches, *Monumenta Germaniae Historica. Scriptores*, VI, p. 475, etc., XXVI, p. 226, etc. and XXVI, p. 216 (extracts only); for William of Malmesbury and Matthew Paris, *Rolls Series,* LII and XC, and LVII. See also, on Otto, L. Grill, *Bildung und Wissenschaft im Leben Ottos von Freising*, in *Analecta sacri ordinis Cisterciensis*, XIV, 1958, pp. 281–334, and, on the Englishmen, V. H. Galbraith, *Historical Research in Mediaeval England*, London, 1951 and R. Vaughan, *Matthew Paris*, Cambridge, 1958.

18. There is an edition of Joseph of Exeter under the title *De bello Trojano*, Amsterdam, 1702; of the *Alexandreid* in *Patrologia Latina*, CCIX, p. 460, etc.; of the *Gesta* in *Fonti per la storia d'Italia. Scrittori sec. XII*, 1887; of the *Ligurinus* in *Patrologia Latina*, CCXII, p. 327, etc.; of the *Anticlaudianus*, by R. Bossuat, Paris, 1955; of the Latin comedies in G. Cohen, *La comédie latine en France au XIIe siècle*, 2 vol., Paris, 1931; of the *Speculum* in *Rolls Series*, I, p. 3, etc.; of the *Isengrinus*, by E. Voigt, Halle, 1884.

19. O. Dobiache-Rojdesvensky, *Les poésies des Goliards*, Paris, 1931. The works attributed to the 'Primate' and the Archpoet and the well-known collection called the *Carmina Burana* have been edited by W. Meyer in the *Nachrichten* of the Göttingen Academy, 1907, p. 89, etc., M. Manitius, *Die Gedichte des Archipoeta*, in the *Münchener Texte*, VI, 2. ed., München, 1929 and J. Schmeller, Stuttgart, 1847 or A. Hilka and O. Schumann, Heidelberg, 1930–41.

20. The finest religious poems of the period have been published by G. Dreves and C. Blume, *Ein Jahrtausend lateinischer Hymnendichtung*, 2 vol., Leipzig, 1909.

21. G. Vecchi, *Pietro Abelardo; I 'Planctus'*, Modena, 1951.

22. L. Gauthier, *Les oeuvres poétiques d'Adam de Saint-Victor*, 3. ed., Paris, 1894 and E. Misset and P. Aubry, *Les proses d'Adam de Saint-Victor. Texte et musique*, Paris, 1900.

23. A. Jeanroy, *La poésie lyrique des troubadours*, Paris, 1934. The same author has compiled an *Anthologie des troubadours*, Paris, n.d.

24. J. Frappier, *Chrétien de Troyes, l'homme et l'oeuvre*, Paris, 1957. Chrétien's chief works have appeared, or will appear, in the *Classiques français du moyen âge*.

25. For one example of the influence of French literature on that of neighbouring countries see I. Frank, *Trouvères et minnesänger. Recueil de textes pour servir à l'étude des rapports entre la poésie lyrique romane et le minnesang au XIIe siècle*, Saarbrücken, 1952.

26. *Histoire de la littérature allemande*, edited by F. Mosse, Paris, 1959; G. Ehrismann, *Geschichte der deutschen Literatur bis zum Ausgang des Mittelalters*, 4 vol., München, 1932–5. The *Nibelungenlied* has been published with a French translation by M. Colleville and E. Tonnelat, in the *Bibliothèque de Philologie germanique*, Paris, 1944. In the same series there are texts, with full introductions but with no translation, of Wolfram von Eschenbach's *Parzival*, by A. Moret, of Hartmann von Aue's *Erec and Iwein*, by J. Fourquet, and an *Anthologie de Minnesang* by A. Moret.

27. E. de Bruyne, *L'esthétique du moyen âge*, p. 209, etc., Louvain, 1947, expounds the intellectualist conception of art which lies behind the composition of these *artes*.

28. The *Wapene Martijn* has been transcribed into modern Dutch by A. E. van Beughem, Damme, 1943; there are extracts from it in a French version by F. Closset, *Joyaux de la littérature flamande du moyen âge*, Brussels, 1949. Van Maerlant's trilogy, *Naturen Bloeme, Rijmbijbel, Spieghel historiael*, has been published by E. Verwijs, Leiden, 1878, M. de Vries and E. Verwijs, Leiden, 1857–63 and J. B. David, Brussels, 1858–69. Brunetto Latini's *Tesoro* has been re-edited by F. J. Carmody, Berkeley, 1948.

29. The Works of Rutebeuf have been edited by E. Faral and J. Bastin, Paris, 1959, 1960.

30. R. Bauerreiss, *Honorius von Canterbury (Augustodunensis) und Kuno I., der Raitenbucher, Bischof von Regensburg, 1126–1136*, in *Studien und Mitteilungen zur Geschichte des Benediktiner Ordens*, LXVII, 1956,

pp. 306–13, is the most recent work devoted to this enigmatic figure. The works of Honorius are in the *Patrologia Latina*, CLXXII.

31. On Roman and Canon Law see M. D. Hazeltine, *Cambridge Mediaeval History*, V, p. 753, etc., Cambridge, 1943; on the Custumaries and the influence of the Romanists and the Canonists on their composition, see S. Gagnée, *Studien zur Ideengeschichte des Gesetzgebung*, Uppsala, 1960.

32. M. Torelli has begun work on a new edition of Accursius's gloss on the *Institutes*. In the meantime there is the old edition by Denis Godefroi, Lyons, 1589.

33. P. Tisset, *Placentin et son enseignement à Montpellier*, in *Recueil des mémoires et travaux publiés par la Société d'histoire du droit et des institutions des anciens pays de droit écrit*, II. 1951, pp. 67–94.

34. The two Norman custumaries have been edited by E. Tardif, Rouen, 1891, and Paris, 1903, and Beaumanoir's work by A. Salmon, Paris, 1899–1900.

35. T. F. T. Plucknett, *Early English Legal Literature*, Cambridge, 1958.

36. The *Sachsenspiegel* has been edited by K. A. Eckhardt, in *Monumenta Germaniae Historica. Fontes iuris germanici antiqui*, 1955, 1956.

37. C. Bernabei, *Bartoli di Sassoferrato e la scienza delle leggi*, Roma, 1881.

38. S. Kuttner, *The Father of the Science of Canon Law*, in *The Jurist*, I, 1941, p. 2, etc. The *Concordia* has been published, with later collections, by E. Friedberg, *Corpus Juris Canonici*, Leipzig, 1879.

39. The *Decretists* are those who wrote commentaries on the *Concordia*, often known as the *Decretum*, of Gratian; the *Decretalists* are those who glossed other collections of canon law.

40. The *Historia* is in the *Patrologia Latina*, CCVIII, col. 1053, etc.

41. J. de Ghellinck. *Le mouvement théologique du XIIe siècle*, 2. ed. Bruges, 1928; P. Delhaye, *Pierre Lombard, sa vie, ses oeuvres, sa morale*, Montréal, 1961.

42. P. Delhaye, *La place de l'éthique parmi les disciplines scientifiques au XIIe siècle*, in *Miscellanea moralia A. Janssen*, I, pp. 29–44, Louvain, 1948, and *Grammatica et Ethica au XIIe siècle*, in *Artes liberales*, ed. J. Koch, Leiden, 1959.

43. A. M. Ethier, *Le 'De Trinitate' de Richard de Saint-Victor*, Ottawa, 1939; the work has been republished by J. Ribaillier, Paris, 1958.

44. The *Ars fidei* is in the *Patrologia Latina*, CCX.

45. On the two kinds of theology see above, note 2.

46. The epithet 'genius' is used of him by Haskins, who deserves respect as a historian of medieval science. One treatise by Leonardo, '*The book of squares*', has been published with a translation into French and introduction by P. Ver Eecke, Bruges, 1952.

47. F. van Steenberghen, *Aristote en Occident*, p. 58, Louvain, 1946.

48. M. H. Vicaire, *Les Porrétains et l'Avicennisme avant 1215*, in *Revue des sciences philosophiques et religieuses*, XXVI, 1937, p. 449, etc., lays stress on the importance of Avicenna.

49. M. D. Chenu, *La théologie comme science au XIIIᵉ siècle*, 3. ed., Paris, 1957.
50. On the philosophers of the period see A. Forest, F. van Steenberghen and M. de Gandillac, *Le mouvement doctrinal du IXᵉ au XIVᵉ siècle*, in *Histoire de l'Église*, by Fliche and Martin, XIII, Paris, 1951; for Bonaventure in particular see C. Wenin, *La connaissance philosophique d'après saint Bonaventure*, in *L'homme et son destin. Actes du premier congrès international de philosophie médiévale*, pp. 485–94, Louvain, 1951.
51. M. D. Chenu, *Introduction à l'étude de saint Thomas d'Aquin*, Montreal, 1950.
52. A. C. Crombie, *Robert Grosseteste and the Origins of Experimental Science, 1100–1700*, Oxford, 1953.
53. The most interesting treatises of Albertus Magnus, the *De animalibus* and the *De vegetabilibus*, have been published by H. Stadler, Münster, 1916–20 and E. Meyer and C. Jessen, Berlin, 1867.
54. This is the leading argument of Crombie's book (note 52 above): 'The modern, systematic understanding of at least the qualitative aspects of the experimental method was created by the philosophers of the West in the thirteenth century. It was they who transformed the Greek geometrical method into the experimental science of the modern world.' F. Masai has cast doubt on this point in his review in *Le Moyen Âge*, LX, 1954, pp. 191–4.
55. The *Speculum majus* was published, amongst other editions, at Douai in 1624.
56. S. Stelling-Michaud, *L'histoire des universités au moyen âge et à la renaissance au cours des vingt-cinq dernières années*, in *XIᵉ Congrès international des sciences historiques, Stockholm 1960. Rapports*. I, pp. 97–143.
57. *Le problème de l'ogive. Recherche*, I, 1939; M. Aubert, *Les plus anciennes croisées d'ogives*, in *Bulletin monumental*, 1934, p. 24, etc.; J. Baltrusaitis, *Le problème de l'ogive et l'Arménie*, Paris, 1936; E. Lambert, *Art musulman et art chrétien dans la péninsule ibérique*, Paris, 1958.
58. O. von Simson, *The Gothic Cathedral. The origins of Gothic architecture and the mediaeval concept of order*, London, 1956.
59. In a note on *Têtes de statues-colonnes du portail occidental de Saint-Denis*, in *Bulletin monumental*, CIII, 1945, p. 243, etc., M. Aubert claims that since the sculpture decorating the door-jambs was not mentioned by Suger in his memorandum on the management of the cathedral it cannot be earlier than 1147, the year in which the illustrious abbot completed his description of the reconstruction of Saint Denis, and that it is probably no earlier than 1151 or even 1155. Thus it is later than the statues at Chartres, which were carved between 1145 and 1155, as Aubert shows in his *Le portail royal de Chartres*, in *Miscellanea L. van Puyvelde*, III, p. 281, etc., Brussels, 1949.
60. See the model of the prototype cathedral in H. Focillon, *Art d'Occident*, p. 71.
61. C. Thérasse, *La cathédrale, miroir du monde*, Paris, 1945.
62. M. Aubert, *Le vitrail en France*, Paris, 1946; M. Aubert and others,

Les vitraux de Notre-Dame et de la Sainte-Chapelle de Paris, in *Corpus vitrearum medii aevi. France.* I, *Seine* I, Paris, 1959.

63. L. Réau, *Histoire de l'expansion de l'art français*, 3 vol., Paris, 1928–33.

64. E. Lambert, op. cit., p. 120 and 164, observes that the Gothic style was used in the North of Spain in the first half of the thirteenth century and that it was replaced by the Mudejar style in architecture and sculpture.

65. R. Wagner-Rieger, *Die italienische Baukunst zu Beginn der Gotik*, 2 vol., Weimar, 1956–7; R. Jullian, *Les persistances romanes dans la sculpture gothique italienne*, in *Cahiers de civilisation médiévale*, III, 1960, pp. 295–305. The latter author sometimes seems to confuse Romanesque with Roman Revival.

66. L. Hautecoeur, *Les primitifs italiens*, Paris, 1931.

67. P. Brieger, *English Art*, 1216–1307, Oxford, 1957.

68. J. A. van Houtte, *Gedachten over de economische geschiedenis van de middeleeuwsche Kerk*, in *Miscellanea A. De Meyer*, I, p. 304, Louvain, 1946 and A. Sapori, *Studi di storia economica medioevale*, Firenze, 1947.

69. For the Church's assimilation of the conception of courtly love, see, for example, J. B. P., *Hadewijck D'Anvers. Poèmes des béguines*, Paris, 1954. For the difficult question of the Arthurian and related legends see J. Marx, *La légende arthurienne et le Graal*, Paris, 1952.

70. P. Renucci, *Dante*, Paris, 1958; A. Masseron, *Dante. La Divine Comédie, traduction, introduction et notes*, 4 vol., Paris, 1947–50.

NOTES TO PART III

CHAPTER X

1. F. Baethgen, *Europa im Spätmittelalter*, Berlin, 1951; several chapters by C. Petit-Dutaillis and R. Fawtier, in volumes IV and VI of the *Histoire générale* edited by G. Glotz, deal with the constitutional development of England and its influence on European countries, especially France.

2. G. de Lagarde, *La naissance de l'esprit laïque*, I, p. 139; S. Mochi-Onory, *Fonti canonistiche dell'idea moderna dello stato*, Milano, 1951. Jurists and other laymen were not alone in reviving the idea of the State. W. von den Steinen, *Der Kosmos des Mittelalters*, p. 194, etc., Bern, 1959, and N. F. Cantor, *The Age of the Gregorian Reform and the Investiture Controversy: New Interpretation*, in *Canadian Historical Association Report*, 1959, p. 28, call attention to the part played by the Gregorians: by making a sharp distinction between the temporal and the spiritual they encouraged the holders of political power to develop independence of religious authority. L. Buisson, *Potestas und caritas*, Graz, 1958, stresses the importance of the Canonists: by laying upon the king the duty of maintaining the rights of the kingdom they bound the king to the kingdom and gave his power a character which transcends the personal.

3. See above, Chap. VI, p. 117.

4. Quoted by G. de Lagarde, op. cit. (note 2 above), p. 195.

5. Taken from Alvaro Pelayo, *De statu et planctu Ecclesiae.* There are many editions of this work; one of the best was printed at Venice in 1560.

6. R. Foreville, *L'Église et la royauté en Angleterre sous Henri II*, Paris, 1943; C. R. Cheney, *From Becket to Langton. English Church Government, 1170–1216*, Manchester, 1956.

7. The opposing theories are set out in J. Rivière, *Le problème de l'Église et de l'État au temps de Philippe le Bel*, Louvain, 1926; the facts are related in G. Digard, *Philippe le Bel et le Saint-Siège de 1285 à 1304*, 2 vol., Paris, 1936.

8. From the Bull *Unam sanctam*, published in Hefele-Leclercq, *Histoire des Conciles*, VII, p. 426, etc.

9. The theories held by these men are set out in M. Pacaut, *Tolérance et laïcité au moyen âge*, in *Cahiers d'histoire publiés par la Faculté des Lettres de Clermont-Ferrand, Lyon et Grenoble*, IV, 1959, pp. 7–18; they are analysed at length by G. de Lagarde, op. cit., II.

10. The growing influence of royal courts in the matter of church preferment is shown, for the Low Countries by E. de Moreau, op. cit., IV, p. 55, etc., for England by A. H. Thompson, *The English Clergy and their Organization in the later Middle Ages*, Oxford, 1947, and J. R. L. Highfield, *The English Hierarchy in the Reign of Edward III*, in *Transactions of the Royal Historical Society*, ser. 5, VI, 1956, pp. 115–38.

11. F. Baix, *La chambre apostolique et les 'Libri annatarum' de Martin V*, I, Brussels, 1947, analyses some concordats on p. clxxxv.

12. G. O. Sayles, *The Mediaeval Foundations of England*, 2. ed., p. 448, etc., London, 1949.

13. On progress in commercial and financial techniques see Y. Renouard, *Les hommes d'affaires italiens du moyen âge*, p. 171, etc., Paris, 1949.

14. For a full list of references on the population problem and the recurrent crises of the later Middle Ages see the bibliography appended to L. Genicot, *Agriculture in Transition*, in the new edition of the *Cambridge Economic History of Europe*, I.

15. The Guilds, whose origins are wrapt in mystery, appeared particularly early in some regions, in some towns and some trades. According to A. Gourdon, *La règlementation des métiers en Languedoc au moyen âge*, Paris, 1958, they date from the twelfth century in that region. But it was only in the fourteenth century that they became numerous, and sometimes even later; in any case it was only then that they acquired legal recognition. From that period on their basic object was the elimination of competition. See H. van Werveke, *L'origine des corporations de métiers*, in *Revue belge de philologie et d'histoire*, XXIII, 1944, p. 506, etc.

16. E. Coornaert, *Draperie rurale, draperie urbaine; l'évolution de l'industrie flamande au moyen âge et au XVIᵉ siècle*, in ibid., XXVIII, 1950, p. 60–98, gives a late thirteenth-century date to these regulations.

17. E. Perroy, *Les crises du XIVᵉ siècle*, in *Annales, Économies, Sociétés, Civilisations*, IV, 1949, p. 172, etc.

18. Above, Chap. IX, p. 180.
19. H. Sée, *Histoire économique de la France*, I, Paris, 1939.
20. E. Perroy, *La Guerre de Cent ans*, 4. ed., Paris, 1945.
21. H. van Werveke, *Essor et déclin de la Flandre*, in *Studi in onore di G. Luzzatto*, p. 152, etc., Milano, 1949; E. Coornaert, op. cit., note 16.
22. G. Luzzatto, *Storia economica d'Italia*, I, Roma, 1949, and Y. Renouard, *Les hommes d'affaires italiens du moyen âge*, p. 81, etc., Paris, 1949.
23. H. Sproemberg, *Die Hanse in Europäischer Sicht*, in *Dancwerc; opstellen D. Th. Enklaar*, pp. 127–51, Groningen, 1959.
24. The influence of economic situations and of the great merchant classes on the development of civilization have been noted by Y. Renouard, op. cit., p. 73, etc. and 247, etc., and by J. Le Goff, *Marchands et banquiers du moyen âge*, Paris, 1956.
25. A graph drawn by J. Harvey in *Gothic England*, 2. ed., p. 160, London, 1948, shows in striking fashion the relation between political troubles and cultural activity.
26. G. Mollat, *Contribution à l'histoire du Sacré collège de Clément V à Eugène IV*, in *Revue d'histoire ecclésiastique*, XLVI, 1951, p. 68; R. B. Betts, *Correnti religiosi nazionali ed ereticali dalla fine del secolo XIV alla metà del XV*, in *Congresso internazionale di scienze storiche, Roma, 1955. Relazioni*, III, pp. 485–513; below, note 22, Chapter XI; J. P. Shaw, *Nationality and the Western Church before the Reformation*, London, 1959.

CHAPTER XI

1. Hefele-Leclercq, *Histoire des Conciles*, VI, p. 647; the Dialogue of Saint Catherine, ch. 130, ed. I. Taurisano, Roma, 1947; Mansi, *Sacrorum conciliorum nova et amplissima collectio*, XXVIII, col. 316.
2. Detailed studies like that of A. H. Thompson, *The English Clergy and their Organization in the Later Middle Ages,* Oxford, 1947, or V. Chomel, *Droit de patronage et pratique religieuse dans l'archevêché de Narbonne au début du XVe siècle*, in *Bibliothèque de l'École des Chartes*, CXV, 1957, pp. 58–137, would lead one to believe that we usually take too gloomy a view of the clergy of the later Middle Ages. O. Vasella, on the other hand, in *Reform und Reformation in der Schweiz*, Munster, 1958, confirms the traditional view in many particulars.
3. The *Visites d'église à la Côte et au Pays de Nyon, XVe-XVIe siècles*, used by J. P. Chapuiset, in *Revue historique vaudoise*, LXIV, 1956, pp. 49–64, reveals that the clergy were guilty of ignorance and absenteeism rather than misconduct.
4. For the part played by rulers in nomination to benefices, see above, note 10, Chap. X.
5. Text taken from the *Correspondance de Philippe II*, published by L. P. Gachard, II, p. 87, Brussels, 1851. The scant education of the clergy is emphasized by F. W. Oediger, *Über die Bildung der Geistlichen im späten Mittelalter*, Leiden, 1953.

6. Below, p. 224.

7. Aeneas Sylvius Piccolomini, *De Rebus gestis Basileae commentarius*, ed. Fea, p. 62, Roma, 1823.

8. J. B. Mahn, *Le pape Benoît XII et les Cisterciens*, in *Bibliothèque de l' École des Hautes Études. Sciences historiques et philologiques*, 285.

9. D. A. Mortier, *Histoire des maîtres généraux de l'Ordre des Frères Prêcheurs*, IV, p. 183, etc., Paris, 1907.

10. G. Mollat, *Les papes d'Avignon*, 9. ed., Paris, 1950, and *Contribution à l'histoire du Sacré Collège de Clément V à Eugène IV*, in *Revue d'histoire ecclésiastique*, XLVI, 1951, p. 22, etc. and 566, etc.

11. P. Pelliot, *Les Mongols et la Papauté*, in *Revue de l'Orient chrétien*, XXIII, 1923, p. 3, etc. and XXIV, 1924, p. 225, etc.

12. A. Fliche, C. Thouzellier and Y. Azaïs, *La chrétienté romaine, 1198–1274*, in *Histoire de l'Église*, by Fliche and Martin, X, p. 460, etc., Paris (1950). The authors observe that both heavy taxation and the custom of nepotism had existed before the Avignon period of papal history.

13. L. Salembier, *Gerson*, in *Dictionnaire de théologie catholique*, VI, col. 1318, etc. and Z. Rueger, *Le 'De auctoritate concilii' de Gerson*, in *Revue d'histoire ecclésiastique*, LIII, 1958, p. 775, etc.

14. E. Vansteenberghe, *Schisme d'Occident*, in *Dictionnaire de théologie catholique*, XIV, col. 1468, etc.

15. B. Tierney, *Foundations of the Conciliar Theory*, Cambridge, 1955; G. de Lagarde, *La Naissance de l'esprit laïque*, II and III, 2. ed., Paris, 1948, 1958, IV, V and VI, Paris, 1942–6.

16. E. Schard, *De jurisdictione imperiali et potestate ecclesiastica*, p. 706, Basel, 1566.

17. Torquemada's work was printed at Cologne in 1480, and reprinted in part at the end of the eighteenth century by J. T. de Rocaberti, *Bibliotheca maxima pontificia*, XIII, col. 283, etc.

18. R. R. Betts and others, *Movimenti religiosi popolari ed eresie del medioevo*, in *X Congresso internazionale di scienze storiche, Roma, 1955. Relazioni*, III, pp. 307–541.

19. G. Gonnet, *Il movimento valdese in Europa secondo le piu recenti ricerche*, in *Bollettino della società di studi valdesi*, 1956, fasc. 6, pp. 21–30 and G. Koch, *Quellen und Forschungen über die Anfänge der Waldenser*, in *Forschungen und Fortschritte*, XXXII, 1958, pp. 141–9.

20. H. Grundmann, *Neue Forschungen über Joachim von Fiore*, Marburg, 1950.

21. The only biography is open to criticism both in its use of sources and in its theological analysis. We refer to H. B. Workman, *John Wyclif*, London, 1926.

22. According to P. de Vooght, *L'hérésie de Jean Huss* and *Hussiana*, both Louvain, 1960, we must make a distinction between Huss himself, who can only be reproached with rejecting the primacy of Rome, like the Fathers of the Council of Constance themselves, and his followers, who were much more heterodox. Other studies recommend caution on another point usually held to be well established, the national character

of the movement; P. P. Bernard, *Jerome of Prague, Austria and the Hussites*, in *Church History*, XXVII, 1958, pp. 3–22, notes in this connection that the Hussites tried to recruit followers in Austria.

23. For the text see Hefele-Leclercq, *Histoire des Conciles*, VII, p. 907, etc., Paris, 1916.

24. The multiplicity of new devotional practices is noted by E. Delaruelle in one of his contributions to the work by Betts and others cited above, note 18. In the same work H. Grundmann observes that the *Imitation* is so concerned with interior and personal piety that it does not pay proper respect to participation in the collective life of the Church.

25. For the text of the Bull see E. Friedberg, *Corpus juris canonici*, II, col. 1151. On the conflict see W. Ullmann, *The Development of the Mediaeval Idea of Sovereignty*, in *English Historical Review*, LXIV, 1949, p. 1, etc. For the first appearance of the idea of 'rex imperator in regno' see E. E. Stengel, *Imperator und Imperium bei den Angelsachsen*, in *Deutsches Archiv zur Erforschung des Mittelalters*, XVI, 1960, pp. 15–72.

CHAPTER XII

1. E. Panofsky, *Early Netherlandish Painting: its origins and character*, 2 vol., Cambridge, Mass., 1953, stresses the part played by Parisian studios in the development of the great painting of the fifteenth century.

2. C. van den Borren, *Geschiedenis van de muziek in de Nederlanden*, Antwerp, 1948, observes that France led the musical revival of the fourteenth century.

3. The first chapter of L. Baldass, *Jan van Eyck*, London, 1952, emphasizes the close contacts between the different schools of painting in the late Middle Ages.

4. The philosophy of William Occam has been the object of considerable study for the last quarter century, but opinions have differed considerably. The recent study by R. Guelluy, *Philosophie et théologie chez Guillaume d'Ockham*, p. 13, etc., Louvain, 1947, attempts to show that Occam was not concerned to purge theology of reason and cut it off from philosophy. His followers moreover continued to confirm the faith by arguments of probability, if not by rigorous proofs. Up to the end the medieval mind remained steeped in the Anselmian ideal of *Fides quaerens intellectum*.

5. This consequence of Occamism is further considered below, p. 241.

6. The introduction to *Hadewijck D'Anvers. Poèmes des béguines*, by J. B. P., Paris, 1954, distinguishes the trends which characterize Dutch and German mysticism. The former is analysed by S. Axters, *La spiritualité des Pays-Bas*, Louvain, 1948. The principal representative of the latter school is treated succinctly by J. Ancelet-Hustache, *Maître Eckhart et la mystique rhénane*, Paris, 1956, and with greater detail by J. M. Clark, *The Great German Mystics. Eckhart, Tauler and Suso*,

Oxford, 1949. A wide selection of his works is to be found in F. Aubier and J. Molitor, *Maître Eckhart, traités et sermons*, Paris, 1942, with an introduction by M. de Gandillac.

7. P. Debongnie, *Dévotion moderne*, in *Dictionnaire de spiritualité*, III, col. 727–47 and S. Axters, *Geschiedenis van de vroomheid in de Nederlanden*. III. *De moderne Devotie, 1380–1550*, Antwerp, 1956.

8. E. van Steenberghe, *Le cardinal Nicolas de Cuse, l'action, la pensée*, Paris, 1920.

9. For the author of this work, of which there is no modern edition, see G. van Dievoet, *Jehan Boutillier en de Somme rural*, Louvain, n. d. (1950).

10. For Petrarch and the other Italian writers of the time see P. Mazzumuto, *Rassegna bibliografico-critica della letteratura italiana*, Firenze, 1953. P. Champion wrote a life of Charles: *Vie de Charles d'Orléans*, Paris, 1916, and published his works, in 2 vol., Paris, 1923, 1927.

11. The origins of the flamboyant manner are as subject to controversy as the origins of Gothic itself. Some hold that it began in England, some in France; according to M. Hastings, *St. Stephen's Chapel and its place in the development of the Perpendicular style in England*, Cambridge, 1955, it was born in the Île de France in the middle of the thirteenth century.

12. The *Messe du Sacre*, which Guillaume de Machault is supposed to have written for the coronation of Charles V, and two of his *Ballades* have been published by '*L'Anthologie sonore*'. Another transcription of the Mass was published by J. Chailley, Paris, 1947.

13. D. Knowles, *A Characteristic of the Mental Climate of the XIVth century*, in *Mélanges E. Gilson*, pp. 315–25, Toronto, 1959, gives a brief sketch of the intellectual atmosphere of Occam's time; P. Vignaux, *Le nominalisme au XIVᵉ siècle*, Paris, 1948, and L. Baudry, *Guillaume d' Occam, sa vie, ses oeuvres, ses idées sociales et politiques*, I, Paris, 1950, analyse his teaching.

14. P. Duhem, *Le système du monde; histoire des théories cosmologiques de Platon à Copernic*, IV, Paris, 1916, details these discoveries; M. Lacoin, *Sur la gestation de la science moderne (XVᵉ et XVIᵉ siècles)*, in *Revue d'histoire des sciences et de leurs applications*, 1956, pp. 193–207, reminds us that very few scientists actually made experiments.

15. R. de Roover, *Monopoly theory prior to Adam Smith*, in *The Quarterly Journal of Economics*, LXV, 1951, pp. 495–500, comments on the part played by the schoolmen in elaborating the theory of price.

16. E. Bridrey, *La théorie de la monnaie au XIVᵉ siècle: Nicole Oresme*, Caen, 1906.

17. There is a Louvain edition of the *Imago* by J. de Westphalia, 1480.

18. For Valla see C. Carbonara, *Il secolo XV*, pp. 51–107, in *Storia della filosofia italiana*, VI, Milan, 1943.

19. R. Schneider and G. Cohen, *La formation du génie moderne dans l'art de l'Occident*, Paris, 1936. For the Low Countries, see J. Lavalleye, in E. de Moreau, *Histoire de l'Église en Belgique*, IV, p. 399, etc.,

Brussels, 1949. For the Italian painters see B. Berenson, *The Italian Painters of the Renaissance*, London, 1952.

20. H. Hauvette, *Boccace*, Paris, 1914; E. Legouis, *Geoffrey Chaucer*, Paris, 1910; S. Battaglia, *Il 'Libro de Buen Amor'*, in *La Cultura*, IX, 1930, p. 721, etc. and X, 1931, p. 15, etc.

21. M. Wilmotte, *Froissart*, Brussels, 1943; his works were published by Kervyn de Lettenhove, for the Académie Royale de Belgique, from 1867 to 1877, in 29 volumes.

22. L. Hommel, *Chastellain*, Brussels, 1945; his works were published by Kervyn for the Académie in 8 volumes, from 1863 to 1866.

23. F. Desonay and P. Champion published the *Petit Jean de Saintré*, Paris, 1926, and F. Desonay wrote *Antoine de la Salle, aventureux et pédagogue*, Paris, 1940.

24. G. Cohen, *Le théâtre en France au moyen âge*, 2 vol., Paris, 1928, 1931, and a new ed., in one vol., Paris, 1948. This scholar also published the Liège morality plays under the title *Mystères et moralités du Manuscrit 617 de Chantilly*, Paris, 1920. For the *abelspel* see G. Godelaine, *Esmoreit*, Brussels, 1942. The *Palatinus Passion* has been published by G. Frank, Paris, 1922.

25. *Maître Pathelin* has been published by R. Holbrook, Paris, 2. ed., 1937, and Gréban's *Passion* by G. Paris and G. Raynaud, Paris, 1878.

26. Villon's works have been published by A. Longnon, 4. ed., revised by L. Foulet, Paris, 1932. There is a study by P. Champion, *François Villon, sa vie et son temps*, new ed., Paris, 1932–3.

27. J. Huizinga, *Le problème de la Renaissance*, in *Revue des cours et conférences*, XL, 1938–9, pp. 163, 301, 524, 603, etc. Many authors date the beginning of the movement from the thirteenth century, even the late twelfth century in Naples or in Sicily. Indeed anyone who has visited Italy sees that the Ancient World was never quite forgotten, which makes it rather difficult to date the 'distant origins' of the Renaissance.

28. An example of the revival of interest in the Fathers about 1400 is to be seen in the Italian translations of the *Moralia in Job* examined by G. Dufner, *Die Moralia Gregors des Grossen in ihren italienischen Volgarizzamenti*, Padova, 1958.

29. G. Toffanin, *Storia dell'Umanesimo*, new ed., Bologna, 1950; E. R. Labande, *L'Italie de la Renaissance*, Paris, 1954.

30. P. Renucci, *L'aventure de l'humanisme européen au moyen âge, IVᵉ-XIVᵉ siècles*, Paris, 1953, emphasizes the nationalist aspect of the *trecento*.

31. K. M. Setton, *The Byzantine Background to the Italian Renaissance*, in *Proceedings of the American Philosophical Society*, C, 1956, pp. 1–76, traces the history of the Greek language in the later Middle Ages; R. R. Bolgar, *The Classical Heritage and its Beneficiaries*, Cambridge, 1954, gives in an appendix a list of the MSS. of Greek works preserved in the libraries of Italy in the fifteenth century.

32. A. Venturi, *Storia dell'arte italiana. VIII. L'architettura del Quattrocento*, 2 vol., Milan, 1923–4; J. Pope-Hennessy, *Italian Renaissance Sculpture*, London, 1958.

305

33. H. A. Enno van Gelder, *De grote en de kleine Reformatie der 16ᵉ eeuw*, in *Mededeelingen der Koninklijke Nederlandse Akademie van Wetenschappen, Afd. Letterkunde*, n.s., fasc. 18, no. 9, describes the effects of the Renaissance in matters of religion; the substitution of a philosophy of the Christian life for a religion of redemption.

CONCLUSION

1. A complete analysis of the medieval legacy to succeeding ages is to be found in C. G. Crump and E. F. Jacob, *The legacy of the Middle Ages*, new impression, Oxford, 1943.

GENERAL BIBLIOGRAPHY

With some exceptions this bibliography will include only general works, neither too voluminous nor too technical for the reader of this book. Those who require more specialized works should consult the excellent *Initiation aux études d'histoire du moyen âge* by L. HALPHEN, 3. ed., revised by Y. RENOUARD, Paris, 1951, or the extensive bibliography compiled by J. LE GOFF, *La civilisation de l'Occident médiéval,* Paris, 1964.

GENERAL WORKS

Three recent works deal with medieval history. The first one, by E. PERROY, J. AUBOYER, C. CAHEN, G. DUBY and M. MOLLAT, *Le moyen âge* in the series *Histoire générale des civilisations,* Paris, 1955, covers the whole period and offers several chapters on East Europe and Asia. The second, by R. S. LOPEZ, *Naissance de l'Europe,* in the series *Destins du monde,* Paris, 1962 (English translation *The Birth of Europe,* Phoenix House, 1966) does not go further than the year 1300 and the western boundaries. The last, by J. LE GOFF, quoted above and published in the series *Les grandes civilisations,* Paris, puts the emphasis on the medieval mind.

The two volumes by J. CALMETTE, in the series '*Clio. Introduction aux études historiques*', *Le monde féodal,* 5. ed., Paris, 1951, and *L'élaboration du monde moderne,* 3. ed., Paris, 1949, provide a simple introduction to medieval history. Each chapter is a concise exposition of the essential facts, with valuable notes on the sources and bibliography and the current views on controversial questions.

WORKS ON MEDIEVAL CIVILIZATION IN GENERAL

Four books, which the student cannot neglect, trace the development and analyse the characteristics of medieval culture. The well-known book by C. DAWSON, *The Making of Europe,* London, 1932, deals with its origins up to the year 1000. The second and the third, R. H. SOUTHERN, *The Making of the Middle Ages,* London, 1953, and W. VON DEN STEINEN, *Der Kosmos des Mittelalters,* Bern and Munich, 1959, deal with the period from the tenth to the end of the twelfth century. The last of the four books is J. HUIZINGA, *Herfsttijd der middeleeuwen*, 8. ed., Leiden, 1952, translated into English as *The Waning of the Middle Ages*, Pelican Books, 1955, which deals with the last phase.

WORKS ON SINGLE COUNTRIES

B. GEBHARDT, *Handbuch der deutschen Geschichte*, Bd. I, 8. ed., Stuttgart, 1958.

A. L. POOLE, *Mediaeval England*, new ed., 2 vol., Oxford, 1958; *Oxford History of England*, of which five volumes, by F. M. STENTON, 1947, 2. ed., A. L. POOLE, 1955, 2. ed., M. POWICKE, 2. ed., M. MCKISACK, 1962, and E. F. JACOB, 1961, cover the history of England up to 1500.

Historia de España, edited by R. MENÉNDEZ-PIDAL; volumes III to VI, published 1940 to 1956, cover the years 414 to 1038. F. SOLDEVILA, *Historia de España*, volumes I and II of which, Barcelona, 1953, cover the medieval period.

G. DUBY and R. MANDROU, *Histoire de la civilisation française. Moyen âge–XVIe siècle*, Paris, 1958.

Storia d'Italia illustrata, of which volumes III to V, Milan, 1937–47, are concerned with the Middle Ages; *Storia d'Italia. Il medioevo*, by F. COGNASSO, Rome, 1958.

Algemene Geschiedenis der Nederlanden, edited by J. A. VAN HOUTTE, J. F. NIERMEYER, J. PRESSER, J. ROMEIN and H. VAN WERVEKE; the first three volumes, published in 1949, 1950 and 1951, cover the beginning to 1477.

WORKS ON LAW AND INSTITUTIONS

F. CALASSO, in *Medio Evo del Diritto*, Milan, 1954, has begun a comprehensive work on the history of medieval law. So far he has dealt only with the sources.

For the study of institutions there are a number of reliable and well-written books: for France there is FR. OLIVIER-MARTIN, *Histoire du droit français, des origines à la Révolution*, Paris, 1948; for England, S. B. CHRIMES, *An Introduction to the Administrative History of Mediaeval England*, Oxford, 1952; for Germany, H. CONRAD, *Deutsche Rechtsgeschichte*. I. *Frühzeit und Mittelalter*, Karlsruhe, 1954; for Italy, A. SOLMI, *Storia del diritto italiano*, 3, ed., Milan, 1930; and for Spain, J. M. FONT RIUS, *Instituciones medievales españolas*, Madrid, 1949.

For private law see J. BRISSAUD, *Manuel d'histoire du droit privé*, 2. ed., Paris, 1935, or the more concise work by J. IMBERT, *Histoire du droit privé (Que sais-je)*, Paris, 1950.

For the history of Roman law, see P. VINOGRADOFF, *Roman Law in Mediaeval Europe*, new ed., Oxford, 1929. The composite work now in preparation, *Ius Romanum Medii Aevi*, will be confined to the external history. P. KOSCHAKER, *Europa und das Römische Recht*, 1947, is concerned with private law.

As for Canon law, A. STICKLER, *Historia juris canonici Latini* has only reached volume I, Turin, 1950, which covers the sources. One volume of the great work edited by G. LE BRAS, *Histoire du droit et des institutions de l'Église en Occident*, covers part of our period: VII. *L'âge classique, 1140–1378. Sources et théorie du droit*, Paris, 1965. The two small volumes of I. A. ZEIGER, *Historia juris canonici*, Rome, 1939, 1940, are useful. H. E. FEINE, *Kirchliche Rechtsgeschichte*. I. *Die Katholische Kirche*, 3. ed., Weimar, 1955, should be read by students who know German.

WORKS ON THE HISTORY OF THE CHURCH

In this field there are many works, and most of them on a large scale. This is true for example of the *Histoire de l'Église depuis les origines jusqu'à nos jours*, begun under the editorship of A. FLICHE and MGR. V. MARTIN; it is to have thirteen large volumes on the Middle Ages, most of which have appeared.

For the regular clergy, the little book by H. MARC-BONNET, *Histoire des ordres religieux*, (*Que sais-je*), Paris, 1949, provides a good introduction. P. COUSIN, *Précis d'histoire monastique*, Paris, 1956, can be recommended for its concision, its notes and its bibliography.

The Church's influence on civilization is very well dealt with in G. SCHNÜRER, *Kirche und Kultur im Mittelalter*, vol. I, 3. ed., 1936, vol. II, 2. ed., 1929, vol. III, 1929.

WORKS ON ECONOMIC HISTORY

PIRENNE'S two hundred pages on *La vie économique* in volume VIII: *La civilisation occidentale au moyen âge, du XIᵉ au milieu du XVᵉ siècle* of *Histoire du moyen âge* (GLOTZ, *Histoire générale*), republished in *Histoire économique de l'Occident médiéval*, Bruges, 1951, are a contribution of great value, but only a few pages cover the early Middle Ages. There is an English translation from an earlier edition, by H. E. CLEGG, London, 1936. They may be supplemented by R. LATOUCHE, *Les origines de l'économie occidentale, IVᵉ-XIᵉ siècles*, in *L'évolution de l'humanité*, Paris, 1956, English translation under the title: *The Birth of Western Economy*, London, 1961. An interesting book, though it devotes too much space to France.

There are two German books which are still of value: R. KOETZSCHKE, *Allgemeine Wirtschaftsgeschichte des Mittelalters*, in *Handbuch der Wirtschaftsgeschichte*, by G. BRODNITZ, Jena, 1924, and J. KULISCHER, *Allgemeine Wirtschaftsgeschichte des Mittelalters und der Neuzeit*, Bd. I, in *Handbuch der mittelalterlichen und neueren Geschichte*, by G. VON BELOW and F. MEINECKE, München and Berlin, 1928.

An essential work is the *Cambridge Economic History of Europe*, the first three volumes of which deal with the Middle Ages: M. POSTAN, *The Agrarian Life of the Middle Ages*, 1966, 2. ed.; II. M. POSTAN and

BIBLIOGRAPHY

E. E. RICH, *Trade and Industry in the Middle Ages,* 1952, is being revised; III. M. POSTAN, E. E. RICH and E. MILLER, *Economic Organization and Policies in the Middle Ages,* 1963. Agrarian history is excellently summarized in B. H. SLICHER VAN BATH, *De agrarische geschiedenis van West-Europa, 500–1850,* Utrecht, 1960 (English translation *The Agrarian History of Western Europe,* A.D. *500–1850,* 1963).

WORKS ON INTELLECTUAL AND ARTISTIC LIFE

There is a good summary of the history of medieval Latin literature in the eighty pages of M. HÉLIN, *Littérature d'Occident,* Bruxelles, 1943. More extensive treatment is to be found in P. J. DE GHELLINCK, *Littérature latine au moyen âge.* I. *Depuis les origines jusqu'à la renaissance carolingienne.* II. *De la renaissance carolingienne à Saint Anselme,* in *Bibliothèque des sciences religieuses,* Paris, 1939. These two volumes are supplemented by the same author's *L'essor de la littérature latine au XIIᵉ siècle,* 2 vol., Bruxelles and Paris, 1945.

In volume VIII of the *Histoire du moyen âge Histoire générale* edited by G. GLOTZ, G. COHEN summarizes the history of vernacular literatures in the earlier period. He has done the same for French literature in *La vie littéraire en France au moyen âge,* Paris, 1949. For the literature of the South of France see A. JEANROY, *Histoire sommaire de la poésie occitane, des origines à la fin du XVIIIᵉ siècle,* Toulouse and Paris, 1945.

There are a number of books of high quality on the history of medieval philosophy. The most important are E. GILSON, *History of Christian Philosophy in the Middle Ages,* London, 1955, E. BRÉHIER, *La philosophie au moyen âge,* Paris, 1937. A more concise work is P. VIGNAUX, *La pensée au moyen âge,* Paris, 1958, a stimulating book. A clear and well-planned book on a rather larger scale is M. DE WULF, *Histoire de la philosophie médiévale,* 3 vol., 6. ed., Paris, 1934–47, of which there is an English translation under the title: *History of mediaeval philosophy,* London, 1935, 1938.

Theology and devotion are treated in a masterly way by F. CAYRÉ in volume II of his *Patrologie et histoire de la théologie,* 3. ed., Paris, 1945. See too H. DE LUBAC, *Exégèse médiévale,* 2 vol., 1959, 1960 and J. LECLERCQ, F. VANDENBROUCKE and L. BOUYER, *La Spiritualité du moyen âge,* Paris, 1961.

Most work on medieval science has been done by English scholars, particularly A. C. CROMBIE, *Augustine to Galileo. The history of science,* A.D. 400–1650, London, 1952.

In the Middle Ages as at other periods art is the most complete and significant expression of culture. The best guide is P. LAVEDAN, *L'histoire de l'art.* II. *Moyen âge et temps modernes,* Paris, 1944; it appeared in the *Clio* collection and has the same arrangement as the book by CALMETTE mentioned at the beginning of this bibliography. J. HUBERT, *L'art pré-roman,* Paris, 1938, is the classic work on the development of art in the earlier part of our period. For the later centuries H. FOCILLON, *Art d'Occident,* 2. ed., Paris, 1947, contains a wealth of information. There is an English translation, *The Art of the West*, 2 vol., London, 1963. If the student cannot afford the time to read the whole of the series of volumes by E. MÂLE, *L'art religieux du XIIe siècle en France*, 5. ed., Paris, 1947, *L'art religieux du XIIIe siècle*, 8. ed., Paris, 1948, and *L'art religieux de la fin du moyen âge*, 5. ed., Paris, 1949, he can at least read the volume of extracts chosen by the author himself, published as *L'art religieux du XIIe au XVIIIe siècle*, Paris, 1945. The volume on the thirteenth century has appeared in English as *The Gothic Image*, London, 1961, and the volume of selections as *Religious art from the XIIth to the XVIIIth century*, London, 1949.

T. GÉROLD has written an excellent handbook on *La musique du moyen âge*, in the series *Les Classiques français du moyen âge*, Paris, 1933. His larger work, *Histoire de la musique des origines à la fin du XIVe siècle*, Paris, 1936, can only be understood by students with a considerable knowledge of music. A better work for the non-specialist is J. CHAILLEY, *Histoire musicale du moyen âge*, Paris, 1950. A selection of medieval music is to be found in A. T. DAVISON and W. APPEL, *Historical Anthology of Music*, new ed., Harvard, 1944.

ATLASES

History is not to be studied without the use of maps. Unfortunately the atlases available to the student are rather dated and attach too much importance to purely political events. We may note F. SCHRADER, *Atlas de géographie historique*, Paris, 1896, K. VON SPRUNER and T. MENKE, *Handatlas für die Geschichte des Mittelalters und der neueren Zeit*, Gotha, 1880 and G. DROYSEN, *Allgemeiner historischer Handatlas*, Bielefeld and Leipzig, 1886, as well as the eight portfolios of maps attached to the *Cambridge Mediaeval History*, 1911–36.

W. R. SHEPERD, *Historical Atlas*, New York and London, 1929, is more up to date and more complete.

The small *Atlas historique* in the *Clio* collection, noted above, which has one section for the Middle Ages, Paris, 1936, is not satisfactory.

INDEX

313

THE AUTHOR

Léopold Genicot is Professor at the
Faculty of Philosophy and Letters at
the University of Louvain.

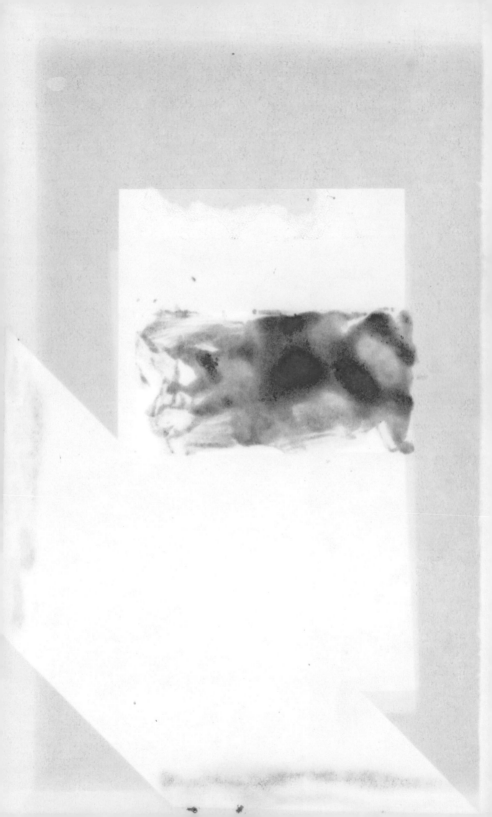